COMPUTER ORGANIZATION AND PROGRAMMING

McGRAW-HILL COMPUTER SCIENCE SERIES

Richard W. Hamming
Bell Telephone Laboratories

Edward A. Feigenbaum
Stanford University

COMPUTER ORGANIZATION AND PROGRAMMING

2/E

C. WILLIAM GEAR

Department of Computer Science
University of Illinois at Urbana-Champaign

McGRAW-HILL BOOK COMPANY

New York St. Louis San Francisco Düsseldorf Johannesburg
Kuala Lumpur London Mexico Montreal New Delhi Panama
Paris São Paulo Singapore Sydney Tokyo Toronto

COMPUTER ORGANIZATION AND PROGRAMMING

34567890 DODO 798765

This book was set in Alpha Gothic by University Graphics, Inc.
The editors were Kenneth J. Bowman and Annette Hall;
the designer was Edward A. Butler;
and the production supervisor was Thomas J. LoPinto.
New drawings were done by ECL Art Associates, Inc.

Library of Congress Cataloging in Publication Data
Gear, Charles William.
    Computer organization and programming.
    (McGraw-Hill computer science series)
        1.   Electronic digital computers—Programming.
2.   Electronic digital computers—Design and construction.   I.   Title.
QA76.6.G38 1974   001.6′42   73-13720
ISBN 0-07-023076-5

FOR ANN   THE SECOND EDITION

CONTENTS

PREFACE
TO THE SECOND EDITION

The second edition introduces some reorganization of chapters. The chapter on input/output has been split into two chapters, one on hardware and one on software, and a new chapter on modern concepts such as multiprogramming and virtual memory has been added. The major changes in the other material are the references to two specific computers, the IBM 370 and the PDP-11, in Chapters 2, 3, 4, and 6. These are chosen because they are representative of modern large and small computer systems. However, this is still not a text on these machines. If one of them is being used, then the student should have access to a *Principles of Operation and Assembly Language* manual. The material is organized so that one or both machines can be omitted completely. (I teach both machines, covering the PDP-11 first. The IBM 370 material can be covered later very rapidly.)

The instructor should pick as much of the material in Chapters 7 through 11 as is of interest to him and his students. For example, it is possible to assign projects that involve writing a simulator of another computer (Chapter 7), a simple assembler (Chapter 9), sorting programs (Chapter 10), or simple compilers or interpreters (Chapter 11).

C. WILLIAM GEAR

PREFACE
TO THE FIRST EDITION

This text is intended for a second course in programming. Students are presumed to have completed a basic course in a procedure oriented language such as Fortran, Basic, Algol, or PL/I and consequently to have been introduced to the fundamental concepts of digital computers and programs. The book discusses machine language and the design of computers as it affects the language. It then continues with an examination of software systems, programming philosophy, input/output systems, interpreters, macro assemblers, and compilers. Because table lookup techniques are important in assemblers and compilers, a chapter is devoted to searching and sorting. The detailed simulation of one computer on another is discussed in order to explain the way in which instructions are executed by the hardware.

The notes for this book have been used for a course at the University of Illinois since 1965. It is a 44-hour lecture course which is essentially identical to ACM course B2 in its proposal for a computer science curriculum. This course has used three different machines on different occasions. In all cases, the *Principles of Operation and Assembly Language* manuals were also used as texts. As material from the book was covered, examples from the machine being used were discussed in class.

Compilers were not covered in depth in this course, since they are the start of a more advanced course in system programming. A chapter has been included here because many students wanted additional material to read, particularly on compilers.

It has been found important to give programming assignments sufficiently complex that the students may use some of the more advanced features of the available operating system. Since the background of incoming students has been varied both in depth and in type of experience, it has been helpful to assign an assembly language problem at the start of the semester. This has consisted of a working, well-documented but simple program which the students first have to keypunch and get running and then modify in a simple manner with the aid of the machine manuals. To complete the problem, they have to use the operating-system control cards, some machine language, and some simple input/output from machine language. By the time they finish, enough of Chapter 2 has been covered in class that a more difficult assignment can be given. Usually this has been the body of a subroutine that will be used in later assignments.

Considerable emphasis has been placed on Chapter 7 by assigning the simulator as a programming task. On different occasions students have been required to write the whole thing, debug a partially working version, and complete and add other features to a working portion of the simulator. The latter approach has been more successful because it provides the weak students with something to build on slowly while giving ample opportunity for the bright students to experiment. In fact, one problem has been the amount of machine time that some of the better students use in fairly sophisticated extensions of the basic machine.

Most of the questions at the end of the chapters are taken from exams used in the course. The students are usually told that some of these questions (with minor changes in numerical values, etc.) will be used on their exams to encourage them to work the problems.

The emphasis throughout the book is that there is no best way of either designing a machine or programming a given problem of any size. Rather, the point is made that there are many methods, any one of which may be the best in a particular situation, but that a general solution is a compromise among many goals. Different machine designs and different programming techniques are introduced in an historical order in most cases because this usually represents the buildup from the simple to the complex and provides a better perspective of the situations in which given techniques are valuable.

C. WILLIAM GEAR

COMPUTER ORGANIZATION AND PROGRAMMING

1 INTRODUCTION

The digital computer arose in answer to man's need for quicker and more efficient ways of completing large numerical computations. Such computations arise in practical situations, as in the solution of engineering design problems, as well as in the course of theoretical endeavors, such as the attempt to locate prime numbers. Tasks such as these *could* be done without the help of computer technology, but in many instances their value would be negated by their cost in man-hours and human endurance.

However, some fairly large computations had to be done even before the development of automatic digital computers, and these were handled in the following way: they were split up into many sections—each relatively independent of the others—which were then computed separately. Each section was broken down into a set of instructions and the data to which they were to be applied. The various sections were then handed on to a number of assistants, who would perform the indicated computations using desk calculating devices. Today, the instructions and data are given to the digital computer, which has replaced these assistants.

After the initial use of computers in numerical problems, workers began to explore other areas of application. It was noted that any finite class of objects could be related to the sets of numbers that the computer would handle, and could be manipulated in the same way. *Nonnumeric* data processing became important. (Even before the automatic digital computer, nonnumeric data processing had become available for some business applications through the use of punched-card machines.)

Nonnumeric processing is basically similar to numeric processing in that various logical processes, or *algorithms,* which manipulate finite sets of objects (either numbers or other data) can be prepared for the same computer. As an example, the letters of the alphabet can be assigned numeric values 1 through 26 and a space represented by 0. (Space, or *blank* as it is usually called in computer usage, is one of the possible characters that a computer must be able to "print" on a page.) A machine capable of manipulating 8-digit decimal numbers can be used to manipulate four-letter words or less by replacing each letter by its equivalent number and adding spaces, or 0s, if there are less than four letters. Thus, MOTH is "represented" as 13 15 20 08 and MAT as 13 01 20 00. Words can be arranged alphabetically by arranging their representations in numerical order. MAT precedes MOTH because 13012000 is less than 13152008.

By such techniques business data processing, usually involving the manipulation of large amounts of data called *files,* has been automated for computers. Nonnumeric processing has been extended to applications involving the manipulation of abstract mathematical quantities, such as groups; to the problems of natural language translation, such as Russian to English; to graphical or pictorial data processing, such as the matching of fingerprints; and to the control of complex processes such as those involved in the running of oil refineries.

As computer applications grow in number and variety, increasingly automatic operation is required. Such automatic operation makes the computer available to people with decreasingly detailed knowledge of the inner structure of the computer. A given computer is capable of a basic set of operations, and various combinations of these can be used to perform different tasks. The user is unconcerned with the details of these basic operations; his only concern is that the job to be done be specified in as direct a manner as possible. The computer operator, in turn, is unconcerned with the details of each job. He simply wants to get the work load processed as quickly as possible with a minimum of delay between jobs. Therefore, to the basic computer *hardware* (that is, the component parts of the computer) is added the *software* of *system programs,* which translate the language of the user and operator into that of the computer, and vice versa. The hardware and the system programs together constitute the *computer system.* The hardware provides the ability to do basic operations, the software the ability to specify the job in a convenient notation and to move from one job to another without delay.

This book discusses computer organization by describing the various ways in which the basic components of the computer are logically connected, the reasons for the different organizations, and the advantages of each. This material is then used as background for a discussion of the basic principles of system programming, which consists of (1) the translation of programs written in a language applicable to a job, called a *source language,* into an equivalent program expressed in a language obeyed by the computer, called a *machine language;* (2) the supervision of these user programs by other programs, usually referred to as *monitor* and *supervisor* programs; and (3) the assistance of the program in execution by *system subroutines* which are typically concerned with input/output and related functions. There is an almost unlimited amount of material that could be included in a study of system programming. We will have to be content with an introduction to the concepts common to most systems.

A computer system should provide a tool for solving problems quickly—in terms of the computer's time as well as that of the user. The hardware should be designed to operate as fast as possible within a given cost. The software should be designed to minimize the amount of computer time wasted and yet provide as flexible a means of controlling the operation as possible. Computer functions that can be expected to be fixed throughout the life of the machine should be provided by hardware where possible. Functions that will change—by increase of capabilities without negation of earlier properties—should be controlled by the software. A computer has no value of itself; it can only be justified on economic grounds. The objective of system design must be one of minimum cost for the whole job, including the cost of programming the problem and of running it.

The programmer who programs at the machine level is frequently a *system programmer,* that is, one who writes programs which will help other *users* access the computer system. However, some *application programmers* find it necessary to work at the machine level in sections of very large application programs. This book is directed at both of these types of programmer.

1.1 THE BASIC CAPABILITIES OF COMPUTERS

A digital computer is capable of basic operations on finite sets of numbers. These include the usual arithmetic operations *add, subtract, multiply,* and *divide.* In addition, a computer has the important ability to compare two numbers or nonnumeric quantities in order to take one action if the comparison is successful or another if it fails. These comparisons usually include tests for *greater than or equal to, equal, less than,* etc. As well as operating on information, the computer must be able to input the initial data from the user, retain it for additional computations, and output the answers to the user. Therefore, in addition to the operational power, it has facilities for *memorizing* numbers, and for inputting and outputting them in a form intelligible to a human. The next few subsections will trace briefly the historical development of these facilities and the importance of each new feature.

1.1.1 The desk calculator

The desk calculator was one of the first computing tools. With its ability to perform the arithmetic operations add and subtract (and multiply and divide by repetitive addition and subtraction), it replaced a lot of tedious human calculation. However, human intervention was still needed, both to control the steps in the calculation and to memorize intermediate results (by *storing* them on scratch paper). In order to use a desk calculator effectively, the steps of a problem must be carefully organized. In other words, the operator must first program *himself.*

More recent desk calculators provide a number of *storage registers* which eliminate the need to copy intermediate results. However, the efficiency of a desk calculator is still limited by the speed with which a human operator can issue instructions manually.

1.1.2 The stored program computer

The step to *stored program* computers, which bypassed the speed limitation imposed by human control, occurred in two stages. The first stage was marked by the introduction of sequence-controlled calculators. A fixed cycle of steps was *programmed* by preparing a punched tape or a plugboard. The calculator could get its sequence of operations from this storage device and repeat the cycle of steps indefinitely. The capabilities provided by such mechanisms were equivalent to those of a computer in which programs consisting of only one or two Fortran statements could be executed repetitively.

These techniques could be used for repetitive operations such as summing numbers punched in cards. With the addition of auxiliary cycles of steps that could be activated under certain conditions (and with a lot of ingenuity), quite sophisticated jobs were tackled. The sequence-controlled calculator was limited by its inability to change its cycle of steps except within narrow confines.

This limitation was overcome by the introduction of the stored program computer, in which the sequence of steps was stored in the same memory as the data. Because operations could be performed on the contents of the memory, this computer could modify its own programs during execution. This feature made it possible to vary the program according to need. It was first thought that this would be an important step toward operating efficiency, but subsequent developments (for example, indexing, to be discussed in Chapter 2) have made it possible to avoid program modification. For reasons to be discussed later, program modification is now viewed with disfavor.

1.1.3 Operating systems and translators

After the introduction of stored program computers, complex tasks could be tackled. However, many errors could be made during the preparation of a program. In the early days, the programmer sat at the console of the machine to run his program. The computer would often stop on errors, and the programmer would then have to examine the contents of registers and other devices to locate the errors. As machines increased in speed, this correction process became uneconomic. A program that would execute for 1 second could take 5 minutes of human intervention. Therefore, the *operating system* was introduced. This took the form of a program that regained control of the machine when an error was committed by the user program. It attempted to provide the user with diagnostic information he would have received before, but at computer rather than human speeds.

Because the operating system allows for no human intervention, the user has to be able to tell it what is wanted. This is done by *commands*. These are similar to the instructions issued to control the machine operation, but they control the operation of the software. Commands can be used to cause standard system programs to be loaded from special storage devices and to control the machine devices (hardware) available to the user program.

With increase in speed it also became necessary to simplify the drudgery of rote programming. Large volumes of code had to be produced, much of it repetitious and similar — if not identical — to code previously written. Conventions for writing standard codes and ways for using these codes were adopted for each machine so that any user had access to a *library* of codes generated by the users' groups. To simplify the programming of a piece of code that could not be obtained from other sources, *higher-level languages* were designed. Each machine executes code in its own machine language which is needlessly detailed for a human statement and understanding of the underlying problem being programmed. These higher-level languages were oriented toward solving the problem rather than detailing the work of the machine. System programs were developed to translate from these user oriented languages to machine oriented languages. These programs are examples of the nonnumeric processing that occurs every day in the most scientifically oriented computer department. In fact, many computers spend up to 50 percent of their time in translations and analogous system activities. It is therefore very important that efficient techniques be integrated into system programs.

1.1.4 Time sharing and remote consoles

Operating systems, and the desire of management to own the most efficient computer organization in terms of actual versus possible running time, took the programmer out of the computer rooms so that he could no longer interact with his program during execution. Although this certainly eliminated much nonsense, it did slow down the maximum rate at which a program could be developed. Long *turnaround times* (the period between handing a job in for processing and receiving the output) and the inevitable occurrence of unexpected conditions left the programmer sitting idle, waiting to correct minor faults. It also led to many inefficiencies not immediately apparent to management. Because the programmer could not predict the types of errors that would be encountered, he found it necessary to have enough data printed so that all probable contingencies were covered. During test runs of programs, a lot of the time saved by the efficient operating system was lost by excessive printing.

In order to allow the user to interact with his program while it was being executed and also to request only the output that he thought significant on the basis of the completed run, many consoles were attached to a single computer. Programs for each programmer were stored in different parts of the computer memory, and the processing section of the computer switched from one program to another while it switched from one console to another. While one program was being executed for a brief period, the other programmers could be examining their results so far and preparing further input. These consoles are often typewriterlike devices and are frequently connected to the computer by telephone lines so that they can be remote.

1.2 PREPARATION OF PROGRAMS

The preparation of programs for computers has been described haughtily as:

"I program,
you code,
** keypunches."†

The first stage, called programming, consists of analyzing the task and reducing it to a set of logically well-defined steps. The second stage involves the coding of these steps into a language acceptable to the computer system. The third and last stage consists of transcribing the language onto a medium, such as punched cards, which can be read by the computer. This is shown in Figure 1.1, page 8.

This book is concerned with the programming process; the other stages are mechanical and can, in principle, be done mechanically. In fact, as computer systems and input devices have become more sophisticated, much of the keypunching and coding tasks and some of the programming task have been automated. In order to examine the programming process, the stages of solution of a typical large problem will be followed. It will be seen that recent advances in computer technology and science have automated many of the later stages.

Consider the problem of analyzing the stresses in a structural network. (A structural network is a set of beams and columns connected together at joints, called nodes, and subject to various specified forces, called loadings.) The problem is to determine the forces in each member (beam or column) of the network, and to determine the member's deflection due to the loading. The stages in the solution of such a problem include:

1 Preparing a precise description of the network for later processing
2 Selecting an appropriate method for converting the description of the physical network into a mathematical model—that is, selecting a method for writing down equations which describe the problem
3 Selecting a method for solving the equations
4 Expressing that method as a sequence of simple steps

---

† It is a sad comment on the last decade that the use of the third person feminine in the first edition of this book went unnoticed. It is a sadder comment on the years since that the overwhelming majority of the "other minority group" in the computer field are still employed as keypunch operators. Happily, scientific and system programming seem to be one field with very little prejudice.

5 Stating each step precisely in terms of basic computer operations—this is frequently done by expressing them in a high-level language such as Fortran
6 Converting the high-level language description of the method of solution into a machine-level language and running it on a computer

It is important to note that each stage of this process after the first one will have many properties in common with the same stage in the solution of a different problem. Thus the same method for converting the network into a

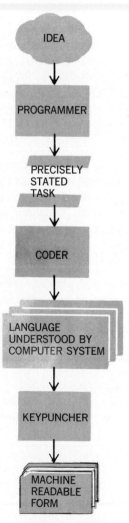

FIGURE 1.1   *Stages of program preparation*

mathematical model may be selected when a different structural network is to be analyzed. The engineer will usually base his choice on his experience in the solution of other problems and his knowledge of the good and bad characteristics of each method. The method selected for solving the equations may be the same as the one which would be selected to solve similar equations for a totally different problem, such as optimization of a business organization. Conversion of the method from a high-level language into machine language will be common to all problems expressed in that language.

In organizing a computer system, an attempt is made to relieve the user of the tasks common to many users by writing programs to do them or by organizing material that can be used to aid in the solution. To make it possible to transmit this material between people and to computers, precise languages have been developed. Thus, there are standards in civil engineering for drawing structural networks so that others can understand them. There are standard ways of expressing the method as a sequence of steps in stage 4. A common one is by using *flowcharts*. A section of a flowchart is shown in Figure 1.2. The rectangular box (formally called a flowchart *symbol*) contains a statement of some processing that must be done. The diamond-shaped box is the *decision symbol,* which is used to ask a question. The *flowlines* are followed in the direction of their arrowheads from one symbol to another. In the case of the decision symbol in Figure 1.2, the flowline labeled YES is followed if A is 0. This says that the next step is to print the message shown in the *print symbol,* then to stop.

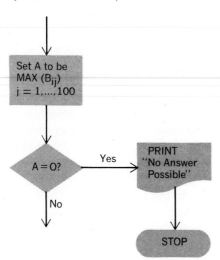

FIGURE 1.2   Section of flowchart

Flowcharts are frequently employed to describe the method to be used on a computer. Apart from a few experimental systems, they are not used to state the solution precisely for the computer to use, but to describe it to other people. Frequently the operations used in flowcharts will not be directly acceptable to the computer, but must be broken down into more basic ones. This is done in stage 5, when the steps indicated in the flowchart are specified very precisely in a high-level language. You are probably familiar with one language, either Fortran, Algol, PL/1, or Basic. We could rewrite the process box in Figure 1.2 in Fortran as shown below:

```
            AM = B(I,1)
            DO 10 J = 2,100
   10       A = AMAX1(A,B(I,J))
```

Languages such as these are commonly used for computer input at the present time. The last stage, conversion to a machine-level language, is almost always done by the computer.

1.2.1 Machine and assembly languages

Ultimately, the program must be expressed in machine language. In machine language every last detail is specified. The basic operations understood by the computer are coded in a numeric form. The place in the computer where a given value is to be found is also numerically coded. Thus if the variable A is to be obtained from the memory, and it is stored in the 123d cell, it must be referred to as the content of cell number 123 in machine language. The first computers were coded in machine language, but it was quickly realized that the excessive detail did not have to be handled by the programmer, and assembly language was designed. Assembly language allows a precise specification of the details of computer code while retaining some *symbolic* and *mnemonic* information. *Symbolic* information refers to names used by the programmer to refer to numbers and other data. Since these names can be chosen arbitrarily, they can be used to indicate their operational significance to the human. A *mnemonic* is a means to aid memorization. In this context it refers to the use of symbolic codes for machine operations which indicate what they do. For example, internal to the machine (in machine language), 112 may be the code for a subtract order. In assembly language this may be replaced by SUB. The assembler replaces each occurrence of SUB by 112. The macrofeature provides an additional symbolic facility that allows the user to define operations consisting of sections of assembly-language code. This enables the input form of the program to be abbreviated and clarified further.

Assembly language can be translated to machine language by replacing the mnemonic and symbolic information by its numeric equivalent. A program that does this is called an *assembler*. Both machine and assembly language allow the programmer to control the basic steps of the computer. For this reason both are referred to as machine-level languages.

1.2.2 Procedure oriented languages

Just as machine language, with its excessive detail, obscures the form of the code, so assembly language, with its detail of each basic machine operation, obscures the nature of the method used to solve the problem. To combat this, languages were developed which are intended to reflect clearly the procedure used for solution. This clarity allows the original problem to be coded more quickly, errors to be more easily removed, and changes to be more readily added — by the original programmer or by another. These languages are called *procedure oriented languages.* They include Fortran (FORmula TRANslation), Algol (ALGOrithmic Language), Cobol (COmmon Business Oriented Language), PL/1 (Programming Language One), Basic (Beginner's All-purpose Symbolic Instruction Code), and others. These languages provide a means of expressing the flowchart of the task in a precise way, a way which the computer has been conditioned to accept in lieu of machine language. Translator programs, usually called *compilers,* are used to convert from the procedure oriented language to machine or assembly languages.

1.2.3 Problem oriented languages

Once a program has been written, it may be desirable to save it for future reuse in order to avoid reprogramming. To implement this, a library of programs is accumulated at a computer installation. Programs with a limited or moderate amount of flexibility are usually used in conjunction with other programs in order to fit them to a particular need. However, it is possible for programs to be written with such flexible input options that they can be used without any additional programming. Suppose, for example, that a number of programs have been written to solve polynomial equations under various conditions. Some may work for real coefficients, others, for complex coefficients, etc. They could be collected together in a package so that the user would see a single program into which he fed his coefficients and some control information requesting action, in this case, to solve the equations.

When this happens, the user does not have to have any knowledge of programming nor need he know any details of the computer hardware and software. A description of the routine will tell him how to prepare his input and how to interpret the output. From the point of view of such a user, the communication with the system is the language accepted as input by the program. This language is normally sufficient to specify what the problem is, but it does not completely specify how to solve it. (The user may be allowed to request one of a number of methods for solution.) It is called a *problem oriented language.*

For each different class of problems, a new program must be written by the computer professional to enable the nonprofessional user to talk to the computer in a suitable problem oriented language. The procedure for solution is specified within the program, not by the user.

A problem oriented language is only a program that accepts a flexible data input. It is therefore difficult to distinguish between any program with data input and a problem oriented language. However, the boundary can reasonably be drawn by asking what the program does with incorrect data input, or, in other words, what happens if there are errors in the input language. A language translator will give numerous diagnostic messages to aid the user in understanding what is wrong. The typical library program will either give wrong answers or just quit with little comment. (Unfortunately, this is a measure under which many procedural language compilers fare badly.)

In the structural analysis example discussed earlier, a method of solving equations had to be programmed. This could have been prepared, or it might have been available as a problem oriented language. However, in that example, one of the major pieces of work was generating the equations from the description of the network. In the early days of computer use, this would have been done by hand, but for large networks, it would be worth using the computer. For example, a program could be written to read a description of the network, such as

NODE 15 IS AT X = 15.2, Y = 17.5, Z = 12.3
BEAM BETWEEN NODES 12 AND 15
. . . etc.

and then to generate the equations for solution. Such a program would obviously be a very useful problem oriented language for the structural engineer. In fact, such a program exists. It is called STRESS, for STRuctural Equation System Solver. With problem oriented languages of this nature, there is very little work for the programmer or the coder, as the user can prepare his network in a form accepted by the language processor and give it directly to the keypuncher. (In fact, with the direct graphical input possible on many computer systems, the user can draw his network on a computer graphical console and avoid the keypuncher also.)

1.3 EXECUTING THE PROGRAM

The task has been described in a language acceptable to the system. From the user's viewpoint, this language is the language obeyed by the machine. In fact, the input usually consists of two or more levels of language—the commands which control the system programs and the statements which will be translated into machine language. If this translation is from assembly language, it is usually called *assembly*; if it is from a procedure oriented language, it is called *compilation.* In either case, the input statements are first processed by a system program to produce machine language. The *source language* is the input to the translator and the *object language* is the output or object of the translator. The object code for each of the translated sections of programs is combined with any required library programs and *loaded* into the computer memory. The loading process links together all the elements of the job and assigns them space in the computer memory.

The next step is the execution phase, during which the user's program is in control of the machine.

Contrast this with the use of a problem oriented language as described above. In this case, the processor for the language is in direct control of the machine. Statements are not translated, rather they cause an action immediately.

From another viewpoint, we can call this *interpretation.* An *interpreter* is a program which executes statements in a language by decoding each statement and immediately executing it, that is, causing the appropriate action. Interpreters can be written to process procedure oriented languages directly. The source language is read into memory and stored there. The combination of the interpreter program and the machine resembles a machine which executes the source language directly.

The distinction between translation and execution on the one hand and interpretation on the other is not clear cut. We can draw a simile from the translation of natural languages. The translator is a professional language expert who accepts input in one language, say French, and produces output in another, say English. If he is working in a technical field like mathematics, for example, the translator does not have to understand his text. That can be checked for sense afterward, by an English-speaking mathematician. Interpretation, on the other hand, is similar to the work done by a mathematician fluent in both English and French. As he reads each statement in the source language, he immediately understands (executes) it.

In practice, both translation and interpretation are involved in reading a foreign-language book. So, in computers, is a mixture of translation and interpretation used to get the best balance of speed and flexibility.

Subsequent chapters will consider the characteristics of various hardware devices. They will also deal with the design and implementation of translators, interpreters, and system programs in relation to these characteristics.

2

HARDWARE ORGANIZATION: THE MAIN MACHINE

The hardware components of a computer system are classified into four groups:

1 Memory
2 Central processing unit (CPU)
3 Input/output (I/O)
4 Control

These units are shown connected together in Figure 2.1. The input/output units are for communication between the internal representation of information by electrical signals used in the computer and the external representation needed by the human, such as printed paper, punched cards, and other *hard copy* media. The CPU is the equivalent of a desk calculator. It contains hardware for performing addition, subtraction, multiplication, and division. The memory is used to store both intermediate results and a copy of the program being executed. The information is read by I/O devices and placed directly into memory in most computers, although in some smaller machines the information passes through the CPU on the way to the memory. This will be discussed in more detail in Chapters 5 and 6 on input/output. Some units, such as magnetic tape units, can be used either as memory devices or as input/output units. This chapter will deal only with the *main* memory (usually called the *core storage*), the CPU, and their relevant control units. Other memory devices, called as a group *auxiliary storage units,* will be discussed in Chapter 5.

The CPU, the main memory, and their controls contain the hardware necessary to perform the arithmetic and logical operations on numeric and non-numeric data. There are many different methods for performing these operations, but there are many similarities between different machines. In

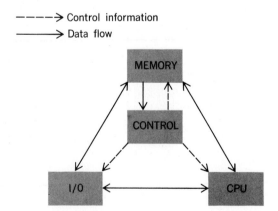

FIGURE 2.1   Computer organization

order to clarify the common problems of software system design, this chapter will discuss the different types of operations in common use. The reader should study the machine (assembly) language of a computer which is accessible to him in order to compare and contrast that machine with the different structures discussed below.

For any given machine, there are a number of programming tricks that can be used to provide shortcuts. Some of these are deliberately built into the computer by the designer, others are "discovered" at a later date by programmers. The fast and effective programming of any given computer in any specified language requires a knowledge of these tricks so that the programmer immediately knows the "best" way to do a given set of operations. However, these tricks are beyond the scope of this book since they depend on the particular machine. They are best learned by direct experience. Rather, the theme of this chapter is that no one machine manual constitutes the "gospel" of machine design. Each machine represents the idiosyncrasies and beliefs of one design team, with the result that some machine features may become drawbacks because of changing needs. (An example of this is the negative indexing on the IBM 7090 series.) In the polytheistic programming universe, it may be necessary to make temporary obeisance to a particular machine design; but it is better to understand the way of machine design in general before becoming a disciple of one specific model.

We shall discuss the various functional elements that make up a computer in order to trace the way in which instructions are executed by the hardware. However, this is not a text in machine design.†

Two particular computers will be discussed in some detail. They are the IBM 370 and the PDP-11. Both are, in fact, classes of machines. The IBM 370 series is the successor to the 360 series, and is very similar to it. Ways in which the two systems differ will be pointed out as they arise. Both the 360 and the 370 series are sets of computers, essentially identical as far as the programmer is concerned, but different in speed, amount of memory that can be attached, and configurations of input/output devices. Basic features are common to all computers, while other features are available at additional cost (much as General Motors provides a range of automobiles, all of which have the same basic essentials—wheels, engine, etc.—and for which extra features, such as a larger engine, may be purchased to increase performance).

†If the student is particularly interested in this subject he may refer to texts such as T. C. Bartee, "Digital Computer Fundamentals," 3d ed., McGraw-Hill Book Company, New York, 1972, and G. Bell and A. Newell, "Computer Structures: Readings and Examples," McGraw-Hill Book Company, New York, 1971.

The PDP-11 family of computers consists of four processors (at the time of writing). The more expensive are faster and can have more memory attached. However, even the fastest is an example of a smaller computer, and PDP-11s are often used as special-purpose processors. Therefore, the discussion will stress the smaller versions of the PDP-11 and generally ignore the advanced optional features. The IBM 370 series computers are often used in large, general-purpose installations, and so some of their optional extras will be discussed. However, both these computer families are discussed in order to illustrate general principles, not with a view toward teaching the best ways of using the particular hardware.

2.1 THE MAIN MEMORY

The main computer processes information which can be obtained from the main memory and the results are returned to the main memory. There is usually a minimum amount of information that can be processed in any one operation and moved to or from memory. This is called a *word*. A word may represent a number to be used in numerical calculations or one or more characters of nonnumeric information. The length of the word differs from machine to machine. On most machines, however, a word consists of a number of *bits,* the most common lengths being between 6 and 64 bits.

Bit is the name for the amount of information that is contained in a number which can only take the value 0 or 1. The word "bit" is a contraction of "binary digit," meaning a digit that can take one of the two values 0 or 1, just as a decimal digit can take one of the ten values 0, 1, 2, . . . , or 9. Although human beings commonly used decimal digits to represent numbers, machines commonly use binary digits because most physical devices used in machines can retain one of two states most reliably (for example, *on* or *off, positive* or *negative, north* or *south* magnetization, etc.).

A word, consisting of a number of bits, may be used to represent anything that the user cares to represent. Each bit of an N bit word can be a 0 or a 1 independently, so that a word can assume any one of 2^N different states. With one word, the user can represent one out of not more than 2^N different objects. These could be different numbers, different letters, different species of trees, etc. The most common use of a word is for number and alphabetic character representation. Much of today's computer terminology reflects the fact that, at the outset, computers handled mainly numbers. If a word consists of N bits, it is usually drawn as in Figure 2.2. The bits have been num-

FIGURE 2.2   *A computer word*

bered arbitrarily from 0 to $N - 1$. Bit 0 is often referred to as the *left-hand bit* or *most significant bit* and bit $N - 1$ as the *right-hand bit* or *least significant bit*. The word is referred to as being N bits *long*.

When a group of bits is used to represent a number, the binary coding scheme is usually employed. In this scheme the bits, starting from the right-hand end, indicate the number of 1's, 2's, 4's, 8's, etc., in the number. Thus if 5 bits, say $b_0 b_1 b_2 b_3 b_4$, are used to represent a number, the value of that number is

$$b_0 \cdot 2^4 + b_1 \cdot 2^3 + b_2 \cdot 2^2 + b_3 \cdot 2^1 + b_4 \cdot 2^0$$

The largest value that this can take is the binary number 11111, representing the decimal value 31. The smallest value is the binary number 00000, representing the decimal value 0. Obviously, such a representation handles positive integers only. One common way of handling negative numbers is to use one more bit to indicate the sign. This is frequently the leftmost bit, with a 0 indicating a positive number and a 1 a negative number. Thus, numbers between -31 and $+31$ could be represented in 6 bits, the first being used as a sign and the remaining 5 for the magnitude of the number. This is called the *sign/magnitude* system. Examples are shown below. Notice that there are

DECIMAL NUMBER	6-BIT SIGN/ MAGNITUDE REPRESENTATION
−31	111 111
−30	111 110
−29	111 101
. . . .	. . . . . .
−1	100 001
−0	100 000
+0	000 000
+1	000 001
. . . .	. . . . . .
+29	011 101
+30	011 110
+31	011 111

two representations for 0, one positive and one negative. If the bits of the word are b_0, b_1, . . . , and b_5 where b_0 is the sign bit, then the number is given by $(1 - 2b_0) (b_1 \cdot 2^4 + b_2 \cdot 2^3 + b_3 \cdot 2^2 + b_4 \cdot 2^1 + b_5 \cdot 2^0)$.

In addition to representing numbers, words are often used to represent nonnumeric data such as alphabetic characters. In program translation, business data processing, and work such as the differentiation of algebraic expressions or word-frequency studies, it is often necessary to represent natural language text such as English or American. To do this, each character (letter, digit, punctuation mark, etc.) is represented by a different bit pattern. The number of bits needed to represent a character is determined by the number of different characters. N bits can represent up to 2^N characters.

N	MAXIMUM NUMBER OF CHARACTERS
6	64
7	128
8	256

A very common representation of the uppercase letters, the ten digits 0 to 9, and the special characters + − * / , . ( ) $ = ' and space (48 characters altogether) uses 6 bits. It is commonly known as the BCD code (Binary Coded Decimal). With a few variations, it is standard over many computers and can be found in most machine manuals. It is shown in Table 2.1. More recently a need has arisen to represent more than 64 characters (other special characters and the lowercase letters, for example). Because 7 turns out to be an awkward number of bits, 8 bits are used. One such code is known as ASCII (American Standard Code for Information Interchange). Not unusually, the largest computer manufacturer has its own standard, known as EBCDIC (Extended BCD Interchange Code).

Both these codes are shown in Table 2.1 for the 48-character set common to all three representations (BCD, EBCDIC, and ASCII). Only one version of the EBCDIC code exists because it has only been used on a few different machines. However, there are several versions of both BCD and ASCII in use because they have been implemented on many different machines by different manufacturers. The BCD code shown is the form that is used internally on the IBM 7094. It is not, for example, the same as that used on IBM magnetic tapes commonly attached to the 7094. The ASCII code shown is the standard for use in an 8-bit environment. Some equipment will produce a different code by changing the bit in position two, so that the number of bits equal to 1 is even in all characters. This is called *parity*.

EBCDIC has one advantage over the two codes. The binary codes are in *collating sequence;* that is, if a character is alphabetically after another character, its code, considered as a binary integer, is larger. Table 2.1 is arranged in collating sequence for EBCDIC. Alphabetizing of data can be done by a numerical sort in EBCDIC. In the other cases, special hardware is needed or a code conversion must be done by software.

2.1.1 Addressing memory

Some uses of a single word have been discussed above. A typical job will have to deal with many thousands of words, be they numbers or strings of characters. Therefore the main memory must store many words and have some way of getting at them when they are needed. The memory can be likened to the boxes at a post office. Each box-holder has a box with a unique number which is his *address.* This address serves to identify his box. Each box or

TABLE 2.1   BCD and EBCDIC codes and card punches and corresponding ASCII codes

CHARACTER	BCD CODE	EBCDIC CODE	ASCII CODE	BCD CARDS	EBCDIC CARDS
blank	110 000	0100 0000	0100 0000	no punch	no punch
.	011 011	0100 1011	0100 1110	12,8,3	12,8,3
(	111 100	0100 1101	0100 1000	0,8,4	12,8,5
+	010 000	0100 1110	0100 1011	12	12,8,6
$	101 011	0101 1011	0100 0100	11,8,3	11,8,3
*	101 100	0101 1100	0100 1010	11,8,4	11,8,4
)	011 100	0101 1101	0100 1001	12,8,4	11,8,5
—	100 000	0110 0000	0100 1101	11	11
/	110 001	0110 0001	0100 1100	0,1	0,1
,	111 011	0110 1011	0100 1111	0,8,3	0,8,3
'	001 100	0111 1101	0100 0111	4,8	8,5
=	001 011	0111 1110	0101 1101	3,8	8,6
A	010 001	1100 0001	1010 0001	12,1	12,1
B	010 010	1100 0010	1010 0010	12,2	12,2
C	010 011	1100 0011	1010 0011	12,3	12,3
D	010 100	1100 0100	1010 0100	12,4	12,4
E	010 101	1100 0101	1010 0101	12,5	12,5
F	010 110	1100 0110	1010 0110	12,6	12,6
G	010 111	1100 0111	1010 0111	12,7	12,7
H	011 000	1100 1000	1010 1000	12,8	12,8
I	011 001	1100 1001	1010 1001	12,9	12,9
J	100 001	1101 0001	1010 1010	11,1	11,1
K	100 010	1101 0010	1010 1011	11,2	11,2
L	100 011	1101 0011	1010 1100	11,3	11,3
M	100 100	1101 0100	1010 1101	11,4	11,4
N	100 101	1101 0101	1010 1110	11,5	11,5
O	100 110	1101 0110	1010 1111	11,6	11,6
P	100 111	1101 0111	1011 0000	11,7	11,7
Q	101 000	1101 1000	1011 0001	11,8	11,8
R	101 001	1101 1001	1011 0010	11,9	11,9
S	110 010	1110 0010	1011 0011	0,2	0,2
T	110 011	1110 0011	1011 0100	0,3	0,3
U	110 100	1110 0100	1011 0101	0,4	0,4
V	110 101	1110 0101	1011 0110	0,5	0,5
W	110 110	1110 0110	1011 0111	0,6	0,6
X	110 111	1110 0111	1011 1000	0,7	0,7
Y	111 000	1110 1000	1011 1001	0,8	0,8
Z	111 001	1110 1001	1011 1010	0,9	0,9
0	000 000	1111 0000	0101 0000	0	0
1	000 001	1111 0001	0101 0001	1	1
2	000 010	1111 0010	0101 0010	2	2
3	000 011	1111 0011	0101 0011	3	3
4	000 100	1111 0100	0101 0100	4	4
5	000 101	1111 0101	0101 0101	5	5
6	000 110	1111 0110	0101 0110	6	6
7	000 111	1111 0111	0101 0111	7	7
8	001 000	1111 1000	0101 1000	8	8
9	001 001	1111 1001	0101 1001	9	9

location in a memory has a unique number, called its *address,* associated with it. This serves to identify it for storage and retrieval. Usually, addresses are integers between 0 and $M - 1$, where M is the number of locations in memory. Each location can store one word of N bits, where N is normally the same for all locations. Thus the memory may be asked to store the bit pattern 1011---0 in location 1027. Later on, if it is asked what is in location 1027, it is expected to reply "1011---0." Here the analogy with the post office box breaks down. If the post office customer fetches the contents from box 342, then box 342 is empty. A computer location cannot be empty. It consists of hardware capable of being in one of 2^N states or bit patterns, and it is always in one of them. Hence, if the contents are fetched from a location in memory, the memory retains a copy of the word. That is, its state does not change.

Section 2.1 defined a word as the minimum amount of information that could be transmitted between the memory and its environment at one time. Some of the more complex computers, the IBM 370 and the PDP-11 in particular, allow the user to refer to varying amounts of information in an instruction. It then becomes difficult to define a word precisely. Physically, the memory may have a certain width, and this could be said to be the word size. However, the physical width may have no effect on the instructions available to the user. Indeed, the IBM 370 is available in various models with different memory widths, but the models are identical from the programmer's point of view. A second definition that could be adopted is to equate the word size to the minimum amount of information that is addressable. The IBM 370 and the PDP-11, for example, allow the user to address any 8-bit character (called a *byte*) in memory. On most machines, one can find at least one instruction that allows a single bit to be specified, so this definition could lead to a 1-bit-word characterization. As usual with computers, we must compromise and say that the word size is that number of bits used in the majority of instructions and therefore probably the most efficient to use in a calculation. With this definition, the 370 can be said to be a 32-bit-word machine, although we shall see that it can address 8-, 16-, 32-, or 64-bit quantities for fixed-length operations, and that it can manipulate strings of n 8-bit bytes for any n from 1 to 256.

Addressing memory with a number is the most common method, and all machines generally available use it. However, there does exist an important concept of *content addressing* which will be discussed in more detail in Chapter 9. In content addressing, a word is specified by stating the value of part of its contents. For example, the first 10 bits could be specified. The memory must return all words which match these bits. Content addressing is performed by an associative memory.

2.1.2 Symbolic addressing

Information to be processed is stored in the memory and brought to the CPU for processing. For example, it may be necessary to add two numbers together and to save the result for later processing. These two numbers are in two locations in memory and the result is to be put back into memory. In Fortran and other high-level languages, this operation might be written as

$$X = Y + Z$$

We think of X as a variable which is assigned the result of adding values of two variables Y and Z.

Corresponding to each of these variables is a memory location. Perhaps location 10571 corresponds to X, location 10732 to Y, and location 27501 to Z. The contents of locations 10732 and 27501 are to be added together and the result stored in location 10571. We shall use the notation (10732) to mean the contents of location 10732.

The Fortran statement

$$X = Y + Z$$

is equivalent to the operation

(10732) + (27501) to be stored as   (10571)

It is not always convenient to use numerical addresses when talking and writing about the computer because the action of an operation is not dependent on the particular locations used. In the above example, the important information (to the user) is that X, Y, and Z are the variables involved. Therefore we shall write

(Y) + (Z) to be stored as (X)

instead.

This is a confusion of variable names and location names which is in common use, so the student should endeavor to become clear on the different uses of X, Y, Z above. In the Fortran statement $X = Y + Z$, we must think of X, Y, and Z as the *names* of variables, not as the variables themselves. The values of variables named Y and Z are to be added and the result is to be stored as the value of the variable named X. In machine language, X, Y, and Z are the names of locations which contain the variables. Therefore, there are two pieces of information associated with the name Z: first, the contents of the location; and second, the actual address of the location. To avoid pedantry, we usually refer simply to Z; the context makes it clear whether the contents or the address of the location is intended. Because a name, such as Z, has an associated address, it is often called a *symbolic address.*

2.1.3 IBM 370 and PDP-11 memory

The IBM 370 and the PDP-11 both allow individual 8-bit bytes to be addressed. If the memory consists of M bytes ($8M$ bits), then these will be addressed 0 through $M - 1$, and the programmer can refer to any one. We say that they are *byte addressable.* However, in most cases, larger units of information are fetched from their memories. The PDP-11, for example, usually works with 16-bit (2-byte) groups, and it is most convenient to describe the PDP-11 as a 16-bit machine. In the PDP-11, a word must have an even address; the word consists of the byte with the even address concatenated with the byte with the next-higher-numbered (odd) address. The even- (lower-) numbered byte is on the right when the information is written in the conventional manner, as shown in Figure 2.3. Notice that the bits are numbered from the least significant to the most significant end. (This has no practical implications in the organization of the machine, and is introduced here simply because manuals for the PDP-11 use the right-to-left numbering system.) Because of the restriction that words must start at an even address, an *alignment* or *boundary* error—an attempt to fetch or store a word with an odd-numbered address—can occur.

The IBM 370 works mainly with 4-byte (32-bit) words. Although it allows words to start on any byte address and continue through the next three higher-numbered addresses, from left to right, the word is processed more rapidly if it is aligned, that is, if it starts at an address divisible by 4. (The 360 series and early versions of the 370 required words to be aligned in this way.) IBM 370 instructions are themselves stored in multiples of 2 bytes which must be aligned (that is, start on even address boundaries).

The IBM 370 allows for 2-byte *halfwords* and 8-byte *doublewords,* whose use will be discussed in Section 2.4. These are also handled more rapidly if they

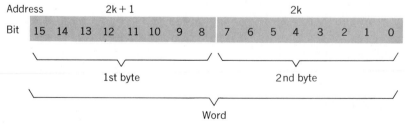

FIGURE 2.3 A PDP-11 word

are properly aligned—that is, if halfwords start at an even address and double-words start at an address divisible by eight. Again, this was a requirement on the 360 series and early versions of the 370.

2.2 THE CENTRAL PROCESSING UNIT (CPU)

The CPU is capable of a number of elementary operations such as addition, subtraction, multiplication, and division. The majority of arithmetic operations require two *operands,* that is, two numbers on which to operate. In addition, the result has to be placed somewhere. In the familiar desk calculator, there is usually a *register* or *accumulator.* An operation such as addition adds the number entered in the keyboard to the number in the accumulator, leaving the result in the accumulator (see Figure 2.4). Addition gets its operands from the keyboard and the accumulator, while multiplication gets its operands from two keyboards. The CPU of a digital computer may have one or more accumulators similar to the desk calculator. These will initially contain operands. The analogy of a keyboard is the memory. CPUs can be classified according to their use of accumulators in instructions. This will be done in the next four sections.

2.2.1 Three-address machines

It is not necessary to have any accumulators available to the user in the CPU if an operation of the form "(X) + (Y) to be stored as (Z)" is to be performed. The CPU could be told that an ADD operation is to be obeyed, and it could be given the three addresses X, Y, and Z. Such an instruction is called a *three-address instruction.* If the CPU predominantly executes three-address instructions, it is called a *three-address machine.* (We shall see that almost all computers will execute mixtures of instruction types, so this definition is necessarily loose.)

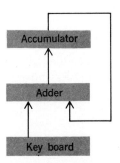

FIGURE 2.4   Addition on a desk calculator

In order to be able to evaluate arithmetic expressions involving addition, subtraction, multiplication, and division, three-address instructions for each of these operations can be provided. The instructions

Add	(ADD)	X,Y,Z
Subtract	(SUB)	X,Y,Z
Multiply	(MPY)	X,Y,Z
Divide	(DIV)	X,Y,Z

perform the indicated *binary* or *diadic* operation (that is, an operation on two operands) on the contents of locations X and Y and store the result in location Z. Thus

DIV   P,Q,R

is equivalent to

(P)/(Q) to be stored as   (R)

The Fortran assignment statement

A = B *(C + D *E − F/G)

is equivalent to

MPY	D,E,T1
ADD	C,T1,T1
DIV	F,G,T2
SUB	T1,T2,T1
MPY	B,T1,A

T1 and T2 are the addresses of two *temporary storage* locations, that is, locations which are used for scratch working storage in evaluating the expression. Note that there are five operations indicated in the expression B * (C + D * E − F/G), and that it takes exactly the same number of three-address instructions. This will be true for all expressions using only the binary operations provided by the computer, regardless of parenthesization.

2.2.2 Two-address machines

The three-address structure is not used in many machines for cost reasons. If A = B + C + D + E + F + G is to be programmed, the three-address code is

ADD	B,C,A
ADD	A,D,A
ADD	A,E,A
ADD	A,F,A
ADD	A,G,A

All but the first instruction needed only two different addresses, but the programmer had to provide three. This is recognized in the two-address machine by providing *two-address instructions.* A two-address instruction has the form

        ADD   A,B

which means

(A) + (B) to be stored as (A)

A *two-address machine* is one which uses predominantly two-address instructions. The four basic arithmetic operations are usually provided in the form

        ADD   A,B
        SUB   A,B
        MPY   A,B
        DIV   A,B

meaning

        (A) + (B)
        (A) − (B)
        (A) * (B)
        (A) / (B)

to be stored as (A). Note that the result is stored in the first address. The second address could have been used equally well in addition and multiplication because they are theoretically *commutative* operations; that is, (A) + (B) = (B) + (A) and (A) * (B) = (B) * (A). However, subtraction and division are not commutative; that is, (A) − (B) is not (B) − (A) and (A)/(B) is not (B)/(A). Because of this, we shall see that it is useful, although not necessary, to have *inverse* subtraction and division operations available.

An inverse operation, as the name implies, produces the "other-way-around" of the result. A two-address subtraction, SUB A,B, forms (A) − (B). A two-address inverse subtraction would form (B) − (A) and store it as (A). A two-address inverse division would form (B)/(A) and store it as (A).

The equivalent of the three-address operation MPY A, B, C can be performed by the two-address instructions as

        SUB   C,C
        ADD   C,A
        MPY   C,B

The effect of the first two instructions is to move the contents of location A to location C by first *clearing* it, that is, setting it to 0, and then adding (A).

Since this is a very common operation, it is usual to have a single two-address instruction MOVE A, B which puts (B) into location A. Then

$$A = B + C + D + E + F + G$$

can be implemented by

```
MOVE        A,B
ADD         A,C
ADD         A,D
ADD         A,E
ADD         A,F
ADD         A,G
```

Note that this sequence contains one more instruction than operations in the expression. In general the equivalent two-address code will contain at least one additional instruction in order to move one of the operands into position. Let us consider the assignment statement $A = B * (C + D * E - F/G)$. This can be performed by the two-address code

```
MPY         D,E
DIV         F,G
SUB         D,F
ADD         D,C
MOVE        A,B
MPY         A,D
```

Notice, however, that this destroys the contents of locations D and F. In fact, F now contains F/G and D contains $C + D * E - F/G$. In general, this is not permissible, because the variables stored in these locations may be needed in the evaluation of other expressions. Therefore, additional move orders must be used, resulting in the code:

```
MOVE        A,D
MPY         A,E
MOVE        T1,F
DIV         T1,G
SUB         A,T1
ADD         A,C
MPY         A,B
```

This is the shortest code which will evaluate this expression without changing any of the variables on the right-hand side; that is, assuming that all of the symbolic addresses A, B, C, D, E, F, and G represent different locations. If there is a possibility that A could represent the same location as one of B, C, . . . , F, then A must be replaced by a temporary location, say T2, in the above code and the additional instruction MOVE A, T2 must be appended.

In many calculations a *unary minus* is used. This is a subtraction operation with only one operand. It is called a unary or *monadic* operation. Thus the subtraction in $A = -B$ is unary. Some two-address machines will provide for this with either a MOVE-NEGATIVE two-address instruction or a SET-NEGATIVE, which only requires one address (the other would not be used).

2.2.3 One-address machines

In addition to saving the programmer work by requiring him to specify only two addresses rather than three, the two-address machine can also result in a lower overall cost, since less information has to be used to present each instruction. If the cost can be reduced by decreasing the number of addresses, we naturally look for ways to reduce the number more. The conventional desk calculator uses an accumulator for one of its operands. In a similar manner, the CPU of a computer can be provided with an accumulator that will always contain one operand of a binary operation. The four basic arithmetic operations are now provided in this form

```
ADD        A
SUB        A
MPY        A
DIV        A
```

SUB A means (AC) — (A) stored as (AC) where AC is the name of the accumulator. Because of the noncommutivity of the subtraction and division operations, it is convenient to have the inverse operations available also. Whereas DIV A means (AC)/(A) stored as (AC), INVERSE-DIV A means (A)/(AC) stored as (AC).

The accumulator of the one-address machine can be used as a scratch working register to evaluate expressions. The equivalent of the two-address MOVE operation is needed to place the contents of a memory location into the accumulator. This is often called LOAD. LOAD A means (A) stored as (AC). B + C + D + E can be calculated in the accumulator by

```
LOAD       B
ADD        C
ADD        D
ADD        E
```

If the result is to be stored back in memory, a MOVE from the accumulator to the memory is needed. This is called STORE A, and means (AC) to be stored as (A). The assignment statement $A = B * (C + D * E - F/G)$ can be calculated by

```
LOAD       F
DIV        G
STORE      T1
LOAD       D
MPY        E
ADD        C
SUB        T1
MPY        B
STORE      A
```

Note that this took two LOAD and two STORE instructions, just as the two-address machine took two MOVE instructions (plus an additional one if A could be the same as one of the right-hand-side operands). The equality of the number of LOAD, STORE, and MOVE instructions can be shown to be true for all assignment statements where only binary operations provided in the machine are used, all operands on the right-hand side are different, and it is stipulated that these operands cannot be changed.

Corresponding to the two-address machine's MOVE-NEGATIVE and SET-NEGATIVE instructions are the one-address machine's LOAD-NEGATIVE and SET-NEGATIVE instructions. The latter requires no address since it operates on the accumulator. Because the names of these instructions are unduly long, they are abbreviated in use to a form determined by the system. On many systems, LOAD will be replaced by a name such as CLEAR AND ADD, abbreviated CLA or CAD. This refers to the way the LOAD instruction operates by first clearing the accumulator to 300 and then adding the operand to it. On other machines, such as the IBM 370, it is abbreviated to L, in order to save the programmer writing. We shall use LOAD in this book, except when discussing specific machines.

2.2.4 Stack (zero-address) machines

If a saving is effected by reducing the number of addresses in instructions, it is natural to examine *zero-address instructions*. Since a binary operation requires two operands, both must be in known places prior to the execution of the instruction. These places could be specified cells in memory or registers in the CPU. Registers are faster than memory cells, so many computer designs have included two or more registers in the CPU. The IBM 370 and the PDP-11 are examples of such designs. In both of these machines it is necessary to specify which of the several CPU registers are to be used as accumulators, so that an address is needed after all. However, there is one type of CPU design in which arithmetic orders do not require any addresses. It uses the *stack* principle, also known as the *push-down list,* the *cellar,* or the *last-in-first-out* (LIFO) *queue.*

The accumulators in a stack machine can be thought of as a stack of registers, one on top of another. We refer to the top register as the *top level,* the next one down as the *second level,* and so on. Each of these registers holds a word of information. A binary operation operates on the top of two registers, puts the result in the second level and discards the top level, leaving the result as the new top level. The operation of discarding the top level is call a POP because it can be thought of as the result of moving each word up one register so that the top one *pops* out. The inverse operation, placing a word on top of the stack as a new top level, is called a PUSH because it can be thought of as the result of pushing a new word on top, causing all of the others to move down one register. A simple analogy to keep in mind is a stack of cards. A new word is pushed into the stack by writing it on a new blank card and placing it on top of the stack. A word is popped out by removing the top card from the stack. In this analogy, the four basic binary operations are equivalent to removing the top two cards, performing the operation on the words written on the cards, writing the result on a new blank card, and putting the new card on top of the stack. The two cards removed are thrown away. The action is shown in Figure 2.5.

A machine that uses this organization for its CPU is called a *stack machine.* It is obvious that if a word is to be fetched from memory or stored into memory an address must be provided, so a stack machine will have some instructions with addresses. Two essential instructions are LOAD and STORE. LOAD A fetches a word form memory location A and pushes it into the stack. STORE A pops a word from the stack and puts it into location A. The six basic operations for a machine are therefore:

LOAD	A	PUSH. (A) STORED AS (TL)
STORE	A	(TL) STORED AS (A). POP
ADD		(SL) + (TL) STORED AS (SL). POP
SUB		(SL) − (TL) STORED AS (SL). POP
MPY		(SL) * (TL) STORED AS (SL). POP
DIV		(SL) / (TL) STORED AS (SL). POP

SL and TL stand for second level and top level respectively. As with two- and one-address machines, an inverse subtract and an inverse divide are useful instructions, although not necessary.

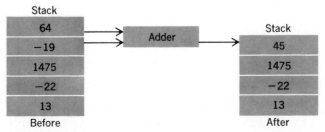

FIGURE 2.5   *Zero-address addition*

An assignment statement can be performed by code in many ways for any type of machine. There is always a way of coding a simple statement for a stack machine such that only one STORE instruction is used. (That one is needed to complete the assignment.) For example, the statement A = B * (C + D * E — F/G) is equivalent to the zero-address code

```
LOAD        B
LOAD        C
LOAD        D
LOAD        E
MPY
ADD
LOAD        F
LOAD        G
DIV
SUB
MPY
STORE       A
```

This form is obtained by writing LOAD VAR in turn for each variable VAR that appears in the expression and by inserting the arithmetic instructions into the code at the first opportunity, that is, when the top two levels of the stack contain the appropriate operands.

There must be a zero-address instruction for each operation in the original expression, a one-address LOAD instruction for each operand on the right and a one-address STORE instruction for the assignment. Since there is one more operand than binary operation in the expression, an N-operation assignment statement will use N zero-address instructions and $N + 2$ one-address instructions.

If we look back over this and the previous three sections, we see that the example A = B * (C + D * E — F/G) was coded, using each of the four structures. It required

5 three-address instructions

7 two-address instructions

9 one-address instructions

or 12 stack-machine instructions, of which 5 were zero-address and 7 were one-address

A computer designer is concerned about many different costs. There is the construction cost of the computer, the cost (in programmers' time) of writing programs, and the costs which increase if it takes longer to compute a result because one particular design is slower than another. Therefore, he will choose a design that, he hopes, keeps all these costs reasonable. A multi-address instruction appears to be better because fewer instructions are used to perform a given computation (in general). On the other hand, the cost of the hardware needed to implement a multiaddress instruction is higher than that for a simple instruction because it is more complex. A multiaddress instruction is also usually executed more slowly than a one- or zero-address instruction for two reasons; it takes more time to deal with the additional addresses, and the time it takes to get information from the memory is typically much longer than the time it takes to perform the arithmetic in the CPU.

For these reasons, the design of a computer represents many trade-offs between cost and speed and involves many judgments by the designer. Consequently, there are many differently organized computers on the market. However, they all use the basic principles discussed here. The next two sections will discuss briefly two particular designs which have many similarities. Since you will probably only want to read about one to avoid confusion, the common features will be summarized first.

Both the IBM 370 and the PDP-11 have been designed to use multiple accumulators. These are also called *general-purpose registers*. There are 8 in the PDP-11 and 16 in the 370. We will refer to them as R0, R1, R2, etc. The basic instructions in both machines are two-address. Thus an addition instruction specifies the address of one operand, then the address of the second, which is to be added to the first and stored back where the first resided. However, in both machines it can be specified that one or both of the operands are in a register. Thus

ADD   R4,A

can be written for the PDP-11, meaning that one operand is in register 4 and the other is in memory cell A. In a sense, register 4 is being used as an accumulator. Looking back at the example of the code for the one-address machine on page 30, it can be seen in the third instruction that it was necessary to store the contents of the accumulator to make it available for use in computing another term in the expression. The availability of several registers as accumulators makes this store unnecessary. Thus, this type of organization uses the smaller number of instructions necessary with two-address code, while using the smaller number of memory references of one-address and stack-machine code.

2.2.5 IBM 370 instructions†

The 370 series of machines has 16 general-purpose registers, each 32 bits long. These will be referred to as R0 through R15. Instructions can be written in the form

†This and subsequent sections will give an outline of the 370 organization. Complete details can be obtained by referring to the IBM System/370, Principles of Operation, IBM form number GA22-7000-2, July 1972.

L   Ri,A

meaning LOAD (abbreviated L) the register Ri from the memory cell A. Anything from 0 to 15 can be used for i. For example,

L   R3,X

puts the contents of memory cell X into register 3. (In fact, it can also be written as "L 3,X." We will use the R to remind the reader that a register is involved.)

The six basic instructions are abbreviated as shown in Table 2.2.

Each one of these uses a register address, followed by a comma, followed by a memory address. Thus the code corresponding to the Fortran statement I = J + K − L could be

```
L     R2,J
A     R2,K
S     R2,L
ST    R2,I
```

Any other register could have been used throughout.

The 32-bit registers in the 370 are said to hold *single-precision* numbers. There is some provision for *double-precision* numbers, which are 64 bits long. This is necessary because the product of two single-precision numbers is a double-precision number. Thus, when the two 3-digit decimal numbers 503 and 311 are multiplied, the 6-digit result is 156433. When two 32-bit numbers are multiplied, 64 bits may be needed to hold the result. This is accomplished by using a pair of registers. Multiplication of a single-precision number in a register (the multiplicand) by a single-precision number from memory (the multiplier) produces a 64-bit result in a pair of registers. The multiplicand and the multiplier are 32-bit integers, the result is a 64-bit integer occupying a pair of registers. These registers must always be an even-odd pair; that is, the most significant part of the result is in an even-numbered register,

TABLE 2.2 *IBM 370 basic instructions*

OPERATION	ABBREVIATION
Load	L
Add	A
Subtract	S
Multiply	M
Divide	D
Store	ST

while the least significant part is in the next-higher-numbered (odd) register. The multiplicand *must be in the odd-numbered register,* but the multiply instruction *must specify the even number,* or the instruction is illegal. The contents of the even-numbered register before the instruction do not affect the result. Thus, to form I * J in location N, assuming that the result is small enough to be a single-precision integer, we can write

L	R5,I
M	R4,J
ST	R5,N

Although the result can be a double-precision integer using R4 and R5, the assumption that the result is small means that it is completely contained in the least significant half, R5. For example, the product of 013 and 024 is the 6-digit number 000312, which can be represented in 3 digits as 312. The action of the multiply operation is shown in Figure 2.6.

Division is also shown in that figure. It starts with a double-precision number similar to that produced by the multiply operation, leaves a quotient in the odd-numbered register and a remainder in the even-numbered register. The divide instruction must also refer to the even-numbered register or an error will result.

Operand from memory or register

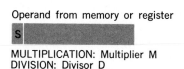

MULTIPLICATION: Multiplier M
DIVISION: Divisor D

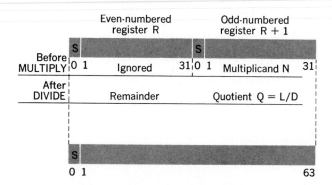

Before DIVIDE: Double–length dividend L

After MULTIPLY: Product R = N * M

FIGURE 2.6   *Fixed-point multiply/divide register usage*

To form J * K/L and to store the result in I, we could use the code

```
L     R3,J        Load J into R3.
M     R2,K        Result J*K is in R2,R3.
D     R2,L        Quotient J*K/L is in R3.
ST    R3,I        Store result into I.
```

This group of instructions is part of a set of 370 instructions known as RX instructions. The X stands for indexing, which will be discussed later. For the moment, think of it as representing the second operand that comes from memory. The first comes from a register; hence the R in RX. When an expression such as I * J + K * L is computed, a different set of registers should be used for the second multiplication because the first set contains the result of the first multiplication. Thus, a start might be

```
L     R3,I
M     R2,J        I*J is in R2,R3.
L     R5,K
M     R4,L        K*L is in R4,R5.
```

Assuming that the products are sufficiently small to be contained in the least significant part of the register pair, the next step is to add the contents of R3 and R5. To avoid storing one of them back into memory so that an A instruction can be used, instructions of the RR class are provided. These use registers for both operands. The instructions are

```
LR    Ri,Rj    Load register i from register j (a move operation).
AR    Ri,Rj    Add the contents of register j to register i.
SR    Ri,Rj    Subtract the contents of register j from register i.
MR    Ri,Rj    The contents of register (i + 1) are multiplied by the contents of
               register j. The double-precision result is left in registers i and (i + 1).
               i must be even.
DR    Ri,Rj    Divide the double-precision number in registers i and (i + 1) by the
               contents of register j. The quotient is left in register (i + 1) and the
               remainder in register i. i must be even.
```

Note that there is no instruction STR, as STR Ri, Rj would be identical to LR Rj, Ri and so is not needed.

Example

The Fortran statement N = (I + J * K) * (L − M) could be handled by

```
L     R3,J
M     R2,K     J * K in R2,R3. Assuming single-precision, it is in R3.
A     R3,I     I + J * K in R3.
L     R2,L
S     R2,M     L − M in R2.
```

MR   R2,R2   This actually multiplies the contents of R3 and R2, leaving a double-precision result in R2,R3.

ST   R3,N   If the result is only single-precision, it is contained in R3.

2.2.6 PDP-11 instructions †

The PDP-11 has eight registers in its CPU. Two of these, R6 and R7, are used for special purposes to be discussed later. The other six, R0 through R5, can be used as accumulators for arithmetic calculations. Each is 16 bits long. They can be specified as operands in the two-address instructions allowed, for example:

MOV   R3,R2   Move the contents of R3 to R2.
ADD   R4,R1   Add the contents of R4 to R1.
SUB   R1,R5   Subtract the contents of R1 from R5.

Note that the first address is the *source* and the second address, the *destination*. That is, the result finishes up in the second address. This is opposite to the instructions discussed in Section 2.2.2 and to the IBM 370 convention.

Either or both addresses can be in memory. Thus

ADD   I,J

adds the contents of cell I to cell J in memory. If the value of I + J − K is to be formed, but the contents of cells I, J, and K must not be changed, the sequence

MOV   I,R0
ADD   J,R0
SUB   K,R0

could be used, leaving the result in R0. If the result is to be returned to cell L, then the instruction

MOV   R0,L

could be used.

In this way, registers R0 through R5 can be used just as the accumulator of a one-address machine is used. However, the PDP-11 has the additional flexibil-

---

†A complete discussion of the PDP-11 instruction set can be found in the PDP-11 Handbook, 2d ed., Digital Equipment Corporation, 1969. This and other subsections will only cover some of the principal instructions.

ity of several accumulators, so that fewer memory references are required, and the capability to do regular two-address instructions.

The PDP-11 is an example of a simple, low-cost machine that is often used for experimental control or in a *hands-on* environment (that is, one in which the programmer has access to the main console of the machine and can control the execution). Part of the reason for the low cost is the "narrow" memory, which is only 16 bits wide. Another reason is that more complex instructions are not provided, at least in the basic model. Thus it has no multiply or divide instruction as a standard feature—although one is available as an optional extra, like a higher-powered engine in an automobile. This is not as serious a drawback as it might seem, as it is possible to program multiply and divide using the ADD, SUB, and other instructions to be introduced in later sections of this chapter. The use of subroutines, similar to procedure oriented language subroutines you have already seen in earlier courses, will make the machine look as though it had as good an instruction set as a larger machine —although it will execute multiplication and division considerably more slowly than it would if the hardware multiply and divide feature were added.

Almost all computers use instructions of several different types. Although the PDP-11 is a two-address machine, it has one- and zero-address instructions for special purposes. Four examples of one-address instructions are:

CLR	Clear—sets the operand to 0.
INC	Increment—adds 1 to the operand.
DEC	Decrement—subtracts 1 from the operand.
NEG	Negate—forms minus the operand.

Thus, we could form $-(I + J)$ in R4 by the sequence

MOV	I,R4
ADD	J,R4
NEG	R4

2.3 THE CONTROL UNIT

The CPU is required to execute a sequence of instructions. In order to make use of the high speed of a typical processing unit (10^3 to 10^6 instructions per second), it is necessary to feed instructions to the CPU at a commensurate speed. This means that they must be stored in a high-speed memory. Some early proposals for computers suggested that this memory should be separate from the data memory. However, the one-memory crowd won the day (although we shall discover that there is now a tendency to separate data and instruction storage for other reasons), so that in addition to representing numbers or alphabetic characters, a word may also represent an instruction.

The way in which the instructions are represented varies from machine to machine, so this section will first discuss the general features. We have seen that there can be zero-, one-, two-, or three-address instructions. Since memory is usually addressed by a positive integer between 0 and $M - 1$, A bits, where 2^A is at least M, are needed to represent each address. In addition, some bits are needed to distinguish between the various instructions. The word may be divided into a number of *fields,* each field representing an address or the instruction. For example, if M is $65,636 = 2^{16}$ and the word length is 40 bits, the "instruction format" for a two-address machine might be as in Figure 2.7. Eight bits of instruction code allow for $2^8 = 256$ different instructions. In practice, a machine may have both one- and two-address instructions, so that more than one format must be used. For example, the IBM 7090 uses one- and two-address instructions with some special zero-address instructions. The formats of the PDP-11 and 370 will be examined later.

A rule must be set up to determine which location in memory is used to provide the next instruction. In some early machines, the address of this location is provided with each order. If the accumulator structure of the machine is two-address, say, this would be referred to as a two-plus-one-address machine. The most widely known machine that provided the instruction sequence in this way was the IBM 650, with a one-plus-one address structure. This technique was used because the main memory of the 650 was a nonrandom access storage drum. The access time for the next instruction depended on the length of the current instruction and the locations of both. In order to keep this time low, the next instruction had to be in one of a set of optimum locations. Machines with a random access storage do not need to use such a technique.

(Advertising usage of computer manufacturers has given the description "random access" to nonrandom access devices, such as drums and disks. The description "immediate access" then has to be used for the truly random access devices such as core stores. Nonrandom access will be discussed in a subsequent chapter.)

If the address of the next instruction is not provided in the current instruction, then there must be a simple rule for calculating it. The most obvious rule is to use the next-higher location in store, and this is what the majority of computers use. A *control counter,* which is a register in the control unit containing an address-length number, contains the address of the next instruction to be obeyed. Each time that an instruction is fetched from memory, the con-

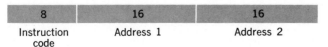

8	16	16
Instruction code	Address 1	Address 2

FIGURE 2.7   *Instruction format*

trol counter is incremented by one. The action of sending the address contained in the control counter to memory, incrementing it, and reading the instruction addressed is called the *fetch cycle.*

If instructions are always stored in successive memory locations, the memory space will be exhausted long before an appreciable amount of computation has been performed. A computer derives a lot of its power from its ability to repeat a sequence of instructions many times. This means that the sequence of successive locations must be broken and control transferred back to an earlier section of the program. A BRANCH instruction is usually provided for this purpose. (It may also be called a TRANSFER or a JUMP instruction.) It is a one-address instruction. BRANCH X means execute the next instruction from location X by putting X into the control counter.

The BRANCH instruction allows a section of code to be repeated indefinitely, but it provides no means for stopping the section of code and starting another. Therefore, *conditional branch* instructions are provided. These can be constructed to test any internal machine condition or even external conditions such as switches. In a one-address machine the accumulator can be tested by these instructions. A typical instruction is BPL (Branch if PLus). BPL X causes *branch address* X to be placed in the control counter if the accumulator is positive or 0. Similar orders include *branch if minus but not zero, branch if zero,* and *branch if non-zero.* If the condition is met, the next instruction is taken from the branch address. If not, it is taken from the next location in sequence.

Two-address machines often provide two-address instructions to test one location and branch to another if the test is successful. Stack machines usually test the top level of the stack and branch in a one-address instruction.

Conditional orders can be used to construct program loops. If, for example, it is required to execute a sequence of instructions a given number of times, say N, a counter can be set to N initially and decreased by 1 after each execution of the loop. It will be 0 after the Nth pass through the loop. Thus if N is greater than 0, 2^N can be constructed by the following code for a stack machine:

	LOAD	NN	NN is the address of a location containing N.
	LOAD	TWO	TWO is the address of a location containing 2.
	BRANCH	B	
A	LOAD	RESULT	
	LOAD	TWO	
	MPY		Multiply result by 2 and store back in result.
B	STORE	RESULT	

LOAD	ONE	ONE is the address of a location containing 1.
SUB		Decrease counter in stack by 1.
BNZ	A	Branch if non-zero.
. . . . . .		

The BNZ (Branch if Non-Zero) instruction is assumed to branch if the top of the stack is non-zero, but not to pop the stack. The location to which control is transferred is indicated symbolically by writing a symbolic address in the branch and on the left of the instruction which is the *object* of the branch. It is evident that this symbolic address may only appear on the left of one instruction.

In some problems it is necessary to execute a sequence of instructions until a given condition is met. For example, the square root of a positive number A is the limit of the sequence X_n, $n = 1, 2, \ldots$

where $X_1 = (A + 1)/2$
$\qquad X_n = (A/X_{n-1} + X_{n-1})/2$

It can be shown that if X_n is calculated to infinite precision, it decreases to $\sqrt{A}$ as n increases. Therefore $X_{n+1} - X_n$ is theoretically less than 0. With finite-precision arithmetic $X_{n+1} - X_n = (A/X_n - X_n)/2$ will eventually become 0 or positive, so this fact can be used to end the *iteration*. The code for a square-root program on a one-address machine is

	LOAD	A	
	ADD	ONE	
	MPY	HALF	Initial approximation X_1.
	BRANCH	L1	
L2	ADD	X	
L1	STORE	X	New approximation X_n.
	LOAD	A	
	DIV	X	
	SUB	X	
	MPY	HALF	$X_{n+1} - X_n = (A/X_n - X_n)^* 0.5$.
	BMI	L2	Stop when no further decrease (Branch if Minus).
	. . . .		

(Result is in X.)

HALF is the address of a location containing ½. A multiply by ½ was used instead of a divide by 2, since multiplication is faster than division by a factor of 2 or 3 on most machines.†

---

†We have not yet discussed how numbers other than integers can be represented in the computer memory. It is obvious that they have to be, but further discussion will be delayed until Section 2.4.

2.3.1 Instruction representation

The word length of a computer is decided by the needs of the data to be processed. The typical instruction may not require as many bits as the word provides, although in some cases it may require more. If all instructions are to occupy the same number of bits, then the maximum must be chosen. This maximum may not be the same as the length of the word. If it is smaller but close to the length of the word, then the word may as well be used as the basic instruction. Historically, this has been the most common choice. If, however, the number of bits required for an instruction is considerably less than a word, then several instructions can be *packed* into a word. The control counter must, in effect, address a part word so that it can *point* to the next instruction.

If the difference between the shortest and the longest instruction (that is, in the number of bits required) is considerable, then it is more efficient to use *variable-length instructions.* Each instruction occupies a certain number of bits, usually a multiple of some divisor of the word length such as 6 or 8, and instructions are packed into memory as tightly as possible.

The IBM 370 and the PDP-11 allow for 16-, 32-, and 48-bit instructions (2, 4, or 6 bytes). This allows for more bits to be used when more information is needed. For example, when both operands are located in general-purpose registers, only a few bits are needed (4 to specify one of 16 registers in the 370, and 3 to specify one of 8 registers in the PDP-11). Both machines then use a 16-bit instruction format. However, if both operands are in memory, 48 bits are needed to specify the instruction with its two addresses.

The reason for going to all these apparent complications is that if fewer bits are used to represent the instructions in a program, less memory will be used for that program. This will lower the cost of the computer needed to execute that program and decrease the length of time taken to fetch the instructions from the memory during program execution. For this sort of reason, the 370 and the PDP-11 use one-address branch instructions. A simple BRANCH only needs one address anyway, but a conditional branch such as BPL (Branch if PLus) needs to specify the branch address and the item to be tested for positiveness. Both machines solve this problem in the same way—the tested quantity is essentially the last quantity calculated. This is handled by having a *condition register* which contains information about the last quantity calculated. It is a very short register, 4 bits for the PDP-11 and 2 bits for the IBM 370. When an operation is performed, the condition code is set to indicate the nature of the result: whether, for example, it is positive, negative, or zero. The branch instructions are called "branch on condition" and branch according to the state of the condition code.

The next two subsections will discuss the branch instructions in the IBM 370 and the PDP-11.

2.3.2 IBM 370 control

Instructions in the 370 are fetched from memory in order. The fetching is controlled by a control counter which is 24 bits long. Instructions can be multiples of 2 bytes in length and must start on halfword boundaries. Therefore, the control counter must always contain an even number. The control counter forms a part of what is known as the "program status word" (PSW). The PSW is shown in Figure 2.8.† It also includes bits of information that indicate the status of the program in execution. The majority of bits in the status word are of no interest to most programmers. The second 32 bits contain the control counter in the last 24 bits; and they contain the instruction-length code, condition code, and program mask in the first 8 bits. The instruction-length code (ILC) indicates the number of 16-bit halfwords in the current instruction (1, 2, or 3).

A branch instruction causes the last 24 bits of the PSW to be changed. This is written as

$$B \qquad\qquad T$$

which causes an unconditional branch to location T. Conditional branching is performed by means of the condition code in the program status word. This code is set as the result of a number of instructions. In particular, the add and subtract instructions set the code to be 0, 1, 2, or 3 as the result is

---

†The format shown for the PSW is that used in the basic control mode. If the computer is equipped with the extended control facility, a second form, the extended control mode, can also be used. This moves some of the fields around, but their position is not important to most programmers. Details can be found in IBM System/370, Principles of Operation, *op. cit.*

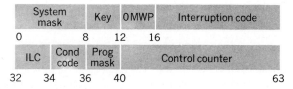

FIGURE 2.8   *IBM 370 program status word in basic mode*

0, less than 0, greater than 0, or overflowed,† respectively. The BC (Branch on Condition) instruction is used to test the condition code. The BC instruction contains a 4-bit group (in place of the usual register address) which specifies the condition to be tested. If the bits in this group are numbered 0 through 3, then a branch occurs if the bit corresponding to the condition code is a 1. For example, the instruction

    BC   10,T

will cause a transfer to location T if condition 0 or 2 is true, since 10 decimal is 1010 binary. Thus it is a branch on ≥ 0 after an add or subtract. To add accumulators 3 and 5 together and to branch to location S if the result is less than or equal to 0, we can write

    AR   3,5
    BC   12,S

The AR (Add from Register) instruction sets the condition code to be 0 if the result is 0 or 1 if negative. The BC (Branch on Condition) 12 branches if code 0 or 1 is set, since 12 decimal is 1100 binary. In order to test a number already in a register, there is an instruction LTR (Load and Test from Register), which loads one register from another as an LR does, but also sets the condition code as for the add instruction. Thus to branch if register 3 is strictly positive, we can write

    LTR   3,3
    BC   2,T

This LTR instruction does not change register 3, but it does set the condition code to 2 if it is strictly positive. Since 2 is binary 0010, the BC 2 branches in this case.

The condition code is set by arithmetic operations, except for multiply and divide, and by most other operations that change data, but not usually by those that only move data.‡ One special set of operations that sets the condition code without changing or moving data is the compare instructions. These are two-address instructions that compare the values of the two operands in

---

†*Overflow* means that that the result of an arithmetic operation is too large to be represented in the space available. This will be discussed further in Section 2.4.
‡Details can be found in the IBM System/370, *Principles of Operation, op. cit.*

order to set the condition code. The result of the condition code after arithmetic and comparison operations is shown in Table 2.3.

Two forms of the comparison operation are

C	Ri,A	First operand in register i, second operand in memory cell A.
CR	Ri,Rj	First and second operands in registers i and j, respectively.

The general form of the branch on condition is BC n,T, where n is an integer between 0 and 15 and T is the branch address. The meaning of n after arithmetic and comparison operations is shown in Table 2.4. To save the programmer the task of remembering the values ·of n, the assembler provides extended mnemonics. For example, BP T means Branch to location T if the condition code is set for a positive result. Hence, it is equivalent to BC 2,T. The extended mnemonics are also shown in Table 2.4.

TABLE 2.3 *Values of 370 condition code*

CONDITION CODE	AFTER ARITHMETIC OPERATION	AFTER COMPARISON OPERATION
0	Result zero	Operands equal
1	Result negative	First operand smaller
2	Result strictly positive	First operand larger
3	Result too large	(Not used)

TABLE 2.4 *Meaning of n in BC instruction and extended mnemonic*

n	AFTER ARITHMETIC OPERATION	EXTENDED MNEMONIC	AFTER COMPARISON OPERATION	EXTENDED MNEMONIC
0	Never—no operation	NOP	Never	NOP
1	Overflow	BO	Never	
2	Plus (strictly)	BP	First operand high	BH
3	Plus or overflow		High	
4	Minus	BM	First operand low	BL
5	Minus or overflow		Low	
6	Not (zero or overflow)		Not equal	
7	Not zero	BNZ	Not equal	BNE
8	Zero	BZ	Equal	BE
9	Zero or overflow		Equal	
10	Not (minus or overflow)		Not low	
11	Not minus	BNM	Not low	BNL
12	Not (plus or overflow)		Not high	
13	Not plus	BNP	Not high	BNH
14			Always	
15	Always (branch)	B	Always	B

2.3.3 PDP-11 control

The PDP-11 fetches instructions from its memory in order of increasing address. The control counter is R7, which is the reason we do not use R7 in ordinary arithmetic. Instructions are 2, 4, or 6 bytes long, so R7 is incremented by 2, 4, or 6 during the execution of an instruction. Instructions must lie on word boundaries, so R7 is always even.

The most flexible form of control transfer instruction is the JMP (jump) instruction.

        JMP   T

transfers control to location T. For reasons which will be apparent in Section 2.5, there is another instruction, called branch.

        BR   T

also transfers control to location T, but T is restricted to a region of core that starts 127 words before the word containing the BR, and ends 128 words after the word containing the BR. (This restriction makes it possible for the BR instruction to fit into one word, whereas the JMP usually requires two. The BR instruction should be used whenever possible.)

Conditional branch instructions have the same format as the branch instruction BR, and so they are also restricted to transferring control to the same area of memory. This restriction does not affect the programmer too much, as the assembler will take care of checking the restriction. Consequently, the programmer simply writes, say,

        BEQ   T

to branch to location T if the result is equal (to zero). If location T is not within the allowable range, the assembler will complain! In that case, the alternative construction

        BNE   X
        JMP   T
X   (next instruction)

can be used. BNE branches to the instruction labeled X if the result is not equal (to zero). If the result is equal (to zero), the branch is not taken, so a jump to location T occurs, as desired.

The condition register in the PDP-11 is 4 bits long. These bits are called

N—for Negative

Z—for Zero

V—for oVerflow (that is, the result is too large)

C—for Carry (to be described in Section 2.4)

These bits are set or cleared by most data manipulation operations and by the compare operation. Thus Z and N may be changed by a move operation. After a move has been executed, Z and N will reflect the value of the data item moved. V and C will not be changed by a move, as no overflow or carry can occur. All 4 bits are set by an add or subtract operation to reflect the value of the result. The compare instruction, written

        CMP   A,B

compares the values of the two operands by forming A — B (note that this is the opposite of SUB A,B, which forms B — A). The condition of the result is stored in the condition bits just as if a subtract had been performed; however, the result is not saved, and so no memory cells nor any of the general-purpose registers are changed. The value of a single operand can be checked with the TST A instruction, which sets the N and Z bits according to the value of the operand A and clears the V and C bits.

The control bits are part of the central processor status register. The format of this register is

unused		priority	T	N	Z	V	C
15		7	6	5	4	3	2	1	0

The priority bits will be covered in Chapter 6. Bit T is described in the PDP-11 manual; it will not be described here as it is only used for program debugging. The remaining 4 bits are described above.

A set of instructions are available for testing the state of the condition bits. They are shown in Table 2.5 on page 48.

(The difference between instructions such as BGE and BPL has to do with overflow. If two numbers are subtracted or compared and the result does not overflow, the operations do the same thing, but if the difference is too large to be represented, they behave differently. Generally, following a comparison BGE, BLT, BGT, or BLE should be used. A full discussion of this must wait until twos complement arithmetic has been discussed in the next section.)

TABLE 2.5   *Conditional branch mnemonics for PDP-11*

MNEMONIC	DESCRIPTION (BRANCH IF . . .)
BNE	Not Equal (to zero)
BEQ	EQual (to zero)
BGE	Greater or Equal (to zero)
BLT	Less Than (zero)
BGT	Greater Than (zero)
BLE	Less than or Equal (to zero)
BPL	PLus
BMI	MInus
BHI	HIgher
BLOS	Lower Or Same
BVC	oVerflow Clear (no overflow)
BVS	oVerflow Set
BCC	Carry Clear—same as BHIS (higher or same)
BCS	Carry Set—same as BLO (lower)

2.4 REPRESENTATION OF NUMBERS

Section 2.1 discussed the representation of integers by sign/magnitude and characters in 8-bit bytes. The previous section discussed how instructions can be represented in a word. It is also necessary to represent floating-point numbers and fixed-point numbers for scientific work. This section will discuss a number of methods used for this, and will finish with a discussion of number representation in the IBM 370 and the PDP-11.

2.4.1 Fractions

Recall that in Section 2.1 integers between -31 and $+31$ in 6 bits were represented using the sign/magnitude convention. If the binary representation is $b_0 b_1 b_2 b_3 b_4 b_5$, the value of the integer represented is

$$(1 - 2b_0) (b_1 \cdot 2^4 + b_2 \cdot 2^3 + b_3 \cdot 2^2 + b_4 \cdot 2^1 + b_5 \cdot 2^0)$$

Assume that a word represents whatever we want it to represent. These 6 bits only represent the integer value above when that is what we want them to represent. It is possible to think of the binary point as being anywhere in the word, rather than immediately after b_5 as it is when 6 bits represent an integer. If the point is thought of as being immediately before b_1, the value represented is scaled by $2^{-5} = 1/32$. This will be called a fraction, although it is an improper use of the word, as a fraction can have any numerator and denominator and in the case of these fractions the denominator is always 32. Another way of looking at this is that the word represents the number of thirty-seconds. The values represented by a 6-bit fraction are:

NUMBER	REPRESENTATION
$-\frac{31}{32} = -.96875$	111 111
$-\frac{30}{32} = -.9375$	111 110
. . . . .	. . . . . .
$-\frac{1}{32} = -.03125$	100 001
$-0 = -0$	100 000
$+0 = +0$	000 000
$+\frac{1}{32} = +.03125$	000 001
. . . . .	. . . . . .
$+\frac{31}{32} = +.96875$	011 111

The value of the number is now given by

$$(1 - 2b_0)(b_1 \cdot 2^{-1} + b_2 \cdot 2^{-2} + b_3 \cdot 2^{-3} + b_4 \cdot 2^{-4} + b_5 \cdot 2^{-5})$$

Fractions are a special case of *fixed-point* numbers, where the point is as-sumed to be in a fixed place. We can always view this representation as an integer scaled by an appropriate amount, For example, if the binary point in a fixed-point number was just before the last bit in the word, then we could view the number as containing the number of halves in the value.

2.4.2 Rounding and range

If the word contained N bits rather than 6, then the sign/magnitude represen-tation of a fraction would end in $b_{N-1} \cdot 2^{-N+1}$, while the *range* of an inte-ger would be from $-2^{N-1} + 1$ to $2^{N-1} - 1$. The range of the representa-tion of a number is the set of values that can be represented. This is necessar-ily a finite set. Thus when numbers between $-\frac{31}{32}$ and $+\frac{31}{32}$ are represented in a 6-bit word, only 63 discrete values can be represented. This is shown in Fig-ure 2.9. If a number which is not one of these discrete values is to be repre-sented, then only an approximation can be made. For example, if $\frac{2}{3}$ is to be represented in a 3-bit machine, then either $\frac{1}{2}$ or $\frac{3}{4}$ must be used instead (see Figure 2.10). As a binary fraction, $\frac{2}{3}$ is 0.101010 . . . ad infinitum. This can be re-duced to 2 bits by chopping off, or *truncating,* all bits after the second, so that $\frac{2}{3}$ is approximately 0.10. However, it is generally better to choose the closest

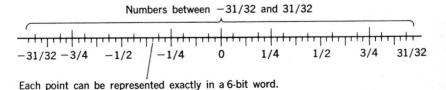

Numbers between $-31/32$ and $31/32$

Each point can be represented exactly in a 6-bit word.

FIGURE 2.9   *Six-bit sign/magnitude fraction values*

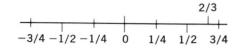

FIGURE 2.10

available value, in this case ¾ or 0.11, since the error is then $-\frac{1}{12}$ rather than ⅙. Taking the closest value is called *rounding*. The error introduced is called *roundoff error* in either case. By rounding rather than truncating, the round-off error can be kept to not more than half the distance between two adjacent representable numbers, or 2^{-N}. It is important to remember that integer arithmetic is exact as long as the range is not exceeded, whereas fractional arithmetic is only exact in those unusual cases where the numbers represented are exact. Generally, fractions will be in error by a small amount. For example, $\frac{1}{10}$ cannot be represented exactly in a binary machine.

Because representable numbers have only a finite range, arithmetic operations will give incorrect answers if the result is not in range. The error can be one of two types. If the answer is larger than the largest representable number, then the answer supplied by the machine will be grossly in error and we say that *overflow* has occurred. In the other case, the answer may be in between two representable numbers, so that the machine can choose one or the other as its answer. This is another example of roundoff error. Multiplication of two fractions, for example, may lead to roundoff error if the answer is to be represented in a single word.

2.4.3 Floating point

It is not always convenient to restrict the representable numbers to either integers or fractions. In many problems, numbers which vary in size from 10^{10} to 10^{-10} must be used. For this reason, floating-point arithmetic was added to machines. We frequently use decimal floating-point arithmetic to write down numbers. For example, we may write

$$
\begin{array}{llll}
& 1052000 & \text{as} & .1052 \times 10^{7} \\
\text{or} & .0000531 & \text{as} & .531 \times 10^{-4}
\end{array}
$$

The first part of the floating-point representation of 1052000, namely .1052, is called the *fraction* or *mantissa*. The second part, 7, is called the *exponent*, in this case the base-10 exponent. In a binary machine we usually use an exponent base which is a power of 2, such as 2, 4, 8, and 16, rather than 10. Part of the word may be used to represent the mantissa as a binary fraction and part to represent the exponent as a binary integer. Figure 2.11 shows the representation used in the CDC 3600. The exponent is a base-2 exponent E between -1023 and $+1023$. The mantissa is a sign-plus-36-bit fraction F

between $-1 + 2^{-36}$ and $1 - 2^{-36}$. The value of the number represented is $F \times 2^E$. Note that in floating-point arithmetic, roundoff error in representing a number depends on the exponent. Thus in the CDC 3600, the error in the fraction can be limited to 2^{-37} (half of the spacing). However, the actual error is limited by $2^{-37}2^E$. Hence it is desirable to make E as small as possible so as to make the error as small as possible. For each unit that E is reduced, the fraction F is doubled. However, the absolute value of F must be less than 1, so it can only be doubled until it is greater than or equal to $\frac{1}{2}$ (unless it is 0). A floating-point number which is represented in the form with a minimum exponent is called *normalized*. The number .001730 can be represented as

$.000173 \times 10^1$
$.001730 \times 10^0$
$.017300 \times 10^{-1}$
$.173000 \times 10^{-2}$

in a 6-digit decimal machine. Only the last form is normalized.

Arithmetic operations on floating-point numbers can cause overflow if the resulting exponent is too large. The exponent may also be less than the most negative representable number, in which case the answer is very small. This is called *underflow*. Some computers will replace the result with a formal 0 consisting of a 0 fractional part and the smallest exponent allowed.

Even if the result of a floating-point operation is not 0, it is important to note that errors which are large relative to the size of the answer can occur. In fixed-point addition, the number of bits and their position relative to the binary point do not change, so the error is in a known bit position. When two floating-point numbers with opposite signs are added, the result may contain very few significant bits. The user may, however, be fooled by printing the answer to high precision. For example, if the two decimal floating-point numbers $.65284 \times 10^{-3}$ and $-.65252 \times 10^{-3}$ are added, the result, after normalization, is $.32000 \times 10^{-6}$. However, it is no longer accurate to 5 digits. If the original numbers had errors as large as 1 in the least significant digit, the result has an error as large as 2 in the second digit. The problems

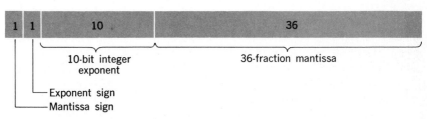

FIGURE 2.11   Floating-point word in the CDC 3600

of floating numerical errors are complex and not a subject for this text or this level: they belong in a study of numerical analysis.

2.4.4 Twos complement representation of numbers

The sign/magnitude system of negative number representation is familiar in everyday life. A number of computers use this system, but there are two other systems that are important. The first is the *twos complement* system. It arises in the following manner: consider a 6-bit machine in which bit 0 is reserved for a sign bit yet to be discussed and the other 5 bits represent a fraction in the usual way. Suppose two numbers are subtracted, such as $\frac{5}{32}$ from $\frac{11}{32}$:

$$
\begin{array}{ll}
0.01011 & \frac{11}{32} \\
-0.00101 & -\frac{5}{32} \\
\hline
0.00110 & \frac{6}{32}
\end{array}
$$

When everything is positive we can consider the sign bit just as any other bit in the arithmetic process. However, if the number being subtracted is larger, we usually perform the subtraction in the other direction. Thus, if you are asked to subtract 43 from 25 in decimal, you say that the answer is minus $(43 - 25)$ and subtract 25 from 43. A computer is not equipped with the foresight to reverse the operation, so a computer which could only perform 2-decimal-digit arithmetic would perform as follows:

$$
\begin{array}{l}
25 \\
-43 \\
\hline
82
\end{array}
$$

The answer of 82 is not correct because a borrow from the next position to the left was ignored. But in 2-digit arithmetic, 82 will act like the true answer of -18. Thus, if we add 34 to 82 in 2-digit arithmetic, we perform the operation

$$
\begin{array}{l}
82 \\
+34 \\
\hline
16
\end{array}
$$

The carry into the hundreds position is ignored because only 2-digit arithmetic is allowed. This is the correct answer of $34 - 18$. Note that 82 is in fact $100 - 18$. The hundred arose because of the neglected borrow from the hundreds position. Suppose that $\frac{11}{32}$ is subtracted from $\frac{5}{32}$ as though the sign bit in a binary representation were a regular bit in the number

$$
\begin{array}{ll}
0.00101 & \tfrac{5}{32} \\
-0.01011 & -\tfrac{11}{32} \\
\hline
1.11010 & -\tfrac{6}{32}
\end{array}
$$

In some sense, the answer, 1.11010, represents $-\tfrac{6}{32}$. Note that the borrow from the top bit of the answer was ignored. Since the first bit of the answer arose by subtracting 1 from 0, it is really a -1, that is, it has a negative *weight*. The word 0.00101 represents $\tfrac{1}{8} + \tfrac{1}{32}$ and the number .01011 represents $\tfrac{1}{4} + \tfrac{1}{16} + \tfrac{1}{32}$. The answer 1.11010 represents

$$-1 + \tfrac{1}{2} + \tfrac{1}{4} + \tfrac{1}{16} = -\tfrac{6}{32}$$

since the weight of the first bit is negative. Now let us add $-\tfrac{6}{32}$ to $\tfrac{11}{32}$ in this representation:

$$
\begin{array}{ll}
0.01011 & \tfrac{11}{32} \\
+1.11010 & +-\tfrac{6}{32} \\
\hline
0.00101 & \tfrac{5}{32}
\end{array}
$$

since the weights of the fraction bits are positive, they are added. The arithmetic in the sign position for this example is "0 + -1 + a carry of 1 is 0." Notice that this is the same as saying "0 + 1+ a carry of 1 is 0, carry 1— forget the carry because there is no place to put it."

The name "twos complement" is derived from the fact that the negative form of the number can be obtained by subtracting it from 2. Two is too large for the representation, but if we ignore this, we can find $-\tfrac{6}{32}$ by the following arithmetic:

$$
\begin{array}{lc}
2 & 10.00000 \\
-\tfrac{6}{32} & -0.00110 \\
\hline
& 1.11010
\end{array}
$$

The result is indeed the twos complement form of $-\tfrac{6}{32}$. This relation will hold for fractions of any length. It is true because the statement that "the weight of the sign position is negative" is the same as the statement that "2 was added to a -1 in the sign position to get a $+1$." A twos complement integer is simply an integer in which the weight of the first bit is negative.

SUBTRACTION IN TWOS COMPLEMENT

The reason for the use of the twos complement representation in the machine is that the addition can be done directly. It is not necessary for the machine to examine the signs of the numbers to decide whether to add or subtract, or, in the case of subtraction, to decide which number to subtract from which.

Rules for subtraction in a twos complement representation can readily be formulated. Alternatively, it can be done by addition of the negative of the number; that is, $A - B = A + (-B)$. Given B, we need a rule for forming $-B$. The value of a twos complement integer $b_0 b_1 b_2 \ldots + b_{N-1}$ is

$$-b_0 \cdot 2^{N-1} + b_1 \cdot 2^{N-2} + \cdots + b_{N-1} \cdot 2^0$$

Hence minus this number is

$$b_0 \cdot 2^{N-1} - b_1 \cdot 2^{N-2} - \cdots - b_{N-1} \cdot 2^0$$

Note that

$$2^{N-1} = 2^{N-2} + 2^{N-3} + \cdots + 2^1 + 2^0 + 1$$

Therefore, by adding and subtracting 2^{N-1} from $-B$ we get

$$-B = b_0 \cdot 2^{N-1} - 2^{N-1} - b_1 \cdot 2^{N-2} + 2^{N-2} - b_2 \cdot 2^{N-3} + 2^{N-3} - \cdots - b_{N-1} \cdot 2^0 + 2^0 + 1$$

$$= -(1 - b_0)2^{N-1} + (1 - b_1) \cdot 2^{N-2} + \cdots + (1 - b_{N-1}) \cdot 2^0 + 1$$

This number is a 1 in the least significant position plus the value of a twos complement number which is the *digit-wise complement*, or simply *complement*, of the original number. The digit-wise complement of a number is formed by writing a 0 for each 1 and a 1 for each 0. Thus -6 can be obtained from 6 by the following steps:

6	000110

complement	111001
add 1 +	1

−6	111010

Hence subtraction can be done by the adder hardware in a twos complement machine equipped with a complementing mechanism which is usually trivial.

Example of subtraction of fractions

$^{11}\!/_{32}$	$-^6\!/_{32}$	decimal form
=001011	−000110	binary form
=001011	+111001+000001	complement subtrahend
=001011		
+111001		
+000001		
=000101		
=$^5\!/_{32}$		

TABLE 2.6   Transformations from decimal to twos complement

DECIMAL	DECIMAL +32	BINARY INTEGER (CHARACTERISTIC FORM)	TWOS COMPLEMENT FORM
−32	0	000000	100000
−31	1	000001	100001
−30	2	000010	100010
. . . .	. . . . . .	. . . .	. . . .
−1	31	011111	111111
0	32	100000	000000
+1	33	100001	000001
+2	34	100010	000010
. . . .	. . . . . .	. . . .	. . . .
+30	62	111110	011110
+31	63	111111	011111

Yet another way of viewing twos complement is as follows. We wish, say, to represent integers between −32 and +31 in a 6-bit word. (There are exactly $2^6 = 64$ such integers.) Add 32 to the integer I that we wish to represent in order to get a positive integer in the range 0 to 63. Represent this as a 6-bit binary integer. This form is frequently used for exponents (for example, in the IBM 7094) and is then called a *characteristic*. Because 0 is now represented by 100000 rather than 000000, the sign bit of every number is complemented. The sequence of transformations is shown in Table 2.6.

The negative form of a number A represented in twos complement is frequently referred to as the twos complement of A. Thus the twos complement of 11010011 is 00101101.

EXTENDING THE PRECISION OF A TWOS COMPLEMENT NUMBER

When the precision of a sign/magnitude number is increased, it is only necessary to add zeros. Thus the 6-digit integer −123456 becomes −000123456 as a 9-digit integer, while the 3-digit fraction +.123 becomes +.123000 as a 6-digit fraction. Similarly, zeros are added to the left or right end of a binary sign/magnitude integer or fraction respectively. However, the twos complement causes problems when negative integers have their precision increased. This arises because the weight of the sign bit is -2^{N-1}, which changes as N changes. No problem arises if the number is positive, as the value of the sign bit is then 0 independent of N, or if the number is a fraction, as the weight of the sign bit is then −1 independent of N, but consider the 6-bit twos complement representation of −19. It is 101101, standing for −32 + 13. As a 12-bit number it is 111111101101, standing for −2048 + 2029. Note that six copies of the sign digit have been added. Formally, the 6 bits $b_0 b_1 b_2 b_3 b_4 b_5$ represent

$$-b_0 2^5 + b_1 2^4 + b_2 2^3 + b_3 2^2 + b_4 2^1 + b_5 2^0$$

To change to an N-bit number we add

$$b_0 \left(-2^{N-1} + 2^{N-2} + \ldots + 2^6 + 2^5 + 2^5\right)$$

which is identically 0 and so does not change the value. We get

$$-b_0 2^{N-1} + b_0 2^{N-2} + \ldots + b_0 2^5 + b_1 2^4 + \ldots + b_5 2^0$$

which is represented by $b_0 b_0 \ldots b_0 b_1 b_2 \ldots b_5$. We see that the length of a twos complement integer is increased by adding copies of the sign digit on the left.

A binary number can be doubled or halved by moving the binary point just as a decimal number can be multiplied or divided by 10 by moving the decimal point. For numbers with the point in a fixed position within a word, the digits of the number must be moved rather than the point. Thus the 6-bit representation of decimal 6, that is, 000110, can be doubled by shifting it left one place to get 001100, which represents decimal 12. When a sign/magnitude number is shifted, the bits representing the magnitude are shifted, but the sign is left unchanged. A right shift of a sign/magnitude number is shown in Figure 2.12. Zeros are shifted into the left-hand end and digits on the right-hand end are discarded. This may result in a loss of accuracy. For example, if -13 is halved, the result of -6 or -7 has to be accepted as an integer. In that case, a sign/magnitude representation of 101101 would change to 100110, the right-hand end 1 being lost in the process.

When a twos complement number is shifted, the same process can be used for positive numbers, as the representations are identical, but a special process must be used for negative numbers in right shifts. Suppose the number is first halved by discarding the right-hand end bit, thus lowering the weight of every other bit by a factor of 2 (assuming each bit represents an integer). Next, the length must be increased back to the original form, and the way to do this is to add a copy of the sign bit. Thus in twos complement right shifting to halve the number must leave the sign digit unchanged and also shift a copy of it to the right, as shown in Figure 2.13.

When a number is doubled by a left shift, it may overflow, as the result may exceed the range of the representation. If it does not, then the sign digit must have the same value as before the shift. In sign/magnitude, digit b_1 prior to the shift must be a 0 or the doubled value will be too large. In twos comple-

FIGURE 2.12   Right shift in sign/magnitude

FIGURE 2.13 *Right shift in twos complement*

ment, digits b_0 and b_1 must agree before the shift or the result will have over-flowed. This can be seen by noting that if the result does not overflow, halving the result by right shifting should return the original value. Since right shifting will cause b_0 and b_1 to agree, the original form must be in that state.

2.4.5 Ones complement representation of number

The other method of representing negative numbers is the *ones complement* system. This is derived by requiring that the negative of a number be the digit-wise complement of that number. Thus the negative of $6/32$, which is 111010 in twos complement, is 111001 in ones complement. The least significant 1 is not added in after the complementation. Because of this the weight of the sign position is $-(1 - 2^{-5})$ rather than -1, so that the value of a fraction with the ones complement representation $b_0b_1b_2b_3b_4b_5$ is

$$-(1 - 2^{-5})b_0 + b_1 \cdot 2^{-1} + b_2 \cdot 2^{-2} + b_3 \cdot 2^{-3} + b_4 \cdot 2^{-4} + b_5 \cdot 2^{-5}$$

The addition rules for ones complement are the same as for twos complement except that the carry from the sign position must be added to the least significant position. This is called *end-around carry*. It arises when a carry into the sign position which has a value of $+1$ is added to a 1 already there which has a value $-1 + 2^{-N+1}$. The result is 2^{-N+1} which is a 1 in the least significant position. Thus if $11/32$ is added to $-6/32$ in ones complement

$$\begin{array}{ll} 0.01011 & {}^{11}\!/_{32} \\ +1.11001 & + - {}^{6}\!/_{32} \\ \overline{=(1)0.00100} & \end{array}$$

$$\begin{array}{l} + 1 \quad \text{end-around carry} \\ = 0.00101 \quad = \quad {}^{5}\!/_{32} \end{array}$$

This can be written out as

$$0 + {}^{0}\!/_{2} + {}^{1}\!/_{4} + {}^{0}\!/_{8} + {}^{1}\!/_{16} + {}^{1}\!/_{32} \quad (001011)$$

$$+(-1 + {}^{1}\!/_{32}) + {}^{1}\!/_{2} + {}^{1}\!/_{4} + {}^{0}\!/_{8} + {}^{0}\!/_{16} + {}^{1}\!/_{32} \quad (111001)$$

Add to get

$$ {}^{1}\!/_{32} + {}^{0}\!/_{2} + {}^{0}\!/_{4} + {}^{0}\!/_{8} + {}^{0}\!/_{16} + {}^{0}\!/_{32}$$

Carry the $\frac{1}{32}$ around to get

$0 + \frac{1}{2} + \frac{1}{4} + \frac{1}{8} + \frac{1}{16} + \frac{1}{32}$ (000101)

EXTENDING THE PRECISION OF A ONES COMPLEMENT NUMBER

One confusing facet of ones complement representation arises when the precision of a fraction is increased, that is, when the number of bits is increased. In ones complement form $-\frac{3}{4}$ is 1.00 in 3-bit accuracy, but 1.001 in 4-bit accuracy. The bits added must agree with the sign bit, because the weight of the sign bit is $-1 + 2^{-N+1}$ and hence is determined by the number of bits of accuracy.

The precision of a ones complement integer is extended in exactly the same way as a twos complement integer — by adding copies of the sign digit to the left.

2.4.6 Hexadecimal and octal

It is frequently necessary to describe the bit pattern in a memory word or in a register. Because words contain many bits (32 in the IBM 370), it is too tedious to write down all the bits. Instead, a condensed notation is used. Two such notations are in common use, hexadecimal and octal, meaning base 16 and base 8, respectively. Rather than think of them as numbers in those bases, it is usually easier to consider them as condensed representations of binary numbers. Consider the 12-bit number 110011101001. Group it as four groups of 3 bits, that is, as 110 011 101 001. Each 3-bit group can be thought of as representing an integer between 0 and 7 and can be represented by the corresponding character. Then we could represent the 12-bit number by 6351. This is the octal representation of the 12 bits given above. If the word was longer, say 16 bits, it could be grouped in 3s from the right to get the octal representation. In this case, the leftmost digit would correspond to only 1 bit and could take values 0 or 1 only. Thus 1010111100000 110 would be represented by 127406 octal.

To get the hexadecimal representation of a binary number, the bits are grouped in 4s, and so 110011101001 is written as 1100 1110 1001. Each group of 4 bits represents an integer between 0 and 15. There are standard characters for the values between 0 and 9, but other characters are needed for the values 10 through 15. The most common convention is to use the letters A through F, respectively. Thus C stands for the integer 12, binary 1100. In this way the binary number 1100 1110 1001 can be represented as CE9 hexadecimal.

If there is any doubt which representation is being used when a number is written, it must be stated explicity. This is done by writing the base as a subscript to the number. Thus 4032_8 means 4032 octal (base 8). Subscript H will be used for hexadecimal, thus $F1A_H$ means F1A hexadecimal.

2.4.7 Conversion of numbers

A number can be converted from one base to another by multiplication or division. Consider the integer N represented by the decimal digits $d_1d_2d_3$. (Note that N cannot exceed 999.) Suppose we wish to find the binary representation $b_1b_2...b_9b_{10}$. (Ten bits are considered because a 10-bit binary integer can be as large as $2^{10} - 1 = 1023$, which is sufficient for the range of decimal integers considered.) If this conversion is to be done by hand, decimal arithmetic is probably preferred. In that case, *divide by the new base.* Thus

$$N = b_1 \cdot 2^9 + b_2 \cdot 2^8 + \ldots + b_9 \cdot 2^1 + b_{10} \cdot 2^0$$

Dividing by 2, we get

$$N/2 = b_1 \cdot 2^8 + b_2 \cdot 2^7 + \ldots b_9 \cdot 2^0, \text{ remainder } b_{10}$$

Hence, the least significant bit of the binary representation (b_{10}) is the remainder after dividing N by 2. The remaining 9 bits represent the integral quotient of N divided by 2, and can be converted by the same process.

Example

Convert 44 decimal to binary:

$44/2 = 22$, remainder 0
$22/2 = 11$, remainder 0
$11/2 = 5$, remainder 1
$5/2 = 2$, remainder 1
$2/2 = 1$, remainder 0
$1/2 = 0$, remainder 1

Hence 44 decimal = 101100 binary = 54_8 = $2C_H$

The conversions to octal and hexadecimal were done by grouping the bits after a conversion to binary. However, a quicker way is to convert directly into octal or hexadecimal, using the rule "divide by the new base." Thus:

Convert 44 decimal to octal:

$44/8 = 5$, remainder 4
$5/8 = 0$, remainder 5

Hence 44 decimal = 54_8

This can be converted to binary by replacing each octal digit by its 3-bit group.

Convert 44 decimal to hexadecimal:

$44/16 = 2$, remainder 12
$2/16 = 0$, remainder 2

Hence 44 decimal $= 2C_H$

When conversion is to be performed in the computer, it is desirable to operate in the arithmetic provided in the computer. In that case, the conversion of integers is done with multiplications by the old base. If the decimal integer is $d_1 d_2 d_3$, the steps

$$P = d_1$$
$$P = 10 \times P + d_2$$
$$P = 10 \times P + d_3$$

assign P the value of the integer. This is confusing until one remembers that the arithmetic is being done in another base.

Example

Convert 473 decimal to octal using octal arithmetic (*note that all numbers below are octal!*)

$$P = 4$$
$$P = 12 \times 4 + 7 = 57 \ (12_8 \text{ is ten})$$
$$P = 12 \times 57 + 3 = 731$$

Hence 473 decimal $= 731_8$

The rule for converting integers is to *divide by the new base* or *multiply by the old base*. The rule for converting fractions is exactly the opposite: *multiply by the new base* or *divide by the old base*. Thus, the decimal fraction F can be converted to the octal fraction $o_1 o_2 o_3 \ldots$ by noting that

$$F = o_1 \cdot 8^{-1} + o_2 \cdot 8^{-2} + o_3 \cdot 8^{-3} + \ldots$$

Multiplying by the new base we get

$$8 \times F = o_1 + (o_2 \cdot 8^{-1} + o_3 \cdot 8^{-2} + \ldots)$$

Hence the integral part of $8F$ is the digit o_1 and the fraction part is represented by the octal number $o_2 o_3 \ldots$, which can be converted in the same way.

Example

Convert 0.6875 decimal to octal

$8 \times 0.6875 = 5.5$, so the first digit is 5
$8 \times 0.5 \quad = 4.0$, so the second digit is 4
Hence 0.6875 decimal $= 0.54_8$

Note that most decimal fractions cannot be converted exactly into octal (or binary). $0.2_{10} = 0.14631463 \ldots _8$, for example.

A person would usually use the method above for converting to octal from decimal by hand, as the arithmetic is done in base 10. However, a computer usually prefers to do the arithmetic in binary (or octal), so it might prefer to divide by the new base. If the decimal fraction was $.d_1d_2d_3$, the steps are

$$P = d_3/10$$
$$P = (P + d_2)/10$$
$$P = (P + d_1)/10$$

Although this may be the fastest way, it is not the most accurate, as each step in the division may introduce rounding error. A better way, the one used in good programs, is to convert $d_1d_2d_3$ as an integer and then do one division by 10^3, causing only one roundoff error.

2.4.8 Arithmetic in computers

A computer designer chooses a method of representing numbers in a computer on the basis of his evaluation of cost and speed considerations, and occasionally on the basis of accuracy (too often accuracy of numerical computations is given insufficient thought in the design). He will then design a computer that has arithmetic operations to handle numbers in that representation. Because one representation is inadequate for a wide range of problems, large general-purpose computers will frequently have more than one form of number representation. Typically there will be integers and floating-point numbers, and possibly also strings of decimal characters. Different operations must be provided for each form of number handled. The IBM 370, for example, has instructions for integers and floating-point in a binary representation, and decimal integers represented in character strings. The integer instructions are standard on all models; floating-point and decimal instructions are optional extras that can be included. The PDP-11 is a smaller computer, and has arithmetic only on binary integers (discussed earlier) and optional floating-point arithmetic. However, it is possible to program arithmetic on other representations in any computer.

2.4.9 IBM 370 arithmetic

The 16 general-purpose registers already discussed contain 32-bit twos complement integers. Conventionally, IBM uses hexadecimal to represent the contents of registers and memory, so it could be said that the registers contain 8 hexadecimal digits. However, remember that the first bit of the first hexadecimal digit is the sign bit with weight -2^{31}. The most negative number that can be represented is $80000000_H = -2^{31} = -2,147,483,648$, while the most positive is $7FFFFFFF_H = 2^{31} - 1 = 2,147,483,647$. Floating-point arithmetic is also provided in a separate set of four double-precision registers, which will be called FPRO, FPR2, FPR4, and FPR6, respectively. (FPR stands for Floating Point Register. The registers could also be called 0, 2, 4, and 6, but the former names will be used in this chapter for clarity.) Floating-point instructions are available for both single-precision (32-bit) and double-precision (64-bit) numbers. These will be discussed shortly.

INTEGER ARITHMETIC

Most of the integer arithmetic instructions have already been introduced in Section 2.2.5. However, that section was deliberately vague about the nature of the double-precision result from multiplication and the double-precision dividend used in division. These are both 64-bit twos complement numbers stored in an even-odd pair of registers. If the value of the integer represented is smaller than 2^{31}, it can be stored in one register. The most significant half of the number will then contain copies of the sign of the number, and the single-precision form can be obtained by discarding the most significant half. However, prior to division, a single-precision number must be converted into its double-precision form. This means that somehow the most significant part of the register pair must be filled with copies of the sign digit. The easiest way to do this is to use the arithmetic right-shift instruction, which shifts the bits right and propagates copies of the sign bit. The instruction

        SRA   Ri,n

shifts register i right arithmetically n places, thus dividing it by 2^n. Thus the sequence

        L   R2,A
        SRA   R2,32

would fill register 2 with copies of the sign bit of A. Prior to division, it is necessary to fill the even register with the sign bit and the next higher register with the dividend. The above sequence could be followed with an L R3,A, but this is inefficient as there is also an instruction

        SRDA   Ri,n

which does a shift of the double-length number in registers i and $i + 1$ by n places arithmetically to the right (i must be an even number). Using this instruction, K = I/J can be coded as

        L   R2,I
        SRDA   R2,32

```
D          R2,J
ST         R3,K
```

A number can be divided by powers of 2 using the right-shift instructions. The condition code will be set according to the value of the result. Similar left-shift instructions SLA and SLDA can be used to multiply a number by powers of 2. Note that the result may overflow, in which case the corresponding condition code will be set.

FLOATING-POINT ARITHMETIC

The format of single- and double-precision floating-point numbers is shown in Figure 2.14. The fraction occupies 3 or 7 bytes, giving 6 or 14 hexadecimal digits. It contains the magnitude of the fraction; its sign is the first bit of the leftmost byte of the number. The exponent is a base 16 exponent, that is, it contains the number of powers of 16 by which the fraction must be multiplied to obtain the value of the number. This is equivalent to the number of hexadecimal digits to the left of the point in the number. The exponent is stored in the rightmost 7 bits of the first byte in a characteristic form obtained by adding 64 to the exponent. Hence the exponent range is from -64 to $+63$. Since this is a base 16 exponent, it corresponds to a floating-point range of about 10^{-78} to 10^{+78}. The principal floating-point arithmetic instructions are shown in Table 2.7.

An even-numbered register is always used. These registers are double length, although they only hold a single-precision result after single-precision operations, except that ME and MER yield a double-precision answer. To form $A = B \times C + D \times E$ we should code

```
LE         FPRO,B
ME         FPRO,C          Form B x C in register 0.
LE         FPR2,D
ME         FPR2,E          Form D x E in register 2.
ADR        FPRO,FPR2       Add products in double-precision.
STE        FPRO,A          Store single-precision result.
```

TABLE 2.7   Floating-point instructions

	SINGLE-PRECISION		DOUBLE-PRECISION	
TYPE	RX	RR	RX	RR
LOAD	LE	LER	LD	LDR
ADD	AE	AER	AD	ADR
SUBTRACT	SE	SER	SD	SDR
MULTIPLY	ME	MER	MD	MDR
DIVIDE	DE	DER	DD	DDR
STORE	STE		STD	

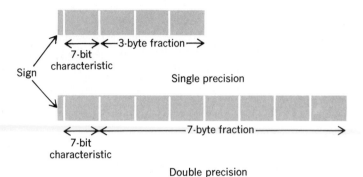

Single precision

Double precision

FIGURE 2.14   IBM 370 floating-point formats

(In fact, this will truncate the sum, and a round instruction should be used. See the Principles of Operation manual for details)

Another optional set of instructions are the decimal arithmetic instructions. These work with numbers in the packed format shown in Figure 2.15. These are variable-length numbers containing between 1 and 16 decimal digits. Each digit is stored in 4 bits. Since the basic unit of storage is the 8-bit byte, 2 digits are stored in each byte. A sign/magnitude number is stored in as many bytes as are necessary to hold its digits and sign. The sign is in the last 4-bit group. If the number contains an even number of characters, the left-most 4 bits of the first byte are ignored. Decimal arithmetic instructions are two-address; both addresses are memory addresses, and so they are of the SS type, meaning Store-Store. The length of each operand can be specified separately. Thus

AP   A(6),B(3)

means "Add the (Packed form of the) 3-byte number *B* to the 6-byte number *A*." It will be seen that the assembler will usually take care of specifying the length of the operands in the instruction, so this could also be written AP A,B.

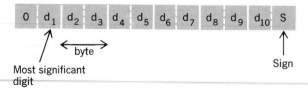

FIGURE 2.15   Ten-digit decimal number in IBM 370 packed format

Example

The following example uses the floating-point and shift instructions to find the square root of a floating-point number moderately rapidly using Newton's method. If the number is in location B with value b, Newton's method consists of computing the sequence

$$x_{n+1} = (x_n + b/x_n)/2$$

starting from any positive value x_0 and evaluating $x_1, x_2, x_3, \ldots$ It is known that as long as b is nonnegative and x_0 is greater than the square root of b, the x_i are theoretically a decreasing sequence. Eventually, computed values will stop decreasing because of roundoff errors, and this can be used to stop the iteration. At that time, the value of x_n is a good approximation to the square root of b. Fewer iterations (a smaller value of n) will be sufficient if the initial value x_0 is close to the square root of b. Thus we would like to calculate such a starting approximation.

If b is stored in normalized hexadecimal, then it has the form

$$b = f \times 16^e$$

where f is between $\frac{1}{16}$ and 1. Consequently

$$\sqrt{b} = (\sqrt{f}) \times 16^{e/2}$$

Suppose that p is the largest integer not greater than $e/2$ (p can be calculated by a right shift of 1 bit).

Then

$$16^{e/2} < \frac{1}{4} \times 16^{p+1}$$

Since f is less than 1, $\sqrt{f}$ is also less than 1; hence

$$\sqrt{b} < \frac{1}{4} \times 16^{p+1}$$

This will be used as x_0. To calculate it, the 7-bit characteristic must be extracted and shifted right one place. Since the characteristic is $64 + e$, the result is $32 + p$. It is necessary to add 33 to get the characteristic $64 + (p + 1)$ and add it to a word whose second byte is hexadecimal 40, representing one-quarter. Then the result can be used in the iteration. The code is shown below.

L	R5,B	Load b into general register 5 and
LE	FPR2,B	floating-point register 2.
LTR	R5,R5	Set the condition code on b.
BM	ERROR	Negative b is an error—no square root.
BZ	ZERO	Answer is 0 if b is 0.
SR	R4,R4	This sets register 4 to 0.
SLDA	R4,7	The top 6 bits of the exponent are now in R4.

	SR	R5,R5	This clears R5, discarding the rest of the word.
	SRDA	R4,8	The characteristic has been halved.
	A	R5,=X'21400000'	The operand is the hexadecimal number with the value inside the quotes. It adds 33 to the characteristic and $\frac{1}{4}$ to the fraction.
	ST	R5,X	This is x_0.
	LER	FPR0,FPR2	b to FPR0.
	LE	FPR2,X	x_0 in FPR2.
LOOP	LER	FPR4,FPR2	x to FPR4.
	LER	FPR2,FPR0	b to FPR2.
	DER	FPR2,FPR4	b/x_n.
	AER	FPR2,FPR4	$b/x_n + x_n$.
	HER	FPR2,FPR2	This halves the floating-point number to get x_{n+1}.
	CER	FPR4,FPR2	Compares x_n with x_{n+1}.
	BH	LOOP	Branches back for next iteration if $x_n > x_{n+1}$.
ZERO	STE	FPR2,X	Result in location X.

The IBM 370 includes many variations of arithmetic instructions and other instructions. Some of these will be discussed in Section 2.6.1, but the reader must refer to IBM manuals for most of the other instructions. Among the arithmetic instructions not to be discussed further are halfword versions of the integer load, add, subtract, multiply, and store instructions in the RX format, and unnormalized versions of the floating-point instructions. The floating-point instructions discussed above produce normalized answers. Halfword instructions are useful so that integers with a small range (up to $2^{15} - 1$) can be stored in only 2 bytes of memory.

2.4.10 PDP-11 arithmetic

The PDP-11 handles 16-bit twos complement numbers in its registers. It can deal with either 8- or 16-bit numbers in memory. The range of a 16-bit number is −32,768 to +32,767; of an 8-bit number, −256 to +255. The 16-bit instructions for arithmetic have already been introduced. The operands for these instructions are pairs of bytes, either from a register or from consecutive bytes in memory. A memory address has to be even. Some of these instructions have a byte form in which an operand from memory is 8 bits and can come from any address. If a register is used for an operand, the eight least significant positions are used. These byte instructions include

MOVB	MOVe Byte
CMPB	CoMPare Byte
CLRB	CLeaR Byte
INCB	INCrement Byte
DECB	DECrement Byte
NEGB	NEGate Byte

These instructions behave in the same way as the corresponding 16-bit instructions. A mixed mode instruction is

SWAB   SWAp Bytes

which must refer to a 16-bit single operand. It swaps the positions of the 2 bytes in a word. Thus SWAB R3 exchanges bits 15 through 8 with 7 through 0 in register 3.

The arithmetic is twos complement to either 8 or 16 bits, according to the instruction. This means that the sign bit is treated exactly like any other bit in addition or subtraction. The condition bits thus have the following meanings:

N   is identical to the leftmost bit (sign bit) in the result.

Z   is set to 1 if all 16 bits (or 8 bits) of the result are 0.

V   is set to 1 if the result is out of range as a twos complement integer. This is detected when an addition of numbers with the same sign gives a different sign, or subtraction of numbers with different sign gives a result with the sign of the source operand.

C   is set to 1 if there is a carry out of the twos complement adder on addition. This happens when the sum of the numbers considered as 16-bit positive unsigned numbers exceeds $2^{16} - 1$ under addition, or when their difference is negative under subtraction.

The carry bit C is useful for performing multiple-precision arithmetic. Suppose there are two 32-bit twos complement numbers stored in locations A0,A1 and B0,B1, respectively, where the most significant parts are stored in A0 and B0, respectively. What we wish to do is to add the least significant parts of the two numbers, and then add the carry into the sum of the most significant parts, as shown in Figure 2.16.

The instruction ADC (ADd Carry) can be used to help with this. It adds the carry bit into the operand specified. Thus the sequence

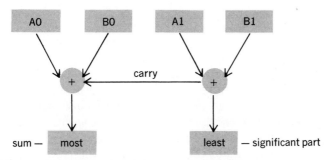

FIGURE 2.16   Double-precision addition in twos complement

```
ADD        A1,B1          Add least significant parts into B1.
                          Carry to C.
ADC        B0             Add C to most significant part.
ADD        A0,B0          Add most significant part of
                          A to B
```

will do the required double-precision addition. This can be extended to multiple-precision addition by continuing to add the more significant parts and the carries together.

The instruction SBC subtracts the carry bit C from the operand. It is used to form double-precision $B - A \rightarrow B$ as follows:

```
SUB        A1,B1
SBC        B0
SUB        A0,B0
```

ADC and SBC also exist in a byte form as ADCB and SBCB, which work with byte operands only.

Left and right shifts are performed by the instructions

```
ASR        X              Arithmetic shift x right 1 bit
ASL        X              Arithmetic shift x left 1 bit
```

In the right shift, the carry bit is loaded from the original rightmost bit (bit number 0) of the operand. The sign bit is propagated and unchanged, so a division by 2 occurs. The left shift moves all bits left one place, loading the C bit from the original sign bit and inserts a 0 into the least significant position. If overflow does not occur, this doubles the operand. The same operations are available in byte form as ASRB and ASLB.

Two other versions of the shift instruction are

```
ROR        X              Rotate X right 1 bit
ROL        X              Rotate X left 1 bit
```

The rotates are similar to the shift instructions except that in a left shift, the low-order bit is loaded with the old carry bit, and in the right shift, the sign bit is loaded with the old carry bit. It is as if the 16-bit operand and the carry bit considered as a 17-bit word have been rotated one place, with the bit falling off one end being fed into the other end. RORB and ROLB are the equivalent byte rotates. The rotates are useful for doing double-precision shifts. Thus a double-precision left shift can be performed by the pair of instructions

| ASL | A1 | Shift the least significant part left. |
| ROL | A0 | Shift the most significant part left, picking up the bit shifted out of the least significant part. |

Similarly a double-precision right shift can be performed by

| ASR | A0 | Right shift the most significant part. |
| ROR | A1 | Right shift the least significant part, inserting the bit shifted out of the most significant part. |

Example

Multiplication can be performed by addition and shifting as follows. Suppose the numbers A and B are to be multiplied. Let us suppose that they are unsigned 16-bit numbers. (If signs have to be handled it is simplest to treat them separately and to multiply the magnitudes.) Suppose A is represented as $a_{15}a_{14} \ldots a_1a_0$. Its value is

$$a_{15} \cdot 2^{15} + a_{14} \cdot 2^{14} + \ldots + a_1 \cdot 2^1 + a_0 \cdot 2^0$$

This is multiplied by B to form

$$a_{15} \cdot 2^{15}B + a_{14} \cdot 2^{14}B + \ldots + a_0 \cdot 2^0B$$

which can be written as

$$(\ldots ((a_{15} \cdot B) \cdot 2 + a_{14} \cdot B) \cdot 2 + \ldots + a_1 \cdot B) \cdot 2 + a_0 \cdot B$$

Thus, start with 0 and add B if a_{15} is a 1. Then the result is shifted left one place to double it. Next, add B if a_{14} is a 1 and shift left. This can be repeated until $a_0 \cdot B$ is added. To test the bits of A it can be shifted left a bit at a time, putting the top bit into the C bit for testing. Since the result may be 32 bits long, a double-precision shift must be done on the result. A can be shifted at the same time by starting with it in the most significant part of the result. After 16 shifts, it will be shifted off completely. The status of the double-precision intermediate result after the first six steps is shown in Figure 2.17. The program is shown below.

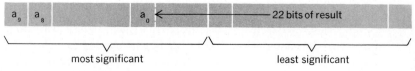

FIGURE 2.17   Intermediate stage of a multiply

	MOV	A,R0	Move A to most significant part.
	CLR	R1	Clear least significant part.
	MOV	B,R2	Move B to R2 for fast access.
	MOV	#−16.,R3	The number −16 is put in R3 as a count.
LOOP:	ASL	R1	
	ROL	R0	Double-precision shift. a_{15} is in C bit.
	BCC	L1	Branch if C clear and do not add in B.
	ADD	R2,R1	
	ADC	R0	Addition of B to R0,R1.
L1:	INC	R3	Increment count by 1.
	BNE	LOOP	If count not 0, repeat process.

The result is in R0,R1 after this program finishes.

The basic PDP-11 does not have floating-point or decimal operations, but it is not difficult to program them, using one or more words for the mantissa and another word or byte for the exponent. The PDP-11 model 45 has floating-point arithmetic as an option. It provides six floating-point registers, AC0 through AC5, each of which can handle 32- or 64-bit floating-point numbers. The format

S	Characteristic	Mantissa

is used, where the leftmost bit is a sign for a sign/magnitude representation of the fraction (mantissa). The next 8 bits are a characteristic, which is obtained by adding 128 to the exponent. Thus the exponent range is −128 to +127. The fractional part is always normalized with respect to the binary exponent, and so the leftmost bit is known to be a 1. Hence it is not stored. The remaining bits of the representation are the second through twenty-fourth bits of the mantissa when single-precision (32 bits) is being used, or the second through the fifty-sixth if double-precision (64 bits) is being used. Any number with a zero characteristic is treated as zero.

2.5 ADDRESS STRUCTURE

A task can be coded using only the simplest of instructions, such as those discussed above. Indeed, neither addition, multiplication, nor division are necessary, but without them an arithmetic task would take longer to program and longer to execute. Since the purpose of a digital computer is to perform a given task for the minimum cost, the job of a machine designer is to provide instructions which reduce the cost of programming and execution. This section will examine some classes of instructions and related hardware that help in this direction.

2.5.1 Index registers

It is frequently necessary to process arrays of data in a sequential fashion. For example, it may be necessary to execute the equivalent of

$$A(I) = B(I) + C(I)$$

for values of I from 1 to 1000. Let us assume that the variables $A(1)$, $A(2)$, . . . , $A(1000)$ are in Locations A, $A + 1$, . . . , $A + 999$ in memory, where $A + 1$ is the address one larger than the address represented by A, and similarly for the arrays B and C. The task can be executed for $I = 1$ by the one-address program.

LOAD	B
ADD	C
STORE	A

but it is certainly not desirable to repeat this a further 999 times. Assuming that the machine contains one instruction per word, that the address in an instruction is on the right-hand side of the word, and that integer arithmetic in twos complement is being used, then the instruction set previously discussed can be employed to *modify* the instructions by making use of the fact that the instructions and data are in the same memory.

X	LOAD	B
Y	ADD	C
Z	STORE	A
	LOAD	X
	ADD	= 1
	STORE	X
	LOAD	Y
	ADD	= 1
	STORE	Y
	LOAD	Z
	ADD	= 1
T	STORE	Z

"$= 1$" is a notation for the address of a location containing integer 1. The instruction sequence LOAD X, ADD $= 1$, STORE X puts a copy of LOAD B into the accumulator, adds 1 to it, which adds a 1 to the address B (which is on the right-hand end) and stores it back where the LOAD B instruction was stored. After the sequence from X to T has been executed, the first three instructions have been modified to

X	LOAD	B+1
Y	ADD	C+1
Z	STORE	A+1

If a counter to loop the required 1,000 times is added, the loop is complete. However, beware . . . at the end of execution, the first three locations have been changed to LOAD B+1,000, etc. If the loop is to be used again, it must be reset. A number of programming tricks can be used to reduce the execution time of a loop such as this. About the best that can be done is

	LOAD	=(LOAD B)†	Load initial value of location X.
	TRA	W	
X	LOAD	B	
Y	ADD	C	
Z	STORE	A	A(I) = B(I) + C(I)
	LOAD	X	
	ADD	= 1	Add 1 to address.
W	STORE	X	Update location X.
	ADD	=(ADD C — LOAD B)†	
	STORE	Y	Update location Y.
	ADD	=(STORE A — ADD C)	
	STORE	Z	Update location Z.
	SUB	=(STORE A +1000)	
	TMI	X	Repeat loop 1,000 times.

Many of the small machines now on the market provide simple instructions that can be used to reduce the length of this program. Two examples are the instructions ADD TO MEMORY, which performs an addition leaving the result in the addressed memory location rather than the accumulator, and INCREMENT MEMORY BY ONE which adds 1 to a specified memory cell. The PDP-11 has both of these.

The code above has 12 instructions inside the loop, an additional 2 outside of the loop, and requires 5 additional storage locations—although =1 is undoubtedly used by other sections of code. Only 3 of the 12 instructions contribute directly to the arithmetic being performed, so, in a sense, the loop is only 25 percent efficient.

Recognizing that what is needed is an efficient scheme to modify addresses of orders in a sequential fashion, the machine designer provides one or more *index registers*. An index register is functionally similar to an accumulator in that it is a mechanism for storing a number. This number only need represent a positive integer in the range 0 to $M - 1$ where the memory contains M locations, so an index register is typically shorter than a regular word. For

† =(LOAD B) is a notation for an address of a location containing a constant equivalent to the instruction LOAD B. =(ADD C — LOAD B) is a notation for an address of a location containing a constant equal to the difference between the binary forms of ADD C and LOAD B.

example, if $M = 65,536 = 2^{16}$, an index register need only be 16 bits long. Each index register is usually assigned an address which must be distinguished from a memory address. It is a small integer, since there are usually only a small number of index registers. For example, if there are 15 index registers, they could be addressed by the integers between 1 and 15. The function of an index register is to provide a displacement to the address of an instruction. Each memory address in the instruction format has an associated index address. The *effective address* for the instruction is the sum of the actual address and the contents of the indicated index register. Figure 2.18 shows a typical instruction format for a 32-bit-wide, 65,536-word memory machine with 15 index registers. If the index address is 0, then the effective address is Y, otherwise the effective address is Y + (XI) where (XI) means the contents of index register I. We can indicate this in our program writing by using Y to mean the unindexed address Y (that is, the index bits are 0) and by using Y(I) to mean the address Y indexed by index register I. Other notations are used in place of this. If we use the code

```
X          LOAD       B(1)
           ADD        C(1)
           STORE      A(1)
```

for the statement A(I) = B(I) + C(I), I =1, 2, . . . , 1,000, it is only necessary to arrange that I is stepped from 0 to 999 in steps of 1. Many schemes can be devised to do this efficiently; each such scheme involves the specification of instructions which act on index registers. We shall examine one design below.

Note that there are four items of information to be specified—the start of the loop in memory (X), the initial value of the index (0), the increment (1), and the end condition on the index (999). Each of these items of information is an address-length quantity. In a one-address machine, therefore, either four instructions will be needed or the value of some of the items must be assumed to be fixed by the machine. The latter approach will yield designs which are efficient for a limited class of problems, but the design should allow for the most general case. Therefore, instructions should be provided which will allow an arbitrary number to be loaded into an index register, to be added to an index register, or to be compared with an index register.

Since the content of an index register is an address-length quantity, the

FIGURE 2.18 *Instruction format with indexing*

number used as data in such instructions should also be address length. This means that either the value of the address contained in the instruction could be used directly as data, or the contents of the cell addressed could be used. The advantage of the former is that it is faster, requiring one less memory reference. The advantage of the latter is that it is not necessary to change the program when the data change. For our present discussion we shall assume that the index instructions LOAD INDEX and ADD TO INDEX refer to the data in another memory location addressed by the instruction.

The end test must compare the contents of an index register with an arbitrary number. In addition to the data, a branch address is needed. This dictates either a two-address instruction in an accumulator machine or a combination of two instructions. The IBM 370 and the PDP-11 use two instructions to terminate a loop, although the 370 does have special instructions that use more than one register to provide all the information. In both machines, the index registers are the general-purpose registers; that is, these registers can be used either as working accumulators or as index registers. Consequently the arithmetic comparison and branch on condition code instructions can be used to test index registers.

A third possible organization uses the idea of a SKIP instruction. This instruction increases the control counter by an additional amount, typically 1 or 2, so that the next 1 or 2 instructions are not executed. A COMPARE instruction could conditionally skip on the basis of the result. The IBM 7094, for example, has a COMPARE ACCUMULATOR WITH MEMORY instruction which skips one location if the contents are equal or two locations if the accumulator is larger.

If a condition-register organization is used, the loop for $A(I) = B(I) + C(I)$ can be written as

	LOAD INDEX	$= 0(1)$	Put 0 in index 1.
X	LOAD	B(1)	
	ADD	C(1)	
	STORE	A(1)	
	ADD TO INDEX	$= 1(1)$	Increment index 1 by 1.
	COMPARE INDEX	$= 1000(1)$	Compare index 1 with 1,000.
	BRANCH LOW	X(1)	Jump if the index was low.

The loop now contains six instructions, three of which contain the arithmetic. There are four additional instructions, each of which provides an address-length item for the basic loop structure.

Index registers are also called *modifiers, tags, B-lines,* or *B-boxes.* On some machines, such as the IBM 7090, their contents are subtracted from the actual address to obtain the effective address. This was done to allow the indexing in a loop to be done by one additional instruction (the TIX instruction). However, it is so specialized that programs produced automatically by compilers do not usually use it. Other machines allow for multiple indexing of an address; that is, the contents of more than one index register can be added to an address. The IBM 370 is in this class.

2.5.2 Indirect addressing and immediate operands

A facility related to indexing is called *indirect addressing.* Indirect addressing may be specified by 1 or more bits in the instruction. If it is specified, the data address is used to fetch a word from memory. This word is not used as the operand; rather, it contains the address of the operand (see Figure 2.19). This is called *single-level indirect addressing.* Since the word fetched from memory may have bits in addition to the address bits, it could contain another indirect address bit. This could lead to *multiple-level indirect addressing.* The *effective address* is the address finally obtained for use by the instruction. Thus for a LOAD, it is the address of the data loaded into the accumulator. Indirect addressing can be used to supplement the number of index registers. If several instructions use the same element of an indexed array, say A(I), the address of A(I) can be kept in a fixed memory location and all references to it made indirect via this address. A second important application is the parameter transfer in subroutines. This will be discussed in Chapter 4. For example, suppose that a program has to square A(I) and

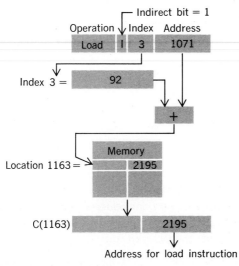

FIGURE 2.19   Indirect addressing

return the result to memory for I from 1 to 1,000. Suppose further that no index register is available for I. In this case the following code could be used (an * before the address indicates indirect addressing):

```
X          LOAD              *AI
           MPY               *AI
           STORE             *AI
           LOAD              AI
           ADD               = 1
           STORE             AI
           SUB               = A+ 1000    Test for end of array of 1,000 elements.
           BRANCH-IF-MINUS   X
```

AI is a location initially containing the address A. It is incremented by 1 on each pass through the loop. This is similar to the instruction modification schemes above, but only one address has to be modified rather than three.

If the word fetched from memory contains enough bits to allow for flags in addition to the indirect address, then additional levels of index modification can be performed. Figure 2.19 showed the indexing being performed before the address was sent to memory. There are situations in which it is preferable to index after the indirect addressing has been done. (Such situations can occur in some of the small machines which permit the address in an instruction to reference only a small part of memory in order to minimize the number of bits used in the instruction. Indirect addressing usually allows a longer address to be fetched for accessing the remainder of memory. Since this is used as a device to get a regular address, the long address after the indirect operation should be indexed. In this case, the index bits in the original instruction should be used for the index specification.) Parameter transfer, discussed in Chapter 4, is a case where indexing is needed before the indirect addressing. Some machines give the programmer the choice. The PDP-11 allows one level of indirect addressing with indexing beforehand, while the 370 does not allow indirect addressing.

The concept of an immediate operand is, in a sense, the inverse of indirect addressing. Many orders will call for the use of simple integer operands such as 0, 1, 2, 10, etc. If the integer is no larger than the maximum address, then the value of the address, rather than the contents of the addressed location, could be used as the operand. A number of instructions therefore will have an *immediate* option. An ADD-IMMEDIATE N instruction, for example, would add the number N to the accumulator of a one-address machine. Care must be exercised in the use of immediate operands since, if they ever have to be changed, it is necessary to modify the program rather than a data location in memory.

2.5.3 IBM 370 address structure

One of the advantages of the 370 organization with multiple accumulators is that these accumulators can and do serve as the index registers. An index register is represented in a 4-bit address in an instruction, so that all 16 registers could be used. However, it is necessary to allow for no indexing, so that accumulator 0 is not allowed as an index register. If the index address is between 1 and 15, the contents of that accumulator is added to the address of the instruction, but if it is 0 it is not. The maximum-size address that is allowed is 24 bits, so after the arithmetic, the top 8 bits of the address are discarded. The remaining 24 bits must specify an address that is within the storage capacity of the machine in use. Many instructions allow double indexing; that is, the address can be modified by two index registers. In the next section we shall see that there is a special purpose for the second indexing, so that it should not be normally used by the programmer. If he does wish to use it, then it can be specified by writing

        L   R4,23(6,9)

which says that register 4 should be loaded from the (byte) location "23 plus the contents of registers 6 and 9."

Because the index registers and the fixed-point accumulators are one and the same, no additional instructions are needed for arithmetic on the index registers. The test instructions for arithmetic results can also be used for the index test. Three special instructions are provided for use in loops. They are BCT (Branch on CounT), BXH (Branch on indeX High), and BXLE (Branch on indeX Low or Equal).

The BCT instruction has two addresses; a register containing a count and a branch address. It is written as

        BCT   Ri,T

Register i is reduced by 1 and a branch to location T occurs unless register i is now 0. (As with some of the other branches, there is an option, BCTR, in which the second address is also in a register.) These instructions can be used by loading an integer into a register before entering a loop and terminating the loop with the BCT(R). Thus:

```
        L              R4,=F'16'        The address is that of a location
                                        containing fixed-point 16. R4 is set by 16.
T       . . . . . . . . . . . . . . . . . . . . . .   This section of code will be executed
                                        16 times.
        BCT            R4,T
```

The BXH and BXLE are three-address instructions, although they specify four operands.

BXH   Ri,Rj,T

adds Rj to Ri. It then compares the contents of Ri with the *comparand*, which is found in register j if j is odd, or in $j + 1$ if j is even. If the value in register i is higher, the branch is taken. BXLE operates similarly, except that the branch is taken in the opposite case. The example below forms the sum of the contents of locations B through B + 19 in register 5.

	SR	R5,R5	Clear register 5 for sum.
	SR	R4,R4	Clear register 4 as index.
	L	R2,=F'4'	Increment is 4 because there are 4 bytes per word.
	L	R3,=F'76'	Terminate when count reaches 19 × 4.
LOOP	A	R5,B(4)	Accumulate sum.
	BXLE	R4,R2,LOOP	Increase R4 by 4 and branch back until R4 is 80.

Indirect addressing is not provided on the 370. The effect of using a location to provide the address of another location is achieved by the load instruction. Thus the sequence

    L   R4,A
    L   R4,0(4)

first loads the contents of location A into register 4, and then loads the contents of location "0 + contents of register 4" into register 4. In other words, A contains the address of the data loaded into register 4. If only single indexing is required, the second index need not be specified, although, of course, one could write for the second instruction above:

         L   R4,0(4,0)
    or   L   R4,0(0,4)

Certain instructions can use immediate operands in the 370. Some are called SI instructions (Store-Immediate). They operate on byte-length data only and will be discussed briefly later in this section. Another is the LA (Load Address) instruction.

LA   R4,X

puts the actual address X into register R4. LA is an RX instruction, and so the address can also be indexed. Hence one way of forming the sum of a register and an integer is to code LA R*i*, *n(j)*. This will sum *n* and the contents of register *j*, then put the result in register *i*.

The memory address in the 370 may need up to 24 bits, depending on the amount of memory available. (Twenty-four bits allows about 16 million bytes to be addressed.) If the designers of the 370 had chosen an instruction format with 24 bits for each address plus 4 bits for each index, a two-address instruction would have needed 56 bits for addresses alone, not to mention the operation code bits. In order to reduce this, several tricks were used. RR instructions, which refer to registers only, need just 8 bits of address. These can be represented in 16 bits of instruction, as shown in Figure 2.20. The formats of other 370 instructions are also shown in that figure. When an actual memory address is needed, it is specified in 16 bits, using the *base-plus-displacement* format. The displacement is a 12-bit integer *D* which is added to the contents of a general-purpose register *B* called the base register. The base register to be used can be specified in 4 bits, for a total of 16. In fact, the base register functions logically exactly as an index register, and so register 0 may not be used as a base register either; however, it is wise to distinguish base and index registers functionally for the reasons given below.

When the programmer writes an address such as X, it cannot be converted directly into binary and assembled into the instruction; rather, it must be

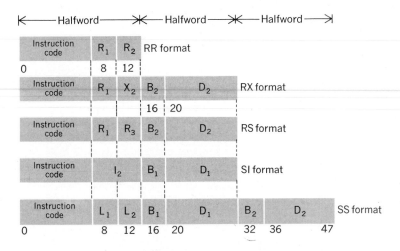

Ri — Register containing operand i, i = 1, 2, 3.

Xi, Bi — Register containing two index quantities for operand i.

D — Address to be added to index register for operand i address.

FIGURE 2.20   *Instruction formats in the IBM 370*

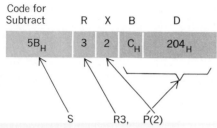

FIGURE 2.21   RX instruction assembled

expressed as the contents of a base register plus a displacement between 0 and 4,095 ($2^{12} - 1$). Fortunately the assembler handles this provided it is told which registers can be used as base registers, as will be discussed in Chapter 3. However, the assignment of the base register must be left to the assembler, it must not be used as an index register. For example, if the user writes the instruction R3,P(2) and the assembler knows that register 12 contains 516 less than the address P, it can assemble the instruction as shown in Figure 2.21.

The SS format shown in Figure 2.20 has space for two operand lengths. These are needed because the SS format is used for the variable-length decimal and character instructions. When the programmer writes the length of an operand explicitly with its address, the assembler fills out the length fields (the integer is 1 less than the actual length, allowing lengths from 1 to 16 to be specified in a 4-bit field). It also converts the address into base-plus-displacement form as shown in Figure 2.22. If the programmer does not specify the length of the operands, the assembler uses the information available to fill out the length field. However, the programmer may always override the assembler on both base register selection and length specification if there is one by specifying them explicitly. Thus he could write S R3,516(2,12) for the example shown in Figure 2.21, or AP DX(4,BX),DY(3,BY) for the example shown in Figure 2.22. Another form of the SS format is used for character operations such as MVC P,Q. This moves characters from Q to P. Since the operands must have the same length, only one length is needed. It can be from

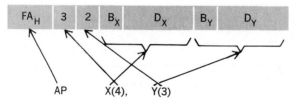

FIGURE 2.22   SS instruction assembled

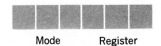

Mode   Register

FIGURE 2.23   General PDP-11 address format

1 to 256 and is specified with the first address P if given explicitly. Alternatively, the assembler will provide it.

The SI format is used for 1-byte immediate data. An example is MVI C'x', B, which moves the 8-bit byte represented by the character x into the byte addressed by B.

2.5.4 PDP-11 address structure

The PDP-11 provides for indexing, indirect addressing, immediate operands, and other useful features such as automatic increment and decrement when an index is used. The general-purpose registers are used as index registers, so that 3 bits are needed to specify an index. An additional 3 bits specify how the address is constructed. These are called *mode* bits. Thus an address consists of 6 bits as shown in Figure 2.23. Two-address instructions use two groups of 6 bits as shown in Figure 2.24. This leaves 4 bits for the op code. Since this would allow for only 16 different operation codes, only a few of the most frequent instructions use two addresses. Many use one address with the format also shown in Figure 2.24. The branch instructions have a special format with an 8-bit address, as shown. In addition, there are some zero-address instructions.

In the two-address format, the first address is known as the source address (src), as it provides the source operand in a move or one of the operands in an ADD or SUB. The second address is the destination address (dst) in a move or arithmetic operation. (It also provides the second operand in an arithmetic

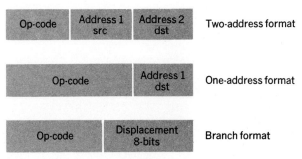

FIGURE 2.24   PDP-11 instruction formats

operation.) The branch address is a twos complement number which is doubled and added to the control counter to get the actual branch address. It is doubled because all instructions must lie on a word boundary, so that an even address is needed. This allows the branch to be taken to a word up to 128 words beyond the word containing the branch or 127 words before. (Note that the control counter contains the address of the next instruction in sequence, to which an integer between -256 and $+254$ is added.)

General addresses using the 6-bit format are constructed independently of whether they are first or second addresses, and independently of the instruction. The four principal modes are shown in Table 2.8. These allow the contents of a register or of a cell in memory to be used as an operand.

In mode 0, the operand is in a register or returned to a register. In mode 1, the 16-bit contents of a register provide the operand address. In mode 6, the contents of a register are added to a 16-bit address to get the effective address of the operand. The 16-bit quantity X is in the word following the instruction. (This means that the instruction is 4 bytes long and the control counter is incremented by 4.) If both addresses in a two-address instruction are mode 6 (or 7), the two values of X required are in the two words following the instruction. The first word contains the X for the src address, while the second word following the instruction contains the X for the dst address. (In this case the instruction is 6 bytes long and the control counter is incremented by 6.) In mode 7, an address is calculated as in mode 6, and the word from that memory location is used to provide the operand address; that is, it is indirect.

The PDP-11 provides a mechanism for automatically incrementing or decrementing the index register. This is done with the four auxiliary modes shown in Table 2.9. The incrementing or decrementing is done by 1 or 2 in the case of modes 2 and 3, depending on whether the instruction is a byte or word operation, respectively. (However, note that if register 6 is specified, the change is always by 2, as register 6 is used as a stack pointer. This will be discussed in Chapter 4.)

Only four of these modes should be used with register 7, as R7 is the control counter. These four modes are 2, 3, 6, and 7. Their meanings are shown in

TABLE 2.8 *Four principal address modes in PDP-11*

DESCRIPTION	MODE	CALLED IN PDP-11 TERMINOLOGY	WRITTEN
Register contents	0	Register	Ri
Register contains address†	1	Deferred	(Ri) or @Ri
Indexed	6	Indexed	X(R)
Indexed indirect	7	Indexed deferred	@ X(R)

†Think of this as indexed with zero address.

TABLE 2.9   Auxiliary addressing modes in PDP-11

MODE	FUNCTION	WRITTEN
2	Same as mode 1, but Ri is incremented afterward.	(Ri)+
3	Same as mode 7 but Ri is incremented afterward; X is 0 and is not specified.	@(Ri)+
4	Same as mode 1, but Ri is decremented first.	−(Ri)
5	Same as mode 7, but Ri is decremented first; X is 0 and is not specified.	@ −(Ri)

TABLE 2.10   Modes used with register 7.

DESCRIPTION	MODE	CALLED IN PDP-11 TERMINOLOGY	WRITTEN
Immediate	2	Immediate	#n
Direct address	3	Absolute	@#A
Relative to control counter	6	Relative	A
Relative indirect	7	Relative deferred	@A

Table 2.10. These meanings can be derived from the earlier descriptions. Thus mode 2 says that the address is in the register and the register is to be incremented after use. This means that the operand address is the value of the control counter. It contains the address of the word following the instruction. Thus the operand is the word following the instruction, which can be viewed as an address to be used as an immediate operand. The register (that is, the control counter) is incremented afterward so that the next instruction comes from the word following the operand. (Note that register 7 is always incremented by 2 so that it is always on a word boundary.) Mode 3 is similar to mode 2 except that it is indirect. This means that the word following the instruction contains the address of the data. This is conventional direct addressing. Modes 6 and 7 specify that the address is to be indexed by the control counter, which means that the address given is a displacement relative to the address of the word following the instruction. When a programmer writes an address A, the PDP-11 assembler automatically generates mode 6 using register 7, although mode 3 with register 7 could be used also. The reason for this choice will be apparent in Chapter 3.

Example

Some of the power of the PDP-11 address structure is illustrated in the following example. It assumes that locations X, $X + 2$, and $X + 4$ contain A, B, and $2n$, where A and B are the addresses of two strings of n 16-bit words containing $16n$-bit twos complement numbers. The address of the most significant word is assumed to be in A and B, respectively, as shown by the diagram:

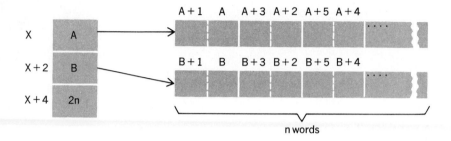

The code below adds these two numbers together, leaving the result in the words addressed by B.

```
            MOV     #X,R0        Put address X in R0.
            MOV     (R0)+,R1     Put address A in R1, increment R0.
            MOV     (R0)+,R2     Put address B in R2, increment R0.
            MOV     (R0),R3      Put 2n in R3.
            ADD     R3,R1        A+2n in R1.
            ADD     R3,R2        B+2n in R2.
            CLC                  Clear carry; sets carry bit to 0.
LOOP:       ADC     −(R2)        Add carry to next word.
            ADD     −(R1),(R2)   Add two words.
            DEC     R3           Decrease R3 by 2 altogether without
            DEC     R3           changing carry bit.
            BNE     LOOP         Repeat loop n times.
```

2.6 LOGICAL OPERATIONS

The logical orders are bit-wise operations; that is, they treat each bit separately and identically. The three basic logical operations are AND, OR, and NOT. If a binary 1 is thought of as corresponding to *true* and binary 0 to *false*, then the result of A AND B is true if both A and B are true individually. A OR B is true if either A or B is true individually, while NOT A is true if A is false. Thus we have the *truth tables*

```
    0 AND 0 = 0
    0 AND 1 = 0
    1 AND 0 = 0
    1 AND 1 = 1

    0 OR 0 = 0
    0 OR 1 = 1
    1 OR 0 = 1
    1 OR 1 = 1

    NOT 0 = 1
    NOT 1 = 0
```

In addition, the EOR (Exclusive OR) is often available. It has the truth table

```
0 EOR 0 = 0
0 EOR 1 = 1
1 EOR 0 = 1
1 EOR 1 = 0
```

Logical instructions are useful for testing the state of bits within words. For example, to see if the second bit of a word is a 1, it can be ANDed with the constant 01000 . . . 0. If the result is identically 0, the second bit was a 0, otherwise it was a 1.

Shifts are another class of logical instructions. Some computers provide "logical shifts" (the IBM 370 does, for example). These shifts operate on bit patterns rather than numbers. A logical right shift of two places would move every bit over to the right two places and insert two 0 bits in the left-hand two positions, whereas the corresponding arithmetic shift would duplicate the sign bit if the arithmetic was twos complement. Some computers (for example, the PDP-11) provide *circular shifts,* which are also called *rotates.* A rotate moves the bits in the designated direction and inserts the bits "falling off the end" into the other end. Thus a rotate right one place of the 4-bit group 0111 gives 1011. Shifts and rotates can often be used to test specific bits. For example, on a twos complement machine, a 2-bit left shift moves the third bit position of a word into the sign position. If a test for negative sign instruction is available, it can be used to test this bit.

2.6.1 Logical operations in the IBM 370

The IBM 370 provides a fairly complete set of logical instructions. All single- and double-length shifts described in Section 2.4.9 are available in the logical form described above. The condition code is not changed by these instructions, so they are not immediately useful for testing bits, but should be used when nonarithmetic work is being performed to avoid setting the overflow condition. The basic logical operations that operate on two operands are

```
N            AND
X            EXCLUSIVE OR
O            OR
```

in the form above, they are RX instruction. For example,

```
X            R3,A
```

forms the bit-wise EXCLUSIVE OR between the data in location A and the contents of register 3. The result is left in register 3. An RR form of each of these logical operations is also available. Thus

```
NR           R2,R5
```

forms the bit-wise AND of registers 2 and 5 and leaves the result in register 2. They also have SI and SS forms.

        OI   X'hh',B

is the OR Immediate instruction. "hh" stands for 8 bits represented in 2 hexadecimal digits which form the immediate operand. They are ORed bit by bit with the 8 bits in the byte addressed by B.

        NC   P(L),Q

is the aNd Character instruction. It logically ANDs the string of bytes of length L starting at location Q with the string of the same length starting at location P. The result is left in the string starting at P. (As with the packed decimal instructions, the length need not be specified. The assembler will fill it in if the address P has been declared properly. In this case, the length of the operands is the same, and so only one length specification is needed. It can be between 1 and 256.)

Two operands considered as unsigned binary integers can be compared by the Compare Logical instruction, written CL. It exists in the four forms

MNEMONIC	DESCRIPTION	TYPE
CL	Compare Logical	RX
CLR	Compare Logical Register	RR
CLI	Compare Logical Immediate	SI
CLC	Compare Logical Character	SS

Compare Logical sets the condition code to 0, 1, or 2, depending on whether the first operand is equal to, lower than, or greater than the second.

A well-worn example of the exclusive or is the following sequence which exchanges the contents of registers 2 and 3 without using any other storage or registers (although it is not clear why one would ever want to do this!).

        XR   R2,R3
        XR   R3,R2
        XR   R2,R3

This uses the fact that P exclusive or Q exclusive or Q = P (check it for both values of Q to prove it).

2.6.2 Logical operations in the PDP-11

Rotates, which can be used for logical shifts, were discussed in Section 2.4.10. The following four logical instructions are available in the 16-bit form given or in an 8-bit byte form obtained by appending a B to the operation code.

BIC	S,D	(NOT S) AND D is stored in D.
BIS	S,D	S OR D is stored in D.
COM	D	NOT D is stored in D.
BIT	S,D	S AND D is formed and Z and N bits are set according to the condition of the result. C is not changed and V is cleared.

There is no exclusive or. However, an exclusive or of P and Q can be obtained by forming ((NOT P) AND Q) OR ((NOT Q) AND P). Hence the following sequence forms the exclusive or of P and Q in R1.

MOV	P,R0	
MOV	Q,R1	
BIC	R0,R1	(NOT P) AND Q
BIC	Q,R0	(NOT Q) AND P
BIS	R0,R1	Result

A final class of instructions in the PDP-11 which is useful in logic allows the C, V, N, or Z bits to be set and cleared. The instructions are CLC, CLV, CLN, and CLZ for clearing; and SEC, SEV, SEN, and SEZ for setting. In the set and clear instructions, 4 bits in the operation code are ORed or complemented and ANDed with the 4 condition bits, respectively. For this reason, up to four of the clear or set operations may occur in one clear or set instruction, respectively. These are written in the form CLV!CLN!CLC. This clears the V, N, and C bits. Similarly, SEZ!SEV sets the Z and V bits.

2.7 INTERRUPTS

A number of unusual conditions can arise from time to time. For example, the result of an arithmetic operation can exceed the range of the representation (this is called *overflow*), or, because of either machine or human error, the bit pattern in the next word used as an instruction may not represent any of the allowed instructions. (This is called an *illegal* instruction.) In the former case, it is possible to design instructions to test for the overflow condition (BOV—Branch if OVerflow), although it is not desirable to have to follow every arithmetic instruction with a test. In the latter case, it is not possible to test for the condition since some action must be taken immediately. Early machines would stop on such conditions, but this only pushes the problem down one level to the operator on duty. With high-speed machines, it is desirable to take action immediately to avoid wasting time. The action required is presumably to gather some statistics about the error or unusual condition and continue with that job, if possible, or else to move on to another job. A modern computer system will use a monitor program to perform these tasks, so it is first necessary to initiate the required program.

When the control unit recognizes an error or unusual condition, it will stop executing whatever it was trying to do and branch to another location. This location is assumed to contain the start of a program to take care of the condition. Some machines will branch to a different location for each condition, others will branch to one location and store information which specifies the condition in another location or register. In either case the net result is the same, a new program has been initiated and it knows what conditions caused the initiation. This feature is called an *interrupt.*

An interrupt caused by the user's program, whether it be by illegal instructions, overflow, or similar conditions, can be likened to a transfer of control to enable the user to handle the programming more easily. This should be contrasted with an interrupt—due to a condition external to the user's program—which is a signal to the machine to initiate or terminate some other process. The latter will happen in input/output processing, to be discussed in Chapter 6, and in time sharing, which is beyond the scope of this book.

After the interrupt program has taken care of the condition causing the interrupt, it may be necessary to return to the user's program and continue execution. Because some interrupt conditions can arise from conditions external to the user's program, it should not be aware of the interrupt. Since the status of all registers and memory locations available to the user's program must not be changed, the interrupt program must save the contents of any index registers, condition registers, indicators, or accumulators that it uses and restore them to their original state after the interrupt. In order to return to the user's program, it is necessary to know the location at which execution should resume. The interrupt hardware will usually save the address contained in the control counter at the time of the interrupt and put it in some convenient register or location.

A typical interrupt mechanism will branch to a fixed location in memory, perhaps location 1, and simultaneously store the contents of the control counter into another fixed location, say 0. The program which starts in location 1 will first save any registers that it plans to use in memory, then take the necessary actions, and finally reload the registers from memory cells before executing an indirect transfer to location 0.

It is possible that other interrupt conditions could arise during the execution of the program initiated by the first interrupt. This could cause problems, because the contents of location 0 would be overwritten and lost. Therefore, during the period in which one interrupt is being serviced, others must be disabled. This is handled by a 1-bit register which contains the interrupt status. If the bit is a 0, interrupts are allowed, but the occurrence of an interrupt sets the bit to a 1, which disables further interrupts. An instruction, often called *return from interrupt,* must be added to the repertoire. This instruction transfers control (back to the interrupted program) and resets the interrupt-status register to 0, thus enabling future interrupts.

During the period in which interrupts are disabled, conditions due to other than the user's program can occur (input/output conditions, for example). Since these must eventually be serviced, they must be saved until interrupts are re-enabled. This is done by means of an interrupt-condition register. This is a register which contains a bit for each interrupt condition that can occur. The corresponding bit is set to a 1 whenever an interrupt condition arises. This register controls the interrupting mechanism and saves the condition until it can cause an interrupt. On some machines, the bits must be reset by program instructions which are included in the repertoire for that purpose. Other machines will automatically reset the interrupt bit when the condition is recognized.

The early interrupt schemes allowed the programmer to read the contents of the interrupt-condition register so that he could determine the cause of the interrupt. This provided for program flexibility at the expense of speed. In particular, it allowed the programmer to assign a priority to one interrupt over another, so that when several occurred nearly simultaneously, one could be given precedence over another. This may be necessary if some of the interrupts have to be serviced within a given period. In some applications, an interrupt can arise from an external source in *real time.* Such an interrupt must be serviced within a given time, typically within a few tens of micro seconds up to a few milliseconds. Such interrupts can also occur from mechanical input/output, such as card readers. They must be given high priority, because after a given time it is no longer possible to service them.

Unfortunately, some of the programs that process interrupts may take so long to execute that other conditions are lost. In this case, it is necessary to enable interrupt during interrupt processing. This can be done by saving the return address elsewhere, and enabling interrupts by executing a return from interrupt. This solution, while possible, is tedious and leads to very complicated programs. Instead, it is common to build the priority into the hardware. In a *priority interrupt* scheme, the interrupts are assigned to groups and each group is assigned a priority level. We can take this priority level to be an integer between 0 and $N - 1$ if there are N groups. If an interrupt condition occurs in group J, then it causes an interrupt provided that no other interrupt condition from the same or higher numbered group is in progress. In order to keep several nearly simultaneous interrupts from overwriting each others' storage, the hardware makes a different transfer for each group. Thus, in a typical design, group I may transfer to location $2I + 1$ after storing the control counter in location $2I$. This reduces the amount of work needed to determine which condition caused the interrupt.

In a large computer installation, many interrupt conditions can occur. For example, there could be as many as 20 different interrupt conditions from input/output units. At any given time, the programmer may wish to disregard some of them. To allow for this, the hardware may include a *mask register.* This is a register which contains one bit for each bit in the interrupt-condition register. The hardware looks at the interrupt-condition register "through" the mask register, that is, the condition bit and the mask bit are ANDed together, and an interrupt only occurs if the result is a 1. This is shown in the logical diagram of a 5-bit interrupt group in Figure 2.25. In this diagram we can distinguish two ways in which interrupts might be ignored. If the status is such that interrupts in this group are disabled, then the condition is saved in the interrupt register. If the mask is set to ignore a given condition, then it will not cause an interrupt regardless of the interrupt status. This is some-times called disarming the interrupt. The mask register can also be connected in such a way that bits cannot be set into the condition register when the mask is off, or so that setting a mask bit to a 1 to reenable an interrupt condi-tion clears the condition bit. This can prevent certain conditions from causing interrupts—conditions that arose far in the past and that are of no interest to the programmer.

The program which handles the interrupt must be in the machine with the user's program, and at least a part of it must be in the main memory. Obvi-ously its purpose will have been defeated if the user's program is allowed to change it, whether by error or by malicious intent. To prevent this from

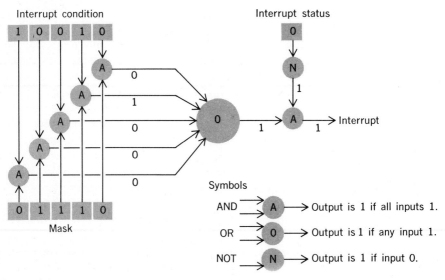

FIGURE 2.25   Interrupt logic

happening, the monitor program is kept in an area of the main memory that is *protected*. When the user's program is in execution, it is not allowed to access the protected area of memory. (This protection is done by hardware devices.) An attempt to access protected memory is itself an error condition that will cause interrupt. Because the contents of the interrupt registers (condition, mask, status) are critical to the operation of the system, the user's program is not allowed to change them. Therefore, all instructions that change them are protected instructions that can only be executed when the interrupt-status register is 1.

The basic types of interrupt that can occur are discussed in more detail below.

2.7.1 Arithmetic conditions

These interrupts are due to unusual arithmetic conditions such as overflow. Although the user could handle them with test instructions, it is preferable to have the hardware continuously monitor the arithmetic register for the occurrence of such conditions. This procedure is more efficient in terms of execution time because it means that no additional orders need be executed until the condition occurs.

The user may wish to specify what action is to be taken after any particular condition. He may, for example, wish some conditions to be ignored and others to ultimately cause a branch to a location in his area of main memory where he has a program to handle the condition. The monitor must accept requests from the user's program to cause these actions when the conditions occur.

In addition to overflow, other conditions in this category include *divide check* (caused by attempted division by 0) and *underflow*. Underflow occurs when floating-point arithmetic gives an answer smaller than the absolute range allowed. This must be represented by 0, but it can give rise to severe inaccuracies in numerical programs. It may therefore be necessary to warn the user.

2.7.2 Illegal conditions

The various illegal conditions that can arise include attempted execution of illegal instructions and attempted access of protected memory. Just as part of the memory is protected from access by the user, so is some of the input/output equipment. Therefore, some of the input/output instructions are protected, so that attempted execution of them by the user program will cause an interrupt. When an interrupt on illegal condition occurs, the job in execution is usually terminated because it can be assumed to be due to a programmer error. Information concerning the error and the state of the user's program is output for printing and another task is initiated. An instruction may be illegal because it is protected or because it is undefined. It is not usually necessary for the system to distinguish them for the user because either is incorrect, however the hardware may distinguish them at the time of the interrupt.

2.7.3 Timer interrupts

It is desirable to time the program in execution for several reasons. Three of these are:

1   To charge the program for the amount of computer time used.
2   To detect infinite loops such as

X   BRANCH   X

which would never stop.
3   To allocate certain quanta of time to each of several programs in turn in a time-sharing environment.

The latter two reasons require that an interrupt be caused after a certain length of time has elapsed. There are two types of clock commonly available, the real-time clock and the interval timer. The latter is a device that can be set to a given number of seconds (or fractions of seconds) and is then counted down to 0. The end of the count provides an interrupt condition. (Some systems allow the interval timer to be reset to 0 and to cause an interrupt when the upward count reaches a quantity stored in another register.) The real-time clock is a counter which is continuously incremented so that — in principle — it provides the time of day. If it is properly initialized, it can be read later to provide the time. Some systems allow an interrupt to occur when the counter reaches a value stored in another register, others allow interrupts whenever a specified position in the clock changes. In a sense, it is identical to an upward interval timer, but it is usually in a form that provides immediate readout in an hours–minutes–seconds–fractions-of-seconds form.

2.7.4 Machine errors

Some errors are automatically detected by hardware in the machine. The design philosophy should be to provide such error detection that the probability of an undetected error will be small enough that, for each basic operation, the expected time between one such error and another will be many hours. Usually all memory devices have some error detection equipment, typically a *parity bit*.

A parity bit is an additional bit appended to a word of N bits. It is always set so that the total number of bits equal to 1 is even (odd). This is called an even (odd) parity scheme. This provides for single-error detection. If a single error occurs in a word, say a bit is changed from a 0 to a 1, then the number of 1 bits is changed from even to odd. Therefore no single error in a word can escape detection, although a double error can. If the probability of a bit error in a word is independent of all other bit errors, and is, say, 1 chance in 10^9 for each memory fetch, then the probability of 2-bit errors simultaneously is 1 chance in 10^{18}. If the memory cycle is 1 micro second (10^{-6} seconds), then the expected time between undetected memory errors has been increased from 10^3 second to 10^{12} seconds or about 3×10^4 years.

If the probability of errors is too large, then it may be necessary to use automatic error correcting schemes.† A simple example will illustrate the point.

Suppose the 5-by-5 array of bits in Figure 2.26 is to be stored. By storing an additional row and column of bits such that the column and row parities are all even, a single-error correcting code is formed. In the example, the circled bit has been changed from a 0 to a 1 so that the parities of the 3d column and the 4th row are incorrect. This indicates that the circled bit is incorrect. A double error will always be detected because there will be parity errors in two rows or columns. A triple error could be mistaken as a single error. For example, if the 3 bits in square boxes in Figure 2.26 are wrong, this would be indistinguishable from a single error in the circled bit.

†A discussion of this much-studied problem can be found in W. W. Peterson, "Error Correcting Codes," M.I.T. Press, Cambridge, Mass., 1961.

1	0	0	1	1	1
0	1	1	0	0	0
1	1	0	1	0	1
1	0	(1)	1	1	[1]
0	1	1	0	1	1
1	1	[0]	1	1	[0]

FIGURE 2.26

Whatever scheme of error detection is used, the monitor program will have to deal with the problems caused by detected but uncorrected errors. An attempt can be made to repeat the operation that caused the error, but if this attempt fails, the task involved may have to be abandoned or repeated from the beginning.

2.7.5   Input/output conditions

These will be discussed in greater detail in the chapter on input/output. We shall see in that chapter that I/O operations can be performed simultaneously with computation. In order to bring the two parallel processes into step when necessary, the input/output events can interrupt the CPU execution sequence.

In a time-sharing environment, interrupts from input/output equipment may not be related to the program currently in execution. It must therefore be possible to save the conditions until the appropriate program *has* been put into execution.

PROBLEMS

1   How many bits are needed to represent an address in a memory with *(a)* 4,096 locations, *(b)* 131,072 locations, and *(c)* 32,768 locations?

2   How many different representations of zero are there in an *N*-bit ones complement number?

3   What is the range of an *N*-bit ones complement fraction?

4   How many bits are required to represent all numbers between −1 and +1, with an error of not more than 0.0001 decimal, in the ones complement representation?

5   What are the answers to questions two, three, and four for twos complement numbers and sign/magnitude numbers?

6   By analogy with the twos complement of a number, what is the tens complement of a number? How would you use this to express signed integers such that there are about as many negative values as positive values represented?

7   The ones complement of a number is simply the bit-wise complement of the binary form, and is equal to the negative of that number if the ones complement representation is being used. By analogy, what is the nines complement of a number? How would you use this to express signed integers with a balanced range as in question six?

8   Express −6, 17, and −23 in sign/magnitude, ones complement, and twos complement for machine using a sign-plus-5 bits of binary information for representing integers.

9 Add the four signed binary numbers 100110, 001101, 010101, and 111101 together as (a) sign/magnitude, (b) twos complement, and (c) ones complement numbers.

10 What is the 10-bit (double-precision) result if 10010 and 10101 are multiplied in each of the three representations as integers?

11 Divide the integer 0001010111 by 01001 to get a 5-bit quotient and remainder in each of the three representations.

12 *a* Using the one-address instructions LOAD and STORE and the zero-address instructions ADD and MPY for a stack machine, write a code to calculate

$$(A * (B + C + D) * E + F * G) * (B + C + D)$$

using as few instructions as possible.

 b If the instruction DUP (short for *duplicate*) puts a copy of the top of the stack as a new top level (so that the sequence

```
DUP
ADD
```

doubles the top of the stack), how short can the code be made?

13 Suppose there is a machine with the three-address instruction

```
SBTST        A,B,P
```

(and no others) which first subtracts the contents of location B from the contents of location A, returns the result to location A, and then branches to location P for the next instruction if the result is 0, otherwise takes the next instruction in sequence. The arithmetic is presumed to be integer. Write a program using only this instruction to put the absolute value of the contents of location Y into location X. (Y) may not be changed. *Hint.* Count (Y) and —(Y) until one of them reaches 0. This program can be written with nine instructions, using only three extra temporary storage locations for scratch work and one location containing a constant. *Note:* As a matter of programming practice, it must not be assumed that the contents of locations changed by the program are initialized. Rather, this must be done at the start of the program. If this rule is followed, the segment can be reused many times during one computer run. You may assume that location ONM contains the integer —1.

14 If memory locations A, B, C, D, E, F, G, and Z are all different, and the contents of all except for Z may not be changed, write programs for the simple three-, two-, and one-address and stack machines discussed above to perform the calculation $Z = (A + B + C)/(D * E * F — G)$, where the letters

A, B, etc., stand for the contents of the cells of the same name. Temporary storage cells T1, T2, . . . may be used in the calculation.

15   Assume that the cost of executing each instruction in any one of the simple machines discussed above is equal to $p + m * q$, where m is the number of addresses in the instruction and p and q are constants. Thus if 5 two-address instructions were executed, the cost would be $5p + 10q$. Discuss the desirability of each of the four machines from the standpoint of the cost of doing the calculation in question fourteen. How does the "cheapest" machine depend on the ratio $r = q/p$? That is, divide the four costs by p so that they depend on r. (Display the results graphically.)

16   If the restriction that the contents of A through G must not be changed is removed, are the conclusions changed?

17   We have noticed that in the case of two- and one-address machines, extra instructions to move information to and from temporary storage are needed. In fact, a relation between the number of extra instructions needed in the two cases is known if the restriction that the operands on the right-hand side must not be changed is enforced. Consider an arbitrary calculation of the type in question fourteen; that is, only the four operations $+$, $-$, $*$, and $/$ are used, each involves two operands (unary minus is not allowed), all the symbolic addresses A, B, etc., are different, and their contents may not be changed (except for the left-hand side). Suppose that in the minimum cost programs (as defined by question fifteen) the two-address machine requires E MOVE orders and that there are N other orders (that means that there are N operations on the right-hand side of the "=" sign). Write down expressions for the cost of executing the minimal cost program for each of the machines in terms of N, E, r, and p. Noting that all of these numbers are positive, show that the two-address machine can never have the cheapest program of all four. Can it ever cost no more for the calculation than the cheapest of the other three?

18   What are the three steps taken in the fetch part of instruction execution?

19   Do you think it preferable that a conditional branch instruction which tests the top of the stack in a stack oriented machine pop the top level of the stack after the test or leave it for reuse by future instructions? Illustrate by examples.

20   Write a program for a typical stack machine to compute the square root of the number in the top level of the stack.

21   Consider a two-address machine with the instructions

	SUB	A,B	(A) − (B) stored as (A).
and	BZN	A,B	If (A) are 0 or negative, then branch to location B for the next instruction.

Indicate how to perform the two-address operations ADD, MOVE, MPY, and DIV using only these two instructions. Assume that arithmetic is being performed on integers.

22 Why was it stipulated that twos complement arithmetic was used in the program modification discussion at the start of Section 2.5? Would ones complement or sign/magnitude arithmetic have worked?

23 Prove that the correct rule for doubling a ones complement number is a left circular shift of one place.

24 Can you suggest a simple rule for dividing a number by 2^n and getting a rounded result?

25 How can overflow be detected during shifting operations?

26 How can the loss of accuracy be detected during right shifts?

27 Consider a machine with $32,768 = 2^{15}$ words of memory and a 15-bit index register holding positive integers. Assume that index arithmetic is done *modulo* 32768; that is, if the answer is greater than 32767, 32768 is subtracted from it. If the contents of index registers are added to addresses, what should be put in index register 1 so that the effective address of LOAD A(1) is A-327?

28 Show by means of truth tables that the following relations between the logical relations AND, OR, and NOT are true.

a (x AND y) AND z = x AND (y AND z)
b (x OR y) OR z = x OR (y OR z)
c x AND (y OR z) = (x AND y) OR (x AND z)
d NOT (x AND y) = (NOT x) OR (NOT y)
e NOT (NOT x) = x

29 Special symbols are used for the logical operations, just as the characters + and * etc. are used for the arithmetic operations. Because most computers are short of characters in their printable character set, we shall use the characters + for OR, * for AND, and — for NOT (this is a unary operation; that is, it only has one operand). This choice is partly governed by the strong resemblance between the character + and OR etc. In fact, many of the rules of logical manipulation are symbolically true for arithmetic. Thus $(X + Y) + Z = X + (Y + Z)$ is true whether + represents OR or addition and $-(-X) = X$ whether X represents subtraction or NOT. Can you give arithmetic relations that are not true logically and vice versa?

30 Design index arithmetic instructions for a typical one-address machine which will use less than three instructions inside the loop. If the increment is assumed to be 1, can it be done with one instruction in the loop?

31 The following IBM 370 program is to test bit 1 of the 32-bit word MDR. At the start of execution, register 9 contains a 12-bit *left* justified integer which is the *position* in an array of 16-bit halfwords in memory whose *address* is to be placed in register 10 if bit 1 of MDR is a 0. The address of the first 16-bit halfword is MCODE, while its position number is 0. The second halfword has address MCODE + 2 and position number 1.

12	20
Integer	Garbage

Register 9 beforehand

Fill in the blanks:

```
        L          ____,MDR
        N          1,MASK         AND INSTRUCTION
        BC         4,NOBRANCH     BRANCHES IF NON-ZERO
        SRL        9,____
        SLL        9,1
        LA         10,_____(____)
NOBRANCH   . . . . . . . . . . . . . .
           . . . . . . . . . . . . . .
MASK       ____      0F,X' _____'
```

32 The following program section is run on the IBM 370.

LOCATION (HEX)		CODE	
E800		LA	10,8
E804		L	3,FIVE
E808		L	8,=F'38'
E80C		LA	12,FOUR
E810		SRDA	8,32
E814		DR	8,10
E816		SRA	8,1
E81A		MR	2,10
E81C		SLDA	2,32
E820	FIVE	DC	F'6'
E824	FOUR	DC	F'4'

What are the contents of registers 2, 3, 8, 9, 10, and 12 when the instruction in location E81C has been executed?

33 Write a program for an IBM 370 which will multiply two 31-bit positive binary integers and produce a 62-bit result stored in a pair of registers. Do not use a multiply instruction!

34 Write a program to multiply two 16-bit twos complement numbers to get a 32-bit twos complement result using shifts and adds on the PDP-11.

35 Write a PDP-11 program to divide a 32-bit unsigned integer by a 16-bit unsigned integer to get a quotient and a positive remainder.

3

SYSTEM SOFTWARE

The system software is a fundamental part of the total computer system, providing an interface between the user needs and the capabilities of the hardware. A job that is normally done on an elaborate system can be done on a very simple computer with few or no system programs, provided only that there is sufficient memory space and time available. However, the amount of user time involved in preparing such programs as well as the difficulty of checking them can make the task prohibitively expensive. It is often pointed out that the computer can do nothing that cannot be done by hand; that it cannot, therefore, provide the human with powers that he did not previously have. It has also been pointed out that the car does not enable the human to go anywhere he could not have previously walked to, but it *does* enable him to go to many more places a lot more quickly. The car is only about 10 times faster than walking; the computer is about 10^7 times faster than hand calculation. The development of automatic programming systems over the last 15 years has increased the speed with which programs can be written by a factor of 10 to 10^2. The addition of a good software system to a hardware system enables the user not only to complete some tasks more quickly and more cheaply, but makes the computer solution of other tasks possible.

The purpose of the system software is twofold: to make it easier for the user to get his job onto the computer, and to make it easier for him to run it and test it when it is on the computer. In this chapter we are going to look briefly at the problem of getting the program onto the computer. We shall also investigate what software is needed once the program is in execution.

3.1 THE RAW MACHINE: INITIAL PROGRAM LOAD

The basic hardware is capable of executing sequences of instructions drawn from the computer memory. It is the job of the user to get his program into the memory and begin execution at the correct point. The input/output section of the computer is capable of reading data into the memory, so this is the hardware that must be used to load the program. Internally, program, numbers, and other data are represented by "words" (or groups) of binary digits; the input instructions on a machine are capable of reading an external representation of these bits into memory. Therefore, if the program to be executed is specified in its binary form exactly as it should appear inside the memory of the computer, input instructions can be used to load it. Unfortunately this begs the question, since these input instructions must themselves be loaded into memory before they can be executed. To get around this difficulty, an *initial load sequence,* also known as an *initial program load* (IPL) or a *bootstrap sequence,* is usually employed.

An initial load sequence is brought into action by pressing a switch on the main computer console. This switch initiates a single short segment of code that is prewired into the computer and represents a program to start the loading process. Very few system programmers need be concerned with this process since it is built in by the manufacturer and is not usually changed. However, it represents the start of a series of more complex loading procedures, so we shall discuss it briefly. The initial load switch requires a section of code to be stored, permanently, somewhere in the computer. It is only used periodically after the computer has been stopped for some reason, and it is therefore desirable to minimize its size. On the simplest computers it can be a single instruction, although typically it consists of several. Let us suppose that the computer has input/output instructions that read single *records* of information (for example, the contents of a card) into certain memory locations. The IBM 1401, for example, can read a card into character locations 1 through 80 with a single instruction. The initial load switch can force the control unit into a *state* in which it thinks that it has just read such an instruction from the memory, and that instruction is therefore executed. The switch should also force the control counter contents to be the address of the first of the set of locations that will contain the result of the read of the single record. After the read is complete, the machine automatically fetches the next instruction to be obeyed. Since this is determined by the control counter, the next set of instructions is determined by the contents of the fIrst record of information read in. This contains no more than a few instructions. What it can contain is enough program to read in additional program. This is the reason for the name "bootstrapping"; it is likened to the idea of pulling oneself up by one's bootstraps.

As additional items of information are read (and we shall assume for the moment that they are on cards) additional program can be read into the memory. It is necessary to decide where this program must be loaded, since both the user and the bootstrap process should agree if the results are to be of any value. It would be possible to agree that each subsequent card is to be loaded into as many locations as necessary following the last card image in memory. Since this is rather restrictive, it is more normal to agree on an input format where each card contains the address of memory locations into which the remainder of the information is to be loaded. Then the user is free to load any location in memory (except the ones containing the loading program). One additional feature is needed as a minimum. This is an indication that the end of the program has been reached and that execution is to start at a specified location. This can be included with an indication of how much (how many words) information is on each card. If the indication is that there is no information on a card, that can be taken to be the last card. The location address can then be used as the location at which execution is to commence.

A program that does this form of loading into memory is called an *absolute loader.* The code that is loaded is called absolute code, since it is written with

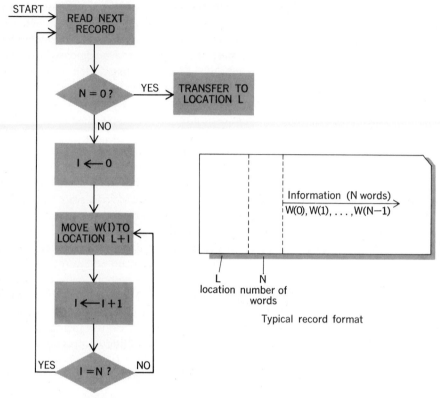

FIGURE 3.1   Absolute loader

each address specified as an actual machine location. A flowchart of a typical absolute loader is shown in Figure 3.1.

3.2 THE ASSEMBLER

The absolute loader requires that the user prepare a program completely, specifying the addresses of all instructions and data words that he uses and giving the machine codes of all instructions that are used. This much detail is not only tedious but unnecessary for the specification of a program. It does not matter to the user if a given variable, which he may call X, is in location 1026 or 21734. Neither does it affect the execution of the program by the machine—provided that the correct address is available every time that the variable X is referenced. For this reason we would like to allow the user to talk about the variable X, or location X, meaning the memory cell that has been assigned for the use of X during the calculation. Thus, instead of using an absolute address, a *symbolic address* is used. If the variable X is to be added to the accumulator in a one-address machine, then an ADD X instruction is executed.

When we write ADD X, we are assuming that the system is going to understand the string of three characters A, D, D. The hardware, however, actually requires a pattern of binary digits such as 01011010 for an ADD instruction. Since we do not want to learn, or repeatedly write, such strings of bits, we would like the machine to accept ADD instead. Terms such as SUB and MPY for the instructions subtract and multiply are called *mnemonic instructions*. A mnemonic is a device to aid the memory. These abbreviations are concise to write, yet they help the memory to recall what they do. For example, it is easier to remember that DIV, rather than 01011101, is the division operation.

The hardware is capable of accepting neither symbols as addresses nor mnemonics as instructions. (This is not to say that a machine could not be so constructed, but most practical machines are not.) To get around this difficulty, we must expand the loading program from the simple absolute loader discussed above to a program that translates the source language of mnemonics and symbols (assembly language) to an object language of binary instructions and addresses. Such a translation program is called an *assembler*. Note that the loading process is becoming more complicated, but as it does, the job for the user is becoming easier. In order to get an assembly language program into the computer it is necessary, first, to obey the initial load sequence to bring in an absolute loader. This, in turn, can bring in an assembly program which is used to translate the source program.

Throughout Chapter 2 we were using a form of assembly language. Without it, we would not have been able to describe machine instructions other than by specifying the actual binary form of the instruction. The latter form is no more necessary to the writing of programs than it is to the understanding of the principles of machine language.

3.2.1   The two-pass assembler

In order to translate the source assembly language, the assembler must replace each mnemonic instruction with its equivalent binary code and replace each symbolic address with its numerical equivalent. The former can be done by keeping a list of all mnemonic instruction names in a table. When a mnemonic is read, the table can be consulted and the equivalent binary code found. In order to do the same for the symbolic addresses, it is necessary to construct an equivalent table. The mnemonics are known ahead of time, but the relation between the symbols that a programmer uses and addresses in memory cannot be known until the program has been coded and read by the machine. Thus there are two distinct actions to be taken for symbols. The first is to set up a table of all symbols used and assign their machine addresses; the second is to take the addresses and substitute them for the symbols. These two phases are usually associated with two scans or *passes* of the source code. On the first pass, a *symbol table* is constructed in memory, giving the equivalent address for each symbol. On the second pass, the substitution is made to translate the code into binary. The first pass has to use rules for determining which location is to be assigned to each distinct symbol.

We will first discuss a common form of assembler, then take a brief look at assemblers for the IBM 370 and the PDP-11. The reader should be aware that there are as many, or more, forms of assembler as there are types of computer, as the assembler has to recognize the idiosyncrasies of the particular brand of computer.

3.2.2 External representation of instructions

The programmer has to be able to specify the name of an instruction and its operand address or addresses, and to indicate if a symbolic address is associated with the location containing the instruction. *Fields* of the input record are associated with each of these items. (We will assume that the input record is a punched card, although it could just as well be a line from an input typewriter keyboard.) Many of the early assemblers used *fixed-format* card input, that is, a format in which each field occupied a fixed set of columns, just as Fortran uses columns 1 through 5 for the statement label. However, more recent assemblers use a variable-format card input. Usually the location field, the one that contains the symbolic address if there is one, is first on the card. It must start in column 1, and it is terminated by one or more blanks. This means that its absence can be indicated by a blank in column 1. The operation mnemonic comes next, occupying as many columns as needed and terminated by one or more blanks. Finally the address field comes, also terminated by one or more blanks. The remainder of the card is available for comments and *should be so used.* (A standard practice is to reserve columns 73 to 80 for a sequence number and identifying code. Thus the thirteenth card in the program named SQRT might contain SQRT0130 in the last 80 columns. This is not necessary in remote time-shared terminal systems which maintain line numbers for the user.)

Since only one blank is needed between fields, a programmer could write a program in the following form:

```
#LOAD#ZZZ
X1Z23#STORE#ABC
#BPL#WR1
KKK#ADD#YRT(3)
WR1###SUB####D4
#BPL##X1Z23
```

The assembler does not care what names are used, does not read comments, and is just as capable of reading the input with one blank between each field as with ten. However, the user also needs to read this program, both to check it and possibly to change it. Consequently, it should be punched so that columns line up, so that symbolic names have some meaning to a user who understands the problem being solved, and with comments. Assemblers often allow full lines of comments on any card started with an asterisk, so the same section of program could appear as:

```
******************************************************************* GOBB0210
*                 THIS SECTION OF CODE FORMS THE GOBBLED GOOK IN GOB.   GOBB0220
*                 SEE PAGE 34 OF REFERENCE 2 FOR A DEFINITION.          GOBB0230
*                 THE STARTING ITERATE IS IN FIRST.                     GOBB0240
******************************************************************* GOBB0250
           LOAD    FIRST       GET FIRST ITERATE.                       GOBB0260
LOOPGOB    STORE   GOB                                                  GOBB0270
           BPL     SKIPGOB     ALMOST DONE IF POSITIVE.                 GOBB0280
SPECGOB    ADD     YDERIV(3)   NOTE. . A BRANCH TO SPECGOB CAN          GOBB0290
*                              OCCUR FROM CARD #120.                    GOBB0300
SKIPGOB    SUB     DECR        DECR IS COMPUTED IN SECTION CAM.         GOBB0310
           BPL     LOOPGOB     REPEAT THE ITERATION UNTIL NEG.          GOBB0320
```

If the rest of the code is changed to agree with the use of symbolic names here, the assembler will produce exactly the same object code and take virtually the same length of time to do it. However, the user may save himself many hours of later frustration.

In effect, a fixed format has been used in punching the program. This is usually possible, as the maximum length of the first two columns can be determined in advance. The maximum size needed for the mnemonic is known from looking at the mnemonics the assembler allows. Most assemblers also restrict the length of symbolic addresses. The IBM 370 allows up to eight characters. The PDP-11 allows any length, but only the first six characters are examined, so there is little point in using too many more. (In long programs, the user will find that it is preferable to use shortish names to save writing.) Six were allowed on the IBM 7090 series machines because six characters could be packed into one word, and this was convenient inside the assembly program. Other machines use a different maximum length. Usually, names are restricted to those combinations of characters which start with a letter and contain only letters and numbers (the *alphanumeric* characters). The only necessary restriction is that it be possible to recognize a name in the address field. Thus A + 3 means the name A followed by + and the number 3. Hence + cannot be allowed as a character in a name. Neither can an all-numeric name such as 31 be allowed, since it cannot be distinguished from the number 31.

The address field is allowed to contain meaningful expressions involving addresses and numbers. The restrictions on the expressions depend on the assembler and loader used, so discussion will be delayed until the chapter on assembler implementation.

3.2.3 Definition of data and storage by pseudo-instructions

By placing a name in the location field, a symbolic address used to reference instructions can be defined. In addition to these addresses, which are typically used in branch instructions, it is necessary to provide a mechanism for defining the addresses of data locations and constant locations. In some assemblers, the symbolic addresses of single-variable locations such as X need not be defined. The assembler recognizes that such symbols have been used and assigns single storage cells for their use at the end of the input code. This is similar in spirit to the action of a Fortran compiler which does not require that simple variables be declared. Dimensioned variables have to be explicitly declared in Fortran. Other languages, such as Algol, require that all variables be explicitly declared. The advantage of not declaring simple variables in Fortran or single cells in assembly language is one of a saving in writing, but its disadvantage is that there is a greater chance of error. If a symbolic address that is supposed to represent the first of a block of storage locations is not defined in assembly language, it would be assigned a single location only, so that, during execution, the program would access other locations. This problem is not as serious in Fortran because the use of the variable name may indicate to the compiler that the variable should have been dimensioned. Consequently, most assemblers demand that all symbolic addresses be defined at some point, so that omitting their definitions is illegal. In either case, it is necessary to provide for the definition of locations containing constants, to specify their contents and to be able to specify blocks of contiguous locations to be used for the storage of arrays and other multiword items. These definitions are handled by *pseudo-instructions*. A pseudo-instruction (pseudo for short) is also called a *directive*. It is an instruction to the assembler rather than an instruction which is to be put in memory for eventual execution by the machine. There are two types of pseudos, those that load data into the memory and those that tell the assembler certain facts about the incoming program.

DATA LOADING PSEUDOS

Typical of those that load data into memory are the pseudos which allow for the definition of decimal, octal, and hexadecimal numbers or character strings as data. Two approaches to this group of pseudos exist. The first method provides several different pseudos which specify the format of the data, whereas the second method provides an all-inclusive pseudo and uses a data format that defines its type. The 370 assembler uses the second method, the PDP-11 uses a combination. A general form of the first type of pseudo is:

```
          CONST       DEC        3.14159
          NUMBER      OCT        173245604
and       STRING      CHR        'ABC DEF'
```

The first pseudo DEC is supposed to convert the constant 3.14159 into binary, put it into the next available location, and define the symbolic address CONST as that location address. It is necessary for the assembler to decide whether to convert into a floating-point or a fixed-point representation (if both are available). This decision can be made in a similar manner to Fortran: if there is a decimal point present, then use floating point. Some assemblers will allow several constants to be specified on one DEC pseudo card by separating each number by a comma. In this case, subsequent numbers will load into consecutive locations. Thus if the pseudo

```
ALPHA       DEC           1.2,4.5,6.546,2
```

is used, then locations ALPHA, ALPHA+1, ALPHA+2, and ALPHA+3 contain the numbers floating-point 1.2, 4.5, 6.546, and fixed-point 2 respectively. The OCT pseudo will work similarly except that, since this is a way of specifying the contents of memory bit by bit (3 bits to each octal digit), there is no need to determine whether the fixed- or floating-point representation is intended. CHR stands for characters. The address is a string of characters enclosed in quotes. Any character except a single quote, including blank, which in this case does not terminate the address field, may appear inside the quotes. Since the quote character is used to delimit the character string, it cannot be used in the string. This can be overcome by using two ' characters. Thus the single ' (quote) character would be input as

```
          CHAR           ''''
```

In addition to specifying constants via pseudos, many assemblers allow the programmer to express the constant required for an operand *literally,* that is, by writing it in the address field of an instruction. This is called a literal address, and is usually written by preceding the constant with an equal sign. For example, if the operand for an ADD instruction is 3.5, the instruction could be written as

```
          ADD           =3.5
```

These literals are equivalent, at the machine-language level, to putting an ordinary address in the ADD instruction and writing the constant in a data-loading pseudo later. The assembler translates them to the latter form.

For a discussion of data loading pseudos of the second type, the reader is referred to the DC pseudo discussed in Section 3.2.5.

ASSEMBLER DIRECTIVE PSEUDOS

The pseudos that tell the assembler what is going on are used to place the code into locations in memory out of the normal sequence, to reserve blocks of locations for multiword items, or to tell the assembler the definition of a symbolic address. Typical of these pseudos are the following examples which are common to many assemblers.

        BSS   NUMBER

BSS (Block Started by Symbol) tells the assembler that a block of length NUMBER locations is to be left free, so that the next instruction will be loaded NUMBER locations further on. A symbolic address in the location field of a BSS pseudo is assigned the value of the address of the first location of the block.

A   EQU   B

EQU (EQUivalent to) tells the assembler that the symbolic address A is equivalent to B. If B is a number, then that number is entered into the table; if B is itself a symbolic address, then the value of B must be found in the table and that value used. This means that B must be defined before such an EQU statement is used.

The ASSIGN pseudo is found in some assemblers. It is used to allocate a number of variables to single cells of storage. This is done by writing their names in the address field of the pseudo, each name separated from the next by a comma. For example, the following line of code

        ASSIGN   A,B,N12345,XYZ

would assign one location each to A, B, N12345, and XYZ in the next four available spaces.

For another approach to allocating storage space for variables, the reader is referred to the DS pseudo described in Section 3.2.5.

The assembler will produce object code to be loaded into locations sequentially, usually starting at location 0. Each instruction or pseudo that allocates space will take space, which is recorded by the assembler in its *location counter,* a memory cell which the assembler uses to know where to assemble the next line. Some assemblers (the IBM 370 and the PDP-11, for example) allow several location counters. The programmer can think of the process as several pads of programming paper. When he switches to a different location counter, it is as if he had switched to a different pad and continued writing from where he last stopped. The assembler assembles the code from each "pad" (called a *control section* in the IBM 370) in such a way that each section follows the previous one in memory. The use of this will be seen in Chapter 4.

The last line in an assembly language program has to be indicated. The usual way is with the pseudo END, which tells the assembler to start the second pass.

It is evident that the address of an instruction or pseudo can be either a symbol or a number. It is convenient to allow arithmetic combinations of symbols and numbers, so many assemblers provide for a variety of possibilities. Addition and subtraction are nearly always allowed, multiplication frequently, while division and parentheses are relatively infrequently allowed.

Once the address field of a card has been terminated with a blank, the remainder of the card can usually be used for comments which help to document the action of the code. Frequently columns 73 through 80 of a card cannot be used as part of the address, but are used conventionally to punch a short identification of two to four characters followed by a sequence number so that the cards can be reordered if they are mishandled. If the initial sequencing is done by 10s or 20s, the additions can be made without frequently resequencing the deck.

3.2.4 The second pass

On the second scan through the input, the assembler produces the binary object code consisting of the machine language and binary constants defined in the source. Where does the assembler put these binary words? One possibility is to place them directly into the memory locations indicated in the assembly language and then to begin execution of the object program immediately after the second pass of the assembler has been completed. Such a scheme is called a *load-and-go* scheme. It suffers from many drawbacks, although it has the very definite advantage of speed over most other schemes to be discussed. Among the disadvantages are the facts that:

1 A program cannot be loaded into locations which are occupied by the assembler code. Fancy assemblers on small machines frequently use the whole of the main memory, ruling out the possibility of such direct input.
2 Each time that the program is to be executed, it has to be reassembled. (This is only serious if the assembler is slow.)

The first problem can be overcome by placing the object code onto an auxiliary storage device during the second pass of the assembler. This is not strictly a load-and-go system, but it can still retain the speed advantages if the intermediate storage is reasonably fast. If a copy of the intermediate storage can also be reproduced on punched cards, for example, then the next execution of the program does not require a reassembly as the cards can be read back in directly. The re-input of the cards is equivalent to the job of loading described earlier. The binary program should be output in a form acceptable to the loader in general use at the installation.

An example of an input to a typical assembler for a one-address machine is given below and followed by the equivalent program with all symbolic addresses replaced with numeric addresses, as would be done by the assembler.

```
START      LOAD       A
           ADD        B
           STORE      C
           BRANCH     D
A          DEC        13,15
B          EQU        A+1
C          BSS        2
D          ADD        =10
           STORE      C+1
           END        START
```

The address field of the last card containing the end pseudo tells the assembler that execution is to start at that location. When this program is assembled, it produces the following code, written below with mnemonics and decimal addresses (although it is in binary in practice):

LOCATION	INSTRUCTION	ADDRESSES
0	LOAD	4
1	ADD	5
2	STORE	6
3	BRANCH	8
4	DEC	13
5	DEC	15
6		
7		
8	ADD	10
9	STORE	7
10	DEC	10

Note that it has placed the literal constant 10 at the end of the program and inserted its address into the instruction at location 8. This program will attempt to execute this location after it has executed location 9. This is a programming error, because data should never be executed as instructions. A branch instruction to return control to the operating system should have been placed after the last instruction, just as a branch instruction was placed so that control jumped around the block of data and working storage in the middle of the program. This system-return instruction will differ from one machine and one system to another. It will be discussed at greater length in Chapter 4.

3.2.5 The 370 assembler

The assembler for the IBM system 370 machines differs in a number of ways from the design just discussed. Some of these differences are due to additional burdens imposed on the assembler by the complexity of the machine; others stem from an attempt to provide a more uniform approach to many of the pseudos concerned with data loading. This section will discuss the assembler briefly in order to point out some of its features.

Input is usually from cards with three principal fields, the location, instruction, and address fields. There can also be comments and a sequence number. The rule for determining the different fields is one of blank separation. Each field must be separated from the next by a string of one or more blanks, except that columns 73 through 80 are ignored (they can contain a sequence number). It is conventional to fix the starting columns of the fields at 1, 10, and 16. A symbolic name can have up to eight characters, so that there is bound to be a least one blank between the location and the instruction field. Similarly, the instruction can have up to five characters, so a blank is bound to follow that field.

The instruction mnemonics for the 370 were used in Chapter 2. They tend to use a single letter to represent each word in the instruction name such as L (Load), A (Add), S (Subtract), and so on. This cannot always be achieved. For example, *store* must be represented as ST, while L also stands for *left* (in shift instructions) and *logical*. Additional letters indicate the particular form of the instruction. Thus, by itself, the mnemonic usually means 32-bit twos complement arithmetic in fixed point. H, E, D, and P added refer to halfword fixed point, singleword floating point, doubleword floating point, and packed decimal respectively. In general, a trailing R means that the operand is fetched from another register. Thus ADR means *add double-length floating point from a register*. The simplicity of the scheme can lead the unwary into the trap of inventing nonexistent instructions. For example, from the LTR (Load and Test from Register) the user might be tempted to use an LT instruction. It does not exist!

The address field conventionally starts in column 16 and terminates at the first blank before column 73. (Character strings used as constants may contain blanks in exception to this rule.) The addresses in the multiple-address instructions are separated by commas, whereas indexing and similar modifications follow the address and are enclosed in parentheses. For example, a register-to-register addition is

> AR   2,4   (two register addresses, separated by a comma)

In Chapter 2 we were writing AR R2, R4 for this instruction to emphasize that a register was involved. In fact, that is specified by the instruction, and so the R is unnecessary, although it is not uncommon for programmers to define the symbolic addresses R0 through R15 as equivalent to the integers 0 through 15 so that they can use the R notation. A memory-to-register addition with indexing is

> A   3,B(7)   (two addresses, the second indexed from register 7)

A memory-to-memory decimal add packed is

> AP   B,C   (two memory addresses)

If it is necessary to supply the length of a decimal operand, it can be stated explicitly in parentheses. Thus, we can write

> AP   B(6),C(4)

meaning the 4-byte packed-decimal number starting at location C is to be added to the 6-byte number starting at location B.

Normally, it is not necessary to specify the length of variable-length operands. The assembler provides the length automatically. Obviously, it does not do this by reading the programmer's mind. It looks at the operand definition. We shall see that when operands and storage areas are defined, the amount of memory space occupied is specified. This information is used by the assembler.

The *branch on condition* instruction can be written as

> BC n,Addr

where n is the number between 0 and 15 that specifies the condition, while Addr is the branch address. n is really a part of the instruction code from the point of view that there are several different types of branches. Therefore the assembler provides a group of *extended mnemonics* to simplify the use of these instructions. They are given in Table 2.4 on page 45. There are mnemonics for each of the useful condition numbers for use after compare, arithmetic, or test-under-mask instructions. Each of these instructions can set the condition register, so that its meaning depends on the type of the last instruction. The mnemonics BP and BH are seen to be the same instruction. The former would normally be used after an arthmetic instruction and the latter after a compare, although either could be used with no ill effects.

The general pseudo for defining storage areas is DS (Define Storage). It appears in the instruction field. The address field determines how many bytes of storage are allocated to the area. The address of the first of these bytes can be assigned to the symbolic name punched in the location field, if any. The DS pseudo can use very complex address fields.† In these notes we shall content ourselves with a description of some of the simpler forms. Different types of operands in the 370 are described by single letters. We have already seen that H, E, D, and P are used to describe halfwords, single-precision fullword floating-point numbers, double-precision floating-point numbers, and packed-decimal numbers for instructions. They are also used for this in the DS pseudo. Suppose we wished to define a storage space for one double-precision floating-point number called B. We could write

B   DS   D

This allocates a field of length 8 in the next group of 8 bytes that start on a doubleword boundary. Thus the assembler has taken care of the restriction that double-precision words must have addresses divisible by 8. Similarly, we can reserve a block of 5 halfwords by writing

C   DS   5H

The first of these is named C. Its address is even. Notice that the number of items is placed before the type of the item. Fullword fixed-point numbers are described by F. Thus 24 bytes of storage, starting on a multiple of 4 bytes, would be reserved by

T   DS   6F

A packed-decimal region is specified by a P. In this case it is necessary to indicate the number of bytes required for each number. This can be done with the length modifier L. PL5 indicates a 5-byte packed number. Thus

K   DS   4PL7

† For these, the reader is referred to the Assembler Language Manual, IBM document number GC28-6514.

reserves 4 groups of 7 bytes. No boundary alignment is necessary since it is assumed that K will be used as an address in a variable-length instruction. If K is used as the address of an instruction such as AP, the length modifier is set to 7 unless it is specified otherwise. Thus

```
        AP          K,K
```

will assemble identically to

```
        AP          K(7),K
        AP          K,K(7)
or      AP          K(7),K(7)
```

and will double the number in location K. On the other hand

```
        AP          K,K+5(2)
```

will add the least significant 3 digits of K to K, since the specified length over-rides the automatically specified form. (The 3 digits and the sign occupy the last 2 bytes of K.)

The other type of descriptor that appears frequently is C for *character*. Characters occupy 8-bit bytes. C behaves identically to P in the DS pseudo, except that the maximum length of a character field in an instruction is 256 rather than the 16 of a P format. Thus

```
H           DS          5C123
```

defines 5 fields of 123 bytes each. These might be used in an instruction such as MVC (MoVe Characters).

```
        MVC         H,H+123
```

would move the second group of 123 bytes into the first group.

The DS pseudo provides the effect of the BSS pseudo of many fixed-word-length machines. In addition, it sets the *length attribute* in the symbol table. This will be used to determine the length of variable-length operations as described later.

The DEC constant defining pseudo and its companions are replaced by the DC (Define Constant) pseudo. It is very similar to the DS, except that the value to be loaded into the storage area must also be specified. This is done by specifying the value of the constant inside quotes. For example, three fixed-point halfword integers equal to 5, 7, and −3 could be specified by

```
X              DC            H'5,+7,-3'
```

Note that several numbers can be separated by commas and that plus signs can be omitted, as is standard practice in both commercial and scientific work. Decimal numbers and characters can be specified in the same way. The length modifier can be omitted, in which case the assembler will generate it. For example

```
X              DC            2PL3'45'
Y              DC            C'1234 A'
Z              DC            P'13',C'AB,CD'
```

X is the first of a pair of 3-byte packed-decimal numbers. Since the length is set to 3 bytes, they contain 5 digits plus sign. Y is a 6-byte character string, starting with 1, ending in A, and including a blank. Z is the first of two constants. This definition introduces the use of a comma between definitions. This is permitted. Z has the length attribute of the first, namely 2 bytes, since '13' requires 2 bytes for storage. The second constant, which begins in storage 2 bytes after Z, is a 5-byte constant AB,CD. In a character string, the comma has no meaning to the assembler, just as a blank does not terminate the address field.

There are several other type letters that can be used in both the DS and DC pseudo. We shall not cover all of them, nor all of the combinations that can be used. Two that will occur frequently in the DC pseudo are X (heXadecimal) and A (Address). X acts like P, except that the digits are hexadecimal, two-per-byte, and, of course, there is no special sign group. If an odd number of hexadecimal digits is given, then a 0 is inserted on the left to make a round number of bytes. The X is a convenient way to specify the binary form of a word. (B for binary can also be used.)

Thus

```
Q              DC            X'55555555'
```

specifies a 32-bit string of alternate 0s and 1s. But beware! It is not word-aligned, and if this is needed, it must first be aligned. This can be done by

```
               DS            0F
Q              DC            X'55555555'
```

The 0F specifies zero 32-bit words, starting on a word boundary. This serves to force the next following item to be loaded onto a word boundary. A is used to define a 32-bit fixed-point word whose right-hand 24 bits are the address of a variable. Thus

```
P           DC          A(T)
T           L           B
. . . . . . . . . . . . . . . . . . . . . . . . .
```

would set P to be on a word boundary and place in the next 32 bits the address of the following load instruction.

LITERALS

Literals follow naturally from the above discussion. A literal is generated by writing an = sign followed by any valid address field of a DC pseudo. Some examples are

```
A           4,=F'23'         Add the fixed-point number 23.
AE          6,=E'13.5'       Add the floating point number 13.5.
AH          1,=H'—9'         Add the halfword —9.
AP          A,=P'—235'       Add decimal to A the 2-byte number
                             —235.
N           6,=X'0000FFFF'   AND the Hex number 0000FFFF.
```

These have the effect of putting the constant at the end of the program and replacing the literal by its address.

BASE REGISTER ASSIGNMENT

We have seen how the length specification will be provided by the assembler on the basis of the length of the data at the time it is defined. The AP instruction in

```
AP          A,B
. . . . . . . . . . . . . . . . . .
A           DC          P'1234'
B           DC          PL2'1'
```

is equivalent to

```
AP          A(3),B(2)
```

We now need to discuss the base register problem. Recall from Section 2.5.3 that the address is represented by a 12-bit displacement and a base register address. The assembler must take a memory address, such as A above, and put it in this form, providing a base register address and calculating the displacement. To do this, it must know the contents of index registers that can be used for base registers. This is done by telling the assembler, by means of the pseudo USING, the contents of a base register. For example

```
                 BAL          15,A
                 USING        A,15
A                next instruction
```

The BAL instruction branches to location A (the next instruction), and places the address of the next location (A) into register 15. The USING pseudo specifies an address (A) and a register (15) to inform the assembler that, from now on, register 15 can be assumed to contain the address A. Note that the USING does not assemble into any machine instructions and therefore occupies no space in the object code. It takes effect at assembly time when it is read by the assembler. It cannot be executed, so it does not have to be in the sequence of the program's control flow.

Actually, this sequence can be specified more simply as

```
                 BALP         15,0
                 USING        *,15
```

The BALR instruction fetches its branch address from a register unless that register is 0 (as above), in which case no branch occurs. The USING makes use of the address *. This is used in many assemblers to mean the address of the current instruction. After such a USING pseudo, the assembler knows that register 15 contains a given address. Consequently, in the sequence

```
                 BALR         15,0
                 USING        *,15
T                AR           5,6
U                BC           4,T
```

the address T in the BC instruction can be assembled as a displacement of 0 relative to base register 15. Thus the BC is assembled as

```
        BC            4,0(0,15)
```

The address U is a displacement of 2 to register 15 since the AR instruction is 2 bytes long.

The programmer *must not* change the contents of registers declared as bases without telling the assembler beforehand. The assembler is told by the DROP command. Its simplest form is with a single register specified.

```
        DROP         15
```

tells the assembler that register 15 can no longer be used as a base register.

It is common to use more than one base register. Often two will be used, one for program and one for data. The only limit imposed by the assembler on the number used is 15, since only 15 registers can be used for indexing.

If the student is going to use the 370, he should refer to the manuals for the precise definitions of many of the pseudos. Their usage and names differ from one type of machine to another.

3.2.6 The PDP-11 assembler

The PDP-11 computer system programs show an orientation toward paper tape and on-line interactive use because, like many other smaller computers, the principal form of input is the Teletype (a typewriter-like device that can be connected directly to a computer or be used to punch or print paper tape). Paper-tape systems have a lower cost than corresponding card systems, both initially and for supplies of paper tape versus cards. However, they are slower, and therefore are used on smaller, slower systems.

When a card is used as an input medium for instructions, it does not matter much where on a card the user is asked to punch each field, as a keypunch for cards provides for spacing to any specified column automatically. Furthermore, a whole card will be used for an instruction, whether the instruction appears at the beginning or near the end of the card. However, punching paper tape is like typing a line. If information is near the end of the line, many spaces must be used to move the typing mechanism over to that position. (Some Teletypes have tab characters that function like the typewriter tab key.) Each key action on a Teletype produces a character in the computer or on paper tape, so that the number of characters is proportional to the length of the line. This means that there is a premium on using short lines. Unlike a card, which always has 80 characters (or some other fixed number), a "line" from a Teletype or paper tape ends when the "line end" character is read. This is usually the carriage return–line feed character or pair of characters.

When these considerations are kept in mind, the format used in the assembler for the PDP-11, called MACRO-11, appears reasonable. It is designed to allow for minimum-length lines. The format is

[label :] mnemonic [separator] addresses [; comments] CR LF

where anything enclosed in brackets [and] is optional. The meanings of the various elements are:

label —a position which defines a symbolic address. It is equated to the address of the first byte of the instruction or data assembled by the line.

If a label appears, it is terminated by the colon character (:). If it does not appear, neither does the colon, and the mnemonic field can start in column 1.

mnemonic—the name of the instruction or pseudo. As we will see, all pseudos start with a period. The mnemonic field is terminated by the separator.

separator—either a space or a nonalphanumeric character (although the period and dollar characters are considered alphanumeric in MACRO-11). Thus we could write the immediate move instruction as MOV #12,R0 or as MOV#12,R0 since either the space or the # sign acts as a separator.

address (or addresses)—characters containing the address field(s) of the instruction or pseudo. Separate elements of the field may be separated by blanks or by a comma, and so we could write either MOV R1,R2 or MOV R1 R2. The address field is terminated by a carriage return–line feed (CR LF) or by a semicolon. In the latter case, comments may appear up to the line-terminating CR LF.

If a card system is being used, a fixed field format can be adopted for punching the programs to aid in reading them; however, it is not essential.

Symbolic addresses in MACRO-11 are strings of alphanumeric characters which must start with an alpha character (which includes period and dollar, although these are normally reserved for system and macro use). Any number of characters can be used, but the assembler only checks the first six (which means it only records the first six), so it is not wise to use more unless it will make the program much clearer to the user.

A series of special characters are used to indicate the type of address structure required. Some were used in Tables 2.8, 2.9, and 2.10 in Section 2.5.4. A complete set is shown in Table 3.1.

Thus, %3 means register address 3, so the instruction

MOV %3,3

would be interpreted by the assembler to mean move the contents of register 3 to memory location 3, while the instruction

MOV #5,%5

would be interpreted to mean move the integer 5 into register 5. Earlier we were using R5 to mean register 5. In order to do this, the programmer must first equate the symbolic address R5 to %5. On the PDP-11 this is done by writing

TABLE 3.1   *Address construction characters*

#	immediate address
@	deferred (indirect) addressing
( )	deferred (from register only) or indexing
—	auto-decrement
+	auto-increment
%	register address

R5 = %5

The equal sign is like a mnemonic and acts as an equivalence. Programs typically start with

R0 = %0
R1 = %1
  . . .
R6 = %6
R7 = %7
SP = %6
PC = %7

This allows the register names R0 through R7 to be used. (Some PDP-11 operating system assemblers do this automatically for the user.) It also allows register 6 to be referred to as SP, meaning Stack Pointer, and register 7 to be referred to as PC, meaning Program Counter, the PDP-11 name for the control counter.

The data-loading pseudos include

.WORD
.BYTE
.ASCII

For the .WORD and .BYTE pseudos, the address field is a series of expressions separated by commas. The value of each expression is computed and stored as a word or a byte, respectively. Any label is assigned a value equal to the address of the first byte loaded. Thus

TAB: .BYTE 1,2,3,4,5,6

causes 6 bytes to be loaded into locations whose addresses are TAB, TAB+1, . . . , TAB+5. Location TAB contains 1.

Expression evaluation is simple in MACRO-11, as expressions are evaluated from left to right unless parentheses are used. Thus $1 + 2 * 2$ is 6 since the plus operator is obeyed first. The conventional result $1 + <2 * 2>$ can be obtained by using angle parentheses. A second trap for the unwary is that all numbers are treated as octal (base 8) unless a statement otherwise is made. Thus

A: .BYTE   13+5

loads a byte with value 20 octal into a cell addressed by A. This applies to any expressions, whether in pseudos or instructions. Thus

$$SR = 5*52$$

assigns the value 322 octal to the symbol SR.

The .ASCII pseudo allows strings of characters to be assembled using the ASCII code. Thus

B: .ASCII   /ABCDEFG/

loads 7 bytes with the characters A through G in ASCII code. The address of the first is B. The division sign is used as a delimiter around the character string.

Assembly directive pseudos include

       .ODD
       .EVEN
       .BLKW
       .BLKB
       .RADIX

ODD and EVEN are used to force the next item to start on an odd or even byte location, respectively. This is done by skipping a byte if necessary. BLKW assigns a block of words of storage, while BLKB assigns a block of bytes. Thus

X: .BLKW   23

assigns the current value of the location counter to X and then increments it by 46 octal, leaving 23 octal words.

Another way of assigning bytes is to write

$$. = . + n$$

Period is the assembler name for the location counter maintained by the assembler. This says that the number n is to be added to it, thus skipping n bytes. Hence the two lines

W = .
. = . + 6

are equivalent to

W: .BLKB   6

The RADIX pseudo allows the user to change from radix 8 arithmetic. Radices 2, 4, 8, and 10 are allowed, and are indicated by writing

.RADIX n

where n is one of the above numbers. Once a new radix has been declared, it is in effect until another declaration is made.

The radix in effect can be overruled temporarily by the constructions shown in the example below:

Q: .WORD   54,↑ D231,↑ B1101,↑ F3.6,↑ O7777

The first word assembled by this example is taken in whatever radix is current. Subsequent words are converted as a decimal integer, a binary integer, a floating-point number in 16-bit format (equivalent to the 32-bit format mentioned in Section 2.4.10 with the bottom 16 bits discarded), and an octal integer.

MACRO-11 has many other features, some of which will be discussed in later chapters.†

3.3 RELOCATABLE LOADERS AND LINKAGE EDITORS

It was stated that the assembler prepared code as though the first instruction was to be loaded into location 0. There are many circumstances in which it is necessary to be able to control the point at which loading starts. If several sections of program are to be placed in memory simultaneously, it is obviously necessary that they not overlap. This can happen when one user combines several sections of codes to form one larger program, or when several programs from different users are placed in memory simultaneously in a time-sharing environment. The assembler does not provide an adequate means for determining the place at which the code is to be loaded for two reasons: first, because it is a time-consuming process to translate from source to object, and second, because the assembler itself may occupy much more space than the object program. It is desirable to be able to load any segment of program anywhere in memory after it has been assembled. In such circumstances, sections of code can be assembled separately and loaded together into memory at execution time.

It is also desirable to leave the decision of initial load point until the last possible minute, so that the system can take account of the current environ-

---

† Readers intending to program in this language should consult the MACRO-11 Assembler Programmer's Manual, Digital Equipment Corporation document number DEC-11-OMACA-A-D, 1972.

ment. (In fact, programming encourages many undesirable habits. As a general rule, it is better to leave all decisions until the last possible minute so as to achieve maximum flexibility. Further, the laziest way of preparing a program is often the best, because it is usually the case that the shortest specification of a task has the most desirable properties!)

Now we are at a seeming impasse. The assembler prepares code as though it were to start at location 0 because the assembler doesn't know any better. The loader is supposed to change the assembler's mind afterward. The solution is to require the assembler to tell the loader what would be changed if loading were to start at a different place in the main memory. Consider the assembly language code

```
          LOAD       A
          ADD        B
          BRANCH     C
A         BSS        1
B         EQU        1207
C         STORE      A
. . . . . . . . . . . . . . . . . . . . . . .
```

for a one-address machine that places one instruction in each word. If this is loaded starting at location 0, the values of addresses used are

$$A = 3$$
$$B = 1207$$
$$C = 4$$

On the other hand, if the program were to be assembled starting at location 2300, the address equivalences would be

$$A = 2303$$
$$B = 1207$$
$$C = 2304$$

The change needed is to add the starting address to some of the addresses used in the code, but not to others. The assembler can tell which addresses are to be changed. Those that are defined absolutely in pseudos such as EQU do not change. The ones that *do* change if the program is moved are those that are defined in such a way that their value depends on (1) the counting mechanism used to assign successive instructions, (2) data definitions, and (3) block declarations to consecutive storage locations. The changing addresses are called *relocatable* or *relative* addresses.

In order to allow the loader to relocate code to any part of memory, the assembler must indicate which are the relocatable addresses in the object code. This can be done by allocating an additional bit position for each address. If this bit is a 1, the loader will add the relocation amount to the corresponding address. The code given in the example above would assemble as the equivalent of

```
0          LOAD       L3
1          ADD        1207
2          BRANCH     L4
4          STORE      L3
. . . . . . . . . . . . . . . . . . . . . . . . . .
```

where the L in front of the address means that it is relocatable. If this program is loaded starting at location 4108, the result will be

```
4108       LOAD       4111
4109       ADD        1207
4110       BRANCH     4112
4112       STORE      4111
```

as required.

The programmer should realize that the use of relocation-of-address fields will restrict his use of arithmetic expressions in address fields. Since only single relocation is provided in the loading method discussed, an address expression such as A+B where both A and B are relocatable would be invalid. There will be further discussion of this in the chapter on assemblers.

The assembler can put the *relocatable object code* in auxiliary storage as the translation proceeds. When the assembly is over, the object code can be punched onto cards so that the programmer has a copy which he can reload later without having to reassemble. Alternatively, or in addition, he may wish to load the translated program along with other object codes for execution. Some of these may have been assembled as part of the same job, others may have been loaded in object code form directly from cards. (In most systems, it is possible to get compatible object codes from all the translators, for example, Fortran, etc.)

With this technique, a number of programs can be loaded into the main memory without overlapping each other. The loader can load each one in turn, noting where it starts and how long it is, so that it knows where it may load the next code. In order to execute these codes as parts of a single job, it is necessary to have communication between the various sections. One of the code sections must be the *main* program that is executed initially, since execution must start at a specific place. The others must be subprograms called into play by the main program, or by programs previously called by the main program.

The user cannot be expected to know where the various code sections are going to be loaded, so a mechanism must be provided to allow him to transfer control to another section and to access data used by another section. There are a number of mechanisms used to achieve these purposes. Some of the common ones will be discussed below.

When the user is writing the assembly language code for one section and he wishes to write a transfer of control instruction to another section (which has, or will be, assembled separately), he would like to indicate the name of that section symbolically. One very common way of doing this is to use the pseudo CALL. This is written in the form

        CALL   SQRT

if the SQRT program is to be called. The CALL assembles as a type of branch instruction which will be discussed later. The assembler does not know what address to place in the branch instruction, since the SQRT program will be positioned in memory by the loader after assembly has finished. There are several schemes for handling this problem.

One method is known as the *transfer vector technique.* During the first pass of the assembly, a table of all subprogram names that are used in CALL pseudos is constructed. A unique integer between 0 and $N - 1$ is assigned to each entry in the table, starting at 0 and working up, where N is the number of entries in this table. The assembled program is displaced down N locations so that the first instruction is assembled as if it were to start in location N. Each time that a CALL pseudo is encountered in the second pass, the address used in the branch instruction is the integer assigned to that subprogram name. It is indicated as a relocatable address. This means that when the program is loaded and the CALL is executed, control will be transferred to the appropriate one of the first N locations of that program segment. It is necessary for the loader to place a branch instruction in each of these locations to the correct location of the subprogram required. In order that it can do this, the assembler places an internally coded representation of the symbolic name of each of the CALLed subprograms in the corresponding location at the start of the program segment. The loader is also provided with an indication of the number N of such names so that it can tell which words are to be interpreted as symbolic names, as shown in the center column of Figure 3.2. It is also necessary for the loader to find out which subprogram segments have which names, so that if the programmer writes CALL SQRT in the first segment, and means by this the third instruction of the fourth segment, the loader can generate the correct branch instruction. To handle this, the user tells the assembler the *entry* points to each segment with a pseudo such as ENTRY or a similar name. For example, to indicate that a given instruction is the place to which all CALLs of SQRT should branch it is necessary to write in assembly language

```
               ....................
SQRT           LOAD        ..........
               ENTRY       SQRT
               ....................
```

The ENTRY pseudo can usually be placed anywhere in the section of code that contains the definition of SQRT. When the assembler sees this, it creates an entry in a table of entry points for that section and makes a note of the address of the entry point. The second pass of the assembler uses this table to create a list of all entry names and the corresponding addresses, which it hands on to the loader. The program that is handed onto the loader will take the general form shown in Figure 3.2.

A second method used to tie several subprograms together employs a *linking loader.* A linking loader, also called a *linkage editor,* is essentially another assembler that accepts partially assembled programs and completes the assembly. As with the transfer vector technique, during assembly some of the symbolic addresses are undefined. A pseudo such as CALL causes a special table of symbols to be generated. These symbols may be left undefined in the

Assembler inputs	Assembler outputs = relocatable loader inputs	Program in memory
1 LOAD A ADD B CALL SQRT CALL SIN ———	1 2 CALLS 0 ENTRY POINTS 0 SQRT 1 SIN 2 LOAD L17 3 ADD L8 4 CALL L0 5 CALL L1 ———	0 BRANCH (SQRT) 1 BRANCH 101 2 LOAD 17 3 ADD 8 4 CALL 0 5 CALL 1 ———
2 ENTRY SIN SIN STORE SIN1 ——— CALL PRINT ———	2 1 CALL 1 ENTRY POINT SIN = 1 0 PRINT 1 STORE L13 ——— 7 CALL L0	100 BRANCH (PRINT) 101 STORE 113 107 CALL 100
etc.	———	———

FIGURE 3.2 *Relocatable binary with transfer vectors*

program segment being assembled, just as in the transfer vector technique. However, in the linking technique, the number of the entry in the table is not put in as the address of the object of the CALL. Rather, the address of the location containing the CALL is placed in the special table. This means that the loader can put the correct address into the object of the CALL when it has associated the name with the correct subprogram. If there is more than one reference to the same name, then either more than one entry must be made in the table of CALLs or a chaining technique can be used. In the latter method, the address of the location containing the object of the first CALL is placed in the address field of the second, the location of the second in the address field of the third, and so on. In this way, a *chain* of addresses starting from the address given in the call table points to successive CALLs of the same name. At load time, the loader moves down this chain replacing the address field with the actual address of the program segment. The input and resulting chain-linked object are shown in Figure 3.3.

One of the advantages of the linking method is that there is one less branch instruction to be executed in order to branch to another program segment. This reduces the execution time by a small amount in the case of very short segments. A more important advantage is that it is not limited to use for transfers of control. If it is necessary to refer to a variable in another segment by its symbolic name, then that variable name can be indicated as an external variable. The assembler can then add it to the list of symbolic names to be linked. The example in Figure 3.3 shows that the technique is independent of the fact that the variables are used in CALL pseudos. Implementation of many of these features will be discussed in the chapter on assemblers.

A chain method of linking is not the most common or most flexible method for a linking loader. A more flexible method is to list the locations to which a given address has to be added at load time. With this method, the output of the assembler for the example in Figure 3.3 would start with

```
SQRT       L2,L5,L7
SIN        L3
SYSTEM     L8
```

indicating that the address into which the square root program is loaded must be added to locations L2, L5, and L7, etc. (In fact, it is not necessary to specify that the locations are relocatable, as they cannot be otherwise.) The reason this is more flexible is that it is possible to allow for names such as SQRT in this example to appear in expressions. Thus, the expression SQRT+6 would assemble as 6 in the address field, leaving the loader to add the address of SQRT to that field. There is no reason to do this with the names of subroutines, but the feature is valuable for accessing addresses defined in a different

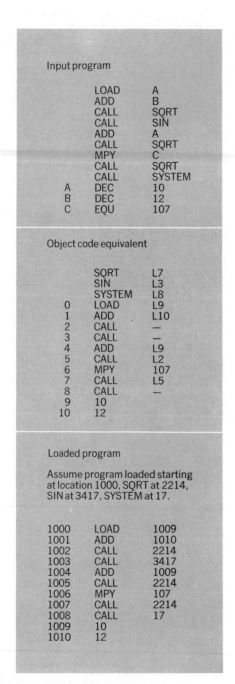

Input program

	LOAD	A
	ADD	B
	CALL	SQRT
	CALL	SIN
	ADD	A
	CALL	SQRT
	MPY	C
	CALL	SQRT
	CALL	SYSTEM
A	DEC	10
B	DEC	12
C	EQU	107

Object code equivalent

	SQRT	L7
	SIN	L3
	SYSTEM	L8
0	LOAD	L9
1	ADD	L10
2	CALL	—
3	CALL	—
4	ADD	L9
5	CALL	L2
6	MPY	107
7	CALL	L5
8	CALL	—
9	10	
10	12	

Loaded program

Assume program loaded starting at location 1000, SQRT at 2214, SIN at 3417, SYSTEM at 17.

1000	LOAD	1009
1001	ADD	1010
1002	CALL	2214
1003	CALL	3417
1004	ADD	1009
1005	CALL	2214
1006	MPY	107
1007	CALL	2214
1008	CALL	17
1009	10	
1010	12	

FIGURE 3.3   Linked chain method

section of code. Such addresses are called *external* or *global*. A common pseudo for defining them is

EXTERNAL   X,WW,I

which defines the three addresses X, WW, and I to be external to the section of code being assembled. The assembler will pass their names onto the linking loader and tell it which locations in the object code have to be modified by having the actual addresses of these symbolic addresses added at load time. Any address declared external in one section of code must be defined somewhere, either in another section of code or in the system library(ies), so that the loader can *resolve* all references. If the user wishes to define them in a section of code, he uses the ENTRY declaration discussed above. (Some assemblers use the EXTERNAL declaration for both purposes, taking the attitude that a name declared external and also defined in the same section of code is obviously an entry point.) Table 3.2 shows an example of two sections

TABLE 3.2   *External referencing for data and subroutines*

	ASSEMBLER INPUTS			ASSEMBLER OUTPUTS		PROGRAM IN MEMORY		
Main program								
				DSUB	17			
	LOAD	X	11	LOAD	L21	511	LOAD	521
	STORE	B	12	STORE	L22	512	STORE	522
	ADD	X	13	ADD	L21	513	ADD	521
	STORE	B+1	14	STORE	L23	514	STORE	523
	STORE	B+2	15	STORE	L24	515	STORE	524
	LOAD	Y	16	LOAD	L25	516	LOAD	525
	CALL	DSUB	17	CALL	0	517	CALL	723
	STORE	Y	18	STORE	L25	518	STORE	525
	. . .			. . .				
X	DEC	5	21	5		521	5	
B	BSS	3		—				
Y	DEC	4	25	4		525	4	
Subroutine								
				DSUB = 0				
	EXTERNAL	X,B		X	2, . . .			
	ENTRY	DSUB		B	1, . . .			
DSUB	STORE	Z	0	STORE	L13	723	STORE	736
D1	ADD	B+2	1	ADD	2	724	ADD	524
	MPY	X	2	MPY	0	725	MPY	521
	. . .			. . .				
	BRANCH	D1	12	BRANCH	L1	735	BRANCH	724
Z	BSS	1		—				

of code using this form of linking loader. The example assumes that the loader has started the main program at location 500 and the subroutine at location 723.

Many current computers (including both the IBM 370 and the PDP-11) are designed so that most addresses within the program do not need to be relocated or linked. This is achieved by holding the part of the address that changes with location in a register and always "indexing" through that register. At some point in the program the register is loaded with an address that depends on the position in which the loader placed the object code, and from then on, all references can be made "through" that register. If the address of an external variable is available in a known location at execution time, then the program can load the register from that location. For example, if there is a pseudo ADDR which forms a word whose value is the address, the programmer could code

```
          EXTERNAL    X
A         ADDR        X
          . . . . . . . . . . . .
          "Load index 1 with the contents of A"
```

say, to load index register 1 with the address of X. The loader would place the address of X into location A at load time. The "constant" A is called an *address constant*. The advantage of coding in this fashion is that the loader does not have to do an enormous amount of address modification because most of it is done dynamically at execution time by the index register.

(Extensions of these ideas lead to the concept of *dynamically relocatable programs.* These are programs which can be moved around in memory at any time. It is very useful to have programs in this form in a time-sharing environment, where, in order to place a new program into memory, it may be necessary to move one already there to another spot. Two levels of relocatability can be sought. Complete dynamic relocatability allows for the program to be stopped at any time, moved, and restarted. A lesser level allows the program to be moved before it has actually started execution or at various check points during execution. The latter only requires that there be no location-dependent information in the loaded form of the program or at the check points. The former requires that location-dependent information never be constructed or that location-dependent information always be in known addresses and registers so that it can be relocated when the program is moved. It is better to have no location-dependent information if the machine design allows it. The simplest way of achieving this with hardware is to provide a relocation register whose contents are automatically added to every memory address. Much more complex schemes have been developed in order also

to tackle the problem of unnecessary program moves in time-sharing environments. This will be discussed under multiprogramming in a later chapter.)

3.3.1 The IBM 370 linkage editor

In assembly language, the 370 programmer uses the pseudos ENTRY and
EXTRN to pass information on to the loader. Symbolic addresses are declared
as external to an assembly program segment by the statement

EXTRN   A,B, . . . ,X

which says the addresses A, B, . . . and X are defined in a separately assembled section of program. They must not, therefore, be defined in the
section containing an external declaration for them. Their symbolic form
will be passed on to the loader for linking. Each variable name declared as
external in any program segment must be declared as an entry point in one
and only one segment. This is done with the assembler statement

ENTRY   P,Q, . . .Z

which says that P, Q, . . . , and Z are entry points to the local program
segment. The symbolic addresses listed in the address field of the ENTRY
pseudo must be defined in the same program segment. The name and associated value can then be passed on to the loader.

The 370 system uses two loaders. The first is called the *linkage editor,* and it
produces a binary form of the program in which all symbolic references
between different segments have been replaced with binary addresses, that is,
in which the linking has been taken care of. A second program is called the
loader. It places the binary program into core memory for execution. For
the sake of simplicity, we shall not distinguish between the two but refer to
them both as the loader.

The major task of the 370 loader is not relocating but linking. This is because
the base register hardware addressing system provides most of the relocating
necessary in the 370. At assembly time, the address field of an instruction
is evaluated. Typically it will be a relocatable address. Since it must be put
into a base-plus-displacement form, the assembler looks for a base register
that is within 4,095 bytes of the expression and converts it to this form.
Since base registers are loaded at execution time (that is, *dynamically*),
they will contain an address relative to the loaded position of the program.
(The most common method for loading a base register is the BALR B,0 instruction, which puts the control counter into register B.) Since the base

contains the relocation factor automatically, the displacement is an absolute amount.

The assembler input that gives rise to relocatable addresses is the A field in a DC pseudo. If B is an address in the program, then

```
DC          A(B)
```

is a 32-bit word which is relocated on loading. The 370 allows expressions to appear inside an A field, but they may only contain single relocation by each program segment.†

If B is an external address in a program segment, then the instruction

```
L           4,B
```

is illegal. The reason is that B must be put into a base-plus-displacement form by the assembler. Since the location of B is not yet known, no base can be assigned. Neither is it possible for the loader to apply a linking method, since 370 machine addresses are 24 bits long, whereas only 12 bits are available in the address field of an instruction. To get around this problem, the code

```
         L           4,AB
         L           4,0(4)
         . . . . . . . . . . . . . . . .
AB       DC          A(B)
         EXTRN       B
```

must be used. The loader now has 32 bits in which to link the address of B at load time.

3.3.2 The PDP-11 loader LINK-11

The PDP-11 loader is of the linking type, containing many of the features of the IBM 370 linkage editor. The assembly programmer defines external variables and entry points using one pseudo, whose mnemonic is .GLOBL. Thus the declaration

```
.GLOBL      X1,AAA,DEF
```

---

† There is a way of assembling several sections of code together, in which case a relocation from each section can be applied. The reader is referred to the CSECT pseudo-instruction in the assembler manual of the 370 for details.

declares the three variables X1, AAA, and DEF to be external if they are not defined in the same program segment, or to be entry points if they are defined in the same segment. The programmer may use expressions involving global variables, but the result must not require more than single relocation by an external variable. Thus the code

```
          .GLOBL     A,B
C = 4
D:        MOV        R1,R2
E:        ADD        R1,R3
          MOV        #A,D—E(R2)
          MOV        D+C,A+C
```

is valid since each address is either absolute or singly relocatable. With the above definitions of symbolic addresses, the instruction

```
          MOV        D+E,A*B
```

contains two errors. The address D + E is doubly relocatable by the origin of the current section, and the expression A * B has a relocation that is impossible to compute reasonably. As a general rule in any assembly language, not more than one relocatable or external address should appear in any expression, except when the difference of two addresses defined in the current program segment is used.

The address structure of the PDP-11 makes it possible to write *position-independent code,* that is, code which contains no absolute addresses or address constants, which can be loaded anywhere just prior to run time. If this is done, the linkage editor can produce a *load module* (which is a linked set of program sections), without knowing where the result is to be loaded. Most instructions are automatically position-independent since they contain register addresses only. Thus each of the address constructs Ri (Ri), (Ri)+, —(Ri), @(Ri)+, and @—(Ri) cannot be relocated. The relative and relative deferred modes A and @A are position-independent if A is a relocatable address because mode 6, indexed by the program counter, is used. Thus if the code

```
          JMP        X
          MOV        R1,R2
X:        ADD        . . . .
```

is written, the address of the JMP instruction will be 2 indexed by PC since the symbolic address X is 2 beyond the value of the program counter when the address of the JMP is calculated. (At that time it is pointing to the next instruction, which is 2 bytes long.) Relative and relative deferred addresses will not be position-independent if they are absolute. For example, the code

```
        D = 10
        MOV          D,R1
```

will not be position-independent. In that case, absolute addressing can be used, for example

```
        D = 10
        MOV          @#D,R1
```

which is position-independent as it is literally deferred immediate. The actual address 10 (D) is assembled in the word following the move instruction.

Conversely, immediate addressing is position-independent if the address is absolute, but not if it is relocatable. Thus the code

```
        N = 10
        MOV          #N,R4          Put number N into R4.
```

is position-independent, whereas

```
A:      MOV          R1,R2
        MOV          #A,R3          Put address A into R3.
```

is not. If it is desired to get the address A into a register as in the example immediately above, it can be done position-independently by the code

```
A:      MOV          R1,R2
        MOV          PC,R3          Put control counter into R3.
        ADD          #A−.,R3        Add difference between A and the
                                    control counter.
```

The first address of the ADD instruction above is not relocatable, as it is the difference between two addresses relocatable by this program section. The first is A and the second is the value of the assembler location counter at the time this instruction is being assembled, which is the address of the first byte of the ADD instruction. This is the same as the value of the control counter PC at the time the preceding move instruction is executed.

Indexed addresses will only be position-independent if the relocatable part of the address is in the index register rather than in the displacement. Suppose, for example, that we wish to add the array A to B and store the result in B, that is, to perform $A(I) + B(I) \rightarrow B(I)$. The code

```
                MOV        #N,R0          Set count for N elements.
                CLR        R1             Index to 0
LOOP:           ADD        A(R1),B(R1)    Add A to B.
                ADD        #2,R1          Increment index.
                DEC        R0             Decrement count.
                BNE        LOOP           Loop until count 0.
```

is a very bad way of doing it for several reasons. One is that the code is not position-independent (although that failing is more a matter of style). The second is that it does not take advantage of the addressing structure of the PDP-11. If registers are at a premium, the code can be made position-independent by writing

```
                MOV        #N,R0
                MOV        PC,R1
                ADD        #B—.,R1        Address B in R1.
LOOP:           ADD        A—B(R1),(R1)+  Add A to B and increment R1.
                DEC        R0
                BNE        LOOP
```

although a better code is obtained by using an additional register as follows:

```
                MOV        #N,R0
                MOV        PC,R1
                ADD        #A—.,R1        Address A in R1.
                MOV        PC,R2
                ADD        #B—.,R2        Address B in R2.
LOOP:           ADD        (R1)+,(R2)+    Add A to B and increment both
                                         addresses.
                DEC        R0
                BNE        LOOP
```

This code uses fewer instruction bytes inside the loop, so that if the loop is executed many times, it is faster (although the whole code uses 4 more bytes than the preceding version).

3.4 THE LIBRARY

In order to avoid loading many programs from external hard-copy input such as punched cards, installations usually will make the commonly used programs available in the program library. This, as the name suggests, is nothing more than a collection of programs which can be used with other programs. In order to make the collection useful and accessible, it is put on a high-speed input device so that the user can obtain a copy for the loading process without obtaining a deck of cards. The loader will first put together those subprogram segments that the user has provided and attempt to link them by one of the above methods. If some of the symbolic names requested are not indicated as entry points or external names in any of the segments, the loader attempts to find a library program of the same name. It does this by first consulting an index of library programs that is maintained for this purpose. When it finds the program required, it is copied into core by the loader in the same manner as the output from the assembler. Thus the programs in the library are kept in an assembled form ready for loading. If a search of the library index fails to find a requested program, then the job is in error. In this case execution is either inhibited or, if it does commence, it cannot be expected to continue beyond a call to one of the nonexistent programs. More advanced systems make it possible for a collection of libraries to be accessed. In such systems, the user can specify which libraries are to be used and in which order they should be searched. (It is possible that two programs in different libraries may have the same name.) These advanced systems are very useful to active programmers. A user may wish to keep a personal library of his own programs, or a group of users — as, for example, a chemistry department — may wish to keep a library of specialized subroutines. Moreover, all users find it convenient to have access to a general library for very standard programs such as SIN, SQRT, etc.

3.5 OTHER TRANSLATORS

The repertoire of the computer will usually include a number of higher-level translators. They are all faced with the same basic task — converting the input, or source program, into a binary program with meaning to the machine. Some translators will translate into assembly language code and then leave the assembler to translate to binary, others will produce binary object code, usually relocatable, directly in one or more passes.

It is highly desirable that all translators that are part of a system produce compatible object code. Then a single loader can be used in all cases and programs written in one language can call on programs written in another. In some instances load-and-go compilers are written. In compilers, the designer is faced with a choice between fast translation or fast execution (in some cases neither may seem to be achieved). The load-and-go compiler is designed as a very fast compile method since it can be kept in memory throughout execution (the program does not load on top of it, since then load-and-go would not be possible). Therefore the compiler does not have to be reread into memory before each compilation. The loading of a compiler can account for a sizable fraction of the job time for a source deck that is only going to take a second or two to compile and execute. Therefore a load-and-go system can be very efficient for short jobs such as, for example, those that occur during program testing.

3.6 RUNNING THE PROGRAM, MONITORING

Once the program is in memory, it can be executed. The programs provided at the installation have assisted the programmer in getting his problem onto the machine. Now he must find ways to check his program during execution.

The most carefully written code will contain errors of various sorts. The programmer may have stated his program improperly so that, say, he forms A — B instead of B — A. Those errors can only be found by the programmer checking his answers with an alternate calculation, or by checking the numerical *invariants* of the problem. (An invariant is an expression that should remain constant if the calculation is exact. For example, in a physical problem, the total energy of the system plus the incoming energy minus the outgoing energy should be constant. It may be easy to calculate this number from time to time. It should stay constant within allowable roundoff error. If it changes drastically, it is an indication that there is a numerical coding error or a machine error.)

Other errors are due to mistakes in transcribing the desired algorithm into the source language or to mistakes in the use of library programs. Frequently, these will lead the program to behave wildly. The program may, for example, try to execute a memory location that was never loaded with a program instruction or that was incorrectly overwritten by data. It may also get into an *infinite loop,* which is a repetitive cycle of instructions that will never terminate. When either of these happens, the programmer can use help. He should be told immediately if his program tries to execute an illegal instruction and, after a certain amount of time has elapsed, he must be told that he either has a program that is longer than he thought or that he is probably in an infinite loop.

To take care of these things, his program is monitored in execution by another program and the interrupt features of the hardware. We shall call this program a *monitor* because of its function. It is frequently referred to as a *supervisor* or an *executive* program. The interrupt mechanisms cause control to be transferred to specific locations in the memory when various unusual conditions arise. When the monitor program — which occupies the locations around the area to which interrupt transfers — senses an illegal instruction interrupt, it will use programs to locate the illegal instruction and report it to the programmer, together with a printout of sections of the main memory of interest to him. A second condition can be caused by a clock or interval timer. It is set by the monitor just prior to execution. When it goes off, much as an alarm clock goes off, an interrupt transfers control to the monitor. Once again, it outputs a message to the programmer, giving him the reason for termination of his program as well as important information from the memory.

Memory protection allows sections of the memory to be declared off limits to the user's program. Any attempt to reference this area of memory can result in an interrupt to the monitor. The program can be restrained from changing or from reading the contents of locations that are protected. Some machines provide separate protection for writing and reading, some use the same signal. Some systems provide memory access keys to various sections of memory, so that a section can only be accessed by a user providing the correct key. A key, in this case, is a binary pattern, perhaps only a few bits long. It is fixed for a given user's program throughout execution.

The chief purposes of memory protection are threefold:

1   To prevent the user from changing the contents of areas of memory which will affect other users
2   To help detect potential errors in the user program
3   To facilitate the assignment of memory space to a user as he needs it

In the first instance, it is obvious that one user should not modify either the monitor or another user's program. The second aim is rather more complex. It would, for example, be reasonable to read a location in the monitor which contained data such as the current time or date—but it would almost certainly be an error to read a location containing arbitrary information (such as another user's program). If such a read were detected and reported immediately, the error could easily be located. This protection can also serve to prevent the user from accessing areas of memory currently in use for input/output. (Chapter 6 will deal with the overlap of input/output operations with computation.) Since input and output may be in progress between the memory and other devices, it is clear that errors could occur if the user read or changed the contents of memory locations involved in I/O transfers before the completion of the transfer. A protection of memory during the transfer can assist in the overlap problem.

Finally, there is the assignment of memory space. In an advanced operating environment, it is possible that other users' programs will be in memory. Although any particular user is unaware of the others, he may have less memory space than he needs. In a fully automatic system each user would refer to memory as needed. If it was not yet allocated, it would be protected and an interrupt would return control to the monitor. The system would use this as an indication that the memory should be reassigned before the first user could continue execution. This will be discussed in a later chapter.

The monitor is stored in a protected area of memory. In order that it may reference memory anywhere, an interrupt status is defined for the machine. If the status is *interrupt allowed,* then the user is in execution and the protected area may not be used. As soon as an interrupt occurs, the status is set to *privileged user* and accesses of protected memory are enabled. While the privileged status is on, interrupts are either disallowed completely or partially inhibited, so that the monitor can complete its analysis of the problem causing the interrupt.

In many larger installations, more than one user's program may be partially on the computer at a time. At a minimum, there may be many other users' programs on an input device waiting to be read. In order to protect these from possible errors by a programmer, the input/output equipment is usually protected also. Thus one user has access to certain devices only, much as he has access only to certain parts of memory.

Many features of the monitor described above are negative — that is, they are designed to *prevent* the user from doing certain things such as, for example, using too much time. However, the monitor also provides the user with a number of positive benefits. The main facilities usually provided are for the use of input/output equipment. The problems and use of I/O devices will be discussed in a later chapter. However, they are generally complicated to use, so that the monitor will normally contain program segments which the programmer can use for accessing the I/O equipment. In many programs, for example, it is desirable to be able to find the actual time in order to control external devices. Therefore the monitor will frequently provide programs that will read the real time clock and give the reading to the user. Programs to take special action on overflow, machine errors, etc., are also usually provided in the monitor, since almost every user requires that such problems be handled.

Additional aids often provided for the user include *dumps, post-mortems, snapshots,* and *traces.* A dump is a listing of all or part of the user's area of memory at the end of execution. It is often in octal or hexadecimal, although it is possible to provide a more useful symbolic listing as follows:

Each translator leaves a copy of its symbol table which lists all symbolic names used and their locations relative to the program section translated. The loader leaves a copy of the *memory map,* which lists each program loaded and its location in memory. (This information could be left on an auxiliary storage device such as a disk file.) With this information it is possible for the dump program to provide a list of the contents of all locations referenced symbolically by each program segment. If information about the type of data stored in each location is also retained, the dump program can convert the binary contents to the most suitable printing format (decimal, octal, character strings, etc.).

A *post-mortem* is an analysis of the contents of memory (after execution has been terminated) to gather as much information as possible that may be of use to the programmer. One such analysis will be mentioned in Chapter 4, after 370 subroutines have been discussed. Another is known as a *comparison post-mortem.* It compares the contents of memory after execution with the contents before. All differences are reported to the user. This enables him to tell very quickly which data locations have been changed, and, more importantly, which program locations have been changed. Present-day programming techniques try to avoid changing the program, therefore such changes are strong indications of error.

A *snapshot* is a dynamic dump of part or all of the memory that can be requested by the user's program. It is essentially a library program that will print sections of the memory conveniently. It enables the user to see when elements of data storage areas are being changed.

A *trace* can be defined as an automatic snapshot feature. It may be possible to request, for example, that certain registers or memory locations be printed every time that a branch is executed. This allows the user to get a picture of the flow of a program, since he knows that flow continues through increasing locations between branches. It may also be possible to print the contents of registers when certain locations are changed; for example, every time that the contents of location AB is changed. A trace may require some hardware features for efficient implementation (an optional interrupt on every successful branch was provided on one of the early machines, the IBM 704). Some of its features can be implemented by arranging for the translator to produce special code when tracing is requested. Alternatively, it can be implemented by interpretation, discussed in the next section.

3.7 INTERPRETATION

Normally the user writes programs in a source language. These programs are translated into a relocatable binary language which, in turn, is then further translated into absolute binary machine language by the loader. It is also possible to interpret any of these languages (source, relocatable binary, or machine language) by an interpreter, which is a program that examines—one by one—each statement or instruction in the language and causes the desired action to be taken immediately. Thus, if a one-address machine assembly language is to be interpreted, a statement such as LOAD A would cause the interpreter to locate the symbolic address A in a table; find out from this table where A was stored in memory; fetch the contents of A; and place them in a location within the interpreter used to represent the accumulator of the one-address machine (since the actual accumulator would be used by the interpreter). We shall discuss interpreters in Chapter 7. They are particularly useful for some forms of tracing because they can easily detect conditions such as the use of variables, for example, by placing flag bits in the name table. They can also provide symbolic error diagnostics because the program being "executed" can be stored in its source form. However, interpretation is slower than translation and execution for long jobs, and should be restricted to program testing and programmer training.

3.8 MULTIPROGRAMMING AND TIME SHARING

Both of these terms refer to the use of memory for more than one piece of code which could be simultaneously executed if more than one processor were available. Some machines have more than one processor. However, if there are more such programs than there are processors, it is usual for a processor to process one program for a while, and then to switch over and process another. This switch is conveniently made when the program being processed has to wait for a slower input/output operation to be completed. Such switching allows the use of the CPU to be maximized. There is no accepted distinction between the terms *multiprogramming* and *time sharing*. In this book we shall use *multiprogramming* to refer to the presence in main memory of two or more segments of code which can be simultaneously executed but which are part of the same job. *Time sharing* will also include those cases when the pieces of code being processed simultaneously are parts of independent jobs.

3.9 TASK AND JOB SCHEDULING, CONTROL CARDS

We have seen that system programs are provided for translation, loading, and monitoring of user programs. In some of the early systems and in current systems on small machines, it is necessary for the user or operator to sequence the separate tasks which comprise a single job through the computer. For example, if a job consists of a section of Fortran code and a section of assembler code and it requires three library subroutines, the operator may have to perform the following steps:

1 Load the Fortran compiler (from cards or paper tape). This would be done with an absolute loader which is either kept in memory or is loaded by an initial load procedure.

2 Fortran compile the Fortran section of code. The output would be saved for later loading.

3 Load the assembler in a manner similar to the loading of the Fortran compiler.

4 Assemble the next section of code. The output would be kept for the loading process.

5 Load the relocatable loader via the absolute loader.

6 Feed the output from the Fortran compiler and the assembler into the machine for relocatable loading. Since three subroutines are required, the relocatable loader would type out their names to the operator. He would obtain copies of the cards or punched tape and input these to the loader.

7 Finally, the monitor must be loaded (it could have been kept in memory to monitor the other system programs). Now execution can commence.

8 When execution is stopped by the monitor, the next job can be processed.

There are two points to be noted. First, the system programs are all being loaded from hard-copy devices such as paper tape or cards, and the intermediate storage between translating and loading is also on hard copy. Second, the operator must manually sequence through the various stages of translation and execution. If backup storage devices are available (and they are in most medium-size systems) then it is not necessary for the system programs or the intermediate storage to use hard-copy devices. If the system programs are on magnetic tape, drum, or disk, then they can be loaded much more rapidly. Since the operator does not have to obtain physical copies of these programs, it is no longer necessary that he issue the instructions for the start of compiling, assembling, etc. Instead, these instructions can be fed in with the source language input and be interpreted by the system programs. This implies the existence of another system program which will perform this interpretation. We shall call this program a *supervisor* since it finds out what tasks have to be done and decides when to do them. In the simpler system, it does them immediately after they are requested. We shall examine such a simple system briefly.

In addition to the input code in Fortran and assembly language and data for the execution phase, the user must prepare a series of input cards which tell the supervisor what is required for the run. The input will normally start with one or more cards which state who the user is (for accounting purposes) and what sort of service is needed (for example, maximum time and output limits, etc.). These are usually called *identification* or *job* cards. Following this will be a series of cards called *control* cards. They are usually identified by means of one or more characters in the first few columns. Some systems use a $ sign in column 1. The 370 uses the characters // in columns 1 and 2. The character(s) will differ from system to system. In each control card will be punched one or more strings of characters which are *commands* to the supervisor. These commands may include FORTRAN, ASSEMBLE, LOAD, PUNCH OBJECT, DATA, and probably many others. Their use is as follows. Commands such as FORTRAN and ASSEMBLE tell the supervisor that the set of records following are to be compiled or assembled by the named system translator. PUNCH OBJECT tells the scheduler to pass on the word to the translator that an object deck must be punched during translation. This enables the user to avoid subsequent retranslations if the program is now correct. Alternatively, this could be supplied as a parameter to the translator. LOAD informs the supervisor that it is time to start loading the programs already translated, and DATA tells the supervisor that the set of records following is data to be made available to the program if it executes.

If the object deck is punched as a result of a translation, then that deck can normally be loaded in place of the symbolic source program and its control cards. Thus if, on the first run, the user submitted a deck with the following form

```
ID CARD
FORTRAN
(Source program in Fortran)
. . . . .
ASSEMBLE
PUNCH OBJECT
(Source program in assembly language)
. . . . .
LOAD
DATA
(Data for the run)
. . . . .
```

he would expect, as output, some information about his programs (listings), a punched deck corresponding to the program in assembly language, and whatever output his own program generated. If now he wished to make a change to the Fortran program only, he could submit the following deck:

```
ID CARD
FORTRAN
(Source program in Fortran)
. . . . .
(Object program from previous assembly)
. . . . .
LOAD
DATA
(Data for the run)
. . . . .
```

In a simple batch processing system, all the user's programs and data will be in the *input stream,* which is the string of successive card images that are read on the primary input device. In some cases, some of the input may come from other devices, such as magnetic tape or disk files. In that case, it is necessary to have a method to refer to the other sources of information. Hence, in more complicated systems, commands such as FORTRAN may be followed by the names of input units or of sets of information on the disk files.

The 370 system uses an assembly-like language called *job control language* (JCL) for system control. Each JCL statement has the form

```
//name      operation     arguments
```

The two / characters must be in columns 1 and 2. No blanks may appear in the name or operation codes, which are terminated by blanks. The argument string may contain blanks only under special circumstances. A few simple examples of JCL will be given and partially explained below.† A job might start with

```
//PROGRAM   JOB      (299899,200,0,5),'USERNAME',MSGLEVEL=1
//FTG       EXEC     PGM=FORTRANG
//SYSPRINT  DD       SYSOUT=A
//SYSLIN    DD       DSNAME=SYS1.SYSLIN,DISP=(OLD,PASS),              X
//                   VOLUME=SER=SYSRE2,UNIT=2314,                     X
//                   DCB=(RECFM=FB,LRECL=80,BLKSIZE=3200)
//FTG.SYSIN DD       *
```

This example is one which will run on at least one installation, but there will be minor differences between installations. In particular, the format and information of the first card, which contains identification and run-control information, are peculiar to the accounting system used on the machine. The names of some of the compilers may also vary locally. In this example, the name FORTRANG is used for the compiler that IBM calls IEYFORT. One of the features of the system is that it is possible for local installations to make minor changes. The first line contains a *job* card. It gives the name of the job (PROGRAM) and of the user (USERNAME). The remaining information on that card contains run-control information such as time limits and amount of output expected. The second card requests the execution of the program Fortran G, which is one of the available Fortran compilers on the 370. The name FTG is called the *step-name,* and can be used to refer to the Fortran compilation step that will follow. The compiler needs to know where certain output is to be placed. In particular, it needs to know where a listing of the program and associated diagnostics should be routed and what to do with the object of the translation. It refers to these as SYSPRINT and SYSLIN respectively. The next three lines define these sets of data. The first DD (Data set Definition) statement defines SYSPRINT by means of the argument field. SYSOUT = A indicates that it is to be placed on the output printer. The next three cards are part of a single DD statement. The first card is continued to the next by an X punch in column 72. The statement defines the set of data SYSLIN to be equivalent to a data set known as SYS1.SYSLIN, and tells the system where it is and what to do with it. In this case, the object data set is passed on to the loader at a later step. The final card defines an input file SYSIN in the step FTG by an *. This means the input card reader. The Fortran compiler is now ready to read its

---

†JCL, the subject of IBM manual number C28-6539, is far too complex for extensive discussion in this book.

input from the input card reader, print a listing of the program with diagnostics, and leave the object in a data set on auxiliary storage. Consequently this group of JCL cards would be followed by a Fortran program. If this program is to be loaded, the next step could be specified by

```
//EDT        EXEC    PGM=LINKEDIT,COND=(5,LT,FTG),                    X
//                   PARM='LIST,MAP'
//SYSPRINT   DD      SYSOUT=A,                                        X
//                   DCB=(RECFM=FBA,LRECL=121,BLKSIZE=726)
//SYSUT1     DD      DSNAME=SYS1.SYSUT1,DISP=OLD
//SYSLIN     DD      DSNAME=*.FTG.SYSLIN,DISP=OLD
//           DD      DDNAME=SYSIN
//SYSLIB     DD      DSNAME=SYS1.FORTLIB,UNIT=2314,                   X
//                   VOLUME=SER=SYSLIB,DISP=OLD
//SYSLMOD    DD      UNIT=DISK,SPACE=(TRK,(99,5,1)),DISP=(,PASS),     X
//                   DSNAME=&G(G)
```

The first card requests execution of the linkage editor (loader). The remaining cards specify the locations or system names of various data sets used by the loader. SYSLIB, for example, is the name of the data set that the loader will refer to as a library. The programmer thus has the option of specifying which library should be used. After loading, it is necessary to request execution. This can be done by the cards

```
//GO         EXEC    PGM=*.EDT.SYSLMOD,COND=((5,LT,FTG),(5,LT,EDT))
//FT05F001   DD      DDNAME=SYSIN
//FT06F001   DD      SYSOUT=A,                                        X
//                   DCB=(RECFM=FBA,LRECL=133,BLKSIZE=798)
//FT07F001   DD      UNIT=(SYSCP,,DEFER)
//GO.SYSIN   DD      *
```

The final card indicates that the input data set named SYSIN in the step GO is the card reader. Since the step GO is the execution of the user's program after translation and loading, and SYSIN is the name of the principal input data set used in Fortran READ statements, this allows the programmer to specify that his data will come from the card reader. A data set stored on one of the auxiliary storage devices could have been specified.

Besides pointing out the highlights of the 370 system, this example shows how generality leads to complexity and length. On the 370, this is overcome by the provision of *cataloged procedures.* A cataloged procedure is a sequence of control-card images that have been stored in a special library of procedures on the disk file or some other storage device. The sequence is given a name so that the user can request the execution of just that procedure. The control cards given above resulted from the sequence of cards

```
//PROGRAM          JOB      (299899,200,0,5),'USERNAME',MSGLEVEL=1
//FTNMAX           EXEC     FTGCLG,PARM.FTG='LIST,ID',PARM.EDT=XREF
//FTG.SYSIN        DD

(Fortran program)
/*
//GO.SYSIN         DD

(Data for execution)
/*
```

The single cataloged procedure FTGCLG contained control cards requesting Fortran G, the linkage editor, and execution of the program. The /* cards terminate an input data set in the same stream as the job control cards. The amount of work has been reduced, but the generality has been restricted. However, the user who requires generality may employ the more complex method of job control.

After a program has been executed and it terminates, whether by user error or intentionally by a transfer back to the system (a location in the monitor program), the monitor program will provide dumps of the memory and other information as requested. Then the machine is vacant until the next user's program is input. In order to minimize the loss of time in the job-to-job transition, the monitor program will immediately transfer to a supervisor program whose job is to take care of any accounting that needs to be done (computer time is normally chargeable to somebody) and then to load in the next user's program. Depending on the complexity of the machine and the sophistication of the system, the next job may be acquired from a number of places. The simplest batch processing system will allow several jobs to be stacked one behind another in the input card reader, so that they can be processed serially. In more complicated systems, there can be several input devices, and the next job can be selected from any one of them. Some jobs may have several inputs from different devices, so that the scheduler will take care of informing the operator that all of the inputs must be present when the job is being read in. The scheduler will also check, by reading labeling information at the front of each input that is read, to see that the inputs have been correctly loaded by the operator.

Complex operating systems, such as those provided on the IBM 370 machines, require a lot of memory, auxiliary storage, and extra computer time. Consequently, small computers provide very limited facilities which must be tailored to the operating environment, so that there is little in common between systems on two otherwise identical computers. We cannot, therefore, talk about *the* operating system for the PDP-11 computer. The user is likely to find one with characteristics similar to the simple description we presented first. Its organization and capabilities must depend on the auxiliary storage and memory capacity of the system.

PROBLEMS

1 What three pieces of information must appear on each record input to the absolute loader?

2 Design an initial load sequence for the following machine:

When the IPL button is pushed, one card is read into words 0 through 19 and control is transferred to location 0. The computer has at least three index registers and an accumulator, and is basically one-address. Its instruction set includes

LOAD	A(I)	Loads the accumulator from location A indexed by index register I.
STORE	A(I)	Stores the accumulator. . . .
LX	I,A	Loads index I with the contents of location A.
LXI	I,N	Loads index I with the number N (immediate operand).
AXI	I,N	Adds the number N to index I (immediate operand).
BZ	P(I)	Branch to location P indexed by index register I if the last value handled (in accumulator or index) was 0.
BNZ	P(I)	Branch if non-zero.

The machine word is 32 bits; index registers and addresses are 16 bits. All arithmetic is twos complement. The instruction format has 16 bits of op code and index register address on the left, and a 16-bit operand address on the right. When a card is read, successive groups of four columns fill up words, with 8 bits coming from each column (do not worry about coding), so that the first 20 words of memory can be set to anything you want. If the objective is to be able to load the memory from cards as flexibly as possible, and you also have the instruction READ A, which reads the next card into the 20 locations from A through A+19, what would you put on the first card (in detail)?

3 What would be the assembled result (using a reasonable assembler) of those of the following programs that can be assembled? Indicate relocatable addresses.

a			
		LOAD	B
	B	ADD	ONE
	ONE	STORE	B
		CALL	SYSTEM
		END	

b	D	LOAD	TEN
		ADD	FOUR
		BRANCH	D
	TEN	DEC	10

```
        FOUR        DEC         4
        D           STORE       E
                    CALL        SYSTEM
        E           BSS         1
                    END

c       N           EQU         10
                    LOAD        TEN
                    STORE       D
                    LOAD        D
                    ADD         FOUR
                    STORE       E
                    CALL        SYSTEM
        E           BSS         1
        TEN         DEC         4
        FOUR        ADDR        N
        D           BSS         1
                    END

d       B           BRANCH      A
                    BSS         2
        A           LOAD        C
                    CALL        SYSTEM
                    END
```

4 Indicate which symbolic names are relocatable and which are absolute in the following section of program:

```
        A           MPY         C
                    ADD         100
        B           EQU         A+10
        E           SUB         D
                    BRANCH      F
        G           BSS         3
        F           ADD         G
        D           EQU         E−A
        C           EQU         7
        H           EQU         C+11
                    MPY         H
                    ADD         G+1
        I           EQU         C+F
```

5 Give the locations and addresses used in the following program assuming that a transfer vector method is used, that this section of code starts loading into location 100, and that the machine has one instruction per word.

```
        START       LOAD        TEN
                    ADD         TEN+2
                    CALL        SQRT
                    STORE       A+3
                    SUB         TEN+1
                    CALL        SQRT
                    BRANCH      B
```

```
A           BSS         7
TEN         DEC         17,21,33
B           STORE       A+1
            END
```

6   What is a transfer vector?

What does the assembler produce as a transfer vector? To what does the loader convert the assembler transfer vector when it loads the program into memory?

7   Indicate what would be assembled as a relocatable object code for the program below if a chained linking method were used by the loader to handle subroutine calls.

```
            LOAD        100
            CALL        SQRT
            CALL        SIN
            ADD         30
            CALL        SQRT
            CALL        SIN
            ADD         30
            CALL        SIN
            CALL        SIN
            STORE       100
            END
```

8   Discuss the action of a relocatable loader in assigning separately assembled sections of code to memory and linking the sections together in a system in which a transfer vector technique is used.

Compare the assignment of memory space to code sections by the loader with the action of an assembler in assigning instructions to memory.

9   What are the differences between a linking loader and a transfer vector method as they affect the *loaded* program in regard to

a   memory space

b   execution speed

For what purpose can a linking loader be used directly that a transfer vector loader cannot?

10   Suppose that we are loading three programs into memory with a relocatable loader which uses a transfer vector technique. Assume one instruction per word.

The relocatable programs have the following characteristics:

Program 1
Entry Points: 0
Called Programs: 3

```
        Names—#0  SQRT
               #1  PRINT
               #2  PUNCH
Length (including transfer vectors): 32 words
Program 2
Entry Points:      1
        Name—SQRT   Value 1
Called Programs:  1
        NAME—#0  PRINT
Length (including transfer vectors): 64 words
Program 3
Entry Points:      3
        Names—PRINT   Values 17
               PUNCH          21
               READ           45
Called Programs:  0
Length: 100 words
```

If they are loaded, starting at location 0, in the order given and immediately following one another, give the locations of all transfer vectors generated by the loader, and the addresses contained in those transfer vectors. *Note:* The value of an entry point is its address relative to location 0 of that program, including its transfer vectors. Give reasons for your answers.

11   Suppose the following DC pseudos are input by the IBM 370 assembler in the order shown.

```
ONE         DC          2F'2'
TWO         DC          PL2'46'
THREE       DC          X'ჳA'
FOUR        DC          F'1'
```

Give the contents of the following byte locations in binary: ONE+7, ONE+9, ONE+10, and THREE−2. If location ONE is byte location 24 decimal, what is the symbolic address FOUR equal to?

12   Suppose the following code is input by MACRO-11:

```
            .ODD
S:          .BYTE       23,12,1
T:          .WORD       12*4,6
R:          .ASCII      /123456.7/
            .EVEN
Q1:         .WORD       ↑D35,↑O32,↑F2.5
```

and suppose that the address S is 375 octal. What is the binary information loaded into byte locations 376, 400, 401, 414, 420, and 421? What is the octal address value of Q1 and R?

13 The following IBM 370 code is assembled and loaded. The BALR instruction is observed to start in location $34E0_H$. Give the hexadecimal contents of the program as loaded, assuming that only register 15 is used as a base register. The hexadecimal form of the op codes and the format of the instruction are given in the comments column.

			Hex op-code	Instruction format
	BALR	15,0	05	RR
	USING	*,15	(establishes R15 as base register)	
	L	4,A	58	RX
LOOP	A	4,B	5A	RX
	LR	6,4	18	RR
	LA	8,B—A	41	RX
	LA	9,B	41	RX
	B	LOOP	47	RX
	DC	0F	(get on a 4-byte boundary)	
A	DC	F'123',F'456'		
B	DC	F'135',A(LOOP)		

What is changed if the BALR starts in location $65F8_H$ instead?

14 The 4-bit op codes for MOV, ADD, and SUB in the PDP-11 are 0001, 0110, and 1110, respectively. The 8-bit code for BNE is 00000010. The following code is translated by MACRO-11 and loaded so that the first byte is in location 526 octal. Give the internal form of the program in octal.

N = 24	MOV	#N,R2
	MOV	PC,R3
	ADD	#X—.,R3
	MOV	#Y,R4
LOOP:	SUB	(R3)+,—(R4)
	SUB	#1,R2
	BNE	LOOP
X:	.BLKW	2*N
Y = .		

Is the program position-independent?

15 Write a program to convert a 32-bit IBM 370 word into 8 hexadecimal characters, where the 16 possible values of the hexadecimal digits are to be represented by 16 different characters, which should be placed in a table of values using the address construct C'xxx. . .x'. For example, if the character for 0 is Z, for 1 is Y, for 2 is X, . . . , and for 15 is K, the construct C'ZYXWVUT SRQPONMLK' should be used. As each hexadecimal digit is extracted, the appropriate character should be looked up in the table by indexing and added to a string.

Write a similar program to convert a 16-bit PDP-11 word to four hexadecimal characters obtained from a table built using the .ASCII pseudo. The representation used in the example above would be specified by .ASCII /ZYXWVUT SRQPONMLK/.

16 Write the shortest IBM 370 and PDP-11 programs you can to convert a 32-bit 370 word to octal (the first digit will be between 0 and 4), or a 16-bit PDP-11 word to octal (the first digit will be between 0 and 1). Generate EBCDIC or ASCII code, respectively.

4

PRINCIPLES OF PROGRAMMING

Modern computers contain many instructions designed to speed up common tasks. The index instructions discussed in an earlier chapter are a good example. These additional instructions are not logically necessary, since a calculation could be done using only a few instruction types; but the resulting programs would be longer, both in numbers of instructions and in execution time. Because of the typical redundancy of the instruction code of a computer, there are many ways in which a job can be coded for any given way of programming it. If the different ways of planning the program and the different methods (algorithms) are also taken into account, then there is a confusingly large number of programs which could be written to handle a single task. One of these possibilities must be chosen — preferably the best or a close approximation to it. Since computers exist only to do a job (not to test the ingenuity of programmers), the "best" solution is always the most economical.

Programming is often spoken of as an art whose works are judged, at least in part, subjectively. Such statements are, however, made mainly because no way has yet been found to evaluate objectively all the criteria of an economical program. In the final analysis, however, the value of a program depends on its cost rather than its beauty. The system programmer may easily be carried away by the fascination of his own work, forgetting that the user, who cares nothing about programming per se, is interested only in getting correct answers as fast as possible.

The cost of a program is determined by a combination of many factors. In addition to the obvious costs of programming and running, there are the costs of documentation and future changes. Almost no large program remains constant throughout its lifetime. Errors are found long after it has been pronounced working, and additional functions must be included to cater to new needs. Many changes will be made after the original programmer has moved or left, so that it must be possible for another programmer to understand the design of the original program in order to be able to update it as necessary. The yardsticks by which a program must be measured are (in alphabetical order)

1   Clarity
2   Debugging time
3   Documentation
4   Flexibility and expandability
5   Portability
6   Programming and coding time
7   Space required in the memory
8   Speed of execution

The clarity of the program will reduce the programming time, reduce the need for documentation, aid in expansion, and reduce the time for debugging (the time used in removing *bugs,* which is colloquial for program errors).

Debugging, which is unproductive in itself, can use up much of the programmer's time as well as that of the machine (50 percent of the total is not untypical). Documentation is the only means by which another programmer can find out in a reasonable manner what a code is supposed to do. It is usually the item most lacking in a computer installation. Well-written, well-documented programs can be expanded and modified. Programs that are obscure or poorly documented are sometimes easier to rewrite completely than to modify. Clarity and documentation are expensive in the early stages of a program, but they pay off handsomely in the later stages.

Portability is the ease with which the program can be taken to another computer installation and run. Programs written in higher-level languages are supposed to be portable to another computer, provided that translators for the particular language are available, as long as the program does not use input/output or other devices specific to a particular installation. Programs written in assembly language are not usually portable to a different type of computer, but they should as far as possible be designed to be portable to another similar computer. For example, sections of code which deal with devices likely to vary between installations should be separated from the bulk of the code, which should run on any similar computer. Then only that section has to be rewritten to adapt the program for another installation.

The space occupied by the program is important in the case of large programs which are executed for relatively short intervals, since the time taken to load the program into memory may exceed the actual execution time. On the other hand, the speed of execution is critically important for small, frequently used programs which are part of much larger programs. For example, a subprogram such as square root may be used very often in a large scientific code. The square root program is normally only a few instructions long (perhaps 15 to 30). It is much more important that a few microseconds be cut from its execution time than that a few instructions be removed from its length. The program is so short that it is unlikely to become too obscure. Therefore the main applicable criterion is one of speed (and of course accuracy, which we assume). Because it is difficult to relate separate documentation to the actual code, it is usually preferable to include the documentation as a part of the program by means of comment cards and meaningful symbolic addresses.

Because there is such a wide choice of programs available, and because the objectives are, in many cases, mutually contradictory, the programmer and coder are faced with decisions that are always open to question. In order to avoid endless argument over what should be optimized and the impossible task of picking the optimum amongst the many possibilities, programming is currently treated as an art and programs are judged subjectively, that is, after they have passed the objective tests of working correctly in a reasonable length of time. The programmer must develop a style of programming by utilizing standard methods in standard situations and by applying these conventions in a consistent manner. This chapter will discuss some of the techniques and conventions that aid in ease of programming, documentation, and modification.

4.1 PROGRAM LOOPS

Consider the following simple tasks:

1   Add the 3 numbers X(1), X(2), and X(3).
2   Add the 10 numbers X(1), X(2), . . . , and X(10).
3   Add the 10,000 numbers X(1), X(2), . . . , and X(10,000).
4   Add the N numbers X(1), X(2), . . . , and X(N).

In the first case, we would undoubtedly write

```
LOAD        X
ADD         X+1
ADD         X+2
```

where it is assumed that arrays such as X are stored in increasing memory locations, starting at the location with symbolic address X. In the second, we might write out seven more ADD operations, but we would probably use a loop with indexing. In the third case, we would certainly use such a loop, since it is out of the question to write 9,999 ADD instructions. In the final case, we have no choice but to write a loop, since, if N is not known until execution time (and it could change each time the set of operations is to be executed), there is no way of writing N ADD instructions.

These examples point out factors that are taken into account in planning the use of a program loop. In some cases it is worth while not using a loop; it is not only faster to use a *straight-line program,* but it also uses less code. Some cases are on the borderline, other cases are quite definitely candidates for loops (although it may still be faster to use a straight-line code), while there is no choice in still other cases. Part of the job of planning a program involves looking for places in which a loop can be used to reduce the work and aid the clarity and ease of debugging. A loop should always be used if there is any chance that the number of times the basic cycle must be executed may change at a later date. A loop should be used if the amount of code is space-wise shorter than straight-line code, otherwise straight-line code should be used. Occasionally, a loop should be written out in straight-line code when speed of execution is essential.

Since the code inside a loop is executed many times each time that the code surrounding the loop is executed once, it is good coding practice to remove as much code from the inside to the outside of the loop as possible. This can be illustrated with the Fortran example below. Suppose the following code is written:

```
        DO 15 I = 1,100
15      A(I)=D*E*(A(I) + S(J))/T(K)
```

One addition, one division, and two multiplications will be executed in each pass through this loop. The program could, and should, be written as

```
        T1 = D*E/T(K)
        T2 = S(J) * T1
        DO 15 I = 1,100
15      A(I) = T1*A(I) + T2
```

where T1 and T2 are two temporary variables. Although there are two multiplications and a division outside the loop, the inside of the loop has been reduced by a multiplication and a division. The saving each time that this section is executed is 98 multiply times and 99 divide times. In fact, on a typical computer the code will run at least twice as fast. It is possible that a very good Fortran compiler would effectively do this reorganization. In machine or assembly-language coding, the programmer will have to do this rearranging himself. It should be realized that the results from the two programs may differ due to differing roundoff errors.

When program loops are used, the programmer should be careful to make it clear in the program and associated documentation what the initial conditions are, where they are set, and what the end conditions are. A common coding error is a transfer to the start of the loop beyond the point where the initial conditions are set. Another is to code one too many or too few passes through the loop. This is particularly easy when the loop has to allow for 0 passes, which requires a jump around the body of the loop. Particular attention should be paid to branches out of the loop. In many instances of complex loops, the variables used in the loop are kept in more accessible registers (for example, the general registers of the 370), and must be stored back in their memory storage locations after exits from the loop.

Early machines used arithmetic operations on instructions to perform indexing of addresses and other forms of modification in loops. This form of programming causes severe problems in debugging, since many errors are caused by incorrect initial conditions and failure to reset instructions back to their original form after a modification has been made. Indirect addressing and indexing have eliminated the necessity of instruction modification, and it is therefore a good philosophy to separate the program from the variables, be they data or program switches, etc., so that no program modification is performed. Apart from making the job of debugging easier, it has a number of advantages in multiprogramming environments. A program segment which has no data or temporary storage within itself and which does not modify itself in any way is called a *pure procedure.* If it uses data, then all references must be made through index registers. It has the advantage that if it is stopped in the middle, for any reason (for example, interrupts), it can be restarted from the beginning without problems. The use of write protection on the memory containing the program will prevent the user from overwriting his program. This is a useful debugging tool.

4.2 SUBROUTINES, COROUTINES, AND MACROS

Frequently the same or similar piece of code must be written in many different parts of a job. There are obvious advantages to designing a system in which the identical piece of code will not have to be rewritten each time that it is used. One obvious approach is to write the code once and then make many copies of the card deck, punched tape, or whatever medium it is on. The copies can be inserted each time that they are needed. This approach is historically called using an *open subroutine.* The piece of code is called a *subroutine* since it is a subsidiary part of a larger routine, and the word *open* serves to distinguish it from *closed subroutines,* which are defined below. A *macro* is an additional facility that will enter, automatically, the section of code without messy card-duplication problems. The basic principle of either scheme is to save the programmer the job of rewriting similar pieces of code many times. Thus, if the job of raising the contents of the accumulator to the fourth power appeared many times, it would be worth while writing the section of code

```
STORE      T
MPY        T
STORE      T
MPY        T
```

once and causing it to be copied into the program each time that it is needed. In many assemblers, this could be done with the sequence

```
MACRO
POWER4
STORE      T
MPY        T
STORE      T
MPY        T
MEND
```

which serves as a *macro definition* at the start of the program to be assembled. The assembler will insert the code sequence each time that the new mnemonic POWER4 is used, so that an input of

```
LOAD        A
POWER4
ADD         B
POWER4
```

would be equivalent to

```
LOAD        A
STORE       T
MPY         T
STORE       T
MPY         T
ADD         B
STORE       T
MPY         T
STORE       T
MPY         T
```

Although the programmer has been saved the job of writing the code by using an open subroutine, the sections of code still occupy space in memory.

If an open subroutine or macro is used many times, the amount of storage space used can become very large. To get around this problem, the *closed subroutine* is used. In the future, we shall refer to the closed subroutine simply as a "subroutine" and the open subroutine as a "macro." The section of code representing the subroutine only appears once in memory. Each time that it is used in the main part of the program, a branch is executed to the start of the subroutine. After the subroutine has been executed, a branch is made back to the instruction following the branch to the subroutine. This immediately poses the problem of how the subroutine knows to which location to *return,* since many different parts of the main program may make branches to the subroutine. This problem can be solved in many ways. On early computers an additional instruction had to be obeyed—prior to the branch to the subroutine—which put the return location into a standard place, such as the accumulator or index register. If, for example, a computer has an instruction LDX 1,A which loads index register 1 with the address A (an immediate operand), then the sequence

```
         LDX        1,T1
         BRANCH     SUB
T1       (next instruction)
```

could be used to enter a subroutine, as it would put the address of the next instruction to be executed into index register 1 before branching. (The subroutine is assumed to start in location SUB.) It would have the form

```
SUB        (first instruction in subroutine)
           . . .
           BRANCH      0(1)
```

The final branch instruction returns to the address held in index register 1. This address is called the *link* address, as it provides the link back to the *calling* program. The sequence of instructions used to branch to the subroutine is called the *call sequence* and is frequently specified by an assembler pseudo or macro with the name CALL. The branch back to the calling program is called a *return.*

Because subroutine *entry* (that is, calling a subroutine) is such a common operation in large codes, most computers provide special instructions to facilitate entry and return. A single instruction that combines loading the index register with the branch as used above is commonly available. On the IBM 370 this is called BAL (Branch And Link). For example,

```
           BAL         14,SUB
```

branches to location SUB after setting the address of the instruction following the branch into register 14. A return can be effected by executing

```
           BR          14              Unconditional branch to address in R14.
```

A stack machine will often provide a subroutine entry instruction that places the return address in the top of the stack before branching and a return instruction that removes the top of the stack and uses it as a branch address. The PDP-11, for example, maintains a stack in memory, using register 6 to contain the address of the top of the stack. The instruction

```
           JSR         R5,SUB          Jump to subroutine.
```

decrements the stack pointer (register 6) by 2 and stores the contents of R5 in the address now in the stack pointer. The control counter (R7) is then placed in R5 (the register address in the JSR instruction), and control is transferred to location SUB. The instruction

```
           RTS         R5              Return from subroutine.
```

does the reverse. The value in R5 is used as a branch address to return, R5 is reloaded from the location addressed by the stack pointer (R6), and R6 is incremented by 2. Thus R5 functions as the top of a stack kept in memory under the control of R6. (More details on the PDP-11 and 370 subroutine instructions will be given in Section 4.3.)

It can be seen that the subroutine approach uses the least amount of storage, but that it uses more machine time because it is necessary to execute at least two additional instructions for each subroutine transfer. For this reason, subroutines should be used only under the following circumstances: (1) when the amount of work within the subroutine is such that these two or more additional instructions are not significant or (2) if the use of a subroutine substantially aids in the clarity and documentation of the program. If, for example, the subroutine were only two instructions in length plus the return branch, then the overhead in time would be 100 percent, while the saving in space would amount to only one instruction per *call*.

As with almost all decisions in programming, there will be many borderline cases, in which case questions of clarity, ease of debugging, etc., must be taken into account.

A subroutine is, in some sense, subordinate to the calling program, as it is executed only when it is called and is expected to return control to the calling program without fail at the end. There are cases, some of which will be mentioned in Chapter 6, where it is not convenient to specify that one program is subordinate to another. These arise when there are two tasks to be performed and their actions must be coordinated. It is always possible to define one as a subroutine of the other and have the dominant one decide when the other should be executed. The subroutine then decides when to stop executing by returning control to the first program. However, this mode can obscure the basic structure of the program, and so *coroutines* are employed. Coroutines are two program sections at the same level which can call each other. The call is of the form, "I have finished all the processing I need to do for a while, so you carry on, but return control to me here when you want to stop." It can be seen that the call and the return are one and the same thing. Further discussion of coroutines must wait until some meaningful examples can be developed.

The next two sections will discuss subroutines and macros. As additional features are added to each facility, the reader will see that they are not interchangeable. Not all systems provide for macro assembly, whereas some form of subroutine facility is essential in any system; therefore, subroutines will be examined first.

4.3 SUBROUTINES

We have already discussed a way in which the link address can be passed to the subroutine. Naturally, each different machine organization will use a different method with the same basic principle — when the programmer writes the subroutine, he does not have to know from where it will be called. We must also examine ways in which data is passed from the calling program to the subroutine and back, and what is necessary for a subroutine to provide a well-documented, easy-to-modify program. Since subroutines will usually represent reasonably self-contained sections of code, it is quite common to want to assemble them as individual units and to retain versions of the programs in binary form suitable for a relocatable loader of the sort discussed in Chapter 3.

4.3.1 Subroutine parameters, data transfer, and common storage

It is necessary for the subroutine to have access to data in the calling program and to return results to that program. Because subroutines may be used from many different points in the program, it is wise to organize this data carefully to avoid errors and to reduce the complexity of the code. If the subroutine appears in the same section of code as the calling program, so that they are both translated at the same time, then they both have access to the same symbolic storage cells. That is, both the calling program and the subroutine could refer to the same variables such as X, TIME, COUNT, etc. However, one of the purposes of a subroutine structure is to enable sections of the code to be assembled separately and to be entered into the machine in a translated form. This is particularly true of commonly used subroutines such as square root, etc., which are coded once and made available to all users via a library. In these circumstances, it is not possible to refer to variables with the same name (except possibly via the external option in Chapter 3), since all record of the names of variables is lost after translation (the input to the loader only contains the binary program, relocation information, and external names). It is therefore necessary to replace this lost facility with some other facility. One means, the external declaration, was mentioned in the last chapter and will be discussed later in this section.

Another method is known as *common* storage. Common storage is an area assigned by the loader at load time for storage of all variables which are used in common by more than one subroutine. Each separately assembled section of code declares the names of variables which are to be stored in common by using a suitable pseudo in assembly language or a declaration statement in a higher-level language (for example, the COMMON statement in Fortran). A typical form for an assembler is the pseudo

```
S               COMMON      34
```

which would assign the symbolic address S in the common area and allocate the next 34 words of storage, which could then be addressed as S, S + 1, S + 2, etc. The assembler will assign the symbolic addresses declared to be in common to consecutive locations in common. Thus if the declarations

```
A               COMMON      3
B               COMMON      1
C               COMMON      5
```

were included, and the common area began at location 1035, then the symbolic addresses A, B, and C would be equivalent to memory locations 1035, 1038, and 1039. One way of handling this in a simple loader is by using additional relocation bits for common storage. The assembler will tell the loader how many common locations are required, and the loader will assign space for the maximum requested by all loaded programs. Thus, if several different sections of code place variables in common, they occupy the same storage area at execution time. However, there is no relation between the names used, because the assignment is made by the loader. Thus, if the pseudos

```
A               COMMON      1
B               COMMON      1
```

appear in one section of code, while

```
B               COMMON      1
X               COMMON      1
```

appear in another separately translated section, the variable A in the first section will correspond to B in the second, while B in the first will correspond to X in the second. Because of this, common storage has to be used with extreme care. A change in one section without a corresponding change in all other sections will cause errors that are very difficult to locate.

If the loader handles common storage by using additional relocation bits, it decides whether to add the program relocation or common relocation to a program address on the basis of these bits. Thus the address fields in the program segment below will be as shown in the comment fields.

```
T               LOAD        A          Relocatable by common base.
                ADD         15         Absolute.
                STORE       A          Relocatable by common base.
                BMI         T          Relocatable by program base.
A               COMMON      1
```

The first and third address fields must be modified if the start of common storage is changed and the fourth if the start of this program is changed, while the second is independent of where the information is loaded.

An alternative way of handling common is preferable if a linking-type loader such as the 370 or PDP-11 linkage editor is used. The address of the first word of common can be viewed as an external name in each program segment. The loader must choose this address and link its value into every program loaded. This uses a mechanism already established for linking external names, although the loader must also allocate an area of memory large enough to accommodate the largest section of common storage used. It has an additional advantage: it is now possible to handle more than one common area. If different areas of common are given different names (*named* or *labeled common*), they can be linked together separately. The assembler must tell the loader the name of each common area used and its length. The loader must allocate space for each area. After that, the linking mechanism will handle the relocation automatically.

Identical storage, by means of either a common area or external names, can be used for data communication between subroutines and the calling programs, but for many needs it is not efficient. Consider, for example, a square root subroutine. This will be used to take the square root of a variety of numbers at different points in the program. If the equivalent of the Fortran statement

$$A = SQRT(X)$$

is to be executed, then a one-address code of the form

Example A

```
LOAD       X
STORE      INPUT
CALL       SQRT
LOAD       OUTPUT
STORE      A
```

would have to be written. INPUT and OUTPUT are assumed to be the locations of the input and output to and from the square root program. The movement of the data from X to INPUT and then from OUTPUT to A is unnecessary if the program can be arranged so that the data links to the subroutine are more convenient. The simplest solution for this case in a one-address machine is to use the accumulator. If the input and output from the square root program are via the accumulator, the code takes the form

Example B

```
LOAD      X
CALL      SQRT
STORE     A
```

We say that there are two *parameters* or arguments to the square root program, the input and the output. (In Fortran, we could call this a *function subroutine* because the output parameter could be represented by the name of the function.) In general, a subroutine can have many parameters, both input and output. If the method of common or external storage is used, it is necessary to copy all of the input parameters into the common area prior to calling the program and to copy the output parameters back into the desired locations after control is returned to the calling program, as was done in example A. This could be very inefficient, so methods similar to the use of the accumulator in example B are used.

The accumulator can only be used for a single input parameter and a single output parameter, so other places must be used to pass data. In order to discuss this, let us examine the various types of parameters that we may wish to pass to a subroutine or to get back from a subroutine. They include

1 A constant (for example, 2. in SQRT(2.))—input only.
2 A variable (for example, A in SQRT(A))—input or output.
3 An array (that is, a dimensioned variable in Fortran). This could be used in input or output; the subroutine would use or change any or all of the elements of the array.
4 The name of another subroutine. This is often restricted to input, but could be used for output.
5 The address of a section of code (a statement number in Fortran)—input or output.

A subroutine call will indicate a list of parameters that are to be used (in Fortran, for example, they are written in parentheses following the name of the subroutine). In machine language, each of the parameters must be in memory or in one of the accessible CPU registers. In a stack machine, the parameters could be put into the CPU stack, since it is arbitrarily large (at least in principle), but on other machines the parameters will have to be put in memory. They are often placed in locations following the call, which is a subroutine entry instruction in machine language, or in a block of storage whose address is passed to the subroutine. In designing subroutine parameter lists for particular subroutines, it is tempting to try to minimize the amount of space and time by taking note of special cases, but this approach can quickly cause problems of compatibility between different translators and lead to errors in use. The parameter list should be made as uniform as possible to avoid these problems. The only item that can be used as a parameter in all cases is an address. For single variables, it must be the address of the variable in memory. This works for both input and output, and takes care of constants. An array can be specified by the address of its first element, and a subroutine or section of code can also be given by its address.

If this form of parameter transfer is used, the machine-language equivalent of the Fortran code

```
DIMENSION A(100)
. . . . . . . . . . . .
CALL PROC (A,B,1.0,X−Y,SINF)
. . . . . . . . . . . .
```

would be similar to

```
A           BSS        100
            . . . .
            LOAD       X
            SUB        Y
            STORE      TEMP
            CALL       PROC
            ADDR       A
            ADDR       B
            ADDR       =1.0
            ADDR       TEMP
            ADDR       SINF
            . . . . .
            TEMP       BSS 1
```

where ADDR is a pseudo which simply loads the value of the address field into the next location in memory, and where some provision is made to put the function SINF into the list of subroutines needed.

When a subroutine is defined, we refer to the parameters as *formal parameters* because they are not the names of variables but place markers for variables that will be substituted when the subroutine is invoked (that is, called). When parameters are specified in a call to subroutines, they are called *actual parameters*. Thus in the section of Fortran code

```
CALL ABC(X)
. . . . . . . . . .
SUBROUTINE ABC(P)
```

P is a formal parameter, while X is an actual parameter.

PARAMETERS IN THE IBM 370

The 370 conventions for subroutines require that a separate list of parameter addresses be provided and that the address of the first member of the list be placed in register 1. Thus the example above for CALL PROC (A,B,1.0, X — Y,SINF) would be implemented by the assembly code

```
              LE          0,X
              SE          0,Y
              STE         0,TEMP
              LA          1,PARLIST
              L           15,ASUB
              BALR        14,15
              . . . . . . . . .
ASUB          DC          A(PROC)         Address of procedure
PARLIST       DC          A(A)            List of parameters
              DC          A(B)
              DC          A(CONST1)
              DC          A(TEMP)
              DC          X'80',AL3(SINF)   Last parameter
TEMP          DS          F
CONST1        DC          E'1.0'
```

The parameter list is a series of 32-bit addresses. The first 8 bits are 0 in a 32-bit address, so the first bit is used to indicate the last parameter. It is set to a 1 by the 1-byte specification in hexadecimal X'80'. This convention allows for variable-length parameter lists. The subroutine can determine how long the list is at execution time. This feature is not provided in Fortran compilers generally, except in the built-in functions similar to MAXOF(A,B, . . .), which find the maximum of a number of arguments.

The subroutine linking convention in the 370 requires that the address of the first word of the program be available in register 15 (as an initial base register) and that the link address for returns be in register 14. The instruction L 15,ASUB loads the word ASUB into register 15, and ASUB is defined to contain the address PROC. [The construction A(X) gives a 32-bit constant whose value is the address X.] In general it is not possible to write LA 15,PROC to load the address PROC directly into register 15 because it will not be possible to put PROC into a base-plus-displacement form unless there is a base register already assigned to an address close to PROC.

PARAMETERS IN THE PDP-11

Parameters are passed to subroutines in the PDP-11 by placing their addresses in the locations immediately following the call. The address structure of the machine makes it very easy to get the parameters. Suppose, for example, we wish to write a subroutine to place the maximum of two n-word positive integers A and B into location C. (Each of these addresses is assumed to be the first of n words.) We could call with the sequence

```
              JSR         R5,MAXN         Standard subroutine entry uses R5.
              .WORD       A               The next four words are parameters.
```

```
        .WORD       B
        .WORD       C
        .WORD       N          This is the address of a location
                               containing n.
```

Control should return to the word following that containing .WORD N. The subroutine can be coded as

```
MAXN:      MOV     (R5)+,R0        Put A in R0.
           MOV     (R5)+,R1        Put B in R1.
           MOV     (R5)+,R2        Put C in R2.
           MOV     @(R5)+,R3       Get n into R3 by indirect addressing.
LOOP1:     CMP     (R0),(R1)+      Compare most significant part first.
           BLO     BLARGE          Branch if B larger.
           BNE     ALARGE          Branch if A larger.
           MOV     (R0)+,(R2)+     Move A to C.
           DEC     R3              Decrement n and test for end.
           BNE     LOOP1
           RTS     R5              Return from subroutine.
BLARGE:    MOV     R1,R0
           SUB     #2,R0           Back up R1 and put in R0.
ALARGE:    MOV     (R0)+,(R2)+     Copy B or A to C.
           DEC     R3              Decrement n and test for end.
           BNE     ALARGE
           RTS     R5              Return from subroutine.
```

The auto-increment feature is used to fetch the parameters. R5 contains the address of the word following the JSR instruction used for entry, and this is the address of the first parameter. As the parameters are loaded into the registers for easy use in the subroutine, R5 is incremented so that it points to the next parameter. When all four parameters have been loaded, it is pointing to the word following the list of parameters, which will be the next instruction in the calling program. The RTS instruction uses this to return to the calling program.

CALL BY NAME

Fortran does not provide for a distinction between call-by-name and call-by-value. Let us consider the subroutine

```
SUBROUTINE EXMPL(A,B,C,D)
A = B
C = D
RETURN
END
```

called by

```
CALL EXMPL(P,1.0,Q,P)
```

The effect of this program may be different on different compilers. The strictest interpretation would be to perform the two operations

$$P = 1.0$$
$$Q = P$$

which would assign a value of 1.0 to Q and P. The value of P is changed by the first statement, and this affects the result of the second statement. Now consider the call

CALL EXMPL(X,1.0,Q,X−Y)

It might be thought that this should be equivalent to

$$X = 1.0$$
$$Q = X - Y$$

so that Q would be set to $1.0 - Y$. This does not happen in Fortran compilers, since the sequence of actions is equivalent to

TEMP$=$X−Y
CALL EXMPL(X,1.0,Q,TEMP)

so that $X - Y$ is evaluated prior to entry and stored in a *temporary*. If actual parameters are evaluated before entry and stored in a temporary, we say that the call is *by value*. If provision is made for evaluating them each time that they are used in a subroutine, we say that they are called *by name*. Algol allows the user to state in the subroutine whether the actual parameters substituted for the formal parameters are to be called by name or by value. Those that are by value are explicitly declared as such; the remainder are by name.

(Before proceeding, the programmer should note the programming error that can be made in Fortran and that can be very difficult to locate. Consider

CALL EXMPL(P,1.0,4.0,P)
$A = SQRT(4.0)$

which will set A to 1.0 on most compilers, as well as have other undesirable effects. Why is this?)

The call-by-name problem introduces problems as well as flexibility into those languages that allow it. For an example of its use, consider the following taken from the Algol report.†

† Revised Algol Report, *Communications of the Association for Computing Machinery*, vol. 6, no. 1, Jan., 1963.

```
procedure  Innerproduct(a,b)ORDER:(k,p)Result:(y);
  value   k; integ k,p; real y,a,b;
  begin real s;
    s := 0;
    for p := 1 step 1 until k do s := s + a × b;
    y := s;
    end  Innerproduct
```

The parameters a, b, p, and y are used by name since they are not declared by value. Consequently, the following use of Innerproduct can be used in the inner loop of matrix multiply.

Innerproduct(A(I,J),B(J,K),N,J,R)

which will calculate the sum

$$R = \sum_{J=1}^{N} A(I,J)B(J,K)$$

This works because the parameters a and b are reevaluated each time that they are used with a new value for J, which is substituted for p.

If a formal parameter is to be used by name, it is necessary for the calling program to provide a section of code which will evaluate the actual parameter each time that it is used. This code section is best made into a subroutine. The main subroutine must know whether to treat the actual parameter as the address of data or as the address of a program that will calculate the data. The subroutine could require that all actual parameters substituted for formal parameters called by name be supplied as subroutines. In that case, it would be necessary for the calling program to know which parameters were by value and which by name. This can only be done if all subroutines in Algol are translated at the same time as their calling programs. This immediately leads to an incompatibility between Algol- and Fortran-compiled subroutines. An alternative solution is to supply all actual parameters by name. If the subroutine requires that they be used by value, then it can request an evaluation initially and save the value in a temporary. If this is done, the subroutines for the actual parameters must return the address of the data to be passed, since the parameter may be used either for output or as a subroutine. Now, in order to pass a constant as a parameter, the called subroutine would get an address from the parameter list and perform a subroutine jump to that address. This code would return an address which could then be used to access the constant. The method is inefficient, but that is the price of flexibility and generality.

An alternative solution is to use additional bits in the parameter words to indicate their type. The subroutine can examine these to determine whether they represent an address, a constant, a subroutine, etc. This provides for a lot of dynamic checking which is very useful. If, in the case of arrays, a complete description of the array (size, etc.) is provided by the parameter (it would then be called a *dope vector*), it is possible to implement languages in which the size and types of arrays are not declared in subroutines. Some of this checking can be done automatically by special hardware. Some of the larger Burroughs computers provide this, for example.

THE CHOICE OF PARAMETERS OR COMMON

In planning a subroutine, the programmer must decide which variables to assign to common storage and which to put in the parameter list. The decision should rest largely on which parameter names change from call to call and which are the same. If a given parameter is always the same variable name, then it is better to place it in common. This saves both writing time and execution time. On the other hand, if it is necessary to store information into common before each call of a subroutine, then it is better to remove the variable from common and to put it in the parameter list.

If the addresses of variables are used as parameters and they are placed in memory cells following the cell containing the subroutine call, indirect addressing can be used to access parameter values. Suppose, for example, that a subroutine is to be written to add the values of the first two parameters and to store the result in the third. (Hardly worth writing a subroutine for, but this is an example!) If the call takes the form

```
        BAL         14,ADD3
        ADDR        A
        ADDR        B
        ADDR        C
```

the subroutine could take the form

```
ADD3        LOAD        *0(14)
            ADD         *1(14)
            STORE       *2(14)
            BRANCH      3(14)
```

The asterisk is assumed to indicate indirect addressing and to occur after indexing. The effect of the LOAD instruction is to first calculate the effective address by adding 0 to the contents of index register 14. This gives the address of the cell containing the pseudo ADDR A. Since indirect addressing is indicated, it uses the address A as the actual address of the data, so the effect is to load the contents of cell A into the accumulator.

4.3.2 Subroutine conventions

Subroutines are used as a means of making code written by one person available to another, since they are written in a form where subsequent users do not have to concern themselves with the inner workings but only with the macroscopic details. For example, if we write a subroutine for complex number multiplication, you can use it as long as you know where the parameters are to be placed. You do not have to know how it does the job.

By collecting general-purpose subroutines written by many of the users of a system, a large program library can be built up which will save a user with a new job a lot of effort. Unfortunately, largeness can become a drawback if the library is not managed carefully. The information-explosion problem is inescapable, since it is bound to take longer to find the right program in a large library; the problem of inconsistent methods, however, *can* be avoided. All programs should have calling sequences which are as similar as possible in order to minimize the chance of errors in calling one program from another. Therefore it is a good idea for the programmer to use the same method in his personal subroutines as is used in the library. In addition to the questions of where the parameters are stored for transmission, there is the question of what is stored as a parameter and in what format it is stored. It is typically impossible to choose a single format that will satisfy all users, some of whom are interested in speed and others in complete generality.

In addition to the transmission of parameters, there is the problem of understanding all of these effects of a subroutine. The write-up should describe the action of the program in terms of how the output parameters are related to the input parameters and what side effects occur. Arguments can be made for the use of side effects in terms of efficiency, particularly when large arrays of data are stored in common storage, but as a general rule the use of side effects should be avoided, since it is easy to forget that variables not in the call sequence can be changed by the program. This applies at the machine- or assembly-language level to the registers on the central processing unit. It would be very difficult to check the write-up of every subroutine used to see if the program changed any registers. The index register used in the BAL instruction is expected to be changed since this is a necessary part of the calling procedure, but it would be very undesirable if information in other index registers were changed. For this reason it is usual always to use the same index register for subroutine calls and to expect every subroutine to leave the contents of all other index registers unchanged. The same attitude could be taken to the accumulator or accumulators, as the case may be, but in a one-address machine it is usual to assume that every subroutine changes the contents of the accumulator. Stack machines will usually expect the stack contents to be unchanged unless they are used for transmission of parameters. This is reasonable, since working space is always available on top of other data in a stack machine. A single-accumulator one-address code will almost always need the accumulator for calculation of answers.

When index-register contents have to be saved, it is certainly not convenient to avoid their use altogether (else why buy a machine that has them?). Therefore, such contents must be stored, temporarily, into cells in memory—so that they will be available during the execution of the subroutine—and then reloaded from memory at the conclusion of the subroutine, just prior to returning to the calling program. Examination of subroutines for a particular computer will usually show that the first few instructions store the index-register contents in memory and the last few reload them from memory. The memory locations used to save the contents of the index registers must not interfere with the execution of any other piece of code; hence they must be separated from the other subroutines' temporary storage. The same applies to any temporary storage used in the arithmetic performed by the subroutine. Therefore, each subroutine will have a set of temporary storage cells associated with it for use by that subroutine. The start of a subroutine might appear on a 15-index machine as

```
        STX         1,A
        STX         2,A+1
        STX         3,A+2
        STX         4,A+3
        . . . . . . . . . . . . . . . .
        STX         15,A+14
```

and the end as

```
        LDX         1,A
        LDX         2,A+1
        . . . . . . . . . . . . . . . .
        LDX         15,A+14
        BRANCH      0(14)
  A     BSS         15
```

if it has no parameters in the calling sequence. LDX and STX stand for *load index* and *store index* respectively.

Since these two sequences of instruction would be very common on a 15-index machine, it might be worth the designer's while to provide two instructions, one of which performs the first set of 15 index stores and the other which performs the last 16. This is sometimes done, but not on many machines. The other possibility is to use a macro for each of them and at least save the programmer the writing time.

Note that index register 14 was saved, although it was changed by the calling BAL instruction. If the subroutine calls on yet another subroutine, this will change index 14, so it is necessary to save and restore its contents in order to make the correct return to the outer calling program.

IBM 370 SUBROUTINES

The IBM 370 requires that most of the general registers be saved if they are used in a subroutine. In general, registers 0, 1, and 13 through 15 will be used in the calling sequence, so they need be saved only if the called subroutine itself calls another. If registers 2 through 12 are changed by the subroutine, they should be restored prior to exit. We have seen that register 15 contains the address of the subroutine, register 14 the return link, and register 1 the address of the parameter list. Register 0 is used to return the output in the case that the subroutine is a function with an integer result. The four floating-point registers may be used by the subroutine if desired. They need not be restored, although registers 0 and 2 are used to return the result of a floating-point function. Floating-point register 0 will contain the real part and 2 the imaginary part if the variable is complex.

The 370 has a pair of multiple-register load and store instructions that are helpful in the subroutine. They are

| | LM | Ri,Rj,A |
| and | STM | Ri,Rj,A |

where the mnemonics stand for *load multiple* and *store multiple* respectively. The contents of registers, Ri, $Ri + 1$, . . . , Rj are moved to or from memory addresses, A, A + 4, ... If Ri is greater than Rj, then registers Ri, . . . , 15, 0, . . . , Rj are copied. The address A cannot be indexed, but it has a base register.

In the example above, the index registers were stored into an area in the subroutine. On the 370 system, the convention requires the calling program to set aside a temporary storage area for the subroutine. This is called a *savearea*, and is 18 words long. The contents of these words is shown in Figure 4.1. The first word can be ignored by the user; the next two will be discussed shortly. The remaining 15 are used for storing the contents of every register except 13. Register 13 is used to pass the address of the savearea from the calling program to the subroutine so that it can store its registers. Figure 4.1 shows the relationship between three subroutines, $I - 1$, I, and $I + 1$. We are looking at the savearea associated with subroutine I, which calls subroutine $I + 1$ and is called by subroutine $I - 1$. The contents of the registers in the savearea are those at the time that subroutine $I + 1$ is called. The second and third words of the savearea contain pointers to the saveareas of the subroutines above and below. SAVEAREA + 4 contains a pointer back to the previous savearea, while SAVEAREA + 8 contains a pointer to the next

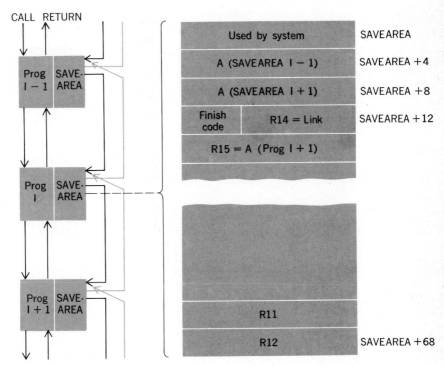

FIGURE 4.1   370 savearea usage

savearea. The former must be stored by program I, while the latter can only be done by program I + 1. These pointers enable the system to determine which subroutines were currently *invoked* when a termination occurs. This provides a useful post-mortem facility. Note that register 15 contains the address of the subroutine itself. Two other conventions are needed to provide a useful diagnostic. The first is an indicator which tells that a subroutine has been completed after it has been called. The first byte of SAVEAREA + 12 in the calling program should be set to 11111111 when the subroutine has completed its task. This enables the system to determine how far back up a chain of subroutines call control has returned at the time of an error. The second convention is to place the name of the subroutine as a character string at the start of the program. (The first 4 bytes contain a branch around the name, the next *n* + 1 contain the length of the name *n* and the name as a character string.)

A typical begin and end sequence for a subroutine is shown below and explained afterward.

```
PROGI      CSECT
           DS        0H         Get on an even word boundary.
           USING     *,15       Use 15 as a temporary base register.
```

B	*+10	Branch around program name.
DC	X'5'	Length of name.
DC	CL5'PROGI'	Name.
STM	14,12,12(13)	Save registers in savearea of calling program.
CNOP	0,4	Get on a word boundary.
BAL	12,*+76	Branch around this program's savearea.
DROP	15	Drop register 15 as a base.
USING	*,12	Use register 12 as a base.
DC	18F'0'	18-word savearea for this program.
ST	12,8(13)	Store address of this savearea in previous savearea.
ST	13,4(12)	Store address of previous savearea in this savearea.
LR	13,12	Address of this savearea in register 13 for calls to lower-level subroutines.

To call a lower-level subroutine, the sequence below is used:

LA	1,PARLIST	Parameter list address.
L	15,ASUB	Address of called subroutine.
BALR	14,15	
		Control returns here.

Exit sequence:

	L	13,4(13)	Address of calling subroutine's savearea.
	LM	1,12,24(13)	Restore registers 1 through 12.
	L	14,12(13)	Restore link address.
	MVI	12(13),X'FF'	Set completion code.
	BR	14	Return.
ASUB	DC	A(SUBROUT)	
PARLIST	DC	A(Par1)	
	DC	A(Par2)	

The pseudo CSECT tells the asembler that a new section of program is being started with the name PROGI. Each section with a different name can be separately relocated. The name in the location field of the CSECT is passed on to the linkage editor as an ENTRY point, so that other programs can branch to this program using the name, in this case PROGI. Since register 15 is known to contain the address of the start of the program, the assembler is told it can be used as a base register until register 12 is loaded. The latter is done with a branch and link instruction after the registers have been saved in the calling program's savearea. (It must not be done before this, or the contents of register 12 at the time of the call will be lost.) Because the branch and link is placed where it is, the address placed in register 12 is the address of this program's savearea. The branch and link also serves to jump around the savearea to the instructions which store savearea addresses before setting register 13 to the address of this savearea. The call sequence to branch to another subroutine has already been discussed. The exit sequence simply reloads the registers from the calling program's savearea, sets the completion code, and returns.

This undoubtedly seems like a lot of code to perform a fairly simple branch to a subroutine. It is, and consequently subroutines should only be used for a significant section of program. Fortunately, it is not necessary for the user to write this every time. The system usually provides macros which handle the entry to and exit from a subroutine. The names vary from one installation to another. One set is ENTER and EXIT. More details on IBM 370 subroutines appear in Section 4.3.6.

PDP-11 SUBROUTINES

Systems for small computers are not usually as standardized as those for large computers, as the user cannot afford the overhead associated with the luxury of standard conventions. The subroutine conventions used on a particular installation are chosen to give the greatest flexibility within that environment. Therefore, the conventions we present here may not agree with those on any computer the reader is familiar with.

The PDP-11 provides a stack in memory addressed by register 6. The subroutine entry and return instructions use this stack to save the register used for the link address. (The stack is stored "backward" in memory: the address of the current top level is stored in R6 and lower levels are in higher-numbered addresses.)

If a simple subroutine in which all parameters can be passed in the registers is to be written (for example, a multiplication routine which forms the product of R0 and R2 as a double-length number in R0,R1), then the simple entry

```
    JSR         PC,SUB
```

can be used. The effect of this is to push the location of the next instruction into the stack and jump to the subroutine SUB. Only registers 6 and 7 are changed. A return is effected with

```
    RTS         PC
```

which restores R6, the stack pointer, and returns to the instruction following the JSR. If, however, a number of parameters are passed in the words following the JSR, it is conventional to use R5 for the link. Because the stack mechanism is available, it is the most convenient place to store the registers that must be saved. In fact, the registers can be saved by another subroutine and restored by yet another, so that one instruction is sufficient to save and another to restore registers. The pair of subroutines below will save and restore registers R0 through R5 in the stack. The routine SAVE pushes R0 through R4 onto the stack in reverse order. Since the subroutine should be entered with JSR R5,SAVE, R5 will have been pushed onto the stack by the entry. The last move instruction puts a copy of the old contents of R5 on top of the stack also, so that the return instruction RTS will restore R5. Note that the auto-decrement addressing feature handles a stack mechanism naturally, as the address is decremented *before* the memory access so that the next higher stack level is accessed. At the end of a subroutine, the routine REST should be entered with a JSR R5,REST. Registers R0 to R5 are restored.

SAVE:	MOV	R4,−(SP)	Push R4 onto stack.
	MOV	R3,−(SP)	Push R3, R2, R1, and R0 onto stack.
	MOV	R2,−(SP)	Note that R5 is already on stack
	MOV	R1,−(SP)	because a JSR was used to enter
	MOV	R0,−(SP)	this program.
	MOV	10(SP),−(SP)	Old R5 on top of stack.
	RTS	R5	Return to subroutine, restoring R5.
REST:	TST	(SP)+	Pop top of stack.
	MOV	(SP)+,R0	Restore R0 from top of stack.
	MOV	(SP)+,R1	Restore R1, R2, R3, and R4.
	MOV	(SP)+,R2	
	MOV	(SP)+,R3	
	MOV	(SP)+,R4	
	RTS	R5	Return to subroutine, restoring R5.

The first instruction in REST removes the value pushed into the stack by the JSR instruction used to enter REST. It tests that value and sets the condition code, but no use is made of the setting, so it functions as a no operation. It is a shorter, faster instruction than ADD #2,SP.

If a subroutine fetches parameters from the words following the call, register R5 will have to be incremented before the return, as REST restores R5 to its value immediately before the entry to SAVE. The following is a typical start and end of a subroutine using SAVE and REST. The case shown is for a subroutine with three parameters whose addresses follow the call.

SUB:	JSR	R5,SAVE	Save registers.
	MOV	(R5)+,R0	Parameter 1 to R0.
	MOV	(R5)+,R1	Parameter 2 to R1.
	MOV	(R5),R2	Parameter 3 to R2.
	. . . . .		*Body* of subroutine.
	JSR	R5,REST	Restore registers.
	ADD	#6,R5	Increment R5 to return point.
	RTS	R5	Return to calling program.

4.3.3 Recursion

It is possible that one subroutine may call another. We say that the second subroutine is at a lower level in this case. An example of such a circumstance frequently arises in library subroutines for integration and quadrature. A library subroutine may be available to integrate a function F(X) from A to B. This requires four parameters, one to tell it what the function F is, two to give limits A and B, and the fourth to return the answer. Numerical integration methods usually evaluate the integrand (F(X)) for a number of different values of X and add these results together in some manner to get an approximation of the answer. Therefore the integration subroutine requires the values of F(X) for values of X that are determined by the integration subroutine, not by the user. For this reason, the most convenient way of telling the integration subroutine about F is to provide it with another subroutine with one input parameter, X, and one output parameter, the value of F(X). This is illustrated in the sections of a Fortran code below.

```
Main program . . . . .
CALL INTGRT(A,B,FUN,RESULT)
. . . . . . .
END
SUBROUTINE INTGRT(C,D,AUX,ANS)
. . . . . . .
CALL AUX(X,F)
. . . . . . .
END
SUBROUTINE FUN(Y,G)
. . . . . . .
G = . . . . . .
END
```

(Not all Fortran compilers will accept this use of subroutine names as parameters.)

It may happen that the function to be integrated itself involves an integration of another function. The simplest example would arise when F(X) is the integral form 0 to X of another function G(X). It would be tempting to write the defining subroutine for F(X) as

```
SUBROUTINE FUN(X,F)
CALL INTGRT(C,X,FUN1,F)
END
```

and define G(X) by

```
SUBROUTINE FUN1(Y,G)
. . . . . . . .
G = . . . . . . . .
. . . . . . . .
. . . . . . . .
END
```

The diagram in Figure 4.2 shows what is happening in terms of levels of subroutine calls, but it must be noted that the same subroutine INTGRT appears below itself, that is, it effectively calls on itself. This is not allowed in most Fortran compilers, and it is easy to see why. At the time of the first call on INTGRT, registers and the link information are saved in temporary storage cells associated with the subroutine. In the middle of executing this

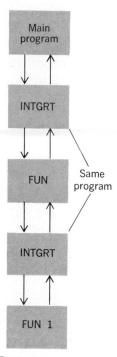

Same
program

FIGURE 4.2   *Recursive use of a subroutine*

subroutine, a call on another subroutine is made. This eventually causes another call on INTGRT which will immediately save the current contents of the index registers, etc., in the temporary storage cells that are still being used to save information at the higher-level call. Thus the information from the higher-level call is destroyed by overwriting, and the program will not work.

It is certainly possible to design ways around this problem. We shall mention some below, but first let us examine the utility of allowing a program to call upon itself, either directly or indirectly via another subroutine. The use of a subroutine by itself is called *recursion* and a subroutine written to allow this is called recursive. We have mentioned one possible application above which could certainly arise in multidimensional integration. Another example often used is the factorial function FACT(N). A factorial can certainly be calculated by iteration, for example by

```
        FACT = 1
        DO 1 I = 1,N
1       FACT = FACT*I
```

It could also be calculated by a recursive subroutine or function were they allowed as

```
              FUNCTION FACT(N)
              IF (N.GT.1) GO TO 1
              FACT = 1
              RETURN
    1         FACT = FACT(N−1)*N
              RETURN
              END
```

It is assumed that N is a positive integer in the above program. This example shows recursion in its worst light, as the program is longer in space and speed than the corresponding iterative program. Generally speaking, recursive techniques for numerical problems will lead to slower programs than the corresponding iterative techniques, but frequently they will give shorter programs in terms of space used. (The integration example is a case in point.) The brevity of the program does lead to clarity. This is particularly true in the case of nonnumerical programs, but we shall have to wait to give meaningful examples in those cases. Since clarity and brevity are important, recursion is a very useful technique, but it should seldom be employed in short, frequently used subroutines.

One of the better examples of its use in numerical subroutines is given below. This is a subroutine function to integrate a function supplied as a parameter with error control. The first program INTG calculates some initial values needed and then calls the second subroutine INTG1. This subroutine calculates the integral by applying Simpson's rule to each half of the interval and compares the result with the integral found by using Simpson's rule over the whole interval. If the results agree within ERROR times the interval, this is the answer; if not, INTG1 is used separately on each half interval. The programs are written in Fortran, but are assumed to be recursive.

```
              FUNCTION INGT(A,B,F,ERROR)
              X = F(A)
              Y = F((A+B)/2.)
              Z = F(B)
              Q = (B−A)*(X + 4.0*Y + Z)/6.
              INTG = INTG1(A,B,F,X,Y,Z,ERROR,Q)
              RETURN
              END
              FUNCTION INTG1(A,B,F,X,Y,Z,ERROR,Q)
              P = (A+B)/2.
              P1 = .75*A + .25*B
              P2 = .25*A + .75*B
              Y1 = F(P1)
              Y2 = F(P2)
              Q1 = (B−A) * (X + 4.0*Y1 + Y)/12.
```

```
            Q2 = (B—A) * (Y + 4.0*Y2 + Z)/12.
            IF (ABSF(Q — Q1 — Q2).LE.ERROR*ABS(B — A))GO TO 1
            INTG1 = INTG1(A,P,F,X,Y1,Y,ERROR,Q1) + INTG1(P,B,F,Y,Y2,Z,ERROR,Q2)
            RETURN
      1     INTG1 = Q1 + Q2
            RETURN
            END
```

To solve the temporary storage problem in recursive subroutines, it is necessary to make provision for different storage for each use of the program while another higher level use is still active. Since the temporary storage that must be accessed is that of the most recent call on the subroutine, a first-in–last-out queue is indicated. In other words, a stack of temporary storage is needed. The accumulator stack could be used on a stack machine, but this is not convenient if it is limited in length. Therefore a stack is usually created in memory. The same stack can be used by all subroutines, since the next subroutine to exit is always the last subroutine to be called. A stack can be created in memory by using a *pointer,* which is an address held either in a known memory cell or in an index register allocated for that purpose. The pointer *points* to the top word of the stack. Words can be added to the stack by increasing the pointer address and storing the words in the memory cells indicated. Words can be removed by decreasing the pointer and reading from the cells indicated. Since care must be taken not to overwrite program and other storage areas in memory, a test must be made to check that the pointer has not, in error, become too large or too small. (A desirable design for a machine includes instructions which perform all these operations simultaneously.) It is convenient to design a set of conventions which allow for such a stack. If register 13 were used as a stack pointer in the 370, then recursion would be straightforward, as the saveareas would be put in the stack. The PDP-11 provides a stack using register 6, and so all subroutines can be recursive.

4.3.4 Reentrant programs: pure procedures

It is highly desirable to avoid instruction modification in subroutines or in any other piece of code. Therefore, parameter addresses should be used by indexing and indirect reference, rather than by planting them into instructions within the subroutine. Temporary storage access within the program should also be by indexed addresses. The index can be set by the calling program in order to take care of possible recursion; it then serves as a stack pointer for the temporary storage. If this is done, an additional desirable feature appears—the program is what is called a *pure procedure.* This means that it can be interrupted at any place during execution and restarted from the beginning. If the index register used to point to temporary storage is changed before the restart, it is possible to return it to its original value when the first execution was in progress and to continue that execution from the point at which it was interrupted. There is normally no reason for a single user to want to restart a program and later return to continue an earlier execution, but, in a multiprogramming environment where there can be several different users' programs in the main memory simultaneously, it may be desirable to switch from one user to another from time to time. If a subroutine is a pure procedure, it is possible for several different users to share the same copy of it in memory. If it is a large subroutine, for example, a Fortran translator, the saving in memory space is considerable. A program that can be executed by several different users in such a way is called *reentrant*. This will be discussed further in a later chapter.

4.3.5 Organization of programs into subroutines

The word *segmentation* is used in two ways. One refers to an advanced method for dynamic memory allocation which will be discussed later. In this chapter, we refer only to the process of breaking a job up into a number of smaller jobs or segments. This is an important part of planning a large program, since it is either going to be programmed by several people or by one person working over a long period. In either case, it is difficult to know the details of one section of a code while working on another section. Therefore, the interaction between different sections should be kept to the necessary minimum. A good way to do this is to make each of the sections a separate subroutine following all the installation conventions. In addition to contributing to the clarity of the total program when it is finished, it aids in the debugging. Each individual subroutine should be checked separately to see that it performs the appropriate operations on its input parameters. This can be done by writing a program whose sole purpose is to call on the subroutine and test the results it gives. Subroutines used by the program being tested can be provided in a form which gives known answers, so that faults will be known to lie within the one subroutine. The hardest part of checking a complex program is isolating an error to a given subroutine. If each subroutine is checked thoroughly first, this problem is greatly reduced. The remaining errors are probably due to misunderstandings by one programmer of what another subroutine does. This is usually partly due to bad documentation.

4.3.6 Subroutines and the 370 assembler

We have already described the subroutine conventions. In this section we will discuss some of the features of the 370 assembler intended to help with subroutine preparation.

The pseudo CSECT was used in an earlier example. It is usually the first statement in a subroutine, and it establishes the name of the subroutine as an entry point. If the subroutine is assembled using a CSECT statement with its name in the location field, separately assembled routines can refer to that name as long as it is declared external in those other routines. The linkage editor will handle the cross-referencing. Using this mechanism, a subroutine can be coded and checked, and then kept on cards or other storage in an assembled form while other parts of the total job are coded. The calling program can use the V-type data definition to define the external name.

```
X              DC           V(SUB)
```

defines a 4-byte, word-aligned number whose value will be the address of SUB at execution time. It is equivalent to the pair of pseudos

```
X              DC           A(SUB)
               EXTRN        SUB
```

namely, it also declares SUB to be external. For example, we could use

```
S1             CSECT
               . . . .        body of subroutine ⎱ one assembly
               END
```

```
MAIN           CSECT
               . . . .        body of main program
               LA             1,PARLIST
               L              15,=V(S1)      Literal which gives address  ⎱ another assembly
BALR           14,15                         of word containing V(S1).
               . . . .
               END
```

The CSECT pseudo establishes a location counter for the named section in the assembler; it can be used to allow several location counters in one assembly. For example,

```
MAIN           CSECT
               a1
               a2
               . . .
S3             CSECT
               b1
               b2
MAIN           CSECT
               a3
               a4
S4             CSECT
               c1
```

```
                c2
S3              CSECT
                b3
                . . .
```

starts assembling in the program section MAIN, and lines a1, a2, etc., are assembled into locations 0, 1, . . . in that section. Then a new location counter named S3 is started at location 0, and lines b1, b2, etc., are assembled for loading at 0, 1, . . . in that section. Assembly then returns to section MAIN and adds on lines a3 and a4 from where it left off last time. A third section S4 is now started with lines c1 and c2, then assembly returns to section S3.

A similar pseudo DSECT is normally used for data. (The D does not, however, stand for data. CSECT means Control SECTion, and DSECT means Dummy SECTion.) A dummy section is not assembled or loaded, but is used to define the layout of a data area that is shared with another program section. Suppose, for example, that a program is passed the first address of a block of storage as a parameter, and that block of storage is known to have a certain layout in the calling program. The same layout can be defined in the called program so that the same names can be used. Consider the example below:

```
S1          CSECT
            . . .
            LA          1,P1
            L           15,=V(S3)
            BALR        14,15
            . . .
            DS          0F              Get on a word boundary.
P1          DC          X'80',AL3(D1)
D1          DS          0D              Note that D1 is known to be on a double-
                                        word boundary.
ALPHA       DC          E'2.35',E'4.5'
BETA        DS          3F,4D
CHAR        DS          20CL120
            END
S3          CSECT                       Start of another assembly.
            . . . .
            L           11,0(1)         Address of D1.
            USING       D1,11           Inform assembler that base is 11.
            . . . .
D1          DSECT                       Definition of dummy data section.
ALPHA       DS          2E              Note that D1 will be address 0 in this
BETA        DS          3F,4D           section, and therefore is on a double-
                                        word boundary.
CHAR        DS          20CL120
S3          CSECT
            . . .                       Continuation of program section S3.
            END                         End of assembly.
```

The calling program in the example above defines a data area named D1 with various fields named ALPHA, BETA, CHAR to which it presumably refers.

(These can be thought of as names of substructures in the structure D1, to use a PL/I analogy.) The called program makes a similar declaration using a DSECT. For example, the DSECT tells the assembler that the name BETA refers to a location that is 8 bytes beyond D1. Since the assembler is also told that register 11 can be used as a base containing D1, it can assemble any reference to BETA in the subprogram S3 as a displacement of 8 from register 11. At execution time, register 11 is loaded with the parameter passed from the calling program equal to the address of D1 in the calling program, so that references to BETA in the called program access BETA in the calling program.

The DSECT technique may seem like a complicated way of accessing data in the calling program, and if that was all that was needed, it would have been simpler to use external declarations. However, the technique above allows the address of any similar area to be passed as a parameter. If, for example, a third program wishes to call S3, it can give a reference to its own area named D1.

Common storage can be defined, but only in blank common, by the pseudo COM. This acts like a CSECT, but all lines following the pseudo are assigned to common until the next CSECT or DSECT. Thus

```
            COM
A           DS          3F
B           DS          5CL4
```

allocates 8 words of storage; the name of the first word is A, and fourth, B. The linkage editor assigns a storage space equal in size to the maximum space needed by all programs for common.

4.3.7 Subroutines and the PDP-11 assembler

MACRO-11, the PDP-11 macro assembler, allows subroutines to be assembled as individually relocatable program sections, either in one or several assemblies. The link editor LINK-11 ties them together. As with many small computers, it is possible to specify absolute memory locations for the object code. This is done by the pseudo ASECT. For example,

```
            .ASECT
= 100
            MOV A,R1
            . . .
```

would assemble the move instruction into locations 100 through 103 (it is a 4-byte instruction). ASECT sets the location counter to absolute zero. The assignment of 100 to . (the name for the location counter in MACRO-11) then starts assembly at 100. The location counter is changed when a CSECT pseudo is encountered. If one is encountered and another ASECT then appears, assembly continues in the absolute section from where it left off. For example:

```
              .ASECT
. = 10
B:            .WORD       34,21
              .CSECT
A:            MOV         R1,R2
              . . .
              .ASECT
C:            .WORD       7
              . . .
```

will cause the word C to be put into locations 14 and 15, since the two words starting at 10 occupied 10 through 13.

Similarly, reappearances of a CSECT cause assembly to continue in that control section at the point where it had stopped previously. CSECTs can be named by putting the name in the address field. There can be 253 named CSECTs and one blank CSECT. Each differently named section has its own location counter. However, these names are not related to external names and cannot be referenced in instructions. If linkage between separately compiled sections is needed, the names must be declared external in the GLOBL pseudo discussed earlier.

The main purpose of nonblank CSECTs is to handle labeled (named) common, as in Fortran. If the user wishes to establish two common areas, say P and Q, he can define sections with those names. For example,

```
              .CSECT      P
A:            .WORD       12,23
B:            .BLKW       15
C:            .BLKB       5
              .CSECT      Q
P:            .BLKW       144
```

The loader assigns separate memory regions big enough to handle each of these sections. However, if a separately assembled code also defines sections with the same name, the loader assigns them to the same area of memory. Consequently, if the storage layout is identical in both definitions, a reference to B in one code will be the same as a reference to B in a separately assembled section of code. Note that the names of sections are not related to other names in the code. In the example above, P was the name of a section and also the name of a location. There is no conflict in such uses.

The blank CSECT differs from named CSECTs in that the loader allocates different regions of memory for each separately assembled blank CSECT. This means that it is possible to break a long section up and assemble the pieces separately, as long as the section is not named and as long as cross references are handled by suitable external declarations.

4.4 MACROS

Macros were introduced in Section 4.2 as open subroutines which are a half-way stage to the closed or regular subroutine. As subroutines, they are not as powerful as closed subroutines because such features as recursion are not applicable. However, we shall see that they have some features of their own that cannot be matched in closed subroutines and should therefore be considered as a tool in their own right. The principal of a macro facility is that a *definition* of an input form can be written so that each time the input form is used, it is replaced by its definition. Elaborate facilities to allow for substitution of *dummy arguments* (similar to the parameters of subroutines) are provided. Macro facilities are not used only in assemblers, although their most common implementation is as part of a system assembler. A macro processor is commonly seen simply as a translator that inputs one string of characters and outputs another in the form of assembly language for eventual input to an assembler. We shall see that the implementation may or may not take that form in practice.

In assembly language, the macro definition is usually accomplished with the pseudo MACRO and MEND. The first appears in front of the definition, while the latter serves to indicate the end of the definition. The macro facility in assembly language defines a new pseudo, called a *macro order,* so that future uses of this new order can be replaced by its definition. The name of the macro order is placed after the macro pseudo. Thus the macro order XYZ can be defined by

```
MACRO
XYZ
LINE 1
LINE 2
. . . .
LINE N
MEND
```

Each time that XYZ appears in the instruction field, N instructions equal to

```
LINE 1
LINE 2
. . . .
LINE N
```

are assembled. The replacement process essentially occurs prior to assembly, so that it is precisely equivalent to inputting the expanded form. In the following subsections, we shall discuss some of the additional features that are added to macros.

It is not necessary to know anything about the instruction set for the particular machine because the macro processor deals only with character strings. Indeed, it is possible to perform macro expansion on assembly language independent of the particular machine for which the output code is intended.

4.4.1 Parameters in macros

Subroutines do not use the same data cells in each call: macros are more useful if they are similarly not restricted. Since the macro substitution is done before execution, it is possible to change the symbolic addresses in the instructions that make up a macro before execution time. Suppose we frequently needed a section of code to add 1 to the contents of a given location. The code

```
LOAD       X
ADD        =1
STORE      X
```

would do it for the location X. However, each time that it is needed the location is different. Therefore, X is made a parameter to the macro, and it is defined as

```
MACRO
INCR       X
LOAD       X
ADD        =1
STORE      X
MEND
```

Because X is listed in the address field of the macro pseudo, it is defined as a dummy parameter. The macro must be called by writing

```
INCR       TCNT
```

where TCNT is the symbolic address of the variable that is to be incremented. This macro call is *expanded* as

```
LOAD       TCNT
ADD        =1
STORE      TCNT
```

so that each use of the dummy parameter is replaced by the symbolic address specified in the macro. A macro can have many parameters. For example,

```
MACRO
EXMP        A,B,ANY,C
ADD         A
MPY         B
STORE       C
ADD         ANY
STORE       A
MEND
```

It is important to remember that the parameters are dummies (that is, they are not defined outside of the macro), so that they can be used over again but cannot be referred to outside of the macro.

When an actual parameter appears in a location field as follows,

```
     MACRO
     EX          A,B
     ADD         A
B    ADD         A
     MEND
```

the use of EX by EX P,Q produces code with the address Q in the location field. This defines Q to the assembler, so that it may only be used once in this form.

KEYWORD PARAMETERS

Complex macro definition can involve a number of parameters, many of which do not really need to be specified on every use of the macro. (It will be seen in the section on conditional expansion that not all of a macro definition need be used in a particular expansion.) In these cases the life of the programmer is made easier by keyword parameters. These are parameters which can be given a *default* value in the definition and which do not have to be specified unless a different value is needed. Keyword parameters are declared in the form

```
MACRO
MULT        AP=VALUE,R=,WRT=23*A

ADD         AP(R)
. . .                   Rest of definition.
MEND
```

The parameters are the symbolic names given on the left-hand side of the equal signs. The corresponding values on the right-hand side of the equal signs are the default values that are used unless another value is specified. Keyword parameters are given values in the same way in the use of a macro. For example, after the definition above, we could write

```
        MULT          WRT=B,R=4
```

and get the expansion

```
        ADD           VALUE(4)
        . . .                          Rest of expansion.
```

The parameter AP is not specified, and so the default value VALUE is used. The parameter R is replaced by 4, and WRT by B. Note that it is not necessary to specify keyword parameters in the order listed in the macro definition, as the assembler can figure out which is which.

Sometimes it is necessary to use a symbolic address in a location field in a macro definition so that the generated code can include a branch. For example,

```
        MACRO
        MNEG          X
        LOAD          X
        BPL           Y
        MPY           =-.5
Y       STORE         X
        MEND
```

Unfortunately, if this macro is used more than once, the address Y will be multiply defined. This can be overcome by putting Y as a second dummy parameter and giving it a new name each time that the macro is called.

However, it is unnecessary for the programmer to do this, as many macro processors provide a mechanism for generating unique labels in each macro expansion. Not untypical of processors using this technique is the 370 assembler, which provides a *system variable* SYSNDX, whose value is a 4-digit decimal string starting at 0001 and incremented by 1 for each macro use (expansion). Since a decimal number is not itself a valid symbolic address, a mechanism for *concatenating* such a string with another name is also provided. Let us use the period character for this, so that, if A and B were macro arguments whose values were P and Q, respectively, A.B would be expanded as PQ. Using such a mechanism, the example above could be coded as

```
           MACRO
           HNEG        X
           LOAD        X
           BPL         A.SYSNDX
           MPY         =-0.5
A.SYSNDX   STORE       X
           MEND
```

When this is called by

```
            HNEG        P
            HNEG        Q
```

the expansion

```
            LOAD        P
            BPL         A0001
            MPY         =−0.5
A0001       STORE       P
            LOAD        Q
            BPL         A0002
            MPY         =−0.5
A0002       STORE       Q
```

results, assuming that these are the first macro expansions. A different symbol is generated in each of the two location fields because the system variable SYSNDX is increased by 1 between the two macro expansions. If more than one location field symbol is needed in the same expansion, different characters can be concatenated with SYSNDX. For example,

```
            MACRO
            MAX         A,B,C
            LOAD        A
            SUB         B
            BPL         A.SYSNDX
            LOAD        B
            BRANCH      B.SYSNDX
A.SYSNDX    LOAD        A
B.SYSNDX    STORE       C
            MEND
```

If this is used as, say, the thirty-fourth macro expansion, the two generated names will be A0034 and B0034.

Macro assemblers will differ as to details, but all will include definition pseudos such as MACRO and MEND, and a means of parameter substitution. The parameters are specified in the address field of the macro call, separated by various characters. These separation characters are called *break* characters, and either can be restricted to the comma or may include others, such as the arithmetic operation characters. At definition time, each parameter is indicated by a valid symbolic name, and at expansion time, all occurrences of that symbolic name are replaced by the specified subfield of the address field. The 370 macro assembler will be discussed in Section 4.4.4, and the PDP-11 in 4.4.5.

4.4.2 Nested calls

In many cases it is convenient to define one macro in terms of previously defined macros. We refer to this as a nested call, in that one call is inside another. If the macro expansion is viewed as a character-string operation, it is easy to understand the steps involved. Consider the two macro definitions

```
          MACRO
          COPY      FROM,TO,COUNT
          LDX       1,COUNT              Load index 1 with count.
L.SYSNDX  LOAD      FROM—1(1)
          STORE     TO—1(1)              Copy one element.
          BCT       1,L.SYSNDX           Decrease index and branch if not 0
                                         (same as 370 instruction).

          MEND
          MACRO
          SWITCH    BUF1,BUF2,SPARE,LENGTH
          COPY      BUF1,SPARE,LENGTH
          COPY      BUF2,BUF1,LENGTH
          COPY      SPARE,BUF2,LENGTH
          MEND
```

When the macro SWITCH is used, say by

```
          SWITCH  A,B,C,L
```

it first expands as

```
          COPY      A,C,L
          COPY      B,A,L
          COPY      C,B,L
```

and then each of the COPYs is expanded using the first definition to get

```
          LDX       1,L                  Load index 1 with count.
L0035     LOAD      A—1(1)
          STORE     C—1(1)               Copy one element.
          BCT       1,L0035              . . .
          LDX       1,L                  Load index 1 with count.
L0036     LOAD      B—1(1)
          . . .     etc.
```

When parameters are handed from one macro to another, it is sometimes desirable to pass a sequence of addresses separated by commas across as a single parameter. Unfortunately, the use of commas indicates the separation of the various parameters. A convention of placing parentheses around single parameters is often used. To process these, parentheses must be recognized in the address field of macros. When a macro use is recognized, the parameters are extracted as character strings by scanning across the address field and counting parentheses, plus 1 for left parentheses and minus 1 for right parentheses. When the count is 0, the occurrence of a comma indicates the end of a parameter. The character string has its leftmost and rightmost parentheses removed. This allows strings with embedded commas to be passed down through several levels of nested macros calls. For example,

```
MACRO
D          X
ADD        X
ADD        X
MEND
MACRO
DD         X,Y
D          X
D          Y
MEND
MACRO
D4         X,Y
DD         X
DD         Y
MEND
```

With these definitions,

```
D4         (A(1),B(1)),(C(2),D(4))
```

expands first as

```
DD         A(1),B(1)
DD         C(2),D(4)
```

where the outer layer of parentheses around the parameters has been stripped. Each of these now has two parameters, and both can be expanded to get

```
D          A(1)
D          B(1)
D          C(2)
D          D(4)
```

No parentheses are removed this time, as they are part of the parameters; they do not surround them. Similarly, each of the macros D is expanded without any parentheses removal.

It is common to allow unnecessary commas to be omitted so that the string can be shortened and, in some cases, given more symbolic meaning. Consider the example below:

```
MACRO
SIN        OP
OP
CALL       SIN
MEND
```

where SIN is assumed to be a subroutine which takes the SIN of the number in the accumulator of a one-address machine and returns the result there. Define a macro COS similarly, and a macro AC by

```
        MACRO
        AC
        MEND
```

which expands to nothing (this should be legitimate). Suppose we want to form SIN(SIN(COS(AC))) where AC is the number in the accumulator. This can be done with

```
        SIN          (SIN (COS (AC)))
```

The first expansion of this results in

```
        SIN          (COS (AC))
        CALL         SIN
```

The second in

```
        COS          (AC)
        CALL         SIN
        CALL         SIN
```

The third in

```
        AC
        CALL         COS
        CALL         SIN
        CALL         SIN
```

and the fourth in

```
        CALL         COS
        CALL         SIN
        CALL         SIN
```

which is the required result.

The 370 macro assembler uses an alternative scheme for handling *lists* as parameters in macros (i.e., a collection of parameters which is handled as a single parameter). They are treated as a *linear array* (similar to a one-dimensional array in Fortran or PL/I) and can be indexed; for example, it is possible to ask for the third or the nth. This means that the example above cannot be constructed quite as simply. However, macro assemblers as powerful as that on the 370 provide many more facilities for manipulating the character strings provided as macro parameters, so that the same result can be achieved. The complexity of the process is increased and the speed of the assembly reduced, but this is usually the price of increased flexibility. The next two sections will give an outline of some of these features.

4.4.3 Nested definition and conditional expansion

Many macro assemblers provide additional features such as nested definition, conditional expansion, and recursive definition. These features make the macro into a powerful tool because with its help, code tailored to the particular situation can be generated at translation time. Such tailor-made code executes more rapidly than a subroutine that must test at execution time to distinguish between the various cases.

Conditional expansion refers to tests that can be made at translation time to decide whether or not to insert lines of code into the expanded form. The conditional mechanism is a pseudo that can test conditions such as the type of parameters (are they numbers, etc.) and, on the basis of the result, can inhibit the expansion of the next line of code.

If nested definition is available, then it is possible for a macro definition to call itself. This will apparently lead to an infinite loop in the expansion process, but the conditional feature can be used to terminate the expansion.

If a macro definition occurs inside another definition, then it is possible to define macros by writing macro calls. For example,

```
        MACRO
        DEFINE      NAME
        MACRO
        NAME
        CALL        NAME
        MEND
        MEND
```

If the macro DEFINE SIN is written, then it expands to

```
        MACRO
        SIN
        CALL        SIN
        MEND
```

which serves to define a macro SIN.

It is impossible to discuss all the possible variations on the general theme of conditional expansion, so in this section we shall content ourselves with a discussion of the general ideas. A conditional expansion, as the name implies, is a method in which the expansion of part of a macro can be suppressed if certain conditions are met. This is useful in defining one macro to take care of several variants of basically the same program. The essential features of a conditional expansion assembler are the ability to test for given conditions on parameter names and the ability to skip over a number of lines in the definition without putting them into the expanded form. The latter can be provided by a pseudo such as

```
        SKIP        D
```

where D is a symbolic name. The assembler skips lines until it finds a line with the symbol D in the location field. The 370 assembler uses the pseudo AGO for skipping forward or backward to a symbol specified in the address field.

Condition testing can be performed by a pseudo such as IF. Existing assemblers have many forms of this pseudo, so the assembler manual must be consulted for the particular assembler used. A typical IF pseudo takes the form

```
        IF          A,COND,B,LOC
```

where A and B are address expressions, COND is a condition by which the two expressions will be compared, and LOC is a symbolic address. If the condition is met, then the assembler should skip to the first card containing LOC in its location field. In the 370, the equivalent pseudo is

```
        AIF         (A COND B)LOC
```

for forward and backward conditional skipping. Conditions which could be tested include string equality, inequality, numerical equality, numerically greater, etc. In the latter cases, the address expression must be purely numeric after all parameter substitution has been completed. As an example of the use of such a conditional expansion pseudo, suppose that we wish to construct a table of increasing powers of 2 ending at any particular value. We would like to call this macro POWER2 and give it one parameter which is the final value of the table entry. Suppose that an allowed condition in the IF pseudo is NUMEQU, standing for NUMerically EQUal. Then the macro

```
        MACRO
        POWER2      X
        IF          X/2,NUMEQU,0,A
        POWER2      X/2
A       MNOP
        ADDR        X
        MEND
```

is an elegant if inefficient way of achieving the result. [ADDR is presumed to be a pseudo which simply causes the address to be loaded as an integer, while MNOP (Macro No-OP) does not expand, so that A is not defined to the assembler]. This macro works as follows. If use of it is made by

POWER2   8

the expansion starts by reading the statements of the definition one at a time. The first statement asks if 8/2 is 0, which it is not, so the skip of one statement is not obeyed. Consequently the next statement, which is another call of POWER2, is obeyed with an address field of 8/2. (This is not evaluated as 4 because macro expansion is simply a string operation except when numerical evaluation is requested, as in a conditional pseudo.) The second level of expansion compares 8/2/2 with 0, which it is not, so again the macro is called, this time with a parameter value of 8/2/2. This process continues, with the macro being called with parameter values of 8/2/2/2 the next time.

During the expansion of the last call on POWER2, the comparison of 8/2/2/2/2 with 0 shows equality numerically, since, in integer division, the result of dividing 8 by 2 four times is 0. Hence, the IF causes a skip of one statement by the assembler. Consequently the pseudo ADDR, with the parameter in the top of the parameter value table, is assembled. This gives rise to

ADDR   8/2/2/2

which after assembly is a 1. Then control pops up, which returns to the next level of use of POWER2, causing an ADDR 8/2/2 to be generated. The complete result is the sequence

```
ADDR        8/2/2/2
ADDR        8/2/2
ADDR        8/2
ADDR        8
```

which is a table consisting of 1, 2, 4, and 8.

Another example of the use of conditional macros is given below. The problem is to create a macro COPY which has five parameters: the first an area of core, the second a preposition (either TO or FROM), the third the name of an auxiliary storage device, the fourth an area on it, and the fifth the length of the area. With this macro, the programmer can write instructions such as

```
COPY        A,TO,TAPE,5,B—A WORDS
COPY        1000,FROM,DRUM,23,500 WORDS
```

The last five characters follow a blank, so they are not part of the address field and are only added to the comment field for additional clarity. The macro definition for copy will have the form

```
            MACRO
            COPY        U,V,W,X,Y
            IF          W,NEQU,DRUM,S1
            IF          V,NEQU,TO,S2
            (Program to call for appropriate I/O tranfer from core to drum.)
            SKIP        END
S2          IF          V,NEQU,FROM,S3
            (Program to call for appropriate I/O transfer from drum to core.)
            SKIP        END
S3          WRONG
            SKIP        END
S1          IF          W,NEQU,TAPE,S4
            (Etc.)
END         MEND
```

The condition NEQU is presumed to be a string comparison for not equal. The result will be true (and the skip will occur) if the parameter provided is not identically equal, character by character, with the character string specified in the IF. The mnemonic WRONG need not be defined, since it will only occur in the expansion if the user does not make the second or third parameter one of the allowed words such as TO, FROM, DRUM, etc. If it does occur and it is undefined, it will cause an error to be listed by the assembler, which will indicate an error in the use of the macro.

In addition to strictly numerical addresses being used in the IF pseudo when numerical comparisons are to be made, there is no reason why symbolic addresses should not appear if they have already been defined. For example, it is quite reasonable to permit another pseudo which is similar to an EQU, except that it allows an existing entry to be modified if it is already defined. Let us use the mnemonic SETTO for this pseudo. The effect of

```
A           SETTO       A+1
```

is to increase the value of A as stored in the name table by 1. Features such as these can be combined with conditional expansion pseudos to provide additional flexibility. Since the mechanisms are so dependent on the particular assembler, details of the 370 and PDP-11 assemblers will be given in the next two sections.

4.4.4 370 macro assembler

The 370 macro assembler is the same in principle as the general form discussed except in the designation of parameters. All parameters must start with the character &. The format of the definition is slightly different. It is written as

```
                MACRO
&P              NAME        &P1,&P2, . . . ,&Pn
                LINE 1
                . . .
                LINE N
                MEND
```

The &P and &Pi are parameters which also appear in text. Thus a macro to extract bits N through M (N < M) of register R1 and place them in R2 could be written as

```
                MACRO
&P              BITS        &N,&M,&R1,&R2
&P              SLL         &R1,&N
                SRL         &R1,31−&M+&N
                LR          &R2,&R1
                MEND
```

The parameter &P is necessary if a location field address will be used when the macro BITS is used. If BITS is used by BITS 4,7,3,5, we get

```
        SLL         3,4
        SRL         3,31−7+4
        LR          5,3
```

Alternatively, keyword parameters can be used. BITS could be defined by

```
                MACRO
&P              BITS        &N = 0,&M = 31,&R1 = 0,&R2 = 0
                etc.
```

which defines the default conditions for the parameters as shown. If it is used by BITS N = 4,M = 7, we get

```
        SLL         0,4
        SRL         0,31−7+4
        LR          0,0
```

The parameters do not have to be specified in order.

The 370 macro assembler allows *positional* parameters (that is, the first type defined) and keyword parameters to be mixed. Positional parameters must be declared first. For example, BITS could also be defined by

```
                MACRO
&P              BITS        &N,&M,&R1=0,&R2=0
```

```
&P              . . .           etc.
                MEND
```

which requires the parameters &N and &M to be specified, but could get default values for &R1 and &R2. Thus

```
A               BITS            8,15,R2=4
```

would expand as

```
A               SLL             0,8
                SRL             0,31—15+8
                LR              4,0
```

Generated names can be handled in a number of ways. The system variable &SYSNDX is a 4-digit decimal number whose value starts at 0001 and is incremented by 1 for each expansion. Items can be concatenated by the use of a period character, although a parameter can be concatenated after anything else without a period because the & character makes the start of the parameter obvious. Thus, X&SYSNDX can be recognized as X concatenated with the 4-digit value of SYSNDX, and a period must not be present because X.&SYSNDX would expand as X.0025 if this were the twenty-fifth macro expansion. However, a period is needed when a parameter is concatenated with an alphanumeric character. Thus &PQRS is the parameter &PQRS, whereas &PQR.S is the parameter &PQR concatenated with the character S. If the value of &PQR is AC, then &PQR.S has the value ACS. For example,

```
                MACRO
&R              MIN             &A,&B,&C,&T=,&R0=0,&R2=2
&R              L&T             &R0,&A          Load first operand.
                L&T             &R2,&B          Load second operand.
                C&T.R           &R0,&R2         Compare both.
                BL              M&SYSNDX        Branch if first low.
                ST&T            &R2,&C          Store second.
                B               M&SYSNDX+4
M&SYSNDX        ST&T            &R0,&C          Store first.
                MEND
```

Use of this by MIN P,Q,R will generate the code

```
                L               0,P
                L               2,Q
                CR              0,2
                BL              M0032
                ST              2,R
                B               M0032+4
M0032           ST              0,R
```

if this is the thirty-second macro to be expanded, whereas MIN X,Y,W,T=D expands to

```
         LD        0,X
         LD        2,Y
         CDR       0,2
         BL        M0033
         STD       2,W
         B         M0033+4
M0033    STD       0,W
```

The string C&T.R is the concatenation of C with the parameter &T and the character R. When T takes its default value of a *null string* (no characters), C&T.R expands to CR, but when &T is given a value of D it expands to CDR (compare double-precision floating-point register-register).

Nested calls of macros are allowed in the 370 assembler, but nested definitions are not. When parameters are passed down through nested calls, parentheses are not stripped off as was discussed earlier. This must be done using the string manipulation facilities provided. (The assembler manual should be referred to for details.) Parentheses around lists of parameters are used for another, more powerful facility—the ability to index through a list. If &S is a parameter in a macro and is specified by the list (A,B,C,D), then &S(n) refers to the nth item in the list. Thus &S(2) would have the value B in this case.

Conditionals allow very elaborate tests to be performed. Some of these are illustrated by the example below. This example also uses "set" variables or symbols. These variables look like macro parameters, but must be declared in a LCL (LoCaL) or GBL (GloBaL) statement. There are three of each type of statement, ending in A for arithmetic, B for Boolean, and C for character string. A local arithmetic set symbol is one which has a numeric value during the course of the current macro expansion only. It "disappears" when the macro is ended. A global character set symbol is one whose value is a character string, and whose value is available throughout the assembly once it has been declared. For example,

```
         GBLA       &D,&T
```

declares &D and &T to be arithmetic set symbols for the rest of the assembly. Once defined, local or global set symbols can be assigned new values by the SETA, SETB, or SETC pseudos. Thus

```
&D       SETA       4
&T       SETA       2*&D
&D       SETA       &T+&D
```

are valid (if not entirely useful).

Example

This example is a macro that constructs a table of character strings and an access table which stores their addresses and lengths. We want to be able to write

TAB	TABLE	('xxx. .x','yyy. . .y', ...)

where the parameter list is a set of character strings. From this we would like to form the following tables:

	DC	0F	Get on a word boundary.
TAB	DC	AL1(nx),AL3(ax)	Length and address of each string.
	DC	AL1(ny),AL3(ay)	
	. . .		Repeat for each string.
	DC	C'xxx. . .x'	First string.
	DC	C'yyy. . .y'	Second string.
	. . .		Repeat for each string.

AL1(nx) assembles a 1-byte address (address of length 1) whose value is nx. In this case nx should be the number of characters in the string xxx. . .x. AL3(ax) is a 3-byte address which should be the address of the first byte of the string xxx. . .x. To avoid generating location symbols, an address of the form "$*+n$" will be used, where * is the name of the assembler location counter. Remember that if TAB is location 1244, then * in

TAB	DC	AL1(3),AL3(*+15)

will be 1245 since the location counter has already been advanced by 1 for the AL1 construction before assembly is started on the AL3 construction.

A definition of TABLE is given below. The lines are numbered for reference in the text that follows.

		MACRO		
1	&P	TABLE	&A	
2		LCLC	&C	Declarations must appear
3		LCLA	&N,&T,&M,&S	first in a macro definition.
4	&M	SETA	N'&A	Number of parameters in list.
5	&T	SETA	4*&M−1	Displacement to string.
6	&N	SETA	1	Running count.
7		DS	0F	Get on word boundary.
8	&C	SETC	'&P'	Address of table.
9	.LOOP1	ANOP		
10	&S	SETA	K'&A(&N)−2	
11	&C	DC	AL1(&S),AL3(*+&T)	
12	&C	SETC	"	Blank future location fields.
13	&T	SETA	&S−4+&T	Update displacement.
14	&N	SETA	&N+1	Increment N.
15		AIF	(&N LE &M).LOOP1	Loop through all parameters.

16	&N	SETA	1	Running count.
17	.LOOP2	ANOP		
18		DC	C&A(&N)	Character string.
19	&N	SETA	&N+1	Increment count.
20		AIF	(&N LE &M).LOOP2	Loop through all parameters.
		MEND		

Line 1 declares the macro to have one parameter, although it is expected to be a list. Lines 2 and 3 declare set symbols. &C will initially be assigned the value &P. This is to appear on the first line generated. Then &C will be set to a null string so that future lines will not contain the value &P. &N will be used for a counter which runs from 1 to the number of strings in the sublist. That number will be carried in &M. Line 4 assigns &M a value, using the construction N'parameter. This has a value equal to the number of items in the parameter. If the parameter is a sublist, this gives the number of elements, in this case the number of character strings, on that sublist. &T is going to be used to compute the displacement in the address field AL3(*+displacement). The first displacement is known to be 4*&M—1 since there will be &M 4-byte words in the first part of the table, but the first AL3 construction will be 1 byte beyond the beginning of the table. Line 6 initializes &N. Finally, in line 7, some code is generated. This gets the alignment on a word boundary. Line 8 initializes &C. Line 9 introduces a new element of the language, called a *sequence symbol*. It is a symbol preceded by a period, and it is used as the "branch address" in the AIF and AGO pseudos, such as that in line 15. A sequence symbol is not expanded; it provides information to the macro processor. In this case, a line to put it on is needed so the ANOP pseudo is used. This is not expanded either, so no code is generated by line 9. Line 10 sets &S to the length of the next character string, using the construction K'&A(&N)—2. This will be examined in pieces. &A(&N) says to select the &Nth item in the sublist specified for parameter &A. Since &N was initially set to 1, the first time through the first item on the list will be selected. For example, if the macro is used as TABLE ('ABC', '123'), the value of &A(&N) would be 'ABC' when &N is 1. The prefix K' stands for *count* and has a value equal to the number of characters in the parameter, in this case 5 (both quotes are counted). Two is subtracted from this value to get the number of characters in the string, namely three. Line 11 is a table entry using a 1-byte and a 3-byte address field. The first byte is set to the value of &S. The 3-byte address in AL3 is specified as *+&T. This is expanded to *+n where n is the decimal representation of the current value of &T. The DC has a location field equal to the value of &C, which was initialized to &P, the location specified in the macro use. Line 12 resets &C to the null string so that future expansions of line 11 in this use of the macro will contain a blank. Line 13 updates the displacement &T by adding the length of the character string, which is &S, and subtracting 4.

The length is added because the next string will be that many characters further on in memory, and 4 is subtracted because the next word containing the address of the string will be 4 bytes further on. Line 14 increments &N by 1 in order to deal with the next item on the sublist &A, and line 15 uses a conditional AIF. If the condition, that &N is less than or equal to &M, is met, the macro expander returns to the card with the sequence symbol .LOOP1 in the location field. This is line 9. Consequently a simple loop is executed (expanded) for &N between 1 and the number of entries in the sublist &A. One DC is generated for each entry. Line 16 resets &N back to 1, and then lines 17 to 20 form another simple loop which generates DC Cxxxx pseudos, where each succeeding xxxx takes on the value of successive elements in the sublist &A. Use of the macro in the following way:

```
T23          TABLE          ('WRE T','123456789','=')
```

generates the code

```
             DS             0F
T23          DC             AL1(5),AL3(*+11)
             DC             AL1(9),AL3(*+12)
             DC             AL1(1).AL3(*+17)
             DC             C'WRE T'
             DC             C'123456789'
             DC             C'='
```

If this is assembled starting at byte location 1200, the pattern shown below results.

LOCATION	BYTE 1	BYTE 2	BYTE 3	BYTE 4
1200–1203	5	1212		
1204–1207	9	1217		
1208–1211	1	1226		
1212–1215	W	R	E	blank
1216–1219	T	1	2	3
1220–1223	4	5	6	7
1224–1227	8	9	=	

CHARACTERS

Location 1227 is the next available for loading. As can be seen, the address in the right-hand 3 bytes of the first set of words is the address of the start of the character string associated with that word, while the left-hand byte contains the length of the string. (This is called an *access table,* or *directory,* and is a common way of handling variable-length character strings. If the *j*th character string is needed, the word in location T23 + 4*j* contains information which allows us to access the string directly.)

4.4.5 PDP-11 macro assembler

The PDP-11 macro assembler uses the definition format

```
.MACRO      name, arg1,arg2, . . . ,argn
LINE 1
LINE 2
. . .
LINE N
.ENDM
```

If desired, the name of the macro can appear in the address field of the .ENDM macro. This is a checking feature, as it allows the assembler to detect when the .MACRO and .ENDM statements are not properly paired. The name of the macro is the first element in the address field. The remaining elements are the arguments of the macro. They are usually separated by a comma, although the PDP-11 assembler accepts spaces and some other characters as separators for elements of the address field of any instruction or pseudo. For example, we could define a macro to call subroutine INTG with two arguments A and B by

```
.MACRO      INTG A,B
JSR         R5,INTG
.WORD       A,B
.ENDM       INTG
```

Writing

```
INTG        P+3,R44
```

is equivalent to

```
JSR         R5,INTG
.WORD       P+3,R44
```

The PDP-11 assembler provides *local symbols* which function as symbolic addresses with a restricted range. Local symbols have the form $n\$$, where n is a decimal integer between 1 and 127. The macro assembler can generate local symbols between 64$ and 127$, but the programmer is free to use any of them. The range of a local symbol extends from the preceding to the following instruction or pseudo which has a location field symbol. Any local symbol defined within that range can be referenced in that range. This means that the same symbol can be reused in another range. For example, the first branch in the program below is to the first line labeled 1$, while the second branch is to the second line, labeled 1$.

```
            MOV        R1,R2
1$:         ADD        A,R2
            BMI        1$
OUT         ADD        B,R1
1$:         SUB        C,R2
            BPL        1$
```

The local symbols can be used for branches within macros. If, in the macro definition, the parameter is preceded by a ? in the first line, and it is not specified in the use of the macro, the next local symbol is created. For example,

```
            .MACRO     MAX A,B,C,?D,?E
            CMP        A,B
            BLT        D
            MOV        A,C
            BR         E
D:          MOV        B,C
E:          .ENDM
```

Writing

```
            MAX        P,Q,R1
```

is equivalent to

```
            CMP        P,Q
            BLT        64$
            MOV        P,R1
            BR         65$
64$:        MOV        Q,R1
65$:
```

(Note that as many location field symbols as desired can be prefixed to a line in the PDP-11 assembler. For example,

```
RE: WTRE: D1:
D2:         ADD        R1,R2
```

is valid, and defines the four addresses RE, WTRE, D1, and D2 all to have the same value, that of the address of the ADD instruction.)

Local symbols can be dangerous, since there can be a conflict if no symbols are defined between two uses of the same local symbol. An alternative scheme is to use the assignment facility and the backslash operator /.

Assignment is written in a Fortran-like fashion as

D2 = expression

where the rules for address expression evaluation are followed to get a value for the right-hand side. This value is then assigned to the symbolic address D2, that is, future uses of D2 will assemble as that address value. Thus

```
D2 = 3
MOV        #D,R2
```

puts 3 in R2 because it assembles as

```
MOV        #3,R2
```

However, D2 may be assigned another value later in the assembly. For example,

```
.MACRO     UP B
B = B+1
.ENDM
```

will increase B by 1 each time UP B is written. Thus

```
A = 0
UP         A
UP         A
UP         A
```

sets the equivalent value of A to 3.

The backslash operator preceding a macro argument converts that argument to a number in the current radix. Thus if the current value of B is 13, \B is equivalent to the string '13'. We could rewrite the MAX macro given earlier as

```
           .MACRO     MXX A,B,C,D
           CMP        A,B
           BLT        M'D
           MOV        A,C
           BR         MA'D
M'D:       MOV        B,C
MA'D:
           .ENDM
           .MACRO     MAX A,B,C
           MXX        A,B,C, \COUNT
COUNT = COUNT + 1
           .ENDM
```

Initially COUNT would have to be set to 0 by writing

COUNT = 0

After that, each use of MAX would increase COUNT by 1 and pass an equivalent numeric string to the macro MXX for the parameter D. The quote sign is used to separate otherwise indistinguishable parameters and symbols, so it performs a concatenation. Hence M'D is the concatenation of the character M with the parameter D. The first use of MAX would generate addresses M0 and MA0, the next use M1 and MA1, and so on.

As can be seen from the above example, nested calls are allowed in the PDP-11 macro assembler. If a list of parameters is to be passed as a single parameter, the angle brackets $<$ and $>$ are used. A pair is stripped off when the parameter substitution is made, as discussed in Section 4.4.2. For example,

```
.MACRO      S A,B
JSR         R5,A
.WORD       B
.ENDM
```

allows us to write a subroutine call to READ, say, as

```
S           READ,<BUF,EOF>
```

and get the expansion

```
JSR         R5,READ
.WORD       BUF,EOF
```

Nested definitions as discussed in Section 4.4.3 are also allowed in the PDP-11 assembler. Conditional assembly is available both inside a macro definition and outside. The basic form of a conditional assembly block is

```
.IF         Cond,argument(s).
...         Block of code.
.ENDC
```

If the condition is satisfied by the argument(s), the block of code is assembled; otherwise it is skipped. The conditions include test on the value of expressions (<0, 0, or >0), whether symbolic addresses have been defined previously, whether or not macro arguments are equal, and whether or not macro arguments are blank. Other features include a repeat block, which allows a section of code to be expanded repeatedly with different values of a single argument, and system variables, which give the number of parameters or characters in an argument list. These are illustrated in an example below. In this example, macros are to be defined so that if SUBC is the name of a subroutine, writing

```
        SUBC        <A,B, . . . ,R>
```

will give the expansion

```
        JSR         R5,SUBC
        .WORD       N
        .WORD       A
        .WORD       B
        . . .
        .WORD       R
```

where N is the number of arguments A, B, etc. If, however,

```
        SUBC
```

is written, the desired result is

```
        JSR         R7,SUBC
```

One such macro definition is DEFINE, given below. It uses both a nested definition and a nested call. Writing

```
        DEFINE      SUBC
```

will expand to a macro definition for SUBC. DEFINE is the macro.

1	.MACRO	DEFINE NAME	
2	.MACRO	NAME A	;Nested definition of NAME.
3	.IF	B,<A>	;B stands for blank. If the ;parameter A is blank, the following ;code is assembled. If not, it is ;skipped.
4	JSR	R7,NAME	;Code for no parameter case.
5	.IFF		;.IFF is a *subconditional.* If the ;earlier condition was false (A not ;blank), the following code is ;assembled.
6	JSR	R5,NAME	;Code for case with parameters.
7	NUM	A	;Nested call of macro NUM. This ;sets N to be the number of ;parameters in the list A.
8	.WORD	N	
9	.IRP	Q,<A>	;.IRP stands for indefinite repeat. ;The code to the next .ENDM is ;repeatedly expanded, with Q taking ;each value from the list A in turn.
10	.WORD	Q	;Parameter for subroutine.
11	.ENDM		;End of .IRP block.
12	.ENDC		;End of .IF block.
13	.ENDM	NAME	;End of nested definition.
14	.ENDM	DEFINE	;End of macro DEFINE.
15	.MACRO	NUM A,B,C,D,E,F	;See text for comment on parameters.

16	.NARG	N	;Sets N to the number of arguments
			;passed to the macro.
17	.ENDM	NUM	;End of macro NUM.

If the macro SUBC is defined by DEFINE SUBC, then it can be written

SUBC   <W1,W5,R>

The macro for SUBC is obtained from lines 2 to 13 above, with NAME replaced by SUBC. The parameter A is replaced by the string W1, W5, R. Note that the angle brackets have been stripped. Since A is not blank, line 4 is skipped. The .IFF in line 5 causes lines 6 to 11 to be assembled. Line 7 uses the macro NUM to find the number of arguments in the list A. NUM is defined in lines 15 to 17. It uses the pseudo .NARG to set the number of arguments into the variable N. (Note that the number is limited to 6, as .NARG will not return a value larger than the number of arguments in the definition. The only way around this is to count the arguments in an IRP loop, to be described below.) Line 8 assembles .WORD N, then lines 9 through 11 form a loop which is expanded repeatedly under the control of the .IRP pseudo. Each pass through the loop assigns a value from the list A to the variable Q. Thus, if A is W1, W5,R the loop will be traversed three times, with Q taking the values W1, W5, and R on successive passes. This causes .WORD Q to be expanded three times with the appropriate addresses. Consequently, the expansion of

```
DEFINE      SUBC
SUBC        <W1,W5,R>
```

causes the code

```
JSR         R5,SUBC
.WORD       3
.WORD       W1
.WORD       5
.WORD       R
```

to be assembled.

PROBLEMS

1   A loop consists of three main parts, the initialization, the body of the loop where the work is done, and the incrementing and end testing. In the discussion, we assumed that they were written in that order. If the loop is to be executed N times where N is a program variable, and N may take a value as small as 0, how should the loop be organized?

2   What are the four items of information necessary to control a program loop?

3 Methods suggested for a subroutine to pick up its parameter addresses included using indirect addressing or moving copies of the variable from the main program storage to storage associated with the subroutine. An example of the former was given in Section 4.3.1. The latter would give the start of a subroutine the appearance

```
LOAD       *0(5)
STORE      T1
LOAD       *1(5)
STORE      T2
LOAD       *2(5)
STORE      T3
```

etc., where index 5 is assumed to contain the link.

From then on, all references to the first parameter would use T1, the second T2, and so on. A copy back in the other direction is needed at the end of the subroutine.

Consider the effect of using each method in the following calls on the subroutine defined in Fortran as

```
SUBROUTINE EXAM(A,B,C,D)
A = B + C
B = B + D
RETURN
END
```

a CALL EXAM(X,X,Y,Z)
b CALL EXAM(P,Q,3.,4.)
c CALL EXAM(1.,1.,2.,1.)

4 Suppose that the following definitions have been made:

```
MACRO
P          X,Y,Z
LEFT       2
X          Y,Z,Z,
MEND
MACRO
Q          X,Y,Z
LEFT       1
X          Y
MEND
MACRO
R          X,Y,Z
LOAD       A
X          Y,Z,Z
MEND
```

What is the result of expanding the following:

   a R   ADD,A,1

b	R	Q,STORE,B
c	R	P,Q,STORE
d	R	P,P,P

5 Propose a set of conventions for parameter transmittal to subroutines such that call by name or by value can be handled within the subroutine. Indicate how the following types of parameters should be handled: (a) constant, (b) variable name, (c) array name, (d) subroutine name, and (e) expression. Discuss the relative merits of always providing a subroutine to get the parameter versus using type codes along with the parameter address.

6 What are the contents of registers 2 through 7 when the following 370 program has been executed? (Note that JCL control cards are not indicated.)

START	L	7,D
	LA	1,LIST
	L	15,VSUB
	BALR	14,15
	L	2,LIST
	L	3,LIST + 4
	LM	4,7,A
	(end of program execution)	
LIST	DC	A(A),A(B)
A	DC	F'78'
B	DC	F'13'
C	DC	F'34'
D	DC	F'17'
VSUB	DC	V(SUB)
. . . .		
SUB	CSECT	
	L	7,4(1)
	L	8,8(7)
	ST	8,4(7)
	L	9,0(1)
	L	4,4(9)
	ST	4,0(1)
	BR	14

7 Write an IBM 370 assembler macro called MOVE which will move N words (32-bit, word aligned) from locations A through $A + 4N - 4$ to locations B through $B + 4N - 4$. N,A and B should be parameters. N may be as large as 8,192. Write a shorter macro which will work for N less than 65.

8 Examine the example of the macro TABLE in Section 4.4.4 (page 203). What happens if the following use of TABLE is made?

T	TABLE	'123,456'

Assume that N'&A is 1 if the parameter &A is given but is not a sublist, and that &A(1) is the parameter itself if &A is not a sublist.

9 Write an IBM 370 macro such that

```
T            CALL         NAME,(P1,XXX,P3,=F'45')
```

would expand to

```
T            L            15,=V(NAME)      Subroutine name.
             LA           1,CL0001         (Or some other number.)
             BALR         14,15            Branch to subroutine.
             B            CL0001+16        Note this skips parameter list.
             DS           0F               Get on word boundary.
CL0001       DC           A(P1)
             DC           A(XXX)
             DC           A(P3)
             DC           X'80',AL3(=F'45')
```

(The last parameter has its sign bit set. Otherwise the parameters are simply copied into the address fields of the DC.) This can be handled using the macro assembler features covered in the example of TABLE in Section 4.4.4.

10   Modify the above macro so that if

```
        CALL         NAME
```

is written (that is, no parameters), then the expansion

```
        L            15,V(NAME)
        BALR         14,15
```

results, but if parameters are given, the previous expansion still occurs. Note that if &P is empty, then N'&P is 0.

11   Write an IBM 370 macro TENTAB such that

```
P            TENTAB       2,5
```

expands to a set of four single-precision floating-point numbers whose values are 10^2, 10^3, 10^4, and 10^5, respectively. P should be the address of the last. If the parameters are specified as M and N (TENTAB M,N), then the table should run from 10^N to 10^M. If M is less than N, no table should be generated.

(Note that a floating-point single-precision number can be defined by

```
        DC           E'3.45E17'
```

where the quantity inside the quotes is any Fortran-like floating-point number.)

12   Consider the example of macro SUBC in Section 4.4.5 (page 210). What happens if we write

SUBC   X,12

13   The auto-increment and auto-decrement address constructs in the PDP-11 can be used to simulate stack machines. For example, assume that R4 contains the address of the top word in the stack, and that lower levels are in increasing memory addresses, that is, the second level is in 2(R4), and so on. Then the equivalent of the stack load instruction LOAD X is the PDP-11 instruction

MOV   X,−(R4)

What are the equivalents of the stack instructions STORE Y, ADD, and SUB? How should the parameters of subroutines MPY and DIV be passed for convenience if simulating a stack machine is desired? Define some macros that allow us to code in stack machine language.

14   Write a PDP-11 macro ACTB such that

ACTB   <PDP,TRW,IBM,1234567,H>

will expand to

```
.WORD        .+12
.WORD        .+13
.WORD        .+14
.WORD        .+15
.WORD        .+22
.ASCII       /PDP/
.ASCII       /TRW/
.ASCII       /IBM/
.ASCII       /1234567/
.ASCII       /H/
```

The first group of WORDs contain the addresses of the corresponding group of character strings. (Remember that addresses are given in octal.) Thus the address of the fifth string is in the fifth word and is 22 octal bytes beyond the start of the fifth word. The character strings can be assumed to contain only alphanumeric characters. In addition to the macro features used in the example SUBC on page 210,

.NCHR   N,string;

will be needed, where string is any string not containing separators. It sets N to the number of characters in the string.

5

INPUT, OUTPUT, AND AUXILIARY STORAGE DEVICES

The function of a computer system is to process information. We have seen how this is done using the memory and processor units. The computer system must also be able to transmit information between itself and its environment. The information to be processed must be input to the system, and the results must be output back to the external world. The computer may be in one of various different environments which affect the type of input/output communication required. In the most familiar systems, the computer primarily communicates with humans who prepare the problem for solution, provide the initial data, and wish to interpret the answers. In other applications, the input can be directly from a physical device. Complex experiments in the physical sciences can be measured automatically by computer. In such a case, the principal inputs to the computer are digital readings taken directly from the various instruments used to monitor the experiment. In other applications, both input and output may connect directly to mechanical or electrical equipment. For example, an airborne computer may be used to calculate the position of the plane at any instant (by use of inputs from gyroscopes and other inertial devices), to compare this position with the desired flight path derived by computation, and then to output correction signals to the control mechanisms of the aircraft. Computers for online instrumentation and process control applications are usually smaller and more specialized than the general-purpose computers that we have been discussing. In this chapter, we shall discuss the input/output that is common to the general-purpose systems. However, the principles involved do not differ from those in online computers.

The general-purpose computer may need to communicate either directly with the user or with a computer-readable medium. The former will be referred to as *input/output,* whereas the latter will be called *auxiliary storage,* since the information is not yet "out" of its computer representation. Auxiliary storage is also called *backup storage.* Auxiliary storage can be used to transmit data to another computer either immediately or at a later time. Immediate transfer can only be accomplished by a direct data connection between two computers. With a direct data connection, each computer looks like an auxiliary storage device to the other. This sort of connection is frequently used between small special-purpose control computers and large general-purpose computers. Delayed transfers are achieved by first storing the information on a machine-readable medium, such as magnetic tape (discussed below), and then transferring the storage medium to the other machine. An important application of this storage is for transferring the information back to the machine that originally wrote it. This provides a mechanism for storing large amount of data for a long period of time without using the expensive main memory. We shall see that some devices have the ability to store information on a medium that can be physically moved from one computer to another, while others do not. This could form one basis for classifying auxiliary storage. Input/output would always fall into the former category. Devices also differ in their speeds and capacities, and this forms another basis for classification which we shall use below. We shall refer to long-term storage devices, which are frequently used to save information over long periods of time, and to medium-term storage devices, which are frequently used to save information from one short computer run to another, for additional storage during a single execution of a program, and to provide rapid access to frequently used system programs. Generally speaking, higher-speed devices have less capacity and are less likely to have removable storage media.

The next four sections will discuss the characteristics of various devices used for input/output and auxiliary storage. Chapter 6 will discuss the ways in which input/output and auxiliary storage devices are controlled by program instruction, and the remainder of that chapter will be devoted to a survey of the software systems of increasing complexity that can be provided for input/output and auxiliary storage access. When speeds and capacities of storage media are given, they are typical figures for large general-purpose installations. Lower numbers are always possible and somewhat greater numbers can be achieved, but they are expensive and technically difficult.

5.1 INPUT/OUTPUT DEVICES

Input/output devices are of two basic types: the *hard-copy* devices which are principally used in an *offline* mode such that the user does not have to be present at the computer at run time; and non-hard-copy devices, which present the output directly to the user in a nonpermanent form or read the input directly as a result of some action by the user, such as typing.

5.1.1 Punched cards

The most common form of input and output is the punched card. The card is a rectangle of heavy card stock (usually about 7½ inches by 3¼ inches) that can be punched with a hole in any one of 960 positions on a 12 by 80 rectangular array of positions. Other sizes of cards—with 51 or 90 columns instead of the 80 columns mentioned above—are in use, but the 80-column card is the most common. Punched cards were used for machine control in the weaving industry long before they were used in data processing. The first major application of punched cards to data handling occurred during the late 1800s, when Herman Hollerith adapted them for use in the 1890 census. Because of his work, the cards are called *Hollerith cards,* and one way in which they are punched is called the *Hollerith card code.* This code is a means of representing alphanumeric data (that is, the alphabetic letters and the 10 decimal digits) and a few special characters such as period, comma, etc. One column is used to represent each character, so that up to 80 characters can be punched on one card. As shown in Figure 5.1, the card rows are labeled 12, 11, 0, 1, 2, 3, 4, 5, 6, 7, 8, and 9. A blank character or space is represented as no holes punched, the numerical digits 0 through 9 by a punch in the corresponding row, and the letters by double punches. A through I are represented by a 12-row punch together with a digit punch from 1 to 9 respectively, J through R by an 11-row punch with the digit 1 through 9 respectively, and S through Z by a 0-row punch with the digit 2 through 9 respectively. Other characters are represented by other combinations of punched holes.

When a card written in this format is read into the machine, it is converted into a string of characters in memory in a suitable code. If the standard 48-character set is used, then only 6 bits are needed to represent 48 characters. Therefore one of the 6-bit codes, such as the BCD code, can be used. This conversion is usually done by hardware, so that the programmer does not have to concern himself with the Hollerith code. In recent machines, such as the IBM 370, the EBCIDIC code is used. This allows for up to 256 characters requiring 8 bits per character.

Each column of the card can contain up to 12 punches, for a total of $2^{12} = 4{,}096$ different combinations. However, less than 64 of these are used in the usual card codes. To combat this inefficiency, the binary card is often used when the desire is to get as much information on the card as possible rather than to make it as legible as possible. The binary card can be punched in any position, so that any column can contain 12 bits of information. If a binary

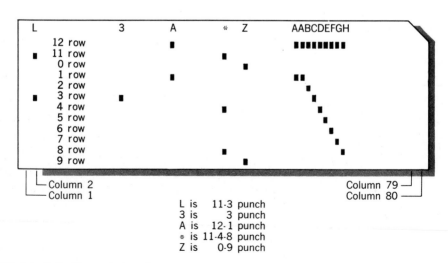

FIGURE 5.1   Hollerith punched card

card is read into the computer, each column is mapped in a direct manner into 12 bits of memory, and vice versa on output punching. Since cards so punched are not readable by most printing equipment, this use of cards is solely for storage of information to be read back in at a later stage. It is very common, for example, to store programs on binary cards after they have been translated by the machine (to avoid having to retranslate them). If the EBCDIC code is used in the computer, there exists a mapping from 8-bit bytes to com- binations of punches in a single column. Since 8 of the 12 bits of informa- tion are being used, the IBM 370 uses this code for storing binary information rather than provide a special set of instructions for handling binary cards. Cards can be read at speeds in the range of 1,000 to 2,000 per minute and punched at speeds of 200 to 400 per minute. Because cards are prone to error, the card reader usually reads each card twice to check for reading errors, and the punches usually also read the punched result to perform similar checking.

5.1.2 Punched paper tape

Punched paper tape is very similar to punched cards in that it consists of a heavy paper stock in which information is represented by the presence or absence of punched holes. It differs from cards in that paper tape is in con- tinuous strips of arbitrary lengths, whereas cards are a fixed size. Tape is commonly used in three different widths containing five, seven, or eight possible information-hole positions across the tape. Each of these positions is called a *channel*. A 1-inch eight-channel tape is shown in Figure 5.2. Notice that, in addition to the eight information positions or channels, there is a ninth position that is always punched with a sprocket hole. This is to lo- cate the position where the information should appear along the tape. Without this sprocket hole, a series of characters consisting of no punched holes

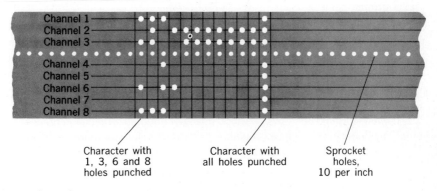

FIGURE 5.2   Paper tape

would lead to a strip of completely blank tape. It would then be impossible to tell how many characters there were in such a string except by measuring the length of the tape, a procedure which would be very prone to error. The sprocket hole is also used to mesh with a sprocket gear on the slower mechanical readers. Since paper tape is prone to error, it is very common to use one of the information channels as a parity bit for the other information channels.

Systems that use paper tape as the primary input to the computer tend to differ from systems designed around cards because of the property that paper tape is continuous. Paper tape is not typically used in the higher-speed installations because it is impractical to join tapes together to make continuous input from one user to the next possible. Secondly, it is more cumbersome to change a paper tape, since the complete strip must be duplicated with the change inserted at the appropriate point. With cards, on the other hand, only the offending cards need be changed. Therefore, in a paper-tape system, the basic input programs should allow the user the ability to follow the initial input with correction tapes which modify a copy of the input internally. In general, paper tape is cheaper (both in terms of the cost of the reading and punching equipment and in terms of the cost of the paper itself) than cards, and hence tends to be used on the small low-speed systems which are becoming very common in special-purpose control applications. Paper tape can be read at speeds of 1,000 to 2,000 characters per second and punched at 300 characters per second.

5.1.3 Printing devices

The most acceptable form of output for general-purpose use is generated by a printer. A large part of the output from a computer consists of numeric and alphabetic informations which will be read by the user. Printers are devices for converting the internal character representation in the memory to the printed page. Although there is no difference in the end result, printers are classified into two basic types because of the great difference in speeds between the two. The *line printer* is a device which prints a line at a time. The computer transmits a complete line of information to the printer unit, and then it is printed. A printing mechanism exists at every print position across the line, which can vary in width from 80 characters to 150 characters in common printers. Because of the parallelism present in such a printer, it can achieve speeds of 1,000 to 2,000 lines per minute by mechanical means. Non-mechanical printing techniques (photographic, for example) can achieve even higher speeds (up to 30,000 lines per minute).

The character printer is similar to a typewriter — in fact, it is very often a modified typewriter which can be controlled by the computer. Since it only prints a character at a time across the line, it is relatively slow, of the order of 10 to 100 characters per second. (Incidentally, the reader might notice that the heavily commercial devices are usually quoted in operations per minute. The numbers are larger.)

5.1.4 Keyboard input

The other half of the typewriter mechanism used for low-speed output, the keyboard, can be used for input. Since this is at human speeds (usually about 2 characters per second and limited mechanically to about 15 characters per second) a keyboard is not an economical input for a fast computer unless its use is for rare events, and its input can be overlapped with the processing of useful work. It is frequently used for small machines as a primary input device so that the programmer types part of his program in directly, rather than typing it first on paper tape and then reading the paper tape. For example, he might make corrections to his program *online*. This type of use is now possible on larger systems by time-sharing techniques, where many keyboards are serviced in parallel to increase the data rate of input to a reasonable total level.

Two basic typewriter devices are in common use today. One is based on the IBM Selectric "golf ball" typewriter, and is marketed as the 2741. The other is based on the Teletype mechanisms. The Teletype Model 35 is a typewriter with numbers, special characters, and uppercase letters only, designed for easy interface to a communication system such as the telephone network. It is now available with lowercase letters as the Model 37. The Model 33 is a low-cost version of the 35. They all use the ASCII code. The IBM 2741 is designed to communicate with equipment using BCD or EBCDIC codes.

5.1.5 Plotters and display devices

Although printer output is very convenient for many purposes, frequently the user needs to present the information graphically in order to be able to understand its significance. This may be in the form of a simple graph plotting one variable against another, or it may be a complex pictorial display representing a multidimensional item. For example, three-dimensional pictures are frequently represented by two-dimensional contour maps, where lines represent the paths of constancy in the third dimension (weather maps, for example, in which the contours of constant pressure are drawn to indicate the high-pressure and low-pressure regions).

If graphs have to be prepared by hand from numerical output by the computer, a large amount of output is typically needed and time-consuming drawing must be undertaken by the human. Therefore, direct graphical output devices have been developed for computer use. There are two basic types of output device, one which allows the user to put a point at any location on the output *page,* and one which allows the user to move a *pen* in any direction a given distance, with the pen either on the paper making a mark or off the paper not making a mark. The words *pen* and *paper* are not meant literally, in that the output could be on any medium which can be marked. In many devices, the two basic techniques are both available, but it is convenient to examine them separately.

The *incremental plotter* is an example of the second form of output. It is a device with a pen and a large sheet of paper. The pen can be moved a small increment in any one of several directions. In a typical plotter, it can move in any one of the eight directions separated by 45 degrees a distance of 0.005 inches vertically or horizontally, or 0.007 inches in any of the four 45-degree directions. All lines must be made up of these short, straight-line segments. The computer commands the plotter with a series of characters to make each basic plot step. The use of a plotter to draw a 45-degree triangle lying on its hypotenuse is shown in Figure 5.3. The computer subroutine library will usually contain subroutines to simplify the use of the plotter. A common package of subroutines for a plotter allows the user to move the pen from where it is currently to any given position on the page with the pen either writing or not, to draw many of the common curves such as ellipses, and to print letters and numbers on the page. The subroutines convert the demands of the user into sequences of the basic steps for the plotter. The time to plot a figure is depen-

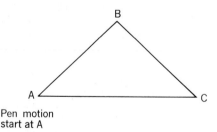

Pen motion
start at A

　　Pen down
　　Move up, right (100 steps)
　　Move down, right (100 steps)
　　Move left (200 steps)
　　Pen up

FIGURE 5.3　*Plotting a triangle*

dent on the linear distance that the pen moves. The speed is of the order of 1 to 10 inches per second.

The cathode-ray-tube output device basically allows the user to illuminate spots on the face of the CRT by specifying X and Y coordinates to the output device. With such a device, a line must be built up from many small points. Typically about 500 to 4,000 points can be displayed in each direction, and adjacent points are sufficiently close that they are joined together as far as the eye can see. Often CRT displays have built-in *vector* and *character* facilities which allow them to generate straight lines and standard characters directly. This serves to decrease the computer time needed to generate a display, but not to increase the flexibility of the display from the user's point of view. The basic operations are used by subroutines to provide the same facilities as are available for the plotter. An important additional facility available with a cathode-ray tube is the *light pen.* This is a photoelectric device, shaped like an ordinary pen, which can be placed on any point on the face of the CRT. When the spot touched is illuminated by the program in control, a signal is generated by the photo-cell. This signal is sent to the computer, usually in the form of an interrupt. Thus the programmer can tell where the pen is positioned. By suitable programs, it is possible to follow the light pen around the screen and store inside the computer the coordinates of the various points indicated by the user. Thus the user can *draw* on the face of the CRT, and the light pen can be used as an input device. Its most common use is for pointing at sections of the total display on the tube.

Other devices can be used for indicating a point on the screen. One is a special tablet that is sensitive to an electronic pen held by the user. Another is a small hand-held box that the user moves over the surface of a table. Pickup devices measure the position of the hand and transmit it to the computer, which then displays a circle or a cross on the screen corresponding to the hand's position.

Many other forms of input and output devices have been developed for special purposes. Optical scanners can *read* sets of typed characters, and some devices have achieved a limited ability to read handwritten characters. Three-dimensional pens that enable the computer to track the user's hand in three-dimensional space have been designed; and analog input and output converters can not only read information directly from experimental measuring equipment but also control experiments directly. Voice output is possible by controlling sets of audio recorders similar to tape recorders, and, experimentally, acoustic input and output has been performed by using the computer to decode the signal from microphones and to generate the signal for a loud-speaker system directly. However, most such equipment is still in a "research" status, so it will not be discussed further in this book.

5.2 LONG-TERM STORAGE AND INTERMEDIATE INPUT/OUTPUT

Problems that involve the use of very large amounts of data and that are run on many different occasions have a requirement for long-term storage devices. Problems in this class include commercial jobs such as the record keeping associated with the maintenance of customer accounts and scientific jobs such as the comparison of data gathered from a particular physics experiment with the data gathered from many previous experiments. Both of these jobs have the characteristic that very large amounts of data are involved (100 million characters should be considered typical in designing systems for this type of problem) and the characteristic that the data is to be changed in a small way (some customer accounts are changed, or some additional experimental data is added to the history file). These characteristics dictate the need for a storage device that has virtually unlimited total capacity, although it only need be accessed in a serial fashion (that is, in sequential order, one unit of information at a time). Since the electronics associated with storage devices is the expensive part of the device, a desirable form of storage is one in which the storage is on a simple medium which can be removed, kept on a shelf, and replaced. To a limited extent, punched cards are a type of long-term storage, since the card reader and punch are, in principle, capable of handling an arbitrarily large number of cards. However, cards cannot be changed (holes cannot be filled in any practical way), and cards have a nonnegligible cost (approximately 0.1 cent per card). Also, card equipment is comparatively slow. However, there are a number of other devices which do not have the drawbacks of card equipment, specifically, magnetic tapes, disk files, and variations on both. These are all forms of the familiar tape recorder used for audio storage. This section will discuss the principles of a number of such devices. It is not intended to be exhaustive, since new versions are marketed almost every day. Although the manufacturer may claim a "breakthrough," the operating principles remain very similar; the speed and capacity may increase and the cost decrease.

5.2.1 Magnetic tape

Magnetic-tape storage was derived directly from audio-tape principles. The storage medium is a long strip of tape with a fixed width. Common tape systems are available with $\frac{1}{2}$-inch and 1-inch tape widths. The length of the tape is typically about 2,400 feet, and it is wound on a reel for easy handling. The tape itself is about $\frac{1}{500}$ to $\frac{1}{1000}$ of an inch thick, and it consists of a backing of flexible material, such as Mylar, with a coating of a magnetic material (an iron oxide). Information is stored on the tape by magnetizing the oxide coating in one direction or another. A *track* on the tape is a section of the width of the tape in which the magnetically coded information is stored. See Figure 5.4. Since a track is less than $\frac{1}{16}$ of an inch wide, several tracks can be placed

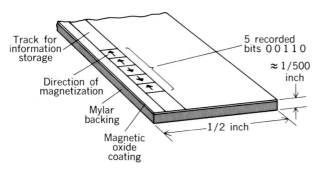

FIGURE 5.4   Magnetic tape

across the tape. Half-inch tape commonly has either 7 or 9 tracks across the width, hence 7 or 9 bits can be stored in *parallel*. In order to read or write on tape, the reel of tape is mounted on a *tape drive*, which is a mechanism with two reel drives, *read heads, write heads,* and a *capstan* which pulls the tape across the heads at an approximately constant speed (see Figure 5.5). When the tape is written, it is pulled across the heads by the capstan, and amplifiers drive current through the write heads in order to magnetize the tape. It is read back by pulling the tape across the read heads with the capstan and sensing the voltages induced in the read heads.

In practice, the bits of information are packed very closely together along the tape; for example, 200, 556, 800, and 1,600 bits per inch (bpi) in each track are standard *densities.* Since the tape is moved at speeds around 120 inches per second, it is out of the question to start or stop the tape between characters. Therefore, the information is usually written on the tape in continuous *records* or *blocks* with gaps between for starting and stopping. These gaps are called *interrecord gaps* and are about ¾-inch long. The length of the blocks is either fixed by the computer or is allowed to vary according to the use by the programmer. It is important to understand the difference between these two possibilities, so we shall first examine the reason for their use.

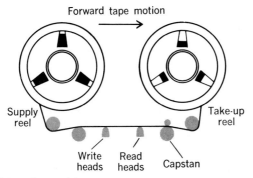

FIGURE 5.5   A tape drive

We recall that paper tape had a sprocket hole in order to allow the tape reader to know where a character was punched on the tape. In a similar manner, it is necessary for the computer to know where a set of bits (a character) is written on the magnetic tape. This is not done by a sprocket hole (it is difficult to punch 1,600 holes to the inch), but in some systems the equivalent—a *timing track*—is used. A timing track is a tape track that contains 1s in every bit position. The tape reader can use this track to indicate when a character position across the tape has been encountered, and then it can read the actual information bits. The alternative is to demand that every character written on the tape contains at least one 1 bit, so that the logical OR of all channels will contain a signal when a character is read. This is not too difficult, since it is normal to use a parity bit in every character. By using odd parity, at least one 1 bit is assured. The important difference is that if timing tracks are used, the tape must be *formatted* before use by writing a timing track all the way along the tape and leaving it there permanently. It is always possible to return to the same point on the tape by counting the timing bits. If, however, a timing track is not used, the tape drive must provide its own timing information via an electronic clock during the writing of new information. Since it is impossible to guarantee that the tape moves at exactly the same speed on two successive operations, a written block of a given number of characters may vary in length from one WRITE operation to another. The effect of this is shown in Figure 5.6. In the top diagram, the tape has been written with two blocks of informa-

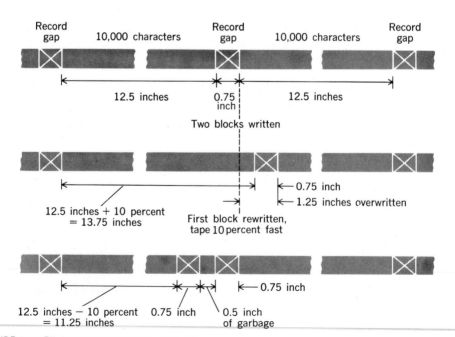

FIGURE 5.6   *Effect of nonconstant tape speeds*

tion of 10,000 characters each at 800 bpi (about 12½ inches each). In the second diagram, the first block has been rewritten when the tape moved 10 percent faster. Consequently, 1¼ inches of the next block has been overwritten. The bottom diagram shows the effect of rewriting the first block with the tape moving 10 percent slower. This time, about ½ inch of the previous block remains. If the user attempted to read the second block, he would get errors in both cases.

Tape that uses timing tracks can be rewritten at any point. In general, tape without timing tracks cannot be used in this manner, but must be used sequentially. That is, before a block can be written, all blocks ahead of it on the tape must first be written. However, some manufacturers are claiming to be able to produce tape units which are sufficiently accurate that blocks can be rewritten at arbitrary points.

A comparison of formatted and unformatted tape is difficult. On the one hand, formatted tape can be changed at any point. On the other, part of the space on the tape is used for timing information that could be used for storage. (The problem of writing precisely where the bit appears in the timing track is also more difficult than writing whenever the tape-unit clock indicates.) If tape is to be rewritten at any point, then it is easier for the programmer to use *fixed-length blocks,* and, indeed, tape is often formatted in this way. However, the tendency has been to use fixed-length blocks even on unformatted tape, for system reasons. The largest computer manufacturer, IBM, uses unformatted tape, and such tape is therefore the most common.

Basic tape operations include writing and reading blocks of information. In addition, tape-handling operations are necessary to enable the program to reach the particular block needed. After a tape block has been written, it is necessary to backspace the tape to the beginning of the block in order to re-read it. (Some systems allow tape to be read or written in either direction, but the majority only allow reading and writing in the forward direction.) Sometimes it is necessary to space forward over one or more blocks in order to reach something further down the tape; therefore a forward space operation is desirable.

Magnetic tape is only sequentially accessible. That is, it is more like a scroll than a book. A scroll is read by unwinding it from one end and, in order to reach a paragraph in the middle, it is necessary to roll through all previous paragraphs. In general, there are no operations to access an arbitrary block on a tape. Instead, it is necessary to skip through all the preceding blocks, one at a time.

Many of the terms introduced below are derived from business data processing. The basic unit of information in business data is the *character,* which may be part of a name, address, or numeric record. Characters are grouped together into *fields* representing the names, etc. Groups of fields are combined into one *record,* which may be the basic block written onto the tape. Historically, the word "record" was used to mean a recorded block of information. We shall reserve the word to signify a logical group of information typically handled as a unit by the user, and we shall use the word "block" to mean the physically recorded group of information. A record might, for example, contain all of the employment information relating to one employee. Finally, all of the employee records are grouped into one *file.* In a large organization, one file may occupy many reels of tape; whereas in a small company, it may occupy only a small part of one reel. (A reel of tape can contain 20 million characters.) The file concept is used in magnetic tape recording by providing a special *end-of-file* mark which can be written by the computer instead of a regular block. When it is read, an indicator is set which can be sensed by the program to indicate that the end of the file has been reached. A common analogy to draw for files, records, and characters on tape is with a book. The paragraphs are similar to records, and the file is the whole book. This does not take into account divisions into sections and chapters. These the programmer must handle by careful use of multiple end-of-file marks or other techniques. Following this analogy, fixed-length blocks are similar to the pages of a book. Blocks do not usually correspond to the natural division of the information into sections, paragraphs, etc., but they *do* provide an easy way of locating a piece of information if an index is provided. On tape, fixed blocks may not correspond to the requirements of the information, but they can be used to advantage if the information is indexed.

To make use of file marks, two operations are usually provided, a backspace file and a skip-to-end-of-file operation. These make it easier to move over multiple files with minimum program effort. The operations allowed on typical unformatted and formatted systems are shown in tabular form below. Many tape units, those with separate read and write heads, check the information as it is being written by reading it back. If a parity bit is used (almost all magnetic recording devices use parity), and if the tape passes over the read head after it has passed over the write head, the information can be checked for parity. This will allow any single error to be detected. If an error is detected, the operation can be repeated, which requires that the tape be backspaced to the start of the block and the write repeated. This repeat operation can be handled by the hardware, although usually an error signal will be passed on to the system programs and they will execute the repeat or take other corrective action as discussed in the next chapter.

When a file of information on magnetic tape is to be updated (that is, some of the information is to be changed), it is necessary to read the original from one tape and make updated copy on another tape on a second tape drive. The only time that this is not necessary is when fixed-block formatted tapes are used and the updated material is not longer than the original. The minimum number of unformatted tape drives for any useful operation is two, while four is a more practical minimum for most data manipulation tasks. Two tapes are needed so that one can be updated onto the other. Four are useful when a *merge,* to be discussed in Chapter 10, is to be done. An unlimited number of reels of tape can be stored on shelves and, given enough time, processed by the computer. Therefore the upper limit of storage is unbounded. The speed of operation varies between different drives and manufacturers, and the range of character rates is from a few thousand per second to 20,000 per second. Moving the tape over records and files takes about the same length of time as reading or writing, while rewinding takes from 1 to 2 minutes maximum. The time to start and stop the tape in the record gap varies from 1 to 20 milliseconds.

5.2.2 Disk files

The use of the word "files" in the name of this device should not be confused with its use to mean a group of records of information. A disk file is a device which resembles a phonograph record and its playback mechanism. Physically, a single disk platter is a circular sheet of metal about 10 to 20 inches in diameter and $\frac{1}{16}$ to $\frac{1}{4}$ inch thick. It is coated on both surfaces with a magnetic material, so that the thickness of the disk is for mechanical strength only. Information is recorded on the disk surface magnetically, just as information is recorded on magnetic tape. The difference between the recording on a phonograph record and a disk platter (in addition to the means of storing information) is that whereas a phonograph contains one continuous groove or track in a spiral, a disk surface contains many tracks arranged in concentric circles. The read and write heads (usually the same head) are mounted on movable

OPERATION	UNFORMATTED TAPE	FORMATTED TAPE
Write	Programmer specifies the number of words.	A multiple of a fixed number of words.
Read	Option. Either the whole block written or a number of words specified by the programmer. Restriction: cannot read downstream of a write operation.	Fixed block as written or a given number of words.
Backspace	Block or file possible.	Block only†
Forward space (skip)	Block or file possible.	Block only†
Rewind	O.K.	O.K.
Write end of file	O.K.	Not available†
Sense end of file on read	O.K.	Not available†

† It is possible to allow an extra character at the start of each block to represent a file mark, in which case write end of file, backspace file, and sense end of file are possible.

arms which can be positioned over any one of the tracks: there may be from 100 to 1,000 tracks on a surface. A diagram of a single disk surface is shown in Figure 5.7.

A disk unit may be able to access a single surface at a time, or it may contain several platters, each with a read/write head on an arm, such that any surface can be accessed. As long as the set of disk platters can be removed, the disk file satisfies our definition of long-term, essentially unlimited storage. It has characteristics similar to magnetic tapes in that it can take a relatively long time to move from the track currently under the head to another track, just as it can take a tape reader a long time to move from one position on the tape to another relative to the transmission time for one character. However, both figures are much faster for disk files, in that a typical maximum head-movement time for a disk file is about $\frac{1}{10}$ second, whereas for a tape it is up to 4 minutes. The data rate for characters from disk is typically between 100 KC (KC = 1,000 characters) and 400 KC per second compared to 30 KC to 180 KC for tape. A large disk file will contain the same amount of information as a tape to within an order of magnitude. (Tapes contain about 1,000 characters per inch over 2,400 feet, for about 20×10^6 characters; disks typically contain from 10 to 400×10^6 characters.)

The method of recording is usually a fixed-block mode rather than a variable-length block mode, since a single track is of a fixed length. A timing track is prerecorded on one surface of the file so that bits are always stored in the same physical position on repeated writes. Hence it is possible to rewrite a single block anywhere on the file without losing other blocks of previously recorded information. Additional tracks adjacent to the timing track frequent-

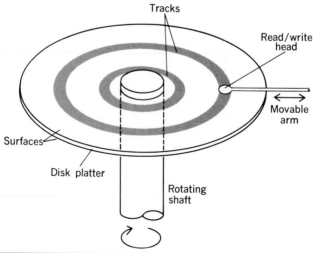

FIGURE 5.7   Disk

ly contain *format* information. This tells the controlling computer where the blocks are around the track and how long they are. Some systems allow this information to be changed, so that the length of blocks can be changed under program control. This is known as *formatting* the disk. It is not a good idea to do this frequently. Usually the installation will settle on a given format and block size.

In order to use a disk file, the heads must first be moved to the right track (assuming that the correct disk platters are already mounted) before the read or write can be done. The former is known as the *seek* operation. More will be said about the use of input/output equipment in the next chapter.

While the heads are fixed in any one position, the computer has access to one track on each surface. If we visualize this set of tracks on the disk surfaces shown in Figure 5.8, we see that they lie on the surface of a cylinder. For this reason, disks are often addressed by the *cylinder address* and the *surface address.* The former refers to the position of the heads, the latter to the surface being used. When several blocks of information are to be transmitted between the disk unit and the computer, it is faster if they are on the same cylinder, so that no head movement is involved.

5.2.3 Variations of tapes and disks

Many devices have been marketed which are in the same class as tapes and disks: that is, they have the characteristics of removability (so that storage is virtually unlimited) and a reasonable speed and capacity for a single load. They take the form of packages of disklike or tapelike storage media which can be accessed so that an individual piece of the medium can be placed under the read/write mechanism. With devices of this form, capacities in

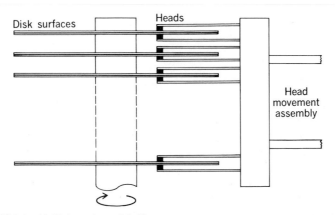

FIGURE 5.8   Multiple-surface disk file

excess of 10^9 characters *online* (that is, in the machine at one time) are achievable.

One such device was the *data-cell,* a unit that contained cartridges, each of which contained strips of flexible base coated with a magnetic material. The read mechanism consisted of a drum around which one of the strips could be wrapped. This was then rotated under read/write heads to record or play back data. A mechanical access system could load or unload any one of the strips. Once a strip was loaded, the speed was about the same as disk speeds, but it took a considerable time to access a strip if it was some distance from the access mechanism. Unfortunately, most devices that rely on mechanical complexity have not proved reliable over the long term, so data-cells were not popular.

The major improvements since 1967 have been decreases in the cost of devices coupled with minor increases in speed. Without reducing the physical size of mechanical mechanisms, it is difficult to move them reliably at a much higher speed than at present. However, reduction in the cost of integrated circuits and the great increase in the number of units produced have served to cut the cost substantially. The number of large-scale disk units available has increased enormously, and small-scale units have appeared on the market at a very reasonable cost. Small, slow tape units based on ⅛ inch-wide audio-style cassettes are well below $1,000 each. Another variation on the disk file that is also low in cost is the *floppy disk.* This is a flexible circular base coated with a magnetic recording medium that can be loaded into a unit and spun over a read/write head. Typically about 100 KC are stored on one disk at data rates ranging from 30 to 120 KC per second.

5.2.4 Long-term storage devices for offline input/output

An important application of long-term storage devices is in the transmission of information from one computer to another. If this transmission has to be fast in the sense of occurring almost immediately, then a direct electrical coupling is necessary; but if the transmission can be delayed as much as an hour or so, then a tape or disk or similar medium can be written by one computer and read by another—provided that they have compatible devices. Large amounts of information can be transmitted relatively inexpensively in this manner. One important specific application of this method is in the use of a second computer to perform the card reading, punching, and printing functions for a high-speed scientific type machine. Since mechanical operations on hard-copy input/output are severely limited in speed, it has been considered unwise to spend the time of a fast machine on such low-speed operations. Therefore, the information from input cards is copied onto magnetic tape or disk files by a cheaper, slower machine, and the tapes or files are loaded onto the faster machine for reading at a higher speed. The output from the faster machine is put onto tapes or disks and sent back to the low-speed machine for printing and punching. This is called *offline* conversion. The use of multiprogramming has made this method obsolete, since the large computer can run a program whose job is to read and print hard-copy input/output to and from disk files simultaneously with user jobs.

5.3 MEDIUM-TERM STORAGE DEVICES

By medium-term storage we mean the retention of information for times of a few seconds to a few days, where it is not practical to *unload* the storage medium for physical storage in a cabinet. Devices in this category are characterized by speeds ranging from those available with the long-term devices to speeds of the order of several million characters per second. The capacities of these devices range from those of long-term devices down to the order of a million characters. Applications of these devices are as extensions of the directly addressable main memory in problems in which there is inadequate main memory, and for the retention of information from one problem run to another when it is not convenient to physically reload a storage medium onto a reader. Typical situations that call for these applications are, in the former case, the sorting of large amounts of input information (probably contained on a magnetic tape) which requires many passes over the data, copying them from one storage area to another, and, in the latter case, the saving of user programs and data in a time-sharing, remote-console system, where it is necessary for the user to have almost immediate access to his information when he sits down at a console.

The needs of the examples given above can be satisfied by the use of the long-term devices mentioned above, but some problems exist for which the maximum data rate, or the average access time (to move the heads or the tape) is inadequate, so improvements must be sought. However, in a typical installation, some of the disk units available will be used mainly as *scratch* storage; that is, for the temporary storage of information during the execution of a program only. In addition, a number of other devices can be used. These will be discussed in the remainder of this section.

5.3.1 The disk file

The disk file was discussed above as a unit with removable disk platters for long-term storage. If the platters do not have to be removable, then it is possible to put more platters in a single unit. In fact, this was the first form of disk file developed. It is physically similar to the removable-platter disk file and is used in the same manner. See Figure 5.8. However, its storage capability can be increased and, by using more than one head to read or write bits on several tracks at once, its speed can be increased considerably. The extreme form of such a disk file is one in which there is one head for every track. This is often called a *drum,* although we shall distinguish between *fixed-head disks* and drums. Since a large disk file can have 8,000 tracks, the one-head-for-one-track arrangement is only possible for the smaller disk units. This type of arrangement does, however, eliminate the positioning of the arms carrying the heads—the slowest part of a disk-file operation. The average access time then drops down to half the rotation time (about half of 35 milliseconds), since the user will have to wait— on the average—a half revolution before the desired information rotates to a position underneath the reading head so that it can be transmitted to the computer.

5.3.2 The drum

Historically, the drum was developed before the disk file, but it is convenient to think of it as a variant of the disk file with fixed heads. Instead of information being stored on a set of disk surfaces, it is stored on the surface of the drum, which may be about 10 inches in diameter and perhaps 20 inches long (although much larger drums have been developed). Because drums are more compact, they can achieve much higher revolution speeds than can disk-file mechanisms. Hence, the average access time (a half revolution) can be reduced. Typically, revolution times are in the range of 8 to 35 milliseconds. Information is usually stored in fixed-length blocks on a drum. A drum is shown pictorially in Figure 5.9. It is like a single cylinder of a disk file but, for engineering reasons, it is possible to get a higher bit density on a drum than on a disk. To achieve high data rates, several tracks may be read in parallel, so that a large number of words can be read in a single revolution. To keep the blocks to a manageable size, the tracks are divided into *sectors.* Each sector contains a block for reading and writing purposes. The computer accesses the drum by specifying a track and a sector address. After one sector has been read or written, the next-higher-numbered sector can be accessed immediately

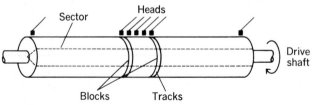

FIGURE 5.9   Drum

because it is possible to switch from one set of heads to another almost instantaneously.

5.3.3 Bulk storage devices

The main memory of the computer is constructed from many identical elements, each of which can store 1 bit, and each of which can be accessed in about the same amount of time. The elements may be cores, or magnetic thin films, or integrated circuit elements. Speeds are typically from $\frac{1}{4}$ to 1 micro second for reading and writing one word composed of from 16 to 64 bits. A bulk store is a similar device in which the number of words has been greatly increased from the typical main memory sizes of 10 to 1,000 KC. A bulk store may hold about 10 million characters. As a consequence of the increase in size, the speed is worse, typically 2 micro seconds or more for an access. One organization, adopted by CDC in their extended core storage (ECS), was to make the "word" in the bulk memory very wide, Whereas the regular memory contains 60-bit words, the bulk memory contains 480-bit words. Thus eight words can be read in parallel from each of four banks of bulk store simultaneously to achieve a maximum rate of 100 nano-seconds per word, which is the peak speed of the main memory, achieved by overlapping four banks of 400 nanosecond memory. Because these speeds can only be achieved if many consecutive words are moved (the first costs 3.2 micro seconds), it can only be used as a block transfer device between the main memory and the bulk store. Thus it looks rather like a drum or disk file, but it is much faster and has no delays waiting for the rotation to the start of a block. It cannot be used to provide instructions and data directly to the CPU.

Other forms of bulk store function logically as main memory. However, their reduced speed slows programs that access data or instructions from them. A related development (that is not new) is the use of small, very fast memories between the main memory and the CPU. These are called *buffer, local,* or *cache* memories. Because they hold a relatively small amount of information (around 500 to 8,000 bytes) they can be very fast (around 0.02 to 0.1 micro second per read or write). Various control organizations can be used to take advantage of such memories. One way is to place information fetched or stored in the main memory in the fast memory at the same time. Frequently programs refer to the same small set of locations repeatedly for a period of time (for example in a loop). Second and subsequent references to a word can fetch it from the fast memory. Actions of this sort are handled automatically by the hardware, so that the programmer is only aware of the increase in speed. He does not have to be concerned with the organization of the computer (unless he wishes to make the most of the speed capabilities by organizing his program to reference a few locations repeatedly.)†

5.4 SPEED AND CAPACITY COMPARISONS

The speeds and capacities of various types of storage media are shown and compared with the speed and capacity of main memories in Figure 5.10.

†See, for example, J. S. Liptay, Structural Aspects of the System 360 Model 85: II The Cache, *IBM Systems Journal,* vol. 7, no. 1, pp. 15–21, 1968.

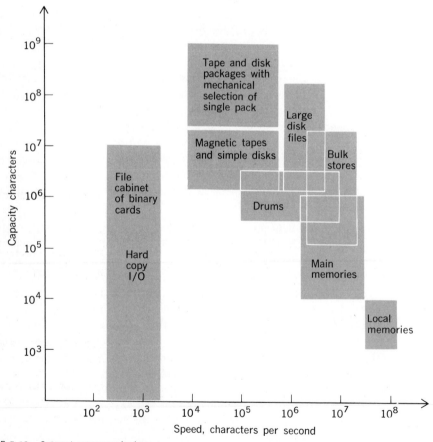

FIGURE 5.10 *Current memory devices*

PROBLEMS

1   How many bytes of information can be represented on one 80-column, 12-row binary card?

2   An early system, the IBM 7090, used a separate computer, the IBM 1401, to load cards onto magnetic tape offline. Cards were read by the 1401 into its memory such that the information was available either as eighty 6-bit BCD characters, one character from each column, or as 160 6-bit characters, two characters representing all possibilities for the 12 bit positions in each column. The 1401 program had to decide whether to copy the BCD (80-character) form or the binary (160-character) form onto tape, since it did not know whether the user's program in the 7090 was going to read a binary or a BCD card. Recognizing that not all 64 possibilities of 6 bits represent valid BCD characters, how would you suggest that the programmer should distinguish between binary and BCD cards, and how should the record of information passed onto the 7090 via magnetic tape distinguish the two?

3   If 8-channel paper tape can be read at 1,000 characters per second, at what speed must 80-column cards be read to achieve the same data rate if the cards contain
a   BCD information?
b   EBCDIC information?
c   binary information?

4   A plotter accepts commands of the form

MOVEP   PEN,X,Y

and

SETP   PEN,X,Y

which move the pen from its present position in a straight line either a distance of X and Y in the x and y directions or to position X, Y, respectively, with the pen down (marking) if PEN is set to DOWN, or the pen up (not marking) if PEN is set to UP, Thus, the command

MOVEP   DOWN,P,=0

draws a horizontal line of length P. (X and Y are assumed to be the addresses of locations containing the values of the coordinates.)
a   Write a subroutine or macro-like program section which will draw a

20 by 20 square whose center is the current pen position, and which will leave the pen in the position in which it started.

b Write a similar program to draw the capital letter L of height 7 and width 5, with the lower left-hand corner in the present pen position, such that the pen is left in a position to draw another letter one unit to the right of the present one by another call to the same subroutine or macro.

c Use these subroutines to draw a square centered at *U, V* with the letter L printed just to the right of the center of the left and right vertical sides without performing any arithmetic on *U* and *V*.

5 Consider a reel of tape written at 1,600 characters per inch with 0.75-inch record gaps. Draw a graph of the average read speed and average density as a function of the number of characters per record if the tape moves at 115 inches per second.

6 Suppose that a movable head disk is such that it takes 5 milliseconds to move the head from one track to the adjacent track. Suppose that the rotational time is 30 milliseconds, and there are 20,000 characters on a track. Draw a graph of the average character rate for a block of *N* characters, where $0 < N < 100,000$, if it is assumed that the first 20,000 characters are on track 1, the next 20,000 on track 2, and so on, and that consecutively numbered tracks are adjacent. Also assume that the disk is in a random position and the read must wait until the start of the track is under the read head, but that the head is over track 1 when the read is requested. (The time for the read is taken to be the time from the read request to the time that the last character is read.)

6

HARDWARE AND SOFTWARE CONTROL OF INPUT/OUTPUT DEVICES

Input/output devices are very much slower than the central computer, so many schemes are used to avoid slowing down the computer while it is controlling input/output. These schemes utilize both complex hardware control units and systems programs so that the user is able to view the device as if it were connected in a simple way. In this chapter we will first look at the computer control of very simple input/output devices such as paper tape and see how an effective speed can be maintained. Other devices introduce a few additional complications, such as positioning tape or moving disk heads to place them over the right track (seeking). These will be discussed in Section 6.3. Then we will look at the organization of typical system programs.

Early computers and modern low-cost computers use the same control unit that sequences the CPU to control the input/output units, whereas large systems use separate control units, called channels, so that the CPU is free to continue processing during an I/O transfer. We will start by considering the simplest scheme so that we can see the way in which hardware has evolved to meet the increasing demands of more complex I/O needs.

6.1 DIRECT CONTROL OF I/O BY THE CPU

An input/output device is a combination of electrical and mechanical components which must be activated in a certain sequence in order to transmit data. The activation is controlled by means of *control signals* sent to the unit along connecting wires, and the computer can determine the state of the unit by *sense signals* sent back from the unit to the computer along other wires. The control signals might mean, for example, "start tape moving," "stop tape," or "rewind tape," while the sense signals might mean "data ready," "tape stopped," or "unit busy." In the simplest of all systems, it is possible for the CPU to execute instructions that send control signals directly to the unit and to test the sense signals in branch instructions. First, consider a paper-tape reader. A paper-tape punch is very similar, and both are typical of the basic operations involved in all I/O devices.

An eight-channel paper-tape reader contains eight sensing devices for the information channels and one for the sprocket hole. When a character of 8 bits has been read, the tape must be moved. A capstan similar to that on a magnetic tape is used. A *pinch-roller* or *clutch* is used to press the tape against the revolving capstan so that it is moved. When it has moved a full character distance ($\frac{1}{10}$ inch), the sprocket hole sense device indicates that the next character can be read from the eight information sensors. It can then be transmitted to the computer. The sequence of steps taken by the paper-tape reader is therefore

1 Start tape moving.
2 Wait until sprocket hole is sensed.
3 Stop tape moving and send character to computer.

If control signals include "start tape," "stop tape," and "read data," while sense signals include "sprocket hole under reader," the CPU could execute a program of the form

```
              Start tape.
X             Branch to X if sprocket hole not under reader.
              Stop tape.
              Read data into CPU.
```

each time a character is needed. Unfortunately, in the 1 to 100 milliseconds it takes a typical paper-tape reader to move the tape 1/10 inch, the CPU can execute between 1,000 and 100,000 operations, which means that it will be wasting its time in the loop at location X every time that a character is needed. To overcome this problem, a simple control unit can be added to the tape reader which will always advance the tape to the next character and stop the tape without being told. Now what is needed is a sense signal that says "character ready." With this, the program becomes

```
X             Branch to X if character not ready.
              Read character to CPU and start tape moving.
```

The first step is necessary because the tape may not have had time to move to the next character after the last one was read. This will only cause a computer wait if not enough time was given between the previous read and this one. After the second step has been completed, the computer need not be concerned with the remaining two steps since a separate control in the tape reader can be used to advance the tape automatically to the next character.

All that this modification does is to eliminate the wait on mechanical motion, but it introduces an important new feature that is used in all future improvements. This feature is *parallelism*. The control of the reader can be busy moving the tape while the computer is busy processing data. Little else can be done to improve the situation until we decide how the data are actually brought into the computer from the tape. The simplest method is to provide instructions to bring the characters directly into an accumulator (if the computer has one—assume a one-address structure for the purposes of discussion). Thus a paper-tape READ instruction can be expected to put the next paper-tape character in the accumulator, and a PUNCH instruction to put the contents of the accumulator, or a set of bits from the accumulator, onto punched tape. The programmer would have to place the READ instructions uniformly in his program to make the best use of the tape reader. In some cases, he may need the character before the reader is ready, so that a wait cannot be avoided; in other cases, the character may be ready before he is, so that the tape reader waits on the computer. It is the desire to avoid these situations that leads to the next development.

6.1.1 Interrupt-controlled I/O

If the user is to achieve better overlap, it is necessary to allow a larger number of characters to be read into the computer ahead of the time that they are needed. Then the user can process them when they are needed, and the reader can be reading further characters at the same time. This is a form of load spreading. If the user needs several characters in rapid succession, they are already available in the machine, and then the reader has time to catch up while he is processing them. The computer or the tape reader will only wait when the average use of the reader is more or less, respectively, than the use of the processor over a longer period.

If the accumulator is to continue to be used for reading characters, how can the user be expected to read in characters ahead of time, and where can he put them? The only reasonable place to put them is in memory, so storage locations are set aside in memory to receive the incoming characters. The problem then is to write a program that will both perform some desired calculation and read in characters at a regular rate from the reader until the memory locations (called buffers) are full. Although this is theoretically possible, it is exceedingly tedious to program, so automatic techniques are usually provided to make it easier. The simplest is the interrupt technique. Interrupts have already been discussed. Let us recall their basic features. When an interrupt signal is received, the current computation in the CPU is temporarily stopped, the control counter is saved so that we know where execution has reached, and a branch to a known location is made. This location could contain a program to read in paper-tape characters and place them in the buffers. Therefore, if an interrupt signal is available that indicates to the CPU that the next character is ready, the current process can be interrupted, the current contents of the CPU registers saved, the next character read into a buffer, the contents of the CPU registers restored, and processing continued in the CPU. A timing diagram for this is shown in Figure 6.1. Note that there are two charts, one for the reader and one for the CPU, since they can run in parallel.

Unfortunately, this program will run into trouble when the buffers are full, since then there will be no place to put additional characters. Therefore, the program must be modified in the section for reading tape to that in Figure 6.2. Here, the buffers are tested to see if they are all full. If not,

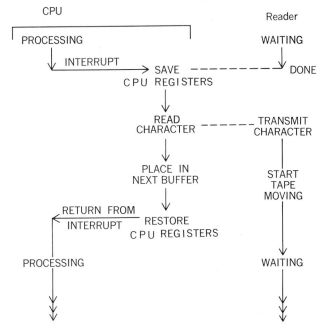

FIGURE 6.1   Basic READ timing diagram

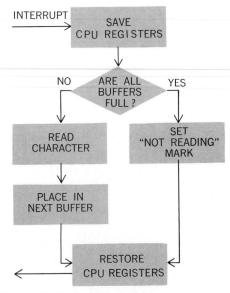

FIGURE 6.2   Modified READ flowchart

flow continues as before; otherwise a mark, indicating that no reading is occurring, is set. A character is not read, so a further interrupt will not be received by the CPU. When a character is removed from a buffer, it is necessary to start the reading process again. This can be done by testing the "not reading" mark in the subroutine used to remove a character from a buffer for use by the program. It is illustrated by the flowchart in Figure 6.3. This particular subroutine first tests to see if there are any full buffers. If there are none, then it waits until there are by simply looping on the test. It appears that this loop is infinite, but what will eventually happen is that the next character will be ready. It will cause an interrupt which stops the program in the loop, put a character in a buffer, and then return control to the loop. But this time, the test gives the answer "yes," so that the com-

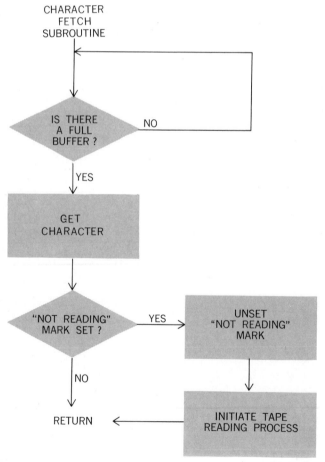

FIGURE 6.3 Reading a character to the accumulator

puter gets the character from the buffer. Finally, the mark for "not read-ing" is tested. If it is not set, then control returns to the calling program. If it is set, it is unset and the reading process is initiated before control is returned to the calling program. This will read the next character and start the tape moving again.

Although interrupt-driven programs are conceptually simple, there are many details to be considered and many ways in which program errors can cause great difficulty. This is because these are parallel operations, and interrupts can occur at any time that an interrupt is enabled. The program in Figures 6.2 and 6.3 illustrates some of the problems. First, buffer or-ganization must be examined, as it is the details that cause the problems.

A set of memory locations B through $B + N - 1$ can be set aside for char-acter buffers. These can be arranged in a *circular* fashion, so that location B logically follows location $B + N - 1$. As the interrupt-driven read pro-gram gets characters, it fills the locations in order, maintaining a pointer, say BI, which contains the address of the next available location. Initially, BI is set to B, and it is incremented at each read. A count of the number of characters in the buffers must be maintained, say in location N1. A mark, say M, must be maintained also. It can be set to 1 when the buffers are full and returned to 0 when there is space in the buffers. The interrupt-driven read program will take the form:

	Save CPU registers.
	Compare N1 and N.
	Branch to W if equal.
R	Read character. (This starts the input reader on the process of reading the next character.)
	Store in location BI.
	Increase BI by 1.
	If BI = B+N, set BI to B.
P	Return from interrupt, restoring registers in CPU.
W	Set M to 1.
	Branch to P.

A second pointer, say BO, can contain the address of the buffer containing the character which will be used next. Figure 6.4 shows such an arrangement of 12 buffers in the state where 7 of the buffers are full. In such a state, the reader can process five more characters before it has to stop until more characters are used by the program, while the program can obtain seven characters before it has to wait for the reader.

Now consider the subroutine which fetches characters from the buffer, as shown in Figure 6.3. It could take the form:

L	Test N1.
	Branch to L if 0.

Get character from location BO.
Decrease N1 by 1.
Increase BO by 1.
If BO = B+N, set BO to B.
Test M.
Return if 0.
Set M to 0.
Branch to R in interrupt-driven read program above.

The first simple error that can occur in the above program is in the first line. On many computers, it is necessary to load a number into CPU registers before that number can be tested. If this is done, it is important to reload the number if the second line branches back. Otherwise the same copy is being tested, rather than the one which will eventually be increased by the read program. A much more serious error can occur when N1 is decremented. If a one-address machine is being used, the code is probably

```
LOAD      N1
SUB       =1
STORE     N1
```

If an interrupt occurs between the LOAD and the STORE, the read program

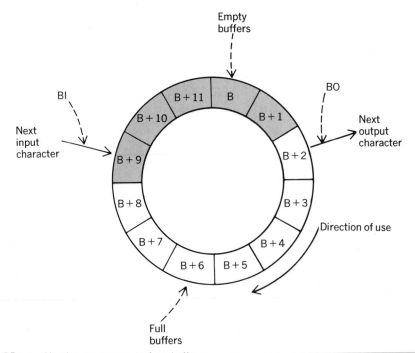

FIGURE 6.4   Circular arrangement of 12 buffers

will increment N1 as stored in memory, then return to this program, which will *decrement the old copy* of N1, so that it will now be 1 too small. Computers which can decrement a number in storage directly in a single instruction (for example, the PDP-11) and which cannot be interrupted in the middle of a single instruction, as is the norm, do not have this problem, since it is impossible for the interrupt-driven program to get control after the value of N1 has been read from memory and before it is restored updated.

This type of problem occurs because more than one parallel process is dealing with the same data. As a matter of programming practice, it is preferable to handle all updating of variables by one section of code only, if several sections can run in parallel or in some undetermined order. Since the last instruction in the character fetch routine branches to the read program anyway, one may as well use one program to handle all changing of the important buffer control words, in this case BI, N1, and M. BO is handled by the character fetch program only and can be left there, but it is more consistent to let it be updated by the read program also. The read program is executed with tape reader interrupts disabled so that it cannot get into trouble. The character fetch program must enter the interrupt-disabled state to request the read program to update its buffer control information. This is sometimes named a *supervisor call.* It looks like a subroutine call from the user's point of view, but it transfers control to the supervisor program by means of an interrupt. A typical organization would require the user to provide the locations for his buffers and to give that information to the supervisor at the start of execution. The supervisor would then take care of filling the buffers by an interrupt-driven program and provide the address of the next available character to the user when he executes a supervisor call for that purpose.

(All timing problems of this sort can be resolved simply by disabling interrupts at every critical point, but this destroys some of the advantages of interrupts. Their purpose is to allow devices to receive service when they are ready so that neither do they have to wait nor does the CPU have to test them continually. If large sections of code are run with interrupts disabled, many devices may have to wait for service. Some devices have to be serviced within a certain time or information is lost or delayed badly, so excessive disabling of interrupts can be expensive. The art of programming I/O devices is largely concerned with careful handling of interrupts so that they can be handled rapidly.)

The next section will give a brief description of the paper-tape I/O in the PDP-11, as it uses the ideas developed above. The IBM 370 uses a more complex scheme which will be discussed in Section 6.2.

6.1.2 Simple I/O on the PDP-11

The PDP-11 assigns "memory locations" to each I/O device. These are not real locations in memory, as addressable memory is limited to locations 000000 through 157777 octal. Addresses above that limit refer to I/O device registers. For example, locations 177552 and 177556 are the data registers for the paper-tape reader and punch, respectively. If a character has been processed by the tape reader, it can be moved to location D by the instruction

        MOVB   177552,D

although we will usually use the name PRB for Paper Reader Buffer and write

        PRB = 177552
        MOVB   PRB,D

Similarly, a character can be punched by writing

        PPB = 177556
        MOVB   D,PPB

Moving a character to the punch buffer starts the punch.

Each I/O device has one or more control and status registers. These are locations 177550 and 177554 for the reader and punch, respectively. Each of these is a 16-bit word. Their formats are shown in Figure 6.5. For now,

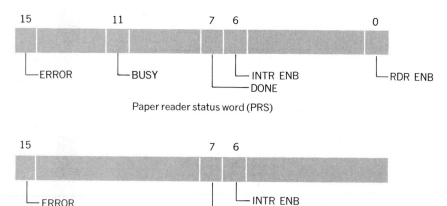

Paper reader status word (PRS)

Paper punch status word (PPS)

FIGURE 6.5 Status words for paper-tape equipment

consider the RDR ENB (ReaDeR ENaBle) and the DONE bits in the reader status word. The reader enable bit is a control line. When it is set to 1 by the computer, the reader transmits a character to its buffer, PRB; and sets the DONE bit when the action is complete. (If there was an error, it would set the ERROR bit instead, but we will delay discussion of that alternative.) The RDR ENB bit is cleared by the reader, so that the following code would read one character into R0 and return to a calling program if there were no errors.

```
READ:    INCB    PRS          ;Sets 1 in RDR ENB bit.
TEST:    BIT     #200,PRS     ;Test bit 7 of reader status word (DONE).
         BEQ     TEST         ;Branch if 0.
         MOVB    PRB,R0
         RTS     R7
```

This corresponds to the simplest non-interrupt-controlled I/O. The interrupt bit would have to be off (INTR ENB zero) or interrupts disabled for this to work. As written, this program waits for the read each time. After the first character has been read by the MOVB instruction, another INCB PRS should be executed before the RTS. This starts the tape moving. Future calls to READ should skip the first INCB PRS. The corresponding subroutine for paper tape is

```
PUNCH:   BIT     #200,PPS     ;Test bit 7 of punch status word (DONE).
         BEQ     PUNCH        ;Branch back until 1.
         MOV     R0,PPB       ;Move character to punch.
         RTS     R7           ;Return to caller.
```

INTERRUPTS

The PDP-11 has a priority interrupt structure. Each I/O device is assigned a priority level between 4 and 7. The paper-tape equipment is level 4. If interrupts are enabled on a particular device and the priority level of the CPU as shown in the processor status register (see Chapter 2, page 47) is less than the priority of the device, that device can interrupt the CPU when an interrupt condition occurs. Hence, paper-tape equipment will interrupt the CPU if the priority of the CPU is less than 4. When this occurs, the processor status word and the program counter are pushed into the stack based on R6. This saves the priority and condition bits of the current task and the return location for continuing processing when the interrupt has been handled. The CPU then reloads its program counter and program status register from two consecutive words whose start is determined by the interrupting device. These locations are 70 and 74 for the paper-tape reader and punch, respectively. Provided that an interrupt by the reader or punch sets the processor priority to 4, further interrupts by these devices are disabled until the priority is reduced. The usual way of doing this is to execute an RTI (ReTurn from Interrupt) instruction, which reloads the processor status register and the program counter from the top two levels in the stack, thus returning to the interrupt program.

Because the stack is used to save interrupt information, multiple interrupts at different priorities are handled automatically. If the CPU is interrupted by a priority 4 service and then that is interrupted by a priority 6 service, the top of the stack contains information that will return control to the priority 4 service program, while the lower levels contain the information to get back to the original program.

Supervisor calls are handled by several instructions which cause interrupts to various locations. The instructions EMT and TRAP cause an immediate interrupt of the current program based on the words at locations 30 and 34, respectively. The address fields of these instructions (the last 8 bits of the word) can be used to tell the supervisor the reason for the call. The use of interrupts and an EMT instruction to fill a buffer from the paper-tape reader and to answer an EMT instruction by getting a character into R0 is shown below. It is assumed that the priority of the user program is less than 4 so that it can be interrupted by the reader. The initial states of the buffer control words are shown. It is assumed that the interrupt is enabled for the paper-tape reader, and that the user program is executing while waiting for an interrupt from the reader.

```
            N = 10                          ;Buffer is eight characters long.
            .ASECT                          ;Start absolute assembly section.
            .= 30
            .WORD       GET                 ;Start of get character routine.
            .WORD       0                   ;Status with priority 0 to allow
                                            ;interruptions.
            .= 70
            .WORD       READ                ;Start of reader service routine.
            .WORD       200                 ;Priority is 4.
            . . .
READ:       CMP         #N,N1               ;See if buffers are full.
            BNE         RD1
            INCB        M                   ;Set M to 1 for not reading.
            BR          RD5
RD1:        MOV         R1,-(SP)            ;Save R1 in stack.
RD2         MOV         BI,R1               ;Input buffer address word.
            MOVB        PRB,(R1)+           ;Tape character to buffer.
            INCB        PRS                 ;Start tape reading.
            CMP         R1,#B+N             ;Check for end of buffer.
            BNE         RD3
            MOV         #B,R1
RD3:        MOV         R1,BI               ;Restore buffer address word.
            INC         N1                  ;Increment character count.
RD4:        MOV         (SP)+,R1            ;Restore R1 from stack
RD5:        RTI                             ;Return from interrupt.
GET:        TST         N1                  ;Check for N1 = 0.
```

	BEQ	GET	;Loop at priority 0 until character ;available.
	MOV	#200,@#—2	;Set program status word (in ;location—2) to priority 4.
	MOV	R1,—(SP)	;Save R1 in stack.
	MOV	BO,R1	;Output buffer control word.
	MOVB	(R1)+,R0	;Move character to R0.
	CMP	R1,#B+N	;Check for end of buffer.
	BNE	RD6	
	MOV	#B,R1	
RD6:	MOV	R1,BO	;Restore output control
	DEC	N1	;Reduce character count.
	TESTB	M	;Test not reading mark.
	BEQ	RD4	;Not set.
	CLRB	M	;Clear not reading mark.
	BR	RD2	;Go read a character.
BI:	.WORD	B	;Input buffer control.
BO:	.WORD	B	;Output buffer control.
N1:	.WORD	0	;Character count.
M:	.BYTE	0	;Not reading mark.
B:	.BLKB	N	;Buffer.

6.2 INPUT DIRECTLY INTO MEMORY

The interrupt method was used to read information into a set of buffers in memory. Existing equipment in the CPU and its accumulators was used to do this at a low cost. It should be noted that the amount of machine time spent per character is fairly high (order of 10 to 20 instructions are needed at least). If the character rate is high (for example, from a magnetic tape unit), all of the CPU time would be spent handling the I/O. We would have gained nothing. In this case, additional equipment can be added to the controller to communicate directly with memory. Since the result desired is to fill a set of memory locations with characters, we can design a controller which will do just that. The controller is given the starting memory address, an indication of the length of the buffer (it could be a fixed-block device, in which case it may be determined), and the actual command (READ, WRITE, etc.). It controls the I/O unit in parallel with processing by the CPU. The result is that the CPU is not interrupted after every character but only after every record. This reduces the amount of CPU time spent on I/O.

A controller which will do these more complex transfers is called a *channel*. In a typical installation, a channel is a relatively expensive device since it contains many of the same facilities as a CPU (registers and counters, etc.), so it is common to share a channel among several I/O devices. One of the devices may be operating at one time. This is shown in Figure 6.6. A channel may receive its commands from the CPU in a straightforward design. Thus a typical input/output order might take the form "Read into memory location 2564, 256 words from channel A, unit 2." Channel A is directed to connect unit 2 and is given the address and count. From then on, the CPU is free until it is interrupted by the end of the instruction. On input, the channel takes care of receiving data from a unit, possibly packing it into words (if it is received as characters), sending the address of that word and the word of data to memory for storage, incrementing the address to the next word, and testing for the end of transmission. Output is similar.

A channel is usually kept busy by a high-speed unit such as a disk transferring data. On the other hand, the seek operation of moving disk heads does not require any channel action once the operation has been initiated. Thus the channel itself may overlap some of the mechanical operations of its units. When a channel is reading information from a low-speed unit such as a punched-card reader, the actual data transfer does not take much channel time. If it had several registers for addresses and counters, it could handle several units simultaneously. These units would actually be staggered in their character transmission times. Several card readers and printers, for example, could each be transmitting characters to the channel. Each character might take about 4 micro seconds, and then there would be a wait of about 500 micro seconds for the next character. By staggering these, the channel can service all of them in rotation. This is called multiplexing. To multiplex means to put a group (plex) of several things into one. If a channel can interleave single characters in this fashion, it is called a *byte multiplex* channel. Some units transmit characters in blocks at a high speed, followed by a delay before the next block. A channel can be designed to handle a block of characters from one unit, followed by a block from another unit before continuing service to the first unit. This is called a *block multiplex* channel. A multiplex

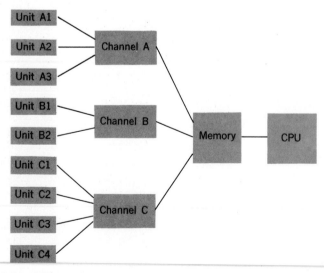

FIGURE 6.6   *Multiple units on channels*

channel looks like several channels to the user, since I/O operations can be started on several units at once. The channel limits the maximum number of units that can be serviced at the same time by the maximum data rate that it can handle (called its *bandwidth*). Obviously, more lower-speed units can be operated at once than high-speed units. Some multiplex channels have a *burst mode* form of operation which takes effect when a unit saturates the channel, using all the available time in a burst of characters.

A channel allows the parallel transfer of data between several I/O units and the main memory while the CPU is processing the program. Each operating channel and the CPU are competing for the use of memory, so the number of units that can be in operation is limited by the speed (bandwidth) of the memory. It is not possible to saturate the memory by I/O devices on most systems, as the speed of most devices is much slower than memory. However, some very fast devices, such as extended core storage or large drums and disks, can use an appreciable number of the available memory cycles. In that case, the speed of the CPU is decreased noticably because it will often have to wait for an I/O device to finish a memory reference before it can use the memory. (The memory unit handles references from the CPU and the channels, usually giving priority to the channels, as I/O devices such as disks cannot be stopped but must be serviced within a certain length of time. The programmer does not have to be concerned with the timing considerations, except to be aware that his program may be slowed down.)

While a channel is transferring a block of data between memory and an I/O device, the programmer has no knowledge of how many characters have been transmitted, as, in most systems, he has no access to the counters in the channels. Consequently, if he wants to read a block of characters and process them, he must wait until the read of the block is complete before starting to process the first character. If he did not start reading the next block until he had finished processing the first block, he would have to wait again for a read to be completed. This mode of operation would be no better than reading a single character, waiting for completion of the read, and then processing the character; whenever a read was being performed, the program would be waiting. Consequently, a program should read more than one block into memory. After the first has been read, processing can start while second and subsequent blocks are being read. In this mode, the blocks of characters are being treated as individual characters were in the earlier discussion on paper-tape reading. A set of buffers, each large enough to hold a block of data, must be provided. The input processing program can try to keep these buffers full with unprocessed blocks of data, while the CPU accesses data a block at a time. If the I/O controller and channel provide interrupts which indicate when the transfer of a block of data is complete, the input process can be interrupt-driven as before. When the CPU needs a new block of data, it can request the address of the buffer containing that data from the supervisor program by a supervisor call. The CPU program can then process all the data in the block, item by item, and not have to call the supervisor again until a new block is needed.

6.2.1 Channel computers

A complex design that provides more flexibility is given by a channel that can execute its own instructions from the memory. In this case, the channel has a control counter and an instruction decoder similar to the CPU. The CPU is usually given the power to set the control counter of the channel to any value. From there on, the channel executes an independent program, performing I/O transfers until it reaches a STOP instruction. The CPU can be interrupted by the channel actions if needed, so that it can initiate actions on other channels and coordinate them with the processing programs.

The control of I/O gets more complicated as it is improved for speed, and the novice programmer is likely to be appalled at the prospect of writing code for all these simultaneously operating devices and keeping all the interrupt signals sorted out. Never fear, the professional programmer would also be appalled if he were asked to do this. The operating system is expected to provide many subroutines that take care of the various I/O units, make their use efficient, and take care of errors which are not infrequent on I/O equipment. They are detected by parity methods and usually cause interrupts. They will be discussed in Section 6.4.

A sophisticated channel is nothing more than a simple computer which is directly connected to the input/output equipment. In a sense, it is like using a separate, slower computer to handle the I/O in an offline manner, but it has the important feature that it works into the same memory as the main computer (CPU) and can be controlled by the CPU. It can indirectly control the CPU by means of interrupts. Thus there is a very rapid communication between the two computers. A program for a typical channel might take the form

SELECT-UNIT	8	This causes unit number 8 to be attached to the channel.
READ-RECORD	A	If unit 8 is a tape unit, this would read the next record into locations A, A+1, A+2, . . . , etc. It would keep a selector channel busy, so the next operation must wait until the read has finished.
TEST-FOR-ERROR	B	This would cause a branch to location B if an error had occurred during the read operation.
STOP		The CPU does not have a STOP instruction, but a channel can stop. It would interrupt the CPU on most machines.

Some I/O channels of this type are small computers, complete with arithmetic and conditional branch instructions. The CPU can start a process running on such channels, and leave tables of complex control information in memory which the channels can use to decide in what order to perform I/O operations in situations where there is a choice. (Such situations can arise when several different parts of a program are referencing the same device. For example, a program could be reading data from a disk file, processing it, and returning the results to the disk file—a compiler usually does this. If the program has requested both reads and writes for the disk file, it does not matter logically whether the reads or the writes are done first. If the heads of the disk file are closer to the area containing the input information, it would be faster to do the reads, then move the heads to the area containing the output information to do the writes. Such a decision could be made by a complex channel processor.)

Most channels can process single instructions only (for example, the PDP-11) or a few data transfer instructions (for example, the IBM 370). The CDC 6600 is an example of a computer with much more sophisticated channels.

6.2.2 PDP-11 and IBM 370 channels

The PDP-11 uses a very simple, extendable design for its channels by allowing the CPU to reference a channel using a set of pseudo memory locations. For example, a unit, such as a disk, will use four memory addresses as the addresses of its registers. These registers contain

Status data (control and sense lines)
Buffer address (location in main memory)
Word count (number of words to be transmitted)
Disk address (block number to be accessed on disk)

When these registers are set, a transfer is initiated. Data are copied between the memory, starting at the buffer address, and the disk, starting at the beginning of the accessed block; copying continues until the desired number of words has been transmitted. An interrupt can be obtained when the transfer is complete so that the CPU can initiate another transfer immediately. The type of transfer (read, write, or seek operation) is determined by the data set into the status register.

The IBM 370 allows up to 16 channels to be connected to memory. Channel 0 is a byte multiplex channel. The other 15 (numbered 1 through 15) can be multiplex or selector channels. The CPU can execute a few instructions that send information to the channels, for example, START I/O, HALT I/O, and TEST I/O. The HALT stops I/O activity on the addressed device. TEST sets the condition code based on the state of the addressed device. START tells the channel which device to connect for an I/O operation. When a channel is started, it fetches the word from absolute location 72. This contains the address of the CCW (Channel Command Word), which is the IBM name for an instruction to an I/O channel. The CCW tells the channel which instruction to execute and where the data are to be found. It also contains a bit that indicates whether the channel is to stop operations on the device at the completion of the operation or is to continue and fetch the next word as another CCW. Hence the 370 can execute channel programs. However, these are very simple programs, consisting of a sequence of transfers and unconditional branches only. The CCW can also indicate whether a CPU interrupt is to occur at the completion of the data transfer.

6.3 CONTROL OF TAPES AND DISKS

Tapes and disks require physical movement of the tape or the disk head in addition to the reading and writing operations. The typical control operations provided by the hardware were discussed in the previous chapter. Tape can be spaced forward or backward to record or file marks, or rewound. Disk heads can be moved to a particular position so that data on a cylinder can be accessed without waiting for further movement. On some systems it is possible to read the position of the disk (or drum) relative to the heads so that it is possible to calculate how long before a given sector is under the read heads. The software use of tapes and disks must be organized to recognize the long mechanical times involved in head or tape motion, or in waiting for a rotational delay. Data on tapes must be organized so that they are generally read in the order written. For this reason, tapes are most suited to input and output data sets that are written and/or read once during a single job. If it is necessary to access data in an arbitrary order, a disk is preferable. Even then, the data should be organized so that not too much head motion is needed in the majority of operations. Later, we will see that the system can take care of some of these problems automatically. Indeed, in most operating environments, the system has complete control of disk use. However, in jobs involving large amounts of data, the programmer must plan the layout of data on the disk if he wishes to get an efficient program.

6.4 ERROR HANDLING

Some of the fundamental subroutines in the system area of memory perform the actual control of the I/O units. These subroutines are provided with parameters which indicate the unit and channel to be operated and the required operation. They must check that the requested operation is legal on the particular unit and then initiate the sequence of instructions to perform the operation. Depending on whether the channels execute independent programs or execute single transfer operations given by the CPU, the operation may require a number of interrupts as the various substeps are completed. These are analogous to the interrupts of the CPU in the simple paper-tape input discussed in Section 6.1.1. If the operation includes steps that transmit data between the unit and the channel, then the channel performs parity checking on the data. (Almost all I/O devices use parity bits in communication with the channel.) If an error is detected, the channel notes it in a 1-bit error register and completes the operation. At the end of processing, action must be taken. In a simple channel that does not execute its own program, an interrupt will be sent to the CPU. When it accepts it, the error bit must be tested so that corrective steps can be initiated. These depend on the type of unit. Some typical actions are given below. A complex channel could execute the steps itself.

Card reader   Since the card that caused the error has passed through the reader, the only thing that can be done is to send a message to the operator (on a console typewriter perhaps), asking him to refeed the card.

Printer   A note can be printed that the last line was in error, and then the line can be reprinted.

Tape unit being read   The tape can be backspaced and the record reread. This process should be repeated several times (five, perhaps), because some errors are due to dust particles lifting the tape off the read heads. These can be dislodged. If it continues to fail, then the processing of that record is impossible.

Tape unit being written   The tape can be backspaced and the write performed again as for read. If it continues to fail, it indicates that there is a bad spot on the tape. On unformatted tape, there is usually a SKIP operation that erases about 3 inches of tape. This can be performed after the last backspace, and then the write sequence can be recommenced. This blank piece of tape looks like an extra long record gap; it does not affect the operation of subsequent reads except to slow them down.

Disk files   These can be handled by rereading or rewriting the record in error. If errors on writes continue to occur, then something is wrong with the track. Its use can be avoided automatically in more sophisticated system programs. Many disk files contain recorded information at the start of each record called the *home address.* The reading or writing program must provide a copy of this information in order to be allowed access to the record. If a match fails to occur, it can indicate either a failure by the hardware or on the part of the programmer to specify the right information. The seek can be tried a second time before the operation request is abandoned.

6.5 SOFTWARE FOR I/O

Because the control of input/output equipment is so complex from a programming point of view, it is necessary to adopt a set of conventions concerning the way in which it is used and to provide most of the direct control by system subroutines. This section will discuss some of the methods used to create an efficient and flexible operating system for the user. In addition to controlling the units themselves, many of the I/O subroutines are concerned with buffers. A buffer was used in the simple example of paper-tape reading given above. In machines with complex controllers, buffers are needed to hold the blocks of characters being read until they are needed by the processor.

6.5.1 The principle of multiple buffering

In the example in Section 6.1.1 above, storage spaces were assigned for many characters and, in this sense, we may say that multiple buffers were being used. In the simple scheme of *double buffering,* two buffers are filled with consecutive blocks of input from the reading unit. As the processor needs characters, it gets them (by subroutine) from the first buffer. When that buffer is empty, a read request is made to the system to refill it. In the meantime, the processor can use characters from the second buffer. The processor will have to wait if the reader does not have time to refill the first buffer before the processor has emptied the second buffer; and, similarly, the reader will be idle if the processor does not have time to empty the second buffer before the first is refilled. If the processor is using input at a more or less constant rate, then two buffers are adequate; but if the rate fluctuates, the double buffering technique can be extended in an obvious way to more buffers. The use of three buffers is shown in Figure 6.7.

Buffering such as that outlined above can be provided completely within the system area of main memory, it can be provided by the user independent of the system, or it can be provided in some combination. Many schemes are available, so in these notes we shall discuss three of the common methods. These discussions apply equally well to output buffering.

6.5.2 Serial I/O through system buffers

By serial input, we mean the sort of input that is read only once. An example of this is the primary data input to the program, probably originating on punched cards. By the time that the system is ready to read the data to the user program, it has usually been copied to a faster medium such as magnetic tape or disk. This discussion also applies to output which is not to be reread, such as the main output destined for the printer.

The user program would like the ability to read in one card image at a time, but it would not like to have to wait for the images to be read into memory. Therefore, the system area of main memory provides two or more buffers which it attempts to keep filled with card images from the input source. A subroutine is provided for the user to request the next card image for processing. This subroutine will copy the contents of the next image into the user area of memory and begin to refill the buffer. Functionally, it is equivalent to the simple paper-tape read program discussed above, except that card images are being discussed instead of characters. The CPU will only have to wait if the overall process time is less than the card read time, while the reader will wait if the process time is longer than the read time. Since card reading is relatively slow, it will usually be done offline, so the appropriate speeds to compare are tape speeds and process speeds.

Output functions in an analogous manner. Two or more buffers are provided in the system area. Each time that the user outputs a line to the system printer, it is placed in one of the buffers. Each time that a buffer is filled, it is written to the output device and output from the user is diverted to another buffer.

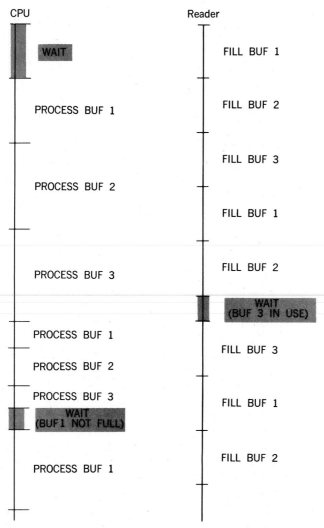

FIGURE 6.7   Use of three buffers

A common method for handling primary input/output involves putting the input and output files (that is, the set of input records and output records for a particular job) onto disk. Card readers and printers are online in such a system, and are used to continuously read new jobs onto the disk file and print completed jobs from the file. This is done by the use of buffers in the system for relaying the data between the disk and the I/O devices, in addition to buffers between the disk and the executing program. The program is "interrupt driven," that is, interrupts caused by the card reader, printer, and disk file are used to initiate further actions. In such a system, the input is read onto the disk file before a job is begun and printed from the disk file after it has been completed. This method is, therefore, similar to offline operation via magnetic tape, but it requires less operator action and is more flexible for scheduling purposes. It is sometimes called "pseudo offline"; by IBM, it is called "SPOOL" (Simultaneous Peripheral Operation OnLine). (A peripheral device is any I/O or auxiliary storage device.)

6.5.3 Programmer buffered I/O

When a computer system has a large number of I/O units available, it may be unreasonable to provide several buffers in the system area of memory for every unit. Also, units that can be used for both input and output are not used in a predictable way; that is, one does not know if the next block on a scratch tape will be read, since it is possible that the user may write something over it instead. It is impossible to predict which is the next record to be fetched from a disk file. Therefore, some units cannot be handled in the manner in which primary input is handled. The simplest provision to make for the programmer is to provide him with a set of subroutines that allow him to read blocks of information from any of the I/O units and routines to test to see if the transfers have been completed. If the programmer can specify which block of memory should receive the input, he is free to use any buffering scheme that he wishes. The important subroutine actions that should be available are

READ (WRITE) into location N, *M* words, from channel J, unit K.

TEST to see if channel J, unit K, is free (that is, that it has finished its previous transfer without error).

If the unit is a serial-access device, then other control operations must be provided. Tape units, for example, have to be backspaced, rewound, etc., while the heads of a disk file have to be moved from one position to another. While this could be done by the user program directly, it is usual to use system subroutines to accomplish these actions. One reason is that it is easier for a single set of subroutines to check for each of the many errors that can occur on an I/O unit. If the user program were to take an action on a unit without the knowledge of the system subroutines, they would have trouble understanding the meaning of interrupts that could occur after an action was completed. A second reason is that there is interference between units on the same channel, and it is easier to let a common subroutine handle such problems. A third and most important reason is that, at this simplest level of operation, it is usual to provide protection for some of the I/O units so that the user program cannot access them. For example, the input may be on a tape, and, in many systems, several jobs are loaded onto a single input tape, one behind another, separated by an end-of-file mark. The serial input program that buffers such input in the system area of memory will prevent one user from moving the input tape beyond the end of his input, and thus protect a user's input from an error by the previous programmer. However, this protection is for naught if the user program can access the tape unit directly and forward space over the end-of-file mark into the next user's program and data. Protection of disk files against unauthorized access allows users to leave files of data from one run to another.

This type of protection can be provided by insisting that all input/output must be done by system subroutine and by designing the hardware so that input/output instructions are protected (or privileged) instructions. This means that if the user attempts to execute them directly, an interrupt to the program monitor occurs. When the system program is called to provide the input/output operation, it first checks to see if the user is allowed the use of that particular unit.

LOGICAL UNIT NUMBERS

Since it is possible that the particular unit available for, say, scratch use may change from one run to another, it is very common to use *logical numbers* or symbolic names for referring to I/O units. The system area of memory contains a table relating each logical number or name to a physical channel and unit number. This automatically takes care of unit protection, since a disallowed unit is simply not put in the table. Thus, in a typical installation, logical units six through nine could be tape units: the first two on one channel, and the second two on a different channel. There could be more tape units physically present but not logically accessible. These could be used to advantage if a job is currently running and the next job waiting requires two tapes to be mounted. They could be mounted on the extra tape drives while the current job is running. When the current job finishes, the operator can instruct the system to change the logical assignment table so that the two tapes mounted are now, say, logical units six and eight. This leaves two spare tape drives which could be used for mounting tapes for the next user. Although better ways of handling this problem will be discussed, the above method is useful because of its simplicity, and it partially solves the important problem of loss of computer time that frequently occurs in short-job environments. If there are a number of 5- to 10-minute jobs, several with tape mounting requirements, then it is not uncommon for several minutes to be lost on a job if the tapes are not mounted ahead of time. If the operator does not start to locate the required tape until the job starts, it can easily take 2 minutes to find it and mount it. This can represent a 20- to 40-percent loss of time.

TAPE LABELING

Most software systems make use of tape labels in a way which reduces the possibility of operator error and improves the efficiency of operation. A tape label should always be used as a guard against error on any system. A tape label is one or more blocks—written on the beginning of a tape—which contain the *name* of the tape. It is always possible that the wrong tape is fetched from the storage cabinet and mounted to meet the user's request. By reading the label and checking it against its known name, such errors can be caught. For example, some systems require that all tapes have labels. These label names also appear in a printed form on the tape reel. During the input phase of the program, the user indicates, on a control card, that a given tape is required on a given logical unit. The system reads the tape labels on all tapes mounted. If the required tapes are present, the units on which they are mounted are assigned the appropriate logical unit numbers. Those that are not present are requested. The operator can mount them on any available tape drive because the system will locate them by means of the tape labels.

6.5.4 Buffer pools and symbolic addressing of files

The last section discussed transfer methods which give the user maximum flexibility, but these methods throw the burden of allocating buffer space onto the user. If he uses many different I/O devices, he will almost certainly have to use some of the buffer space for several different purposes in order to conserve memory space for program. This can create a difficult planning problem in jobs where various tapes and disk files have to be accessed almost at random, since it can be impossible to predict which units are never accessed nearly simultaneously and hence which can share buffer space.

To overcome this problem, a *buffer-pool* technique can be used. A buffer pool is a set of buffer areas in main storage that can be allocated by subroutine for use with any unit. To use a buffer-pool, it is necessary to make all blocks the same length, or, less efficiently, to specify a maximum length. Each buffer is large enough to hold one block. Subroutines are written to allocate buffers from the pool when they are needed and to return them to the pool when they are free. In the simplest such system, the user would call for buffers when he needed to start a series of input or output transmissions to an I/O device. Typically, he would request two buffers in order to do double buffering. When that sequence of transfers had been completed, he would call to return the same two buffers. The pool subroutine would contain a list of all available buffer addresses. When buffers were requested, it would find them and remove them from the free list. When they were returned, it would add them to the list. It would be up to the user to write his subroutines for I/O so they could use the buffer addresses provided by the pool subroutine.

The simple buffer-pool solution does not take care of situations in which many files of data are being accessed simultaneously from many different I/O units. In that case, a request for two or more buffers for each active unit is likely to exhaust the available buffer space very quickly. At that point, the pool subroutine can do nothing except return control to the monitor indicating an error. If many files are active, in the sense that the program is in the middle of reading or writing them, then it is unlikely that all of them are being used at the same time. If there were a burst of activity on one or two files for a while, we would like to allocate buffers to those files and ignore the others. If there were an excessively large amount of activity on one file for a short period, it would be advantageous to allocate several buffers to that one file so that a backlog of input or output could be accumulated rather than having the main processor slow down. Output is easier to organize, because the actual transmission occurs after the buffer has been filled with data. If there is a sudden burst of output, then it is possible to arrange for several buffers to be filled in order and for these to be written as soon as possible thereafter. Input, however, presents problems, because the computer is unaware of the burst of activity until it actually happens. In order not to lose time, however, it is necessary to prefill several buffers before the first is requested. This must be handled either by means of a request from the programmer which warns the system that activity is about to commence on a particular file or by letting the system guess about future activity on the basis of previous activity. The latter is the basis of some systems, so let us take a closer look at the details.

The user will have a number of *commands,* probably in the form of subroutine calls, with which he can *open* and *close* files. The files are names of groups of records on tape, disk, or similar devices which are available to the user. The OPEN command tells the system that the file specified is to be used by the programmer. It therefore makes preparations to provide it with buffer space when it is needed. At this time, it is just an entry in a table in the system area of memory. The CLOSE command is used to tell the system that the file has been completed (if it is output) or will not be needed again (if it is input). Other subroutine entries are used to request input data or to hand over output data. Because the files have fixed block lengths to simplify the buffering problem, the user works with logical records which may be of variable length. Several logical records may be packed into one physical block on the I/O device to save space. The programmer would build up an output file by calling the output programs with successive logical records of information. The system would handle them as follows:

1 If there is no buffer allocated to that device, allocate one.

2 Precede the logical record with a few characters which tell the system its length and other characteristics.

3 Copy the logical record and its heading information into the next available space in the buffer.

4 If the buffer is full, call the subroutine which handles output writing with a request to write this buffer on the specified unit. Allocate another buffer, and return to 3.

5 When the logical record has been copied, return to the calling program.

This technique will allow as many buffers as are available to be used on one output unit. In order that the buffers be returned to the pool after the output writing has been done, it is necessary for the system to process interrupts on the termination of writes and to return the buffer involved to the pool.

Input is more difficult. Unless restrictions are placed on the use of files, the system cannot tell in advance which files will be input and which will be output. The best that it can do without further information is to read one block from each file into a buffer. Any read request can be filled by copying from the buffer. The heading information for each logical record tells how many characters to copy. When a buffer is empty, it should be returned to the pool and another filled. Operations such as backspace, forward space, etc., must be interpreted by the program, since the user is talking in terms of logical — not physical — records. If a burst of reads of a single unit is to be reasonably efficient, then several buffers should be filled in advance. This can be partly done by keeping a record of the average activity of each file over a short period and allocating more buffers to the active files. Whatever scheme is used, it is possible to fool it by performing a number of reads on a given file, to the point where it has kindly filled up several buffers, and then by rewinding the file to the beginning so that all the buffer contents can be discarded.

Since all the I/O reads and writes to the actual devices are done by a central system program working from system buffers in a complex pooling scheme, it is possible for the system to rearrange the order of the operations to maximize the speed. If many of the files are scattered over disks, then there will be considerable head movement from one file to another. Head movement is one of the slowest operations on a disk unit, so its time should be minimized. Since the time for movement increases with the distance of movement, the system should minimize the distance moved as much as possible. This can be done by arranging for the system to select, from all transfers waiting, the transfer with the smallest head movement. This algorithm can be dangerous in situations with two or more independent jobs being time-shared. Consider a system in which one area of core contains a user program and another contains an interrupt-driven program for reading cards to disk (SPOOL). It is possible for one program to give a series of disk references in a small region which will prevent the heads moving to service the other program, thus halting it. The access time of head movement can also be reduced by trying to place the files over different disk modules with separate head-positioning mechanisms.

TYPE OF ACCESS

The techniques discussed above have been aimed at making the I/O access mechanisms look like magnetic tape units, which provide *sequential access* only. This is done by providing — for logical record transmission — operations equivalent to those provided for transmission of physical records. In the discussion of tapes, it was pointed out that there is an advantage to using formatted tape if the information can be indexed and accessed via a search through a much smaller index. In a sophisticated system, it is possible to provide for accessing via an index of contents. The index will contain the reference and the physical location of each logical record, so that the user can request to access a certain record, leaving it to the system to perform the index look-up, positioning of read heads, and extraction of the logical record. This is called *indexed* accessing. Another form of organization is to use *keys* stored with the data and to reference a record by means of the key. If the data are stored with the keys in "alphabetical" order, a combination of indexing and searching can be used to locate data for reading and the place where data should be written. This type of organization is useful for handling "line-numbered" files, which occur in many time-sharing systems. The user or the system attaches a line number to every logical record stored in a file so that records can be fetched, changed, or deleted by line number. It is evident that a lot of time could be spent searching for a given line in such an organization. This is reduced in one implementation† by keeping a directory of the range of line numbers stored in each physical block recorded on disk. When a new line is added, the block that should logically contain it is located. If there is no space, an unused block of disk is obtained from a free storage allocation program, and the data from the old block plus the new line is divided between the two blocks, thus leaving space for several more additions. If lines are deleted until a block is empty, it is removed from the directory and returned for use by the storage allocation program. In this way, the programmer is unaware of which physical locations he is occupying on the disk.

DISK SPACE ALLOCATION

When files are being built on the disk, whether sequential, indexed, or organized in ways such as the line-numbered system discussed above, a program must allocate space on the disk as it is needed by the various files that are growing, and must remember which space is available. Disk space is normally

†D. Whaley, A Failure Tolerant Filing System, *Software Practice and Experience,* vol. 2, no. 3, pp. 287–292, July–September 1972.

allocated in blocks. One block, often several thousand characters, is the amount of data transferred in one disk I/O instruction. Individual files often use *pointers* to know where succeeding blocks of the file can be located on the disk. A pointer is the disk address of the next block; it is contained either in the preceding block or in a directory. As a file is built, new blocks are obtained from the allocation subroutine, and their addresses are placed in the pointer variable. When this is done, it is very important to be certain that the state of the file is always valid. If a pointer to block B is placed in block A, it must not be done until any pointers in block B have been set to reasonable values. If, for example, the pointers in block B were pointing to another user's data stored on disk, and a system failure occurred immediately after the pointer to B had been placed in A, subsequent use of the file might result in this other user's data being changed. Consequently, disk space must be allocated by a system program that properly initializes pointers.

There are several ways of keeping a list of free blocks. The simplest is to use a *bit map.* This consists of a region of memory in which 1 bit is assigned to each block. Bits are set when a block is assigned to a file, and cleared when they are freed.

SYMBOLIC ACCESS OF FILES

The final step in relieving the user of input/output problems is to provide for symbolic access of files of information. A file of information is a group of logical records which are usually related in some sense. The only actions that interest the user are writing groups of logical records as a file, accessing files written previously in order to read the records they contain, and requesting that some files be saved permanently, that some be saved until he makes his next run, and that some be destroyed because they are of no further use. (The latter is particularly important because a constantly increasing part of the cost of computers is in saving information, a lot of which will probably never be used again.) It would be of a lot more value to the user if files were given names and the system took care of matching names against positions on physical units. In such a system, the user would create a file by telling the system that he wanted to write a file whose name was "filename" and that it was to be saved for reuse within 48 hours, for example. The system would use this information to decide, on the basis of current demands on storage space, where to put the file (on tape or disk, etc.). Future calls to the system would be used to pass logical records of information for packing into buffers and subsequent writing onto the storage unit. Each time that a file was completed, the system would index it; that is, its name would be placed in a table of file names for that user with an indication of where it was physically located. When the user returned another day and requested access to the given file, it could first be looked up in the index table. If it was indicated as being on an attached storage unit such as a disk file, the buffers would be loaded directly. If it were not immediately available, then the operator would be instructed to load the tape or other medium that contained the file. (This information is contained in the index.) When the storage medium is loaded, it should first be checked (the operator could have loaded the wrong one) by reading the label. Assuming that the operator had loaded the correct tape or other medium, a table of contents would be read from the device and consulted to find out where the file was currently located. It could then be accessed and read into the buffer area.

It is apparent that there are many inefficiencies in a completely symbolic system such as the one described above. In order to maintain some degree of efficiency, it is almost mandatory to have some form of multiprogramming system in which at least two programs are in core at one time, so that, while one is waiting for I/O transfers, the other can be using the central processor. However, simple machine efficiency is not the only criterion to be applied. If the total system is easier for the user, to the point that he uses fewer machine runs to complete a job, those runs can afford to be less efficient. No more machine time would have been used and less human time would have been used—which is, after all, the purpose of a computer system.

By their nature, complex input/output system programs are restricted to large computer systems because of their heavy demands on space and computer time. Consequently, small systems, such as the PDP-11, provide very basic input/output routines tailored to a particular installation. In the next section we will look at the IBM 360/370 system briefly, as it is typical of large systems.

6.6 IBM 370 I/O SYSTEMS

This section will give a summary of some of the facilities available in the IBM system 370 when Operating System 370 is being used. The purpose of this summary is not to provide complete documentation of any feature, but rather to give the reader an idea of a specific system that has been implemented to supplement the general discussions of the preceding sections. Readers who need to make use of the 370 will have to obtain details from appropriate publications. Many installations make available short write-ups which describe the most frequently used methods of input/output for their particular environment, and these are usually the easiest to start using.†

† The full details are spread across many IBM manuals. In particular, the student can refer to Operating System Data Management, form number C28-6537; Operating System Job Control Language, form number C28-6539; and Operating System Supervisor and Data Management Macro-Instruc-

A user of the 370 must first learn a new set of names for the items that we have been discussing. This has been done by IBM partly to avoid some of the ambiguities of earlier names. (Files, for example, which refer to sets of records or to physical memory devices.) A single storage device, such as a reel of tape or a removable set of disk platters, is now called a *volume*. A group of logical records is now called a *data set* (a name unfortunately also used by communications people for a data-transmission device). In order that access to a volume be as symbolic as desired by the programmer, many volumes contain, in addition to a label, a *volume table of contents*. This contains the names of the data sets that have been stored on that volume. Operations are provided within the system for *cataloging* and *uncataloging* data sets by name.

The system provides operations, by means of subroutines, that allow the user to access specific data sets by name, to read or write records within them, to block and unblock records from longer physical blocks, to check labels (which can appear on both volumes and data sets), to write labels on data sets for future checking, and to get control if error conditions arise. These are provided in a way which attempts to minimize the dependence of the input/output code written by the user on the type of device actually used. In this way, a program can be run on one of many different installations with different input/output configurations. Buffers can be provided by the user, supplied on request by the system, or provided automatically by the system.

A data set may be stored on a volume in a number of ways, depending on the type of volume and the type of data. The simplest way to store records is sequentially. The *sequential* organization is the only one allowed on sequential devices such as magnetic tapes. In this organization, input or output of the next record is permitted, together with some control functions analogous to the various magnetic tape functions discussed. A *partitioned data set* is one that is broken into a number of sequentially organized members. This system provides a *directory* of each subdata set within the set at the start, and the user may access any of its members by name. The subdata sets may only be accessed sequentially. A partitioned data set is useful when groups of related data sets are to be stored. A library of programs, for example, can be stored as a partitioned data set, and each member can be accessed by symbolic name when it is needed for loading purposes. When records each have control information on which the records are to be retrieved, then an *indexed sequen-*

---

tions, form number C28-6647. The first manual presents an overall picture of the system, the second can be used to find details about the DD statements, while the third can be used to find out about the various macro instructions—such as OPEN, CLOSE, DCB, READ, WRITE, GET, PUT, GETPOOL, and FREEPOOL—available to the assembly language programmer.

tial organization can be used. In this organization, the control information, called a *key,* is stored in an index for the data set. The keys are stored in order, so that access to the data set can be either in order of the keys (that is, sequentially as stored), or by reference to a particular key. This mechanism allows the programmer the flexibility of addressable storage when needed. The keys function as symbolic addresses for records. Because the system must perform searches for the keys, this method can be very slow. If addressable storage is needed for speed, then the *direct organization* can be used. This permits the user to specify a track address on a direct-access volume (a device with disklike or drumlike properties) and to write a block on the next available space on that track. Retrieval is again by means of a key, but the programmer can specify on which track the search for the key is to commence.†

6.6.1 Control of I/O

In order to gain access to a specific data set, the user issues an OPEN macro instruction, which is a call on the system. The system then locates the data set, assigns buffer space if necessary, and prepares itself so that future calls on the input/output routines will be connected with the data set. The OPEN macro refers to a block of storage called a *data-control block.* This block contains all of the information that identifies the data set and the way in which it is to be accessed. In particular, it specifies the type of organization (sequential, indexed sequential, etc.), the record format (fixed-length records, variable-length records, etc.), the type of input/output operations to be used, the number and size of the buffers, and what is to happen if error or end-of-data-set (similar to end-of-file) conditions occur. The information in this block can be obtained from four different places. At assembly time, the user can specify most of the block of storage. The easiest way of doing this is by use of the DCB (Data-Control Block) macro instruction. It is desirable to leave the specification of some of the parameters until the program is loaded and run. This can be done by using the DD statement in JCL (Job-Control Language). Some information, such as the size of blocks, is specified in the data set label. If an existing data set is used, then it is not necessary for the programmer to specify this information. The OPEN macro will fill out all unspecified data in the data control block by obtaining the information first from the DD statement and then from the data-set label. Finally, it is possible for the executing program to set information into the control block.

After the OPEN has been executed, the data set can be accessed. There are various ways in which this can be done and in which buffers can be provided.

---

†Details of these storage organizations can be found in the IBM manual Operating System; Supervisor and Data Management Services, form number C28-6646-0.

In the *basic access methods,* which can be used with any of the data set organizations, buffering must be provided by the user. READ and WRITE macro instructions are used to initiate the corresponding operations. The completion of either of these macros does not mean that the actual operation has been completed; rather, it means that the information in the data-control block and system area has been set so that it will eventually be completed. To check for completion, the user issues a CHECK macro which checks for errors and waits for completion. These macros allow the user to program any buffer method that he desires. The system provides a buffer pool service for basic access methods by means of four macros. GETPOOL obtains a group of buffers for a specific data-control block. FREEPOOL returns them to the system when the user is through with them. GETBUF obtains the address of one of them for use in a READ or WRITE macro, while FREEBUF returns it to the group.

The basic methods of access force the user to consider his own buffering and his own blocking-unblocking, as the input/output operations are in terms of physical blocks. *Queued-access methods* are more automatic, in that the system performs the buffer overlap and does the blocking and unblocking. After a data set has been opened for queued access, the user can obtain logical records by means of the GET macro and write logical records by means of the PUT macro. The data-control block contains the addresses of buffers, which can either have been obtained by a GETPOOL macro or assigned automatically in the event that the user made no specification of buffers. The system keeps the buffers refilled or emptied in the case of input or output respectively. The information is copied from or to the buffers to or from the user work area when the GET or PUT is issued, so that the completion of the macro implies the completion of the I/O as far as the user is concerned.

For sequentially organized data sets, a typical set of access macro instructions would be

```
OPEN    (dcbname,(INPUT))
. . . . .
GET     dcbname,line
. . . . .
GET     dcbname,line
etc.
. . . . .
CLOSE   (dcbname)
```

for input under queued-access methods. The *dcbname* is the address of a DCB macro discussed below, while *line* is the address of the first of a group of characters for input. For output, the word OUTPUT would be substituted for IN-PUT above, and the PUT macro would be used instead of GET.

Basic access would be performed in a similar manner. The data set would be opened for input, output, or both, and then READ or WRITE macros could be issued. These take the form

> READ   decbname,type,dcbname,area-address

Optionally, a character length can be placed on the end of this macro. The *decbname* is the address assigned to a block of storage generated for the *data-event-control block* which contains information about the status of the transfer while it is happening. It is used in the CHECK macro which waits for termination and checks for errors. Type indicates with an SF or SB whether the information is read forward or backward. The *dcbname* is the address of the DCB macro which gives details of the data set, while the *area-address* is the memory address for the first byte into which the data is to be transmitted (that is, the buffer). Before the information is used, a CHECK macro should be issued in the form

> CHECK   decbname

The data set must be closed when its use is terminated, just as for queued-access methods.

6.6.2 The DCB macro

The initial specification of the data-control block is by the DCB macro.†
The macro is written in the form

> dcbname   DCB   parameter1,parameter2, . . . , parameter n

More than 25 different parameters can be specified. In order that each one need not be given, all parameters are written in the form

> SPEC=value

where SPEC is the name of one of the parameters and *value* is the value to be assigned. Parameters not specified are filled out by information from other sources or by default values, that is, by values assumed by the system. Some of the parameters are given below.

---

†The reader is referred to the IBM manual Operating System Supervisor and Data Management Macro-Instructions, form number C28-6647, for full details.

DSORG = This parameter gives the data-set organization. Its value is two or three letters: DA for direct access, IS for indexed sequential, PO for partitioned organization, or PS for sequential organization. U may follow any of these to indicate that the data set cannot be moved. (This can happen if it contains the absolute addresses of its own locations, for example.)

MACRF = This indicates which type of access will be used, and whether the data set will be input, output, or both. R and W indicate READ and WRITE for basic access methods, G and P indicate input and output for queued-access methods. An M or a T after G or P indicates that the data are to be transmitted between the work area and the buffer, or that the buffer is to be substituted for the work area.

RECFM = This specifies the format and characteristics of the records in the data set. It need only be specified if the user wishes to force a particular format. Thus, if the data set already exists, its characteristics can be obtained from the label. Typical letters that can appear here include F for fixed-length records or V for variable-length records.

LRECL = Length, in bytes, of a record. This specifies the length of a fixed-length record or the maximum length of a variable-length record.

BLKSIZE = This specifies the maximum length of a block, in bytes. This is needed so that the system knows what size buffers to allocate.

BUFNO = Number of buffers to be used. If the user is leaving the buffering to the system, he may indicate the number of buffers that he requires. For some access methods, two buffers are obtained unless specified otherwise.

EODAD = This specifies the program address to be given control when the end of an input data set is reached. Control is transferred here when a GET or READ attempts to read beyond the end of the data set.

DDNAME = The name of a DD statement must be specified. This is discussed below.

There are many other parameters that can be specified, and there are many restrictions on the use of these. The reader is advised not to attempt to write his own DCBs without consulting the appropriate IBM manual or instructions prepared by his own installation.

6.6.3 The DD statement

The DD statement is a JCL command which provides additional information for the data-control block. It is related to the DCB macro by means of its name, which appears in the DDNAME parameter in the DCB. The DD statement is punched as //ddname DD parameters. The blanks are the separators between the fields. The advantage of using the DD statement to specify parameters rather than specifying them in the DCB macro is that a change in the DCB requires a reassembly, whereas the DD statement is handled just prior to execution. Some of the parameters that can appear in a DD statement are listed below.

DSNAME = This provides the name of a data set. It should be specified if a previous data set is to be referred to or if the data set being constructed will be referred to by a later process. This allows the output of one process (*job step* in 370 terminology) to be provided as input to a later step.

UNIT =
VOLUME = $\Big\}$ These allow the user to specify the location of the data set.

DISP = The disposition of the data set can be specified. It can be a new set or an old one. It may be cataloged or uncataloged. It can be kept for a later job step or deleted.

DCB = Information not provided by the DCB or the data-set label must be provided here. It can be obtained by using the characteristics of an existing data set or by providing a list of parameters that was not specified in the DCB.

As an alternative, the data set might be the system input or output stream. These are handled by the DD statements

> //ddname   DD   *

and

> //ddname   DD   SYSOUT=A

respectively. The attributes of the two data sets are specified, so that all unfilled parameters in the DCB statement can be completed.

PROBLEMS

1   Suppose that there are six records on tape, and that some computation is to be done on each record. Two buffers, B1 and B2, each capable of holding one record, are available. Suppose the instructions available are

> READ   B1
> READ   B2
> COMPUTE   B1
> COMPUTE   B2

and WAIT

where the READ instructions read the next record into B1 or B2 as indicated and the COMPUTE instructions perform the required computation on the buffer named. (These might be implemented as macro instructions.) Assume that the READ instruction starts the read into the buffer, but that it only waits for the previous input operation to finish. That is,

> READ   B1
> COMPUTE   B1

is not a usable program. The WAIT operation holds up program flow until the last input operation (into either buffer) has finished, and the COMPUTE operation completes the computation before proceeding to the next instruction. One way of performing the calculation is to repeat the sequence

```
READ        B1
WAIT
COMPUTE     B1
```

six times, but it is slow because of the waits. Write a program that will not perform any unnecessary waits, using two buffers.

If the compute time is exactly equal to the read time, how much faster is the double-buffered program than the "bad" program given?

2   Suppose that we wish to copy blocks of information from one tape unit (U1) to another (U2) via main memory. The only instructions available are

```
READ        U1, Bi
WRITE       U2, Bi
WAIT        U1
WAIT        U2
```

where Bi, $i = 1, 2, 3, \ldots$, are buffers in memory. READ, WRITE, and WAIT each wait until the previous operation on the specified unit has finished before control can continue to the next instruction.

a   Write a program using two buffers, B1 and B2, to transmit six blocks from U1 to U2 as fast as possible.

b   Write a program using three buffers, B1, B2, and B3, and a minimum of instructions to do the same.

3   Discuss the use of buffer pools. What are they for, how are they organized and what are their limitations?

4   Consider a process which involves reading blocks of a fixed size B from tape, processing each to produce another block of size B, and then writing each onto an output tape in blocks of size B. (Note: block = physical record.) The average calculation time for each of any 30 consecutive blocks is precisely equal to the time T to read or write each of those 30 blocks, including time for record gaps. (It is a two-channel machine.) In theory, it is possible to keep both tapes spinning and the CPU busy. If the maximum process time for one block is $2T$ and the minimum is $T/2$, how many buffers of size B are needed to keep the tapes spinning?

5   Discuss the stages of output overlap that are similar to the successively more complex stages of input overlap described in Sections 6.1 and 6.1.1.

6   Consider a system in which blocks of disk space are allocated by a system program. Suppose these blocks are kept on a free list, that is, each free block has a pointer to the next free block except that the last has an indicator to say

end of list. Each time a block is used, it is removed from the beginning of the list, and the system records the next available free block. Suppose the system passes the address of the free block to the requesting program, and that program uses it for the next block in a file being written. Suppose also that this file *chains* its blocks using similar pointers from one to the next. What would happen if there was a *system crash* (that is, the programs in the CPU failed for some reason and the CPU had to be reloaded, thus destroying pointer information saved in the main memory) between the time that the block was allocated to the requesting program and the pointer in that block was updated if the program put a pointer to the block from the preceding block:

a Before the new block pointer was updated?

b After the new block pointer was updated?

7 Frequently, systems that use large disk files must recognize bad tracks by keeping a record of which tracks cannot be used because of defects. (It is not possible to manufacture a large, high-density disk platter without occasional blemishes. If every platter with a blemish had to be rejected, they would be unbelievably expensive. Instead, the system programs make it possible to use such disks.) How can this be handled if the bit map scheme is being used for disk allocation?

7

CONTROL STRUCTURE, LOGIC, AND MICRO PROGRAMMING

This chapter will discuss some details of the design of a simple hypothetical computer. A brief summary of the principles of data flow and logic will be given, followed by an overview of the hardware in the control unit. Many more details of microprogram control will be covered, as this is an area in which there is considerable interaction between computer design engineers and programmers. The detailed structure of a particular microprogram control will be examined by studying a simulator, that is, a computer program which imitates the organization of the control structure of the hypothetical computer. This approach is taken so that the structure can be illustrated clearly without a need to understand digital circuitry.

Before starting the simulation, let us ask what is the difference between a computer simulator and an interpreter of the machine language for that computer. The former is certainly also the latter, since a simulator will execute the machine language of the simulated machine. A simulator, however, is a little more than an interpreter. If the only need is to interpret the language, then it is of no importance to the user how this is done. However, a simulator should mimic the machine as closely as is necessary to derive the required measurements. When a computer manufacturer has a simulator written, he wishes to use it to determine whether some of his ideas will work. Therefore he must follow the proposed machine design as closely as possible, simulating features that are not apparent to the eventual programmers when the machine is constructed but that do affect the method of operation internally. The example to be treated later falls into the category of simulators, since it models all internal registers and data paths explicitly and generates sequences of operations that would be identical to the control signals in the machine, were it to be constructed.

7.1 AN OUTLINE OF COMPUTER DESIGN

This section will discuss some of the ways in which the central processing unit of a computer can be constructed and controlled. The building blocks which will be used consist of *registers, adders, memory units, gates,* etc. The memory unit and the idea of a register were introduced in Chapter 2. A CPU contains a number of registers connected to one or more adders and one or more memory units. These connections are called data paths. Physically, they consist of wires feeding the output signal from one register to the input of another. *Gates* control the movement of data from one register to another. If two registers P and Q are connected as shown in Figure 7.1, the gate G con-

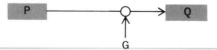

FIGURE 7.1   Gated transfer

trols the information flow. When G is turned on *(opened)*, a copy of the information in register P is placed in register Q. This is necessarily a simplified account of the process, which can vary in detail from one hardware implementation to another. This process takes a finite amount of time, currently in the range 5 to 200 nanoseconds. (1 nanosecond $= 10^{-9}$ seconds.)

During the period in which the gate is open, the contents of the register supplying the information (P in the example) must not be changed. If it is necessary to move information into P after the current contents have been gated elsewhere, there must be some guarantee that the gate has closed on the output of P before an input gate is opened. This is done by performing the basic register-to-register transfers in periods of time called "cycles." One cycle is the time to open the gate, move the information from one register to an adjacent one, and to turn the gate back off again. Many machines have a *clock* which times each of these basic cycles. The machine is controlled by a sequence of gate signals, each occupying one time cycle. These signals are generated by the control section of the computer. The next two subsections will discuss possible arrangements of registers and ways in which the gate signal sequences can be generated.

7.1.1 Actual data flow

The programmer is only aware of some of the registers in a machine and of certain of the interconnecting data paths. This is because most of the registers are not accessible to the programmer but are used to implement the instructions that affect the accessible registers. For example, the IBM 7094 manual mentions the AC, MQ, and sense-indicator registers, in addition to the index registers and the control counter. In fact, there are several other registers in the CPU. We shall discuss some of them below. In some of the lower-cost machines, the registers which the programmer is told about do not exist as separate registers. For example, the IBM system 360/370 can have four 64-bit floating-point registers and sixteen 32-bit fixed-point registers for programmer use. The model 30 version of the 360 cannot afford the hardware to implement all those registers in transistors, so they are stored in memory locations that are inaccessible to the programmer.

Medium- and high-speed machines employ a certain amount of parallelism in their use of gates in order to gain speed. A typical organization of a machine in the IBM 7090 speed category is shown in Figure 7.2. This is a simplified diagram and only shows some of the word-length data flow. Index registers, the control counter, and other necessary registers are not shown. In an organization of this form, the upper and lower parts of the accumulator are normally in the registers labeled AC and MQ, as in the IBM 7090. If an addition is to be performed, the address is sent to memory using data flow not indicated, and a read returns the operand to the MDR. The circuitry in the adder

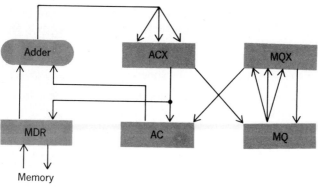

FIGURE 7.2   A simple data flow; gates are indicated by arrows

produces the sum of the registers AC and MDR. The gate into the register labeled ACX is opened in one cycle, and then the gate back down into the AC is opened in the next cycle, returning the result. The gates shown at an angle into ACX and MQX are for shifting. The angle indicates that the gate moves bits over. Thus, if the left-shift gate from MQ to MQX is opened, bit 1 of MQ would be placed in bit 0 of MQX, bit 2 in bit 1, and so on. Repetitive use of this gate can be made for arbitrary-length shifts. In a double-length shift, the AC register would be gated, through the adder, into ACX at the same time. A similar pattern of shifts is used in multiplication and division. The reader is invited to work out the details of these operations with such a data flow. (*Hint:* For multiplication, put the multiplier in MQ, the multiplicand in the MDR. Shift right, testing the bottom of the MQ register. For division, shift the other way.) In lower-cost and hence lower-speed machines, parallelism of data flow is too expensive. In this case, the concept of a *bus* is used. In electrical engineering, a bus is a piece of wire (usually thick) which distributes power to a number of devices. A *data bus* is, by analogy, a piece of wire that distributes data to various registers. Two buses are shown in Figure 7.3. They serve to route information from any one of the three registers A, B, and C to either of the registers X and Y and back again respectively. Because only one number can be on a bus at one time, the number of transfers that can be done in parallel is reduced. Also, because of additional gates (both onto and off the bus) that

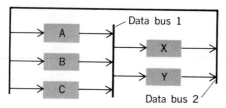

FIGURE 7.3   Data buses

are used, the transfer time is increased by a small amount. However, a bus can reduce the amount of hardware needed to accomplish an instruction execution. Figure 7.4 shows the data paths for the hypothetical machine that we are going to simulate. These data paths use three buses, two for input to the logical unit and one for output. In the future, we shall refer to this as the *simulated* or S machine. All registers are 32 bits wide except for the IR register, which is 5 bits wide. The logical unit is a group of circuits which can form a number of combinations of the input buses. In particular, the twos complement sum can be formed. A 32-bit register, called a *latch* register, is included in the logical unit. This serves to retain the output of the logical unit when the inputs are turned off. In this way it is possible to return a result to a register which contained an input operand. For example, it will be necessary to add the content of the A register to the content of the MDR register and return the result to the A register. Although this is actually a two-step operation, consisting of first opening the gates from A and MDR onto the input buses and then opening the gate from the output bus back to A, we shall call this operation a single cycle.

The S machine will be a stack machine with one instruction per 32-bit word, although addresses will be *to the byte,* that is, an address will indicate one 8-bit byte in memory. Because the memory will be 32 bits wide, the bottom 2 bits of an address will be ignored in memory READ and WRITE operations. MAR and MDR stand for Memory Address Register and Memory Data Register, respectively. The memory is a device which can be requested to read or write. When a read is requested, the memory accesses the location whose

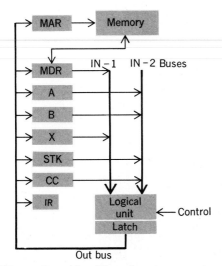

FIGURE 7.4   S-machine data paths

address is in the MAR. The data at that location is placed in the MDR. Similarly, a write copies the data from the MDR into the location whose address is in the MAR. The A and B registers are working registers; A usually holds the top level of the stack. X is a single-index register, CC the control counter, IR an instruction register whose use will be discussed later, and STK a register used to implement a stack scheme. The contents of the accumulator stack are actually stored in memory, starting from the maximum available address and working down. The current top level of the stack is kept in the memory location contained in the STK register. If an item is to be pushed into the stack, STK is decreased by 4 and then sent to the MAR as the address of the new top level. The bottom level is always in location $2^{32}-4$. Let us examine the way in which a typical instruction would be executed by this machine. A stack machine should provide an instruction ADD, which combines the top two levels of the stack by addition and stores the result back into the second level, subsequently discarding the top level. Prior to the execution of the ADD instruction, the STK register contains the address of the top of the stack. The second level is in the location numbered 4 larger, as shown in Figure 7.5. In order to execute the ADD instruction, the address in STK must be sent to the MAR register. A READ can then be used to access the top level of the stack and place it in the MDR register. We can write this as

$$STK \rightarrow MAR \quad READ$$

meaning that the data paths are used to transmit the contents of the STK register onto the IN-2 bus, that this number is passed through the logical unit

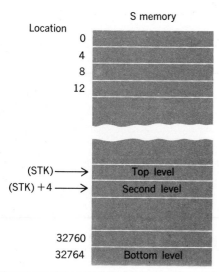

FIGURE 7.5 Stack storage

onto the OUT bus, from whence it is gated to the MAR register. A memory READ operation is then requested, which places the top level of the stack into the MDR. This can be followed by the sequence of steps

$$
\begin{aligned}
\text{MDR} && \to \text{A} \\
4 &+ \text{STK} & \to \text{STK} \\
& \text{STK} & \to \text{MAR} \quad \text{READ}
\end{aligned}
$$

which put the top of the stack into A register in order to leave the MDR free for the second level of the stack, which is fetched by sending its address to the MAR and reading. The operation $4 + \text{STK} \to \text{STK}$ is performed by gating the contents of the STK register onto the IN-2 bus, a constant 4 onto the IN-1 bus (think of this as another register always containing this constant, although it is simpler to implement than that), performing an addition in the logical unit, and gating the result on the OUT bus into the STK. This operation updates the contents of the STK register so that it points to the new top level of the stack.

The addition can be performed between the A and the MDR register and the result returned to the stack by the operation

$$\text{MDR} + \text{A} \qquad \to \text{MDR} \quad \text{WRITE}$$

Collecting these operations together, we arrive at the add sequence

$$
\begin{aligned}
0 &+ \text{STK} & \to \text{MAR} \quad \text{READ} \\
\text{MDR} &+ 0 & \to \text{A} \\
4 &+ \text{STK} & \to \text{MAR} \quad \text{READ} \\
4 &+ \text{STK} & \to \text{STK} \\
\text{MDR} &+ \text{A} & \to \text{MDR} \quad \text{WRITE}
\end{aligned}
$$

They have been written in this way to show that each operation consists of a specification of the gate that is opened onto the IN-1 bus, a specification of the gate that is opened onto the IN-2 bus (0 means that no gate is opened), a specification of the operation of the logical unit (in the example only plus is used), a specification of the gate opened from the OUT bus, and an indication of whether a READ or WRITE is to be requested of memory. The execution of an S-machine instruction such as ADD requires that a sequence of such gate signals be generated in the appropriate order. In future we shall not write the arrow, since it would appear in every line.

Let us consider two other instructions which will certainly be needed in a stack machine, the LOAD instruction and the BRANCH instruction. These will have addresses. For the moment, let us assume that the address of the instruction has been calculated and placed in the B register. The LOAD instruction is executed with the gate sequence

```
0    + B     MAR   READ
−4   + STK   MAR   WRITE
−4   + STK   STK
```

while the BRANCH instruction only requires

```
0    + B     CC
```

under the assumption that the CC register contains the address of the next instruction to be executed.

Each of the instructions in the repertoire of the S machine must be executed by such a sequence of gate operations. After we have constructed these and presumably built hardware to perform them, we still have to face the problem, "how does the machine know which sequence to execute?" The user has placed his S-machine program in the S-machine memory and wishes it to be executed starting at a given location. This location has been put in the CC register, and it is now up to the S-machine hardware to examine the instruction in that location and initiate the correct sequence of gate signals. The instruction can be fetched from memory, and the control counter CC can be incremented to point to the next instruction by sequence

```
0    + CC    MAR   READ
4    + CC    CC
```

This puts the instruction to be executed into the MDR register. The hardware must look at it and determine the instruction type, place its address into the B register, and begin the necessary gate sequence. In order to follow these steps through, we need to know the form of the S instructions in detail.

7.1.2 The S-machine instruction set

Each S instruction will be assumed to occupy a 32-bit word, so that its location address is always a multiple of 4. The format of the instructions is shown in Figure 7.6. There are two types, one-address and zero-address instructions. They are distinguished by the first bit of the instruction code, that is, bit 2 of the 32-bit word. It is a 0 for one-address instructions. Instructions with addresses such as LOAD and STORE will always contain a 0 in this position so that they can be readily distinguished from the zero-address instructions. (This is known as bit significance. We shall see that it will allow the control necessary to handle both type of instructions to be simplified.) In the tables below, the code for each instruction is shown, followed by its name, the amount by which the STK register is changed during its execution, and a brief description of its action. Note that the code for one-address instructions is between 0 and 31, whereas the code for zero-address instructions is greater than 32 because of the bit significance of the top bit. Zero-address instructions will not use the indirect bit, the index bit, or the 24-bit address. (This suggests that the design of the S machine is far from optimal.) For one-address instructions, the address is formed by adding the contents of the X register to the 24-bit address if the index bit is on, and performing indirect addressing with the resulting address if the indirect bit is on (that is, equal to 1). If indirect addressing occurs, then a new 32-bit word is fetched from memory, and it is also checked for indexing and indirect addressing. In this way, multiple-level indirect addressing is allowed.

One-address instructions

CODE	INSTRUCTION	STK CHANGE	ACTION
0	LOAD	− 4	Load stack from memory location.
1	LDI	− 4	Load immediate. Loads top of stack with address.
2	STORE	+ 4	Stores top of stack in memory.
3	BRANCH	0	Branches to specified location.
4	BPL	0	Branches if top of stack is positive or zero.
5	BMI	0	Branches if top of stack is negative (non-zero).
6	BZE	0	Branches if top of stack is zero.
7	BNZ	0	Branches if top of stack is non-zero.
8	ENTER	− 4	Enter a subroutine by placing CC on top of the stack and branching.
9	LDX	0	Load index with contents of memory location.
10	LDXI	0	Load index immediate, that is, with the address of this instruction.
11	LOOP	0	Increment index register by 4 and branch if it is non-zero.
12	LS	0	Left shift N places, where N is the address.
13	RS	0	Right shift N places.

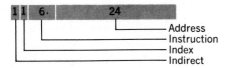

FIGURE 7.6   S-instruction format

Zero-address instructions

CODE	INSTRUCTION	STK CHANGE	ACTION
32	ADD	+ 4	Add top two levels of stack.
33	SUB	+ 4	Subtract top two levels of stack.
34	AND	+ 4	AND top two levels of stack.
35	OR	+ 4	OR top two levels of stack.
36	EOR	+ 4	Exclusive OR top two levels of stack.
37	NOT	0	Complement top level of stack.
38	XTS	− 4	Index to stack. Puts contents of index register on top of stack.
39	STX	+ 4	Stack to index. Removes top of stack and places it in index register.
40	ADX	+ 4	Adds top of stack to index.
41	SBX	+ 4	Subtracts top of stack from index.
42	RET	+ 4	Branches to address contained in top of stack.
43	POP	+ 4	Discard the top level of the stack.

7.1.3 Decoding the instruction and instruction sequencing

We have already seen how the instructions can be fetched in sequence by use of the control counter. Having fetched the next instruction from memory into the MDR, it is necessary to decode the instruction bits in order to determine its type. If it is a one-address instruction, it is also necessary to form the address in the B register for use by the gate sequence for the particular instruction. Since this is a common requirement for all one-address instructions, it should be done before the remaining 5 bits of instruction code are examined. Therefore, if the first bit of the instruction code is a 1, the next 5 bits should be used to select one of 32 gate sequences for the 32 possible zero-address instructions (not all of them are defined in this example); if it is a 0, the effective address should first be calculated and then a 32-way test made for one-address instruction types. This means that the S-machine control needs some mechanism for testing bits 0, 1, and 2 of the MDR register in a way which can influence subsequent actions. It also needs to be able to test bits 3 through 7, but it will turn out to be more convenient to test these in the instruction register IR, so a test on the 5 bits of IR will be provided. If a one-address instruction is being treated, then the address bits in the lower 24 positions of the word must be extracted and sent to the B register. This can be done with a *partial gate*, which gates only the lower 24 bits onto the IN-1 bus from MDR, or it can be done by providing the constant, called *mask*, consisting of 24 least-significant 1s, for gating onto the IN-2 bus. We shall use the latter method. This constant can be logically ANDed with the contents of the MDR and the result sent to the B register. Bit 1 of MDR can then be tested to see if it is a 0. If not, then the contents of the X register must be added to B. Bit 0 of MDR can then be tested for 0. If it is not a 0, then the B register contents must be sent to the MAR register in order to fetch another word and to repeat the process. In order to write these steps down, we shall number all operation cycles in the gate sequence and write the testing step as

TEST   BIT0 N

where N is the number of the operation cycle that is to be executed next if the test is successful. Using this notation, the instruction fetch sequence can be written as

1	0 + CC	MAR	READ	Fetch instruction.
2	4 + CC	CC		Update CC.
3	MDR + 0	IR		Save instruction bits.
4	TEST BIT2	6		Test for one-address instruction.
5	TEST IR	32		Branch on zero-address instructions.†
6	MDR AND MASK	B		24 bits of address to B.
7	TEST BIT1	9		BRANCH if no indexing.
8	X + B	B		Index.
9	TEST BIT0	12		Branch if no indirect addressing.
10	0 + B	MAR	READ	Read word containing address.
11	TEST	6		Branch unconditionally to step 6.‡
12	TEST IR	64		Branch on one-address instructions.†

Since, for example, the instruction code for the BRANCH instruction is 3, the step numbered 67 (= 64 + 3) would be

67	TEST	125	Branch unconditionally to step 125.

while step 125 would be

125	0 + B	CC	Change the control counter for BRANCH.
126	TEST	1	Execute the next instruction.

Number 125 was used as the step number for an example; it could, of course, have been any other number.

---

† The TEST IR step is assumed to select one of 32 steps as the next, based on the 5 bits in the IR register. These are assumed to be steps 32 through 63 in the case of zero-address instructions and 64 through 95 in the case of one-address instructions.
‡ Since no condition is given, step 6 is always executed next.

7.1.4 Logic and hardware control

This section discusses the way in which data flow can be implemented using logic circuits, and how these same circuits can be used to generate the *control sequences* for instruction execution described above. This will necessarily be a brief summary and can be skipped without loss of continuity, as nothing in later sections on micro program control requires a knowledge of this section.

Signals in a computer are usually transmitted along wires as voltages. In order to be able to distinguish between allowed states reliably, only two states are recognized, a high voltage, say about +3V, meaning a 1, and a low voltage, say below zero, meaning a 0. Thus 1 bit is represented on one wire. *Logical operations* are performed on these bits using circuits that combine them in simple ways. In fact, the usual operations that can be performed are the already familiar AND, OR, and NOT operations. An *AND gate* is a circuit with two or more inputs and one output such that the output is a 1 only if *all* the inputs are 1. A conventional diagram of an AND gate is shown in Figure 7.7a. An *OR gate* is a circuit with two or more inputs and one output such that the output is a 1 if *any* of the inputs are 1. A conventional diagram of an OR gate is shown in Figure 7.7b. A NOT element is a circuit with one input and one output such that the output is the opposite of the input. These elements can be interconnected to perform complex logical tasks. For example, suppose we wish to form the sum of two binary digits x and y. The result is shown in Table 7.1. The rightmost digit of the sum is a 1 only if x or y, but not both x and y, is 1. This is called the *exclusive or*. There is no simple gate to perform an exclusive or, but one can be constructed using ANDs, ORs, and NOTs. Looking at the rightmost digit, we see that it is a 1 if (x is a 1 and y is a 0) or (x is a 0 and y is a 1). This is precisely a logical statement. Where we see "y is a 0," we know that NOT y is a 1. Thus (x is a 1 and y is a 0) is a 1 if x AND (NOT y) is a 1. Thus the rightmost digit of the sum is a 1 if (x AND (NOT y)) OR ((NOT x) AND y) is a 1. If we call this digit s, and write + for OR, · for AND, and x' for NOT x, we can write

$$s = x \cdot y' + x' \cdot y$$

and implement it by the diagram in Figure 7.8. This is also known as a half adder.

TABLE 7.1   *Sum of two bits*

X	Y	SUM
0	0	0
0	1	1
1	0	1
1	1	10

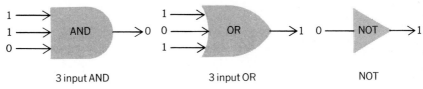

3 input AND   3 input OR   NOT

FIGURE 7.7   *Conventional logic diagrams*

Using similar ideas, any logical combination of two or more bits can be constructed if enough logic elements are used.

Another important element that can be constructed from these basic elements
is a *flip-flop*. A flip-flop is a single-bit memory element used in the construction of registers. One type of flip-flop is shown in Figure 7.9.

If the two inputs are held to 1s, the output of the AND gates is the same as the
inputs that are fed back from the NOT elements. Thus

$$g'=f \quad \text{and} \quad f'=g$$

We can see that this is satisfied if g is 1 and f 0, or if g is 0 and f 1. Thus the
device has two stable states and can store 1 bit. If f is the output, we will say
that it holds a 1 if f is a 1, a 0 otherwise. If p is set to a 0 and back to a 1 again,
f will be set to a 0, so we can say that this action clears the flip-flop. (When p
is set to a 0 g' goes to a 0, so g goes to a 1. This in turn sets f' to a 1 and f
to a 0. Returning p to a 1 causes no change, as the other input to the top AND
gate is now a 0.) Similarly, setting q to a 0 and back to a 1 again sets the flip-
flop to a 1.

A register can be constructed with a set of flip-flops. It can be cleared by setting all the p input lines to 0 and back to 1. A number can be gated in by setting q to a 0 for those bits which are to be set to a 1. Arithmetic, such as addition, can be performed by combining logical circuits in straightforward

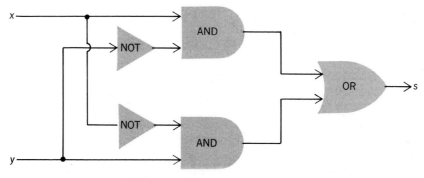

FIGURE 7.8   *Exclusive or (half adder)*

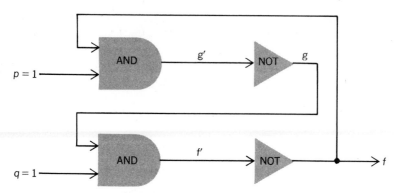

FIGURE 7.9   Flip-flop

ways, and so it is clear that it is possible to build the data flow (although the detailed design of an efficient, high-speed data flow is a very complex process). The remaining problem is to generate the necessary gate signals according to the control sequences discussed above.

One way of doing this is to assign a flip-flop to each step and arrange for the flip-flop to be a 1 when that step is to be performed. The signal to the gates in the data flow can be controlled by the output of the flip-flop so that the gates are opened when the flip-flop is a 1. When the gates have been open long enough for the information to be transferred through the gates, a clock signal can be used to set the next flip-flop to a 1 and the previous one to a 0. The clock signals are derived from an *oscillator,* a device that produces a series of electrical pulses at a given frequency, and a *counter,* a combination of logical elements and flip-flops that counts the pulses from the oscillator.

Modern computers use *integrated circuits,* which are very small devices containing many logical elements. Usually it is convenient to work with logical elements that are combinations of the primitive elements AND, OR, and NOT that we have discussed. (See question 2, p. 311.) Many different types of flip-flops which increase the speed of a computer can be constructed, but the purpose of this section is not to discuss machine design in detail, but only to indicate how it can be accomplished.†

7.1.5 Micro program control

We have investigated the way in which the data flow of the S machine is used to execute the S instructions, one at a time, and to sequence from one to the next. It is done by a fixed sequence of gate signals, interspersed with tests on

---

†More details can be found in texts on computer design, such as T. C. Bartee, "Digital Computer Fundamentals," McGraw-Hill Book Company, New York, 1972.

the top 3 bits of the MDR register and bits 3 through 7 of the IR register. Toward the end of the 1950s, the similarity between the gate sequences and the sequence of steps of any program was utilized in the construction of the control of computers. Prior to that time, the sequences of gate signals were generated by circuits designed for that purpose. This area of the machine was complex, because there was little similarity between the sequences used for, say, the ADD instruction, and those used for the LOAD instruction. Now machines are often built using the concept of *micro program control.* In this concept, the gate sequences are generated by what, in effect, is another simpler computer, called the micro computer. Referring to Figure 7.10, we see that the control unit of the S machine is a black box which can input the states of the MDR register and the 5 bits of the IR register and can output signals to each of the gates, the logical unit setting, and the READ and WRITE requests of memory. The flow of control can be thought of as sequences of program steps which consist of either outputting signals to the gates or of inputting the states of the test conditions and performing conditional branches. Each step, or cycle, in the gate sequences given above is equivalent to a program step in the micro machine. Therefore, each program step must either specify the test condition and the branch address within the micro program, or it must specify the setting of the gates onto each of the three buses, the setting of the logical unit, and whether to READ, WRITE, or just do the gating process.

An organization of a micro program control for the S machine is shown in Figure 7.11. It contains a memory in which the micro program is stored. Each step in the micro program is stored as a word in this memory, which we shall call the micro memory. Since these steps are fixed if the instruction code of the S machine is fixed, it is common to use a *read-only memory* for the micro memory. This is a memory which can be read but not written. Its contents are initially set by the manufacturer, who decides the instruction set of

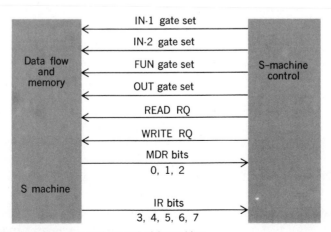

FIGURE 7.10   *Data flow and control of S machine*

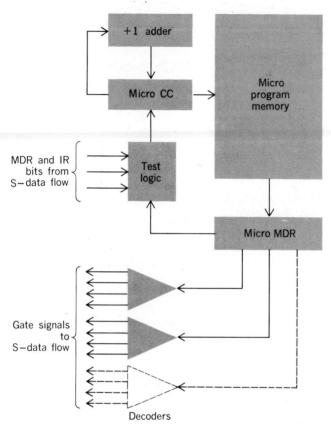

FIGURE 7.11   The micro machine

the S machine. The advantage of using a read-only memory (ROM for short) is that it is cheaper and faster than an equivalent read-write memory.

The micro organization shows a memory address register with an attached adder for incrementing by 1. This serves as a control counter for the micro machine. Since the machine only executes control instructions and does not read data into or out of the micro memory, the address register is only used for accessing micro instructions, hence it can serve as a control counter without any interference. It always contains the address, in the micro memory, of the next micro program step to be executed. Each micro instruction is fetched from the micro memory in turn, and decoded from the memory data register to determine which gates to open, or which conditions to test. If conditions are tested and are true, then a new address is gated from the data register to the address register in the micro machine.

Who, we may ask, controls the micro machine? Do we need a micro-micro machine to control that, and so on, ad infinitum? At some point, hardware control must be used to sequence through the steps of one of the micro-micro . . . machines. We can see that the micro machine is already quite simple compared to the original S machine, and that its control is much simpler. Remembering that the S machine is a grossly simplified machine compared to a typical commercial machine, and noting that the micro control of a much more complex machine is not particularly more complex, we realize the micro control can effectively reduce the amount of circuitry needed in the control area. It is true that a micro memory has to be added, but the cost of this is usually offset by the savings in circuitry and the increased flexibility for implementing more complex instructions for the programmer's use.

Additional advantages accrue to the manufacturer of micro controlled machines: they are often easier to check out during the design stage because the micro control can be easily simulated; they are easier to check out during the construction phase because checking micro programs can be plugged in (by replacing the micro memory temporarily), and these can be used to trace construction errors more readily than the regular instruction set can be used. The micro instructions are stored in the micro memory in a binary code. For the machine discussed, two different formats are needed, one for operation steps, and one for testing steps. The way in which each of these can be stored in a 16-bit-wide micro memory is illustrated in Figure 7.12. If the top bit of the word is a 0, then the word represents an operation on the gates. Each group of bits, called a *control group,* contains a coded representation of the gate action to be taken. The first 2 bits indicate whether the memory is to be accessed for a READ or a WRITE at the completion of the cycle, the next 3 bits indicate which gate is to be opened onto the IN-1 bus, the next 3 the IN-2 bus, and so on. The codes used for each of these control groups are shown in Tables 7.2 through 7.6 below. If, on the other hand, the top bit is a 1, the 16-bit word represents a test action. In this case the micro machine examines the indicated bit or bits in the S-machine data flow and performs a branch if the condition is met. This branch is effected by gating the bottom 12 bits of the micro word into the micro control counter. The conditions

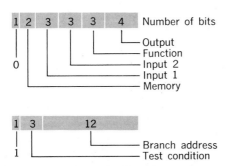

FIGURE 7.12 *Micro instruction format*

TABLE 7.2   Memory control (2 bits)

CODE VALUE	ACTION
0	Nothing
1	READ†
2	WRITE†
3	Not allowed

TABLE 7.3   Input bus 1

CODE	REGISTER OR NUMBER GATED ONTO BUS
0	0
1	MDR
2	X
3	− 4
4	Not allowed
5	Not allowed
6	Not allowed
7	+ 4

TABLE 7.4   Input bus 2

CODE	REGISTER OR NUMBER GATED ONTO BUS
0	0
1	1
2	77777777 octal
3	A
4	CC
5	B
6	STK
7	+ 4

TABLE 7.5   Output bus

CODE	OUTPUT BUS GATED TO
0	MAR
1	MDR
2	X
3	A
4	CC
5	B
6	STK
7	IR
8 to 15	Not allowed

TABLE 7.6   Function

CODE	OUTPUT FUNCTION
0	IN1 + IN2 (twos complement)

† The READ or WRITE action is taken
after the rest of the micro instruction
execution occurs.

1	IN1 — IN2 (twos complement)
2	IN1 "AND" IN2
3	IN1 "OR" IN2
4	NOT (IN1 + IN2)
5	IN1 "EXCLUSIVE OR" IN2
6	Half (IN1 + IN2) (Right shift 1)
7	Double (IN1 + IN2) (Left shift 1)

tested are shown in Table 7.7 for each of the eight code values of bits 1 through 3 of the micro word. Code 0 always causes a branch, so it is an unconditional transfer. Codes 1 through 3 test bits 0 through 2 of the MDR respectively. If the tested bit is a 0, the branch is taken. Code 4 tests all bits of MDR. If they are all 0, the branch is taken. (This will be needed for conditional instructions in the S machine.) Codes 5 and 6 are not used in this example, while code 7 is used to perform a test of the instruction in the IR. The 5 bits in the IR are ORed with the 5 bits in the bottom of the branch address bits in the micro word, and the result is gated to the micro control counter. An OR function is used because it is simpler to implement in hardware than, say, an addition. Since this code will only be used twice in the S-machine implementation, the bottom 5 bits of the branch address may be made 0 by judicious placement of the micro instructions. Under that condition, the OR is equivalent to an addition. After such a micro instruction, the next one to be executed will be one of 32, depending on the contents of IR.

7.2 MICRO PROGRAMMING THE S-INSTRUCTION SET

The instruction set, given in Section 7.1.2 for the S machine, can be implemented by means of micro programs using the micro instructions given above. This section will discuss the micro programming of the S-machine

TABLE 7.7   Test conditions

CODE	BRANCH IF
0	Always
1	MDR Bit 0 = 0
2	MDR Bit 1 = 0
3	MDR Bit 2 = 0
4	MDR = 0
5	
6	
7	The 5 bits in the IR register are ORed with the bottom 5 bits of the branch address and used for a branch.

instructions by means of an annotated micro program. The micro program can be written in any way that provides a unique representation of each micro instruction. We shall write it as if each instruction were either a one-address instruction or a four-address instruction. The one-address micro instructions will be the test instructions, and will be written as follows:

OPERATION		DESCRIPTION
T0	J	Test MDR bit 0, branch to micro location J if 0.
T1	J	Test MDR bit 1, ...
T2	J	Test MDR bit 2, ...
TMDR	J	Test MDR for all 0s, branch if true.
TI	J	Branch on 5 bits of IR.
TRM	J	Always branch.

The four-address micro instructions will be written as follows:

OPERATION	ADDRESS FIELD
ADDM	I1, I2, OUT, Z
SUBM	I1, I2, OUT, Z
ANDM	I1, I2, OUT, Z
ORM	I1, I2, OUT, Z
NOT	I1, I2, OUT, Z
EOR	I1, I2, OUT, Z
LS	I1, I2, OUT, Z
RS	I1, I2, OUT, Z

where I1 is the IN-1 bus, I2 is in the IN-2 bus, OUT is the OUT bus, and Z is either P, R, or W, meaning process only, process followed by READ, or process followed by WRITE. The address in the four-address format may take on any of the allowed values for the specified bus. Thus I1 can be one of 0, MDR, X, MFOUR, or FOUR, where MFOUR and FOUR select the constants —4 and 4 respectively. I2 can be one of 0, ONE, MASK, A, CC, B, STK, or FOUR, where ONE and MASK select the constants 1 and 77777777 octal respectively. OUT can be one of MAR, MDR, X, A, CC, B, STK, or IR. Thus, to add the contents of the MDR register and the A register and to return the result to the MDR without any memory operations, we shall write

ADDM   MDR,A,MDR,P

In writing the micro program, we shall make use of symbolic addresses for branch addresses. These will have to be translated into binary by an assembly process before the code can be used in the micro memory. In the program below, the left-hand column is the actual micro memory location of the instruction; the next column is used for a location symbolic address if it is needed. Then the operation field and the address fields of the instruction are written in the usual manner. Some absolute addresses are used, because the test of the IR register requires that the branch address contain 5 least significant 0s.

The micro code below differs from that given earlier in that the top of the stack is normally kept in the A register (rather than being returned to memory after every operation, only to be fetched back at the start of the next). This serves to shorten the micro program and increase the speed of the S machine.

LOCATION		OPERATION	ADDRESS	COMMENTS
20	FETCH	ADDM	0,CC,MAR,R	Fetch next instruction from S memory.
21		ADDM	FOUR,CC,CC,P	Increment instruction counter.
22		ADDM	MDR,0,IR,P	Move instruction bits to IR.
23		T2	ONEADR	Branch if one-address instruction.
24		TI	32	Test for 32 zero-address instructions.
25	ONEADR	ANDM	MDR,MASK,B,P	Move 24 address bits to B register.
26		T1	NOINDX	Test for no indexing.
27		ADDM	X,B,B,P	Index address in B.
28	NOINDX	T0	NOINDR	Test for no indirect addressing.
29		ADDM	0,B,MAR,R	Address to MAR and read next address.
30		TRM	ONEADR	Return to test for more indexing.
31	NOINDR	TI	64	Test for 32 one-address instructions.
32		TRM	SADD	Branch to micro code for the S addition instruction.
33		TRM	SSUB	Similar for subtraction.
34		TRM	SAND	Etc., for each S instruction.
35		TRM	SOR	
36		TRM	SEOR	
37		TRM	SNOT	
38		TRM	SXTS	
39		TRM	SSTX	
40		TRM	SADX	
41		TRM	SSBX	
42		TRM	SRET	
43		TRM	SPOP	
44		TRM	ILLORD	Branch to micro code to handle illegal instruction.
45		TRM	ILLORD	Ditto.
. . . .				
63		TRM	ILLORD	
64		TRM	SLOAD	Branch to micro code for one-address instructions.
65		TRM	SLDI	
66		TRM	SSTORE	
67		TRM	SBR	
68		TRM	SBPL	
69		TRM	SBMI	

LOCATION		OPERATION	ADDRESS	COMMENTS
70		TRM	SBZE	
71		TRM	SBNZ	
72		TRM	SENTER	
73		TRM	SLDX	
74		TRM	SLDXI	
75		TRM	SLOOP	
76		TRM	SLS	
77		TRM	SRS	
78		TRM	ILLORD	More illegal instructions.
. . . .				
95		TRM	ILLORD	
96	SADD	ADDM	FOUR,STK,MAR,R	Get second level of stack.
97		ADDM	MDR,A,A,P	Perform addition.
98	DECR	ADDM	FOUR,STK,STK,P	Change stack pointer.
99		TRM	FETCH	Return to fetch next instruction.
100	SSUB	ADDM	FOUR, STK, MAR,R	
101		SUBM	MDR,A,A,P	
102		TRM	DECR	
103	SAND	ADDM	FOUR,STK,MAR,R	
104		ANDM	MDR,A,A,P	
105		TRM	DECR	
106	SOR	ADDM	FOUR,STK,MAR,R	
107		ORM	MDR,A,A,P	
108		TRM	DECR	
109	SEOR	ADDM	FOUR,STK,MAR,R	
110		EOR	MDR,A,A,P	
111		TRM	DECR	
112	SNOT	NOT	0,A,A,P	Complement top of stack.
113		TRM	FETCH	
114	SXTS	ADDM	X,0,B,P	X to B.
115	SLDI	ADDM	0,STK,MDR,P	Stack address to MDR.
116		TMDR	SLD	Skip if stack empty.
117		ADDM	0,STK,MAR,P	
118		ADDM	0,A,MDR,W	Top of stack to memory.
119	SLD	ADDM	0,B,A,P	New top level to A.
120	INCR	ADDM	MFOUR,STK,STK,P	Change stack pointer.
121		TRM	FETCH	
122	SSTX	ADDM	0,A,X,P	Top of stack to index.
123	SPOP	ADDM	FOUR,STK,MAR,R	Get second level of stack.
124		ADDM	MDR,0,A,P	And copy to register.
125		TRM	DECR	Change stack pointer.
126	SADX	ADDM	X,A,X,P	Add stack to index.
127		TRM	SPOP	And pop.
128	SSBX	SUBM	X,A,X,P	Subtract stack from index.
129		TRM	SPOP	And pop.
130	SRET	ADDM	0,A,CC,P	Gate stack to CC.
131		TRM	SPOP	And pop.
132	SLOAD	ADDM	0,B,MAR,R	Get operand.
133		ADDM	MDR,0,B,P	Place in B.
134		TRM	SLDI	
135	SSTORE	ADDM	0,B,MAR,P	Address to memory.
136		ADDM	0,A,MDR,W	Write top of stack in store location.
137		TRM	SPOP	And pop.

LOCATION		OPERATION	ADDRESS	COMMENTS
138	SBR	ADDM	0,B,CC,P	Branch address to CC.
139		TRM	FETCH	
140	SBPL	ADDM	0,A,MDR,P	A to MDR for testing.
141		TO	SBR	Branch if positive.
142		TRM	FETCH	
143	SBMI	ADDM	0,A,MDR,P	A to MDR for testing.
144		TO	FETCH	
145		TRM	SBR	Branch if negative.
146	SBZE	ADDM	0,A,MDR,P	A to MDR for testing.
147		TMDR	SBR	Branch if 0.
148		TRM	FETCH	
149	SBNZ	ADDM	0,A,MDR,P	
150		TMDR	FETCH	
151		TRM	SBR	Branch if non-zero.
152	SENTER	ADDM	0,B,MDR,P	Switch B and CC.
153		ADDM	0,CC,B,P	
154		ADDM	MDR,0,CC,P	
155		TRM	SLDI	Now put B on top of stack.
156	SLDX	ADDM	0,B,MAR,R	Fetch word from memory.
157		ADDM	MDR,0,B,P	And place in B.
158	SLDXI	ADDM	0,B,X,P	Place word in index.
159		TRM	FETCH	
160	SLOOP	ADDM	X,FOUR,X,P	Increment X by 4.
161		ADDM	X,0,MDR,P	Move X to MDR for testing.
162		TMDR	FETCH	If 0, no transfer.
163		TRM	SBR	Else transfer.
164	SLS	ADDM	0,B,MDR,P	Move B to MDR for testing.
165	JLS	TO	LEFT	Left shift if B is positive.
166	REPRS	RS	0,A,A,P	Shift one place.
167		ADDM	MDR,ONE,MDR,P	Decrease count.
168		TMDR	FETCH	Finished shifting.
169		TRM	REPRS	Repeat shifting.
170	LEFT	TMDR	FETCH	Zero shifts left.
171		LS	0,A,A,P	Shift one place.
172		SUBM	MDR,ONE,MDR,P	Decrease count.
173		TRM	LEFT	
174	SRS	SUBM	0,B,MDR,P	Minus count to MDR.
175		TRM	JLS	Joint left-shift program.
176	ILLORD	. . . . .		(This is discussed below.)

The above code handles the 26 S instructions in 156 micro instructions. The illegal instructions cause a branch to micro location ILLORD, which has not been programmed. A system decision has to be made concerning the action that should be taken on illegal instructions before it can be completed. In this example, we shall not complete it further (see the discussion on simulation in the next section). In practical machines, an interrupt should occur. This would mean adding at least 1 additional bit to the data flow that could be set and reset by micro instructions and that could be tested. Such bits would be used to indicate the interrupt status, and would be set after an illegal instruction in the S machine.

A more practical machine would have to provide a much larger instruction set, including multiply and divide operations in both fixed- and floating-point forms. In order to make these operations practical, additional gates should be provided. These additional gates would make it simpler to extract sections of words, particularly the exponent part of a floating-point number. It is not the intention of this chapter to discuss all of the tricks that can be used to make micro programming an efficient means for the control of a medium-speed computer, so we won't discuss these problems further. In particular, we shall not discuss input/output, which is very device-dependent at the hardware level and the most difficult to simulate realistically. In practice, it runs concurrently with the central processor, but at its own speed. The simulation of unsynchronized operating processes is beyond the scope of this book.

In the next section, we shall discuss the simulation of the micro machine and the data flow so that the micro program given above can be used to implement a simulator of the S machine. This is the point at which a number of students become confused. So far we have described the S machine and its machine language. We then described a method of controlling it which involved writing program language used to control the gates of the S-machine data flow in a manner that caused S programs to be executed. In a sense, the micro program is interpreting the S-machine language. Now we are going to simulate the micro machine on a real machine, that is, we shall write a program in yet another language in order to make this other machine behave like the data flow and micro machine discussed. Because we are writing a simulator rather than building the machine out of hardware, we shall be able to add other features to the simulator that will make it easy for us to check out our micro program and simulator. Also, we shall see that the macro assembler on the machine being used for simulation can be used to save ourselves the work of writing any systems programs for the S machine until we are happy with its design.

7.3 SIMULATING THE S MACHINE

It is assumed that we have access to a machine that is somewhat larger than the S machine that we have been discussing, so that there is adequate space for the simulator, the micro program, and the S-memory contents to be stored. Since simulation is not efficient, it is also desirable that the available machine be fairly fast and that its word length be at least 32 bits. The available memory must be divided up into sections, so that the various pieces of the S machine can be represented. A suitable number of words, preferably a power of 2, should be allocated to the S memory. Words must be allocated to each of the registers in the data flow, and a block of memory must be allocated for storing the micro program. The remainder of the memory can be used for the simulator. Thus the allocation of memory may be as shown in Figure 7.13.

The S memory can be simulated by writing two subroutines, called READ and WRITE. When READ is called, it should take the address in the MAR register (that is, in the word in the memory being used to simulate the MAR register), AND out the bottom 2 bits and the top $30 - N$ bits—where the number of words allocated to the S memory is 2^N—and use the remaining N bits as the address. If these N bits are added to the address of the first word of the S-memory representation in the actual memory, the result is the location in the actual memory which contains the desired word. It should be copied to the MDR register. Conversely, the WRITE subroutine should form the address in a similar manner and then copy the contents of the MDR register into the address location. Note the N-bit address should be right justified two places before performing the addition in order to remove the two least significant 0s, unless, of course, a machine such as the IBM 370 is being used, since this machine addresses to the byte and therefore requires that addresses be multiples of 4 when 32-bit words are being accessed.

The simulator program must include a cell that contains the address of the next micro instruction. This represents the micro control counter, but it is easier if the actual address of the next micro instruction in the memory of the simulating machine is stored in the simulator. A flowchart of the simulator is shown in Figure 7.14. Notice that it is essentially the same flow as that used in the micro program. The next instruction is fetched from the micro memory and the micro control counter is increased by 1.

A test is made to see whether it is a gating step or a testing step, and simulating code handles each case. The code can be kept very short by fetching the

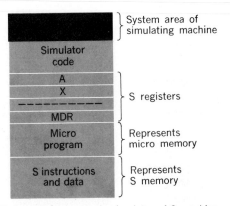

FIGURE 7.13 Memory use in simulator of S machine

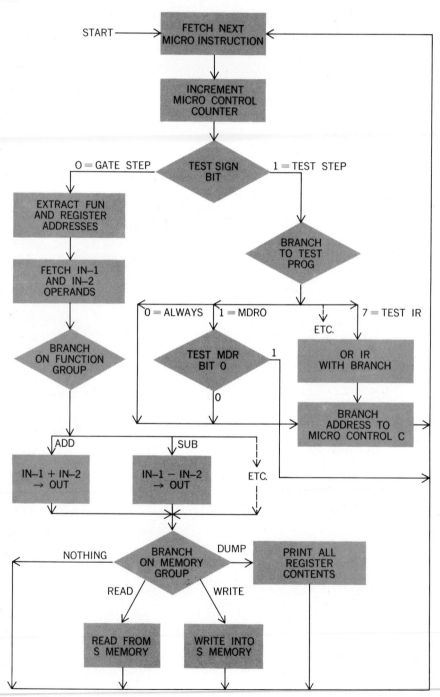

FIGURE 7.14   Simulator

operands that are to be placed on the IN-1 and the IN-2 buses to fixed cells before the function bits are checked. After the function bits are checked, the operation can be performed on the fixed cells directly, and the result can then be stored back into the out register. After the gate operations have been completed, the memory bits are tested, and reads or writes are requested as necessary. The flowchart shows one addition at this point. If the unused code 3 is placed in the memory control group, a printout of all registers in the data flow is indicated. This is not a feasible thing to do in an actual machine, but in the simulator it only consists of suitable output requests. This can prove very handy for debugging both the simulator and the micro program because a trace of the execution of the program can be made. Part of this simulator is shown below in IBM system 370 machine language. It is not complete, but it does indicate some of the techniques that can be used. The micro control counter is kept in fixed-point register 2. The micro instruction, which is assumed to occupy a 16-bit halfword, is fetched into register 3, and the sign bit is examined to see if it is a test micro instruction. If it is not, the five control groups are extracted and placed in registers 4 through 8, each multiplied by 4 because of the addressing to the byte. The effect of indirect addressing (which does not exist in the 370) is achieved by performing a reference through a table which gives the address of the actual registers or program to be used. The contents of the IN-1 and the IN-2 registers are placed in fixed registers 4 and 5 prior to a branch to a program which handles the operation.

```
            MACRO
&A          BITS      &N,&R,&TAB
&A          SR        8,8           Clear register 8.
            SLDL      9,&N          Move N bits from 9 to 8.
            SLL       8,2           Quadruple 8.
            A         8,&TAB        Add address of table.
            L         &R,0(8)       Fetch table entry to register R.
            MEND
. . . . . . . . . . . . . . . . . . . . . . . . . . . . . . . . . . . . . . .
INITIAL     L         2,AMCODE      Initialize micro control counter.
NEXT        LH        3,0(2)        Load next micro instruction.
            A         2,=F'2'       Increment micro control counter.
            LTR       9,3           Test sign bit.
            BM        TEST          Go to test types if negative.
            SLDL      8,17          Remove sign bits.
            BITS      2,6,TMEM      Next 2 bits to REG 6, indirect through
                                    MEM table.
            BITS      3,4,TIN1      3 bits to REG 4 indirected through IN-1
                                    table.
            BITS      3,5,TIN2      Ditto for REG 5 and table In-2.
            BITS      3,7,TFUN      Ditto for REG 7 and table FUN.
            BITS      4,8,TOUT      4 bits to REG 8 indirected through
                                    table OUT.
            L         4,0(4)        IN-1 operand to R4.
            L         5,0(5)        IN-2 operand to R5.
            BR        7             Branch to function program.
```

TMEM	DC	A(MEM)	Addresses of tables.
TIN1	DC	A(IN1)	
TIN2	DC	A(IN2)	
TFUN	DC	A(FUN)	
TOUT	DC	A(OUT)	
MEM	DC	A(NEXT)	Table of branch addresses for control group.
	DC	A(RMEM)	
	DC	A(WMEM)	
	DC	A(DUMP)	
IN1	DC	A(ZERO)	Table of addresses of S registers or constants.
	DC	A(MDR)	
	DC	A(X)	
	DC	A(MFOUR)	
	DC	A(ERR)	
	DC	A(ERR)	
	DC	A(ERR)	
	DC	A(FOUR)	
IN2	DC	A(ZERO)	
	DC	A(ONE)	
	DC	A(MASK)	
	DC	A(A)	
	DC	A(CC)	
	DC	A(B)	
	DC	A(STK)	
	DC	A(FOUR)	
FUN	DC	A(ADDM)	Table of addresses of programs for functions.
	DC	A(SUBM)	
	DC	A(ANDM)	
	DC	A(ORM)	
	DC	A(NOT)	
	DC	A(EOR)	
	DC	A(Rᶜ)	
	DC	A(LS)	
OUT	DC	A(MAR)	Addresses of registers for output.
	DC	A(MDR)	
	DC	A(X)	
	DC	A(A)	
	DC	A(CC)	
	DC	A(B)	
	DC	A(STK)	
	DC	A(IR)	
	DC	A(ERR1)	
	DC	A(ERR1)	
	DC	A(ERR1)	
	DC	A(ERR1)	
	DC	A(ERR1)	
	DC	A(ERR1)	
	DC	A(ERR1)	
	DC	A(ERR1)	
ZERO	DC	F'0'	
ONE	DC	F'1'	
FOUR	DC	F'4'	
MFOUR	DC	F'−4'	
MASK	DC	X'00FFFFFF'	24 one bits (hexadecimal constant).
ADDM	AR	4,5	Function program for ADDM.

```
              ST        4,0(8)
              BR        6                      Branch to memory control group.
    RMEM      L         10,MAR                 Memory control group program for read.
              N         10,=X'00003FFC'                    Extract 12-bit address.
              A         10,AMEMORY             Add address of start of memory.
              L         10,0(10)               Fetch word from memory.
              ST        10,MDR                 Place in MDR.
              B         NEXT                   Return to next micro instruction.
    AMEMORY   DC        A(MEMORY)              Address of memory location 0.
    AMCODE    DC        A(MCODE)               Address of micro memory location 0.
              etc.
```

7.3.1 Assembling micro program and S-machine language

The simulator can be written symbolically using the assembler facilities provided by the system. If the system also provides a macro assembler, then it can be used to assemble the micro program and S-machine language programs. Macro assemblers differ in their capabilities and their formats. In this section we shall discuss typical macro assemblers and indicate how they can be used to assemble the micro program and S language. If a manufacturer were considering building machines, it would probably be worth his while to write a special assembler for this purpose. Such an assembler could provide more error diagnostics than are possible with a reasonable use of macros, although a flexible macro assembler could be used to perform almost any amount of checking at a sacrifice in assembly time.

We would like to input the micro program into memory in exactly the form we wrote it earlier, that is, as an outside symbolic address (optional), an operation, and an address field. This is to be assembled into the appropriate binary patterns. There are two ways in which this can be done in many macro assemblers, by the use of conditional expansion pseudos or by the use of a binary packing pseudo. Conditional expansion can be used to test for erroneous usage of micro instructions, but it takes longer. Many assemblers provide a pseudo which allows binary patterns to be assembled easily.

The equivalent 370 macros can make use of the bit-length specification with an A-type field in a DC pseudo. AL.3(2), for example, generates 3 bits whose value is the binary integer 2. Using this, the two examples given above would be written as

```
              MACRO
    &B        TO        &A
    &B        DC        AL.4(9),AL.12((&A—MCODE)/2)
              MEND
```

This assembles as 1001NNNNNNNNNNNN where NNNNNNNNNNNN is the binary form of A—MCODE. The initial 1 indicates that it is a test step, the next 3 bits indicate that MDR bit 0 is to be tested, while the final 12 bits are the

the address. MCODE is the first address of the set of micro instructions. It is subtracted from A so that the address stored in the micro memory is relative to 0 in the micro memory rather than to 0 in the actual memory. (This will present a problem if an absolute address is written in a micro test instruction. For example, T0 68 would be subject to the same translation of origin and division by 2 whereas the address 68 is wanted unchanged. Either this must be avoided or a conditional assembly technique must be used to check for numeric addresses.)

Similarly, each of the test micro instructions can be implemented as macros. The process steps can be implemented with eight macros, one for each function. The ADDM, for example, can take the form

```
            MACRO
&A          ADDM      &I1,&RI2,&OUT,&Z
&A          DC        AL.1(0),AL.2(&Z),AL.3(&I1),AL.3(&I2),AL.3(0),AL.4(&OUT)
            MEND
```

The function bits are set to 0 to indicate addition in the logical unit. The addresses provided will have to have the appropriate values from the tables of codes. This can be done by means of EQU-type pseudos. This means that the micro program must be assembled separately from the simulator to avoid conflict between different uses of the same symbolic names. For example, MDR stands for the location of the MDR register in the simulator. It must represent the integer 1 in the micro code, because the MDR register has code number 1 in the IN-1 table and the OUT table.

The S-machine language can be assembled in a similar manner by defining each S instruction as a macro. The equivalent 370 macro for the STORE instruction would be

```
            MACRO
&B          STORE     &A,&X,&1
&B          DC        AL.1(&1),AL.1(&X),AL.6(2),AL3(&A-MEMORY)
            MEND
```

For the 370 system, the complete simulator could be put together in the following fashion:

Job control language for first assembly

```
SIMULATR    CSECT
            . . . . . . . . .            Set up instructions.
            EXTRN     MEMORY,MCODE       Addresses of S memory
                                         and MCODE.
            Simulator program for executing micro instructions.
MDR         DC        F                  Definitions of S registers.
```

```
MAR         DC          F
            etc.
            END
```

JCL for second assembly

```
            EQU definitions of S-register names as numbers.
            Macro definitions of micro instructions.
            DC          OF              Start on fullword boundary.
            ENTRY       MCODE           MCODE address for simulator.
MCODE       ADDM        ZERO,ZERO,CC,P  First micro instruction.
            . . . . .
            END
```

JCL for third assembly

```
            Macro definitions of S-machine instructions.
            ENTRY       MEMORY
MEMORY      DC          OF              Get on fullword boundary.
            S-machine instructions.
            . . . . .
            END
```

7.4 EMULATION, SIMULATION, AND INTERPRETATION

When an installation changes from one machine to another, it frequently writes simulators for the new machine to run on the old, so that code preparation can begin well ahead of machine delivery. Code may also be written for the old machine on the new, so that existing codes can be run while they are being converted. In many installations, a large amount of machine time can be used in this mode because of the lower efficiency of a simulator. To combat this problem, the idea of writing the simulator completely, or nearly completely, in the micro language of a micro programmed machine has been used. This has been given the name emulation. Because the data paths of the host machine are designed to ease the task of micro programming its machine language, the emulator does not run as fast as the original machine would were it constructed with the same technology. However, efficiencies of better than 50 percent are easy to achieve. Interpretation usually refers to the simulation of the code of a nonexistent computer on another computer, although the term is also applied to the simulation of code on a computer that could execute that code.

Interpretation was compared with translation and execution in the introduction. The basic difference is that, under interpretation, a statement is translated every time that it is executed, whereas only one translation is necessary if the result of translation is saved for repeated execution. For example, if the Fortran program

```
DO 1 I = 1,100
1 A(I) = B(I) — C(I)
```

is translated and executed, it is only necessary to translate statement number 1 once, whereas, if it is interpreted, it is translated 100 times. Why, one might ask, should we ever use interpretation? The answer is partly that interpreters are easier to write, and that it is sometimes possible to represent the job more compactly as an interpreter plus the source language rather than as machine language. Interpretation is also used in preference to translation for some of the more complex languages that manipulate objects that are not particularly adapted to the computer being used. An early example of this was the interpretation of floating-point instructions on machines that only had fixed-point arithmetic. Recent examples can be found in string-manipulation languages. If the length of execution of an operation is long compared to the translation time, then the overhead of interpretation is not important.

Interpretation finds its chief uses in debugging programs written in other than machine language. It is also used to interpret languages for which compilers have not yet been written nor machines been built, mainly because an interpreter is shorter than the corresponding translator and less expensive than a prototype machine. When programs are being debugged, the speed of execution is not as critical as the speed of locating the bugs in the program. If a program has been translated into machine language and the symbolic information has been removed by the translator, errors that occur must be reported in terms of machine language and machine locations. Many programmers are all too familiar with the problem of reading an octal dump of memory in order to try and find out what went wrong. It is possible to add system programs that retain copies of the name tables generated by the assemblers and compilers in order to give symbolic dumps to the programmer. In such systems, the dump returned by the computer when an error is detected could list the value of each symbolic address used for data storage and an indication of those program locations that have been changed (the *comparison post-mortem* that helps detect erroneous overwriting of the code). However, this information is returned after the damage has been done. A common error in assembly language or compiler languages is to overwrite sections of program when array limits are incorrectly calculated in a loop. The damage will not be apparent until the overwritten section is executed. In the worst cases of this, the whole program has been erased when the damage is noticed and it is virtually impossible to determine the cause from a dump at termination.

Some compilers prepare codes that check all array store operations to determine that no error has been committed. In such a scheme, the attempted execution of, say, A(101) = X, if A was only dimensioned to be 100 elements, would be an error and be caught before it was executed. Such an object code can be fairly inefficient, and it would not be desirable for such a translator to be used for production programs. If two translators, an efficient one and a diagnostic one, were available, it would partly alleviate the situation, but a symbolic dump and post-mortem program would still be needed. If the source language is retained in memory without translation, then an interpreter can immediately determine when an error that attempts to access outside of the data area occurs. The diagnostic information given will indicate precisely the statement in execution at the time, and it can also indicate the value of each of the variables used, by symbolic name, because the variables must be stored by name in order for the interpreter to relate them to the names used in statements.

A trace may consist of an interpretation of machine code for a given machine by a program for that same machine, although it is usually more helpful to interpret a partially translated assembly language for the machine so that symbolic information is present for diagnostic printouts.

The use of emulation and interpretation has been made much easier by the introduction of read/write memories fast enough to be used to hold the micro-program. In such an organization, the micro program can be reloaded when the mode of operation is to be changed. Thus, at one minute the computer could be executing code for machine A, then quickly switch to handling code for machine B. One such computer is the IBM 370, model 145, which uses part of its main memory to store the micro program. The micro program is loaded from a floppy disk when the initial load sequence is executed.

PROBLEMS

1 Refer to the table for the sum of 2 bits (Table 7.1). What logical function of x and y gives the leftmost bit of the sum?

This bit is usually called the carry bit c. A *full adder* is a logical circuit that adds 3 bits, x, y, and ci (c in), to get a sum and a carry s and c. Write down the *truth table* that gives s and c in terms of x, y, and ci. (A truth table is simply a list of all cases of the inputs with the corresponding outputs.) If you have a circuit for an exclusive or, can you construct a circuit which gives the digit s? Now try to construct a circuit for the carry c using three AND gates and one OR gate.

2 With current technology, it is easier to construct NAND and NOR gates. These are the same as AND and OR gates with a NOT on the output as shown below. They are drawn in the conventional way shown on the next page.

A NAND, for example, has a 0 output only if all inputs are 1. Thus, if p and q are the inputs of a two-input NAND, the output is a 1 if either p' is a 1 or q' is a 1. Thus we see that

p NAND $q = (p \cdot q)' = p' + q'$

Derive a similar relation for p NOR $q = (p + q)'$

Notice that a one-input NAND or NOR is the same as a NOT. Using these rela-

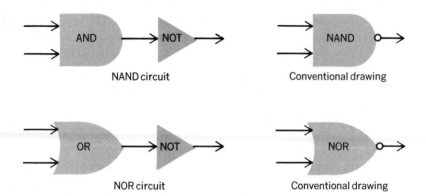

tions, draw a half adder using (a) NAND gates only and (b) NOR gates only.

3   The micro program for the S machine is too forgiving of S-programmer errors. If, for example, he attempts to execute an ADD when there are less than two levels in the stack, the computer performs nonsense. Which instructions do not make sense if the stack has too few operands in it?

Write micro code to correct these defects by branching to an (undefined) error handler when they occur.

4   Why is interpretation useful during debugging of programs?

5   What is ROM (Read Only Memory), and why can it be used for micro programs? Could it have any use for S-machine programs?

6   How can the S-machine data paths and micro machine control be modified to allow for single-byte (8-bit) instructions in the case of zero-address instructions? Note that instructions would no longer start on word boundaries, so it would be necessary to be able to move words by multiples of 8 bits fairly easily.

7   How can an interrupt feature on the S machine be implemented? What instructions have to be added to the S-machine language, and what to the micro machine language?

8   Why is micro program control useful?

9   Can a micro program control system be used on a machine with the data paths shown in Figure 7.2? Why?

10   Using whatever assembler with macro features there is available, implement a macro for the S-instruction LOAD such that it can be written as

LOAD	A	with no indexing
LOAD	A,X	with indexing

Design a similar notation and implement it for indirect addressing of the LOAD instruction.

8

MULTI-PROGRAMMING, MULTI-PROCESSING, AND TIME SHARING

Modern computer systems are organized to try to meet a number of conflicting goals, including efficiency, short turnaround, and user convenience. Each of the techniques in the title of this chapter is aimed principally at one of these goals. This will be a short chapter whose purpose is to review the ideas, examine some of the software problems introduced, and discuss the effects of such organizations on user software. (The implementation of some of these systems introduces ideas, such as virtual memory, that have a profound effect on the organization of large programs.)

Multiprogramming refers to the existence of more than one program in different parts of the main memory at the same time. Its principal purpose is computer efficiency, as it is hoped there will be enough programs ready for execution to keep most of the equipment (CPU and channels) busy at all times. A related technique is multitasking, or the existence of several tasks that are part of the same job and can be executed simultaneously. Multiprocessing refers to the use of two or more CPUs in a single computer system. These CPUs are attached to the same memory so that all can be executing parts of the same or different programs. Several CPUs are used in order to increase the total processing capability of the system, often measured in *mips* (millions of instructions per second). Several CPUs, each with its own memory, can be connected via channels, each of which looks like an I/O device to the other computers. This is not multiprocessing, but a multicomputer system, also called a *computer network*. A computer network practices load sharing, passing jobs to the computer that has available processing time on the required facilities. Networks will not be discussed in this book. Time sharing refers to the servicing of many customers or other remote terminals, each of whose average instruction rate is low because interaction between the terminal and the computer delays the execution of the program associated with that terminal.

8.1 MULTIPROGRAMMING

In a multiprogramming environment, several different jobs are loaded into different areas of the main memory in the hope that they will provide work for most of the equipment that can be run simultaneously. The supervisor program takes care of allocating work to different units by keeping lists of steps that are ready for execution on each of the units. When a unit completes a step, the supervisor can check its lists for new work. In the case of input/output units, completion of a step is indicated by an interrupt which signals the CPU to stop processing the current program temporarily and to allocate more work to the I/O unit if there is any. In the case of the CPU, completion is indicated when the CPU program either comes to the end of a job or requests I/O buffers that are not yet available—that is, if an input has been requested, the system has not yet filled the buffer, or if an output has been requested, the system has not yet emptied previous buffers so that there is space for new ones.

Since the CPU is called into action each time there is a change of job on any unit, it is evident that it must be possible to change from one job to another very rapidly, or much time will be lost. When the CPU returns to continue processing an interrupted task, the *state* of that task must be exactly as it was when the interrupt occurred. That means the contents of its memory cells must be unaltered, and the contents of all CPU registers that can affect program execution must be unaltered. As long as the supervisor, or any other program, is not allowed to change a particular user's memory area (this is accomplished by memory protection), the only problem arises with the CPU registers. When an interrupt occurs, these must be saved, much as on a subroutine entry, and restored when execution is restarted. Many machines provide a "return from interrupt" instruction which restores some of the CPU registers. On the 370 and PDP-11, this instruction restores the control counter and the condition register; that is, it restores the program status or state word. The interrupt service program must restore the general-purpose registers if they have been changed.

An important task for the supervisor in a multiprogramming system is scheduling jobs. This involves both macroscopic scheduling—deciding which jobs to load into memory when several are waiting in a job queue—and microscopic scheduling—deciding which task to allocate to a particular unit when there are several tasks waiting for programs that are already in memory. No one criterion is used to decide on a scheduling algorithm. Macroscopic scheduling is usually done on some basis of priority—the more important job is loaded before the less important job when space is available. In many systems, microscopic scheduling leans more toward increasing efficiency, although priority information can be used also. The *mix* of jobs loaded in memory at any one time affects efficiency. For example, if every program is *CPU bound* (that is, spends more time on CPU processing than on I/O work), it is not going to be possible to keep the I/O units busy. For that reason, a system may try to mix CPU bound jobs with I/O bound jobs in macroscopic scheduling. Once the mix has been chosen, microscopic scheduling must be used to maintain efficiency. Although at first sight it appears that it is only necessary for as many jobs as possible to be loaded in memory so that there is sure to be work for all units, decisions by the scheduler crucially affect efficiency. Suppose there is one heavily CPU bound job in memory which does no I/O for a long time. Once that gets into execution, no more I/O requests will be issued, and eventually activity on all I/O units will cease. A supervisor should interrupt the CPU bound job periodically to let other I/O bound jobs execute long enough to create I/O work.

Memory cost is a nontrivial part of a multiprogramming system because more memory than is needed for a single job must be purchased. Hence, a scheduler that can maintain a given degree of activity using less memory is a better scheduler.

It can be seen that a scheduler has to balance several needs, so that there can be no absolute statements made about the correct algorithm to use. The scheduler must reflect the needs of the particular installation. We will not discuss this further here.

The major software and hardware problems caused by multiprogramming are memory allocation, relocation, and protection. When several jobs are in memory simultaneously, each must be able to function as though the others were not present; otherwise, an error in one program could destroy another user's data. That is the problem of protection. When a program is loaded, it must be able to use the available area of memory. This means that it must not depend on using particular addresses. This can be handled with software, which is a relocation problem. However, it is more convenient to do it with hardware relocation and allocation. The next section will examine a number of schemes that have been used for this.

8.1.1 Memory allocation, relocation, and protection

Relocation was introduced in Chapter 3 as a means of loading preassembled programs into any area of memory. This is called *static relocation*. When the program is loaded, addresses that depend on the program's position in memory are set into the program. This means that the program cannot be moved once it has been loaded unless some addresses are modified. Let us consider the effect of such a system on multiprogramming.

When there are no jobs in memory, available memory forms a contiguous set of addresses, say from M to $N - 1$. (Usually, the lower-addressed part of memory contains the system programs, such as the supervisor. We are assuming that these are in locations 0 through $M - 1$.) Programs can be loaded until the memory is full. These programs can be assigned contiguous sections of memory, say from M to $N_1 - 1$, from N_1 to $N_2 - 1$, etc. A relocating loader can load each program into its place without trouble. Now, suppose programs 1 and 3 are completed, leaving a total of $N_3 - N_2 + N_1 - M$ words of free storage as shown in Figure 8.1. Unfortunately, this storage is not contiguous; it has been *fragmented*. If the only programs waiting to be run are larger than either of the separate free areas, problems arise. One of three things can happen—the system can wait until a smaller job arrives or more memory becomes available, a program can be loaded into noncontiguous areas, or some of the programs already in memory can be moved to make the free storage contiguous. The first approach is not conducive to efficiency! The second approach is used in some systems, but it has limited application. If the program to be loaded consists of a number of separately relocatable sections

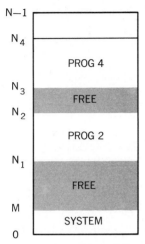

FIGURE 8.1   Fragmentation of free memory

(for example, subroutines, data areas, etc.), the loader can try to package them into the available sections of space. Since a good program is segmented into a number of manageable pieces, this is usually possible. However, if a large data area is needed for a big array, a program may have to wait a long time for a contiguous piece of memory to be available. Alternatively, the scheduler will have to hold on to smaller pieces of memory until several adjacent ones are free, forming a larger contiguous area. The third solution is not possible unless the program abides by some conventions. Consider a program which puts the address of a memory cell into one register (say by a subroutine branch instruction) and a constant into another register. If the program were to be moved, the contents of the first register would have to be relocated, but the contents of the second would not. Consequently, the "reloader" that moved the program would have to know which registers to relocate if a program were to be moved in the middle of execution. Similarly, it would have to know which memory cells to relocate. If the program keeps an up-to-date record of which memory and register cells are relocatable, the reloader can move programs, but that puts a burden on the programmer, as he must write code that keeps such records. It could also lead to program errors that would be hard to detect, since failure to keep a correct record causes an error only if a program is moved while the record is incorrect.

Either of the latter two schemes, assigning noncontiguous storage or moving programs, is an acceptable solution if certain hardware features are added. Historically, the first feature added was *dynamic relocation.* This allows code to be moved without the need to relocate addresses, either in memory or in registers. A *relocation* register is added to the hardware. It is set to contain the lowest address of a user's program in memory. Whenever a memory reference is made by that program, the contents of the relocation register are added to the memory address to calculate an actual address. The user's program is assembled and loaded as though it started in location 0. However, since all memory addresses are displaced by the relocation amount, all memory references are to a contiguous section of memory starting at the address held in the relocation register.

The user cannot change the relocation register. It is set by supervisor instruction at the time the user's program is given control of the CPU. Consequently, the relocation register is part of the program state and must be set by the return from interrupt instruction or by related code. (Memory references by I/O instructions must be relocated also. However, if I/O is handled by calls to the supervisor, it can perform the relocation by software.)

If dynamic relocation is available, the supervisor can move a program simply by copying it from one area to another and by resetting the relocation register. All program references to memory are changed automatically, since no data in the program are dependent on the contents of the relocation register. This is illustrated in Figure 8.2.

The major drawback to using dynamic relocation and moving code is the time spent in the move. In a multiprogramming system in which jobs stay in memory until they have been completed, this is not too serious, as a move will not be necessary more often than each time that a new job is initiated. If jobs take

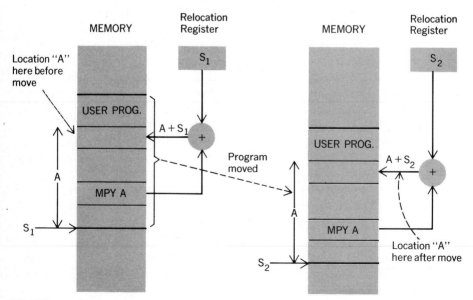

FIGURE 8.2   Effect of dynamic relocation

an average time T and there are an average of J jobs in memory, the average time between moves is T/J, which is large as long as T is large and J is small. However, in most modern systems some part of memory is used for time-sharing work in which many jobs are being loaded frequently. To overcome the high overhead of moving, hardware has been developed to allow for allocation of noncontiguous memory areas.

The desirable feature of such a system is that the program can be prepared as if it had a set of N contiguous memory locations, but the memory space allocated to the program is not necessarily contiguous. If there are N locations free, it is desirable that the program be executed. Consequently, what is needed is a relocation scheme that relocates different addresses by different amounts as shown in Figure 8.3.

It is evident that such a *mapping* is time-consuming and expensive if an arbitrary fragmentation must be handled. Consequently, the memory is broken up into *pages* of 2^p words each, and space is allocated by pages only. Typically p is between 8 and 12 in different systems. If the address used by the programmer is $n + p$ bits long, he can effectively address up to 2^n different pages of 2^p words each. The leftmost n bits of an address determine the page and are called the *page address*, while the rightmost p bits determine the word within the page. Suppose that the programmer refers to addresses in the range 0 to $K \cdot 2^p$; he needs $K + 1$ pages of memory. If there are that many pages free, they can be allocated to him. Then a mapping device must convert each of his memory addresses so that it refers to the correct page. This can be done by a

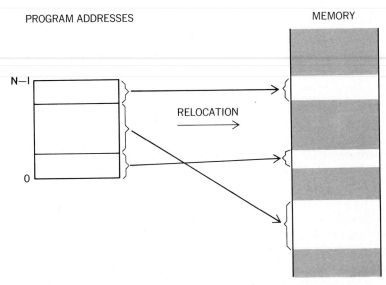

FIGURE 8.3   *Address mapping for relocation*

page table, which lists, for each page used by the programmer, his number for it and the actual number in memory. This can be illustrated by an example. Suppose the programmer refers to addresses 0 to 4095 in a system in which the page size is 1,024 words. Suppose memory locations 1024–2047, 4096–6143, and 8192–9215 are free. Consequently, the following mapping should be performed:

PROGRAM ADDRESS	→	MEMORY ADDRESS
0–1023		1024–2047
1024–2047		4096–5119
2048–3171		5120–6143
3172–4095		8192–9215

When these addresses are expressed in binary, the following are the results:

PROGRAM ADDRESS	→	MEMORY ADDRESS
000000xxxxxxxxxx		000001xxxxxxxxxx
000001xxxxxxxxxx		000100xxxxxxxxxx
000010xxxxxxxxxx		000101xxxxxxxxxx
000011xxxxxxxxxx		001000xxxxxxxxxx

assuming that a 16-bit address is used. The 10 x's represent the 10 least significant bits of the address—the word address. They need not be converted in the address mapping. Consequently, the mapping can be performed by a small *page memory* that is 6 bits wide and 64 words long in this example. The leftmost 6 bits of the program address, the page address, can be used to address the page memory. The 6 bits read from the page memory can be used to replace those 6 bits in the address sent to main memory. With such a device, the example above could be handled by storing 000001, 000100, 000101, and 001000 in locations 0 through 3, respectively, of the page memory.

Several other benefits can be obtained from this system, which is called *paging.* Additional bits can be stored in the page memory to indicate memory protection—whether the program is allowed to access the page for reading, for writing, or not at all. It is also possible to handle *virtual memory.* This is a system in which the programmer is allowed to "reference" many more memory locations than are physically assigned to his program in main memory at any one time. Space for the user's program and data are assigned on an auxiliary storage device such as a disk or drum, and the program is stored there. The page memory for that program indicates that the pages are not in main memory. When the program starts execution, one or more pages are transferred into main memory, and the page memory is set to indicate their positions. The program is executed from main memory until it attempts to reference a location that is still in auxiliary storage. This is indicated in the page memory and causes an interrupt to the operating system, which records a request for free memory and a transfer from auxiliary storage to that free memory. Later, when memory has been assigned and the transfer completed, the program can resume. Until that time, another program is executed. Since the system cannot rely on memory being freed by terminating jobs, it must use a scheduling algorithm to take memory pages away from programs that are not currently executing from them. The contents of these pages can be stored back on the auxiliary storage device and the page memory updated to note that fact. The idea, and hope, of a paging system with virtual memory is that those pages of a program being used frequently will tend to stay in the main memory, while those that have not been referenced for some time will tend to be banished to auxiliary storage. Obviously, the organization of user code has a significant effect on the efficiency of such systems. A program that references a large collection of data randomly will be less efficient than one that concentrates on a small collection of data for a while, even if it performs more work with the latter organization.

Paging solves some problems but introduces others. The contents of the page memory are part of the program state and must be preserved with the rest of the state when the CPU program is changed by an interrupt. Since it is not feasible to reload the contents of the page memory at each interrupt, a different part of the page memory is associated with each program. One way of doing this is to use dynamic relocation in the page memory. The relative origin of the page memory can be held in a relocation register so that only this register need be changed when the program is changed. The easiest way of thinking about this is in terms of page addresses and the page memory. Each program is assigned a contiguous part of the page memory so that it can address a number of contiguous pages. An address generated by the program is split into a page and a word address. The page address is relocated dynamically, and the new page address is used to find an actual page address, which is sent to memory with the word address to access the desired data. This is shown in Figure 8.4.

When a program is removed from memory, space in the page table becomes available for allocation to another program. The problem of noncontiguous free space now occurs in the page memory rather than the main memory. Once again, it can be solved by moving data in the page memory or by using a scheme for allocating noncontiguous page memory. Moving is not as expensive a scheme as before, as the number of words in the page memory assigned to a program is equal to the number of pages assigned to that program, so the information can be copied much more rapidly. (If there are 1,024 words to a page, it can be about 1,000 times as fast.) However, in a virtual memory system, it is desirable to have a large number of addressable pages, even if not all are in main memory at the same time. Consequently, another level of paging is frequently used to avoid this copying. This level is called *segmenta-*

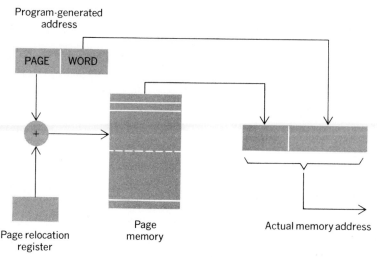

FIGURE 8.4 Relocation and paging

tion. In segmentation, the first part of the page address is called the *segment address.* It is used to do a table look-up in a segment table for an actual segment address. This is concatenated with the page address bits to look up the actual page address in the page memory. The actual page add is concatenated with the word address to get the actual memory address. The process is shown in Figure 8.5.

Segmentation has additional benefits for the programmer. One of the problems in programming is memory allocation for jobs which use large, variable-

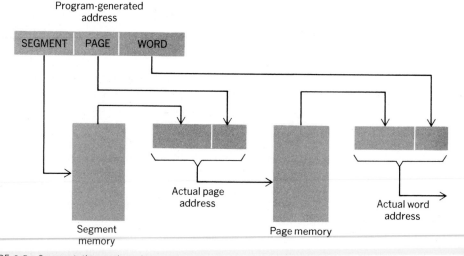

FIGURE 8.5 Segmentation and paging

size arrays whose size will not be known until run time. It is desirable to be able to increase the size of various storage areas as needed. However, if the program must declare the amount of memory it needs at load time and allocate space within the area assigned, it may have to resort to moving information around as arrays change in size. It would be much easier to start each array at an address so far from the adjacent array that there is certain to be space. For example, if it seems likely that no array will exceed 32,768 ($=2^{15}$) words, the arrays could be assigned starting addresses that far apart. Without paging, that much memory would have to be assigned to the array, even if it was not used. With paging and virtual memory, only the space used need ever be placed in main memory. With segmentation, each array could be started in a different segment. Only those segments used need be assigned space in the page memory, while only those pages used in the active segments will have to appear in the main memory.

There is, of course, still the problem of allocating space in the segment memory used for the segment table look-up. One could propose yet another level of mapping, and so on. . . ! However, the number of bits in a segment address is small, and the number of segments used by most programs is very small. Therefore, it is possible to consider reloading the segment information when a program is changed, or using a dynamic relocation register and moving information in the segment memory when a program is removed from memory.

MEMORY PROTECTION AND SHARED PROGRAMS

Segmentation and paging allow for very flexible memory protection. Either pages or segments can be protected against reading and/or writing. (A location can be protected against both by not making it accessible in the page table.) Write protection is useful for communication between programs, particularly between a program and the supervisor. Information such as the real-time clock can be stored in areas which can be read by any program but not changed by any but the supervisor. It is also useful for sharing subroutines. If several programs in memory require the same subroutines or system utilities, these subroutines can be stored in an area of memory that is write-protected for all users. If these subroutines are reentrant and use data areas in the calling programs, they can be shared, thus saving memory space for extra copies. Write protection will also prevent a program from overwriting itself. Programs written as pure procedures are generally better code, and if write protection is applied to them, one common form of program error that is difficult to locate is caught.

SEGMENTATION AND PAGING IN THE IBM 370

Segmentation and paging are an option in the 370 series. The address field of 24 bits is split into a segment, page, and word address. The size of a page can be set to either 2,048 or 4,096 bytes. The size of a segment can be set to either 65,536 or 1,048,576 bytes, giving either 256 or 16 segments of 16, 32, 256, or 512 pages each.

The segment and page memories are areas of the main memory that are not accessible to the user program. The address of the first word of the segment table is part of the program state, so that it acts as a relocation register for the segment table. The address fetched from the segment table is added to the page bits, rather than concatenated, so that the page table can start anywhere. (Actually it is restricted to starting on a doubleword boundary.) The address fetched from the page table is concatenated with the word address as described earlier.

The cost of paging and segmentation is both financial — the extra hardware — and in speed — the delay caused by additional memory references. This is partially offset in many systems by the use of buffer or cache memories (as described in Chapter 5). The currently used segment and page addresses can be kept in the faster buffer memory to save time in the address mapping.†

8.2 MULTIPROCESSING

Two or more CPUs are used in computer systems both to increase the *throughput* and to guarantee *uptime*. The latter is critical in many *real-time* systems which are controlling experiments or handling important allocation problems. For example, if a large processing plant such as a steel mill were under computer control, the cost of a computer malfunction would be high if the plant had to stop production. Similarly, an airline would lose much business if its reservation system did not function while a hardware malfunction was being repaired. The problem can be alleviated by connecting more than one CPU in an organization which allows the second CPU to continue processing when the first is down for maintenance. When both are running, less critical jobs, such as record production and payroll, can also be processed. These jobs can be delayed when one CPU is down so that the critical work can be performed.

Multiprocessing systems usually also perform multiprogramming, so that there is a list of jobs waiting for CPU service. If the additional CPUs are attached to increase the speed of particular jobs, then multitasking can also be used. (An example of a job for which speed is essential is air traffic control.

---

†For further reading, the student is referred to P. J. Denning, Virtual Memory, *Computing Surveys*, vol. 2, no. 3, pp. 153–189, September 1970, and J. B. Dennis, Segmentation and the Design of Multi-programmed Computer Systems, *Journal of the Association for Computing Machinery*, vol. 12, pp. 589–602, October 1965.

If a program is computing the flight patterns of aircraft arriving at an airport, the computation must be done in time to inform pilots of evasive action necessary to avoid collisions.)

The major additional problem caused by multiprocessing involves the synchronization of related tasks. We have already seen this problem in interrupt-controlled I/O. Similar, but more complex, problems arise here. If two or more processors are accessing the same data base, great care must be taken to keep one processor from modifying data between the time that another processor has read the data and the time that it has had a chance to return the modified data to memory. Since multiprogramming systems usually keep lists of waiting tasks in memory, there is a possibility that two processors may try to add to the list or remove tasks at almost the same time. Suppose, for example, that a count of the number of tasks on a list is stored in memory. If a processor adds a task to the list, it must increase this count. If another processor removes a task at almost the same time, it must reduce the count. If the sequence of steps is as shown in Table 8.1, the count will not be correct.

If the computers have increment and decrement instructions that are executed in a single memory cycle, the above problem does not arise. However, much more complex modifications are needed on common data bases in multiprocessing. For example, the list of waiting jobs has to be modified. It is unreasonable to expect a single instruction to handle these, so the problem of locking one processor from a section of code while another processor is changing data must be faced. It is possible to write code that will do this.†
However, such code is slow, and it is something of an intellectual exercise, as there is a very simple hardware approach to the problem. The solution is to use one bit of a word as a flag to indicate that certain data are being changed by one processor and must not be touched by other processors. Let us suppose that one processor has set this bit to a 1, and is modifying the data. When it has finished, it resets the bit to a 0. Any processor that wishes to

TABLE 8.1   *Memory conflict in multiprocessing*

PROCESSOR A		PROCESSOR B		VALUE OF N IN MEMORY
LOAD	N			5
		LOAD	N	5
ADD	= 1			5
		SUB	= 1	5
STORE	N			6
		STORE	N	4

†See, for example, E. W. Dijkstra, Solution of a Problem in Concurrent Program Control, *Communications of the Association for Computing Machinery,* vol. 8, no. 9, p. 569, 1965.

access the data checks the bit and does not proceed until the bit is 0. When it gets "permission" to proceed, it sets the bit to a 1 to block other processors from proceeding until it is finished. This is not quite sufficient, because two processors arriving to test the bit at about the same time can both sneak through without either being aware of the other. This is shown in Table 8.2. (SETONE is assumed to set the bit to a 1.)

The problem occurs because between the time that processor A can test the bit and the time it can change it, processor B has tested the bit and also found it to be a 0. This can be solved by providing an instruction that reads a bit from memory and sets it to 1 in the same memory cycle. The old value of the bit should be tested, but because the bit is set to 1 in the same cycle that it is read for testing, it is guaranteed that no other processor can read the bit during this time. The instruction is called TEST AND SET in the 370.

8.3 TIME SHARING

Time sharing was introduced in the early 1960s to make the facilities of large computer systems available to the user who wanted to sit at the computer console and interact with his program. This is extremely useful during the debugging phase, when minor errors stop the execution of a program before much information has been obtained, and it is useful when new methods are being explored. It arose from a desire for the "good old days" of the middle 1950s when computers were so slow that the normal mode of execution was for the programmer to sit at the operating console and sequence his program through various phases. Since the amount of computation performed between programmer actions is fairly small, the obvious solution is to share the computer between many programmers, servicing each program for a short period. Multiprogramming provides a mechanism for such a solution provided that all programs can be loaded into memory simultaneously, but there is no guarantee that the programs are particularly short and so a lot of memory space may be required. Since fast memory is expensive, many techniques must be used to implement a system that provides time sharing to a large number

TABLE 8.2   *Failure of blocking*

PROCESSOR A			PROCESSOR B			VALUE OF BIT
	. . .			. . .		0
X1	TEST	BIT				0
			X2	TEST	BIT	0
	BNE	X1				0
				BNE	X2	0
	SETONE	BIT				1
				SETONE	BIT	1
	. . .			. . .		

of programmers. In this section we will mention some of the techniques that are used.

A virtual memory system is one approach to providing a large amount of apparent memory. It has the advantage that all programs in the system are treated equally, so that a program developed in one environment, for example, batch, can be run in an interactive mode later if the need arises. Virtual memory will probably be used on all large systems in the future, but it has only recently become commonly available on standard computers such as the IBM 370. Many other techniques have been used in the past and will probably continue to be used on smaller systems because of the cost of virtual memory.

One of the earliest techniques used was simple swapping of programs between main memory and fast auxiliary storage such as disk. When it was a program's turn for execution, it was loaded into memory and started. When it had used its allocated amount of time, or when it requested input/output that caused a wait, it was stored back on the disk and the next program was loaded. Such a system could be improved by several techniques. For example, if enough memory for several programs was available, one could be executing while others were swapped in or out.

Some swapping can be avoided if tasks common to many users are handled by common programs. Consequently, the greatest savings in the cost of a time-sharing system can be achieved by a careful analysis of user requirements and an effort to provide the common, frequently used processes efficiently. Typical common needs are:

Input and output of data to and from the terminal

Storing programs and data from one run to another

Editing programs stored in the computer

Checking programs for syntactic accuracy (seeing if they will assemble or compile)

The first three of these are provided by almost all time-sharing systems. If, for example, the user wishes to read a line from his terminal to an area of memory in his program, he will request a system input program to perform the read. It will read each character from the terminal until it detects the end of the line, then hand the complete line to the program when it is next in execution. If the programmer had read each character directly, his program would have had to be executed for a few instructions between each character read. This would create a high overhead because of the need to swap the program into memory after each character.

Filing systems are an integral part of a time-sharing system. They allow the programmer to input a program, either from a terminal or via other input devices such as card readers, and to leave it on the disk for later use. If a programmer is only typing in a program at a remote terminal, there is no need for him to have his own input program. A system program can process all such input and store it on the disk under the programmer's identification. Similarly, if he wishes to edit data or a program that is already stored on the disk, the editing can be done by a system program.

It is also possible to provide system programs that check the syntax of programs, either a line at a time as they are typed in or a subroutine at a time as the user requests the check. This type of operation is more feasible in an operating environment in which few different languages are in use. If, for example, users are restricted to one language only, it is probably economical to keep a compiler for that language in memory at all times, as a large number of users' programs can be checked at the same time. If there are many different languages, it is less likely that many users will be requiring a check of programs in the same language at any one time. Time-sharing systems have been based on relatively small systems by restricting the use of languages. For example, the early Basic time-sharing system allowed only that language and was very effective for a limited class of problems.

It is always dangerous to make predictions, but it appears that time sharing is becoming relatively less important as a mode of operation. The cost of simple computers has dropped drastically in the last few years, so that small computers can be included in a terminal for very little more than the price of the relatively expensive input/output part of the terminal. We can expect these small computers to handle much of the simple work that was previously handled by time-sharing systems. The larger jobs must still be sent to a large system, but this is done more as a type of *remote batch* in which a complete job is transmitted and processed and the results returned. The large computers are frequently grouped together as a computer network in which load sharing can be practiced. Further, special-purpose computers can be part of the network, so that users with special problems can get access to the most suitable computer.†

PROBLEMS

1   What is the simplest convention for making 370 programs dynamically relocatable? How about PDP-11 programs?

2   In a multiprogrammed system, would it be better to give priority on the CPU to CPU bound programs or to I/O bound programs when both are loaded? What about priority on the channel?

†For additional information on time-sharing systems, the reader is referred to M. V. Wilkes, "Time Shared Computer Systems," 2d ed., MacDonald/American Elsevier Computer Monographs, London, 1972.

3 If 10 jobs of equal duration are loaded for processing simultaneously in a multiprogrammed system, and none of the jobs perform I/O until the end of the CPU execution, what is the best scheduling strategy to maximize efficiency, assuming that there are no other jobs in memory?

4 If a user program is in control in a time-sharing system, is it sufficient to wait for that program to make an I/O request before switching to another program? Why?

9
THE ASSEMBLER

The assembler is a program which accepts input from the user or possibly from the output of a compiler and produces machine language, usually in a relocatable form. The input or source language is frequently in the form of card images. It has four well-defined fields containing

1 The location name (may be blank)
2 The mnemonic instruction or pseudo
3 The address field
4 The comments field

Most assemblers allow comment cards to be included at any point. Such cards are distinguished by a special punch, for example, an asterisk in column 1. We shall not discuss comment cards further, assuming that the section of the assembler which reads the input will arrange to skip over such cards immediately.

The output will be presumed to be in binary format acceptable to the loader. Normally, this output is only punched if specifically requested; the copy that the loader uses is retained on tape or disk. The decision whether to punch the output or not can be made within the scheduler by interrogating the punch option and then outputting a copy of the binary object file. In addition to the binary output, there is usually some form of printed output so that the user can check his input and have enough information to enable him to understand diagnostic results from the memory. A typical output consists of a listing of the input in 80 columns of the page and an octal or hexadecimal version of the object alongside the input. Since the object is produced in a relocatable form and the assembler does not know where the program will be loaded, the object form is given without relocation. Errors will be indicated on the listing in some form, either at the end of the listing with references back to the program or by means of markers alongside the program line in error.

Most assemblers take two basic passes through the input program to produce the object. The first pass is used to produce a table of all symbolic addresses used and their address values. The second is used to substitute these values into the original symbolic form to get the binary form. If too many complications are introduced, then two passes are no longer sufficient, but it is desirable to keep the number of passes to a minimum in order to make the assembly process as fast as possible. The input for short problems can be kept in memory during the translation process, but longer programs would occupy too much space, so they must be kept on auxiliary storage. Since such storage is typically much slower than the main memory, the time spent in each pass is largely determined by the time it takes to fetch the information from the backup device. Thus doubling the number of passes can effectively double the translation time, although very little actual computation may be done in the extra passes.

9.1 PASS I: THE LOCATION COUNTER

The major task of the first pass is to construct a table of all names used in the program and to associate a memory address with each name. To do this, all input lines of code are read, one at a time. If a name appears in the location field, then it is put into the table (with some exceptions to be discussed later). The assembler assumes that the first instruction to be read is placed into location 0, the next into location 1, and so on. For the moment we shall ignore the problems of pseudos and macros and just study the two tasks to be performed in constructing the name table. In order to know what address value to associate with a name in the location field, an account must be kept of the space used by instructions read. We call this the location counter, because it contains the address of the location into which the instruction will be loaded if no relocation is applied. This location counter is maintained during pass I and pass II in order to tell the assembler into which location the line of code currently being translated will load. After each instruction is handled in either pass I or pass II, the location counter is incremented by the length of the instruction (1 in the case of one-word instructions; 2, 4, or 6 in the case of IBM 370 or PDP-11 instructions which can occupy 2, 4, or 6 bytes).

When a name is found in a location field, it is put into a table along with its address value. Thus each entry in the table consists of at least two parts: the name and the associated address value. Since nothing else need be done with names during pass I, this table could be constructed by simply placing each pair of items in the next free words of an array of pairs of words. If, however, it is decided to check for double definition of names during pass I, then it is necessary to determine if the name just read in the location field is already present in the table. This involves some sort of table lookup procedure. We shall delay discussion of techniques for this until the next chapter and content ourselves with some general comments at this stage. What is actually needed is called an *associative* memory. An associative memory is a memory device that is not addressed in the way we have discussed so far, that is, by a numeric address which refers to a specific location in memory. Rather, an associative memory device is addressed by means of its contents. Initially, an associative memory is assumed to contain no information. That is, there is a state of each word in the associative memory which represents *not used*. When a word is written into an associative memory, no address is given; the memory device stores it in any available (not used) location. When a word is to be read from an associative memory, the contents of part of the word are specified. The memory is expected to locate all words which match the specified contents.

We can see that an associative memory is just what is needed for a name table. When a name is first read from a location field, it can be entered into the associative memory along with its address value. (We consider the pair of items as a single entry.) When another name is read, it can be checked for double definition by reading from the memory any word whose name part agrees with the name just read. If the name is doubly defined, there will be an entry already in the memory on the second and subsequent occurrences. If it has not been previously used, then it can be entered (stored) into the associative memory.

In this particular use of the associative-memory principle, the same field of the stored information is always used for matching with the name in the READ operation. In this case, we call this field a *tag* or a *key* since it is an identifying piece of information which serves as the address for user reference to the memory. Associative memories have been constructed directly from hardware, but they are not yet economical for most applications. Therefore, we simulate the functions of an associative memory using the CPU and the regular memory. The mechanics of the simulation will be discussed in the next chapter. The specific operations that may have to be provided are

STORE   Place a set of information into a new location in the associative memory or table.

READ   Locate any entries in the table that match a given tag or key.

CHANGE   Locate any entries in the table, and change them in a specified fashion.

DELETE   Remove an entry with a given tag from the table.

In the remainder of this chapter, we shall assume that these operations are available. In practice, they are provided by suitable subroutines.

If the input lines contain only instructions, then the simple mechanism of incrementing the location counter by 1 for each line is sufficient. However, there has to be one pseudo in any code, the END pseudo. This tells the assembler that the complete deck has been read and that the next pass can begin. In practice, many other pseudos must be interpreted because they affect the location counter in various ways. For example, a BSS 23 should increment the location counter by 23.

In order that pass I may recognize the difference between the instructions and pseudos, it must examine the mnemonic coding. The mnemonic is usually a string of characters similar to a symbolic name, so that similar techniques can be used to handle mnemonics.

In this case, the table of mnemonics (in other words, the contents of the associative memory used for mnemonics) is permanent, having been set up by the assembler designer. It contains each legal mnemonic together with identifying information. The information needed in pass I tells whether the mnemonic is an instruction (possibly what type of instruction if variable-length instructions are possible) or what pseudo it is. Since pass I will contain a number of sections of code for each instruction type and each pseudo, an easy way to handle the testing for mnemonic type is to store, with the mnemonics, a branch address which gives the address of the code used to handle the mnemonic. This is shown in Figure 9.1. The typical flow of pass I of an assembler is shown in Figure 9.2. The input line of code is read and the mnemonic extracted. The mnemonic code is looked up in the mnemonic table. If it is not present, there is an error (unless macros are allowed, as discussed later). If it is present, a branch is made to the address found in the table. Then the appropriate section of code takes care of the rest of the line. If it is a one-word instruction, the name, if any, is placed in the name table together with the contents of the location counter, and then the location counter is increased by 1. If it is an END pseudo, pass I is terminated. A BSS pseudo places a name from the location field into the name table together with the contents of the location counter, and then it increases the contents of the location counter by the appropriate amount. The code for the pseudos will be discussed in detail in a later section.

9.1.1 Coding the basic assembler: pass I

The manner in which the basic code discussed above is written will depend to a large extent on the machine being used. This section will discuss the general problems that occur and mention typical solutions of these problems. The first step is to read in a new line of program for translation. This is usually a card image from magnetic tape or disk file. The operating system will normally provide a read subroutine which will pass the image of the next card from the input file to the program area. The call to this subroutine will have to specify an area sufficient to store 80 characters. The operating system subroutine takes care of buffering the input file in ahead of the READ request so that there is no need for the user to worry about a multiple buffering scheme for input. However, later passes of the assembler will need to reread the input file, so additional steps depend very much on the flexibility of the system. If the system allows the input file to be read a second time, nothing additional need be done; otherwise, a copy of the input must be produced for later use. This is also a good idea if the input is relatively slow compared to other available devices, or if the number of cards per input block is low. By producing a second copy on a high-speed auxiliary storage device with many cards packed in each block, the read time in the second pass can be reduced.

When a card image has been read into the program area of memory, the assembler must extract various fields from it in order to form names, mnemon-

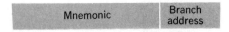

FIGURE 9.1   *Entry in mnemonic table for pass I*

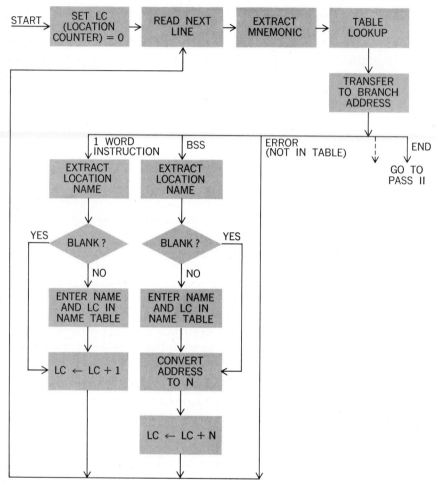

FIGURE 9.2   Pass I flowchart outline

ics, and addresses. For example, the address field of an instruction might contain ABCX + 312 in one case and S — 21 in another. The assembler will have to extract the name ABCX in one case and S in the other, and the numbers 312 and 21. These numbers start in different columns and are of different lengths. If the machine is character oriented or possesses instructions and addressing with these properties (such as the IBM 370 and PDP-11 systems), then it is fairly simple to work a character at a time. If the machine does not have these properties, then it is usually easier to construct a subroutine which extracts characters one at a time from the input card. The characters from the card must be examined, one at a time, to determine where each field and the various subfields and elements of subfields start and finish. This is usually done by a *lexicographic* scan, which only looks at the type of the characters that appear and does not concern itself with more detailed meaning. Most assemblers separate fields and subfields by *break* characters, also called *separators*. For example, the blank character and the comma are used as break characters in the 370 assembler, while the colon, comma, semicolon, and sometimes the blank character are used in the PDP-11 assembler. The logic of a lexicographic scan can often be described by a *state diagram.* This shows the state of the program in terms of what it is doing and indicates how the state is changed when certain characters are read. Partial state diagrams for the 370 and PDP-11 assemblers are shown in Figures 9.3 and 9.4. States are shown in circles, while the arrows leaving the circles indicate the control path to be followed when a character in the indicated class is read as the next character. These state diagrams are incomplete, as the address field must be broken down into its basic components by looking for the separators allowed. The valid separators may change as the state of the scan changes. For example, once the character used to define a string has been read, all characters are part of the string until the character terminating a string has been read. The assembler rules make many character combinations invalid; for example, a plus sign is a separator between elements in an address field, but it is an invalid character in either the location or the mnemonic field in most assemblers. Consequently, the lexicographic analysis is a substantial piece of code for most assembly languages and should therefore be segmented from the rest of the assembler.

One way of achieving this segmentation is to make the lexicographic analysis into a subroutine which returns the next element from the card each time it is called. This is not completely convenient, as it has to be aware of what is happening in the main program. For example, analysis of the address field depends on what has been found in the mnemonic field. Another way is to make it the main program and let it call other subroutines to handle the various fields and subfields. This is not totally satisfactory either, as the purpose of having a lexicographic scan is to separate a well-defined part of the task for clarity and debugging ease. If it is also the main program, it will be confused by many other details. This is the type of situation in which a coroutine can often be used to advantage. Coroutines are able to view each other as subroutines so that both can be written as though they had control of their own domains.

The lexicographic coroutine should extract one item from the input card at a time and go back to the pass I coroutine. For example, it might extract the following list of items:

Location field name (or mark that there is no name)
Mnemonic
First element in address field

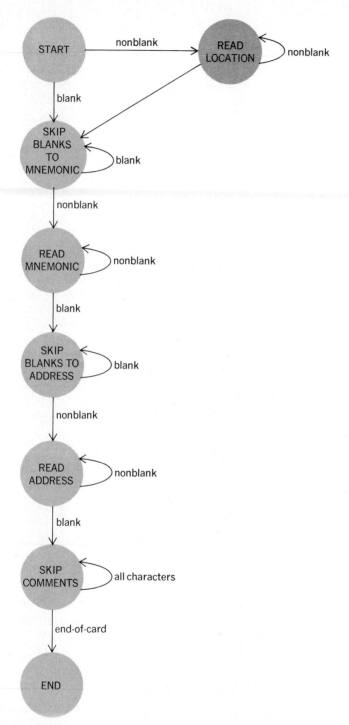

FIGURE 9.3 Partial state diagram for the IBM 370 assembler

Second element in address field

. . .

Last element in address field
End of card or line

The determination of location and mnemonic fields is indicated in Figures 9.3 and 9.4 for two particular assemblers. Breaking up the address field will become much more complex as the types of separators allowed, and the number of different possible constructions, are varied. Generally speaking, numbers and names can be easily recognized, as numbers always start with a digit and contain only digits, while names always start with an alphabetic

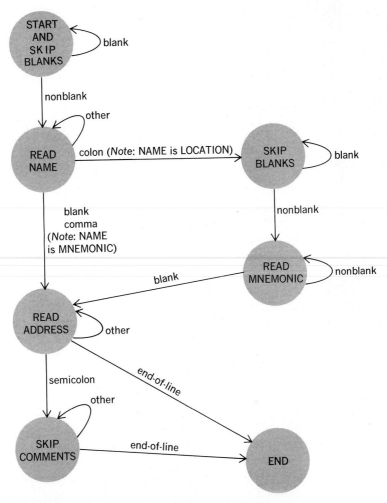

FIGURE 9.4 Partial state diagram for the PDP-11 assembler

character and contain only alphanumeric characters after that. Hence, the first character of the wrong type can be used as an indication that the number or name has been completely read. Most other characters except for blanks are separate elements that will have to be passed on to the pass I coroutine for more analysis. Thus, a coroutine might analyze

| ABCD | LOAD | 3+R,W21 | COMMENT |

to get

ABCD
LOAD
3
+
R
,
W21

The comments would be skipped, as they are not relevant to pass I processing. The pass I coroutine would analyze this output to see if it was a valid assembler statement; if so, it would define the location field and suitably change the location counter, depending on the mnemonic. In many cases, the address field will not have to be analyzed completely in pass I, as its value is not necessary for determining the amount by which the location counter should be changed. However, some pseudos, and instructions whose addresses determine the length of the instruction (such as many PDP-11 instructions), have address fields which must be analyzed in pass I. For this reason, it is common to analyze the address field completely in pass I and to try to avoid repeating the analysis in the second pass. Ways of avoiding a second analysis will be discussed in Section 9.4. In the next few subsections we will mention some techniques that are useful for programming the analysis.

9.1.2 Programming techniques

The lexicographic analysis program has to examine the type of character just read to determine which state to go to next. A bad way of doing this is to test for all cases of interest. Thus, if it is necessary to find out if the next character is alphabetic, 26 comparisons must be made, although the character code used may make it possible to use fewer tests. However, it is desirable to write the program in a way that is independent of the particular coding used so that alternative character sets can be accommodated without rewriting. A fast way of performing the test is to construct a character table which contains an entry for each character. Since characters are 6 or 8 bits in most systems, there need not be more than 256 entries. These can be arranged so that they can be indexed using the binary value of the character as the index. The entries in the table can consist of several fields, each only a few bits long. For example, one field of 1 bit could be used to indicate whether the character is an alphabetic character or not, another 1-bit field can be used to indicate whether it is a numeric digit or not. Another 4-bit field can be used to hold the value of the character if it is a numeric digit.

Using such a technique, a test to see if a character is in a certain class can be executed using an indexed LOAD, an AND with a mask, and a test for 0. For example, suppose the 8-bit character code for 2 is 11110010. This has the numeric value 242. The 242d entry in the table would indicate that the character is a numeric digit, not an alphabetic character, and that its value is 0010 in binary. Other bit fields can be used to indicate whether the character is a separator for location fields, for mnemonic fields, for address fields, etc. A possible format, and the entry for the character two, is shown in Figure 9.5.

In the scan of the location and mnemonic fields, it is known that the only valid element is a name—at least in the assemblers discussed here. Consequently, the lexicographic scan need only check for names in those fields. However, many other forms are possible in the address field, so the lexicographic scan must test for many cases there. The problem is to take a string of characters such as A123+123*123—B123 and to recognize that A123 and B123 are names, and that 123 is a number. In other words, we would like to break up the string into A123, +, 123, *, 123, —, and B123. This recognition can be performed very simply by scanning from left to right and noting the following:

Names start with a letter and contain letters or digits.
Numbers start with a digit and contain only digits.

Starting from the left, the next character is examined. If it is a letter, then a name is recognized. A subscanner called a *name recognizer* examines consecutive characters until a non-alphanumeric character is read. This signals the end of the name. (There may have to be a check for excessive length if names are restricted to a maximum length.) After the string of characters representing the name has been scanned, control returns to the basic recognizer. Simi-

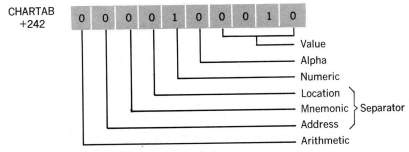

FIGURE 9.5 *Format for a character table and the entry for 2*

larly, if the first character is a digit, a subscanner for recognizing numbers can be used to read the characters constituting the number. Most arithmetic characters form elements directly, although, if exponentiation is allowed (it seldom is) using the notation ** for the operator, the appearance of the first asterisk must cause a check for a second. Character strings in the address field also call for a special recognizer, as all characters inside a character string are valid except for the terminating character, and there is usually a special convention for allowing that also.

Because there is usually very little uniformity between different instruction types and different pseudo-instructions, it is usually easiest to code a separate recognizer for each possible address structure. Generally, they can be detected by the first character so that a branch to the appropriate recognizer can be made after the first character has been read by the main scanner.

CONVERTING NUMBERS TO BINARY

The principles of this were covered in Section 2.4.7. The number recognizer scans the characters, testing to see if they are numeric digits. If they are, the value of the digit is taken from the table and used in the conversion process. The steps are:

1 Set the accumulated value of the number $N = 0$ initially.
2 Table lookup the next character.
3 Test the "digit" bit.
   a If it is 0, the end of the number has been reached.
   b If it is a 1, go to the next step.
4 Multiply N by 10 and add the recoded form of the character.
5 Return to step 2.

If floating- or fixed-point numbers have to be recognized, additional characters must be accepted. One of the better ways of converting floating-point decimal numbers to binary is to convert the mantissa to an integer using the above process. The position of the decimal point should be noted when it is read. This can be stored as the number of digits after the decimal point. This number can be subtracted from the exponent, and the integer multiplied by the appropriate power of 10. If the powers of 10 are stored in a table, only one rounding error need occur, as the initial conversion of the mantissa to an integer will be exact. An example of this is the conversion of 34.532E+6. The recognizer will convert the mantissa to get the integer 34532 represented in binary. It will record the value 3 for the number of digits after the decimal point. The character E causes the exponent to be read as an integer. When 3 is subtracted from the exponent, the result, 3, is used to get the third power of 10 from a table. This will be multiplied by the mantissa currently stored as an integer to get the result 34532000. The powers of 10 will have to be stored in floating-point binary form because they will be too large or small for integer representation in most cases. The integer form of the mantissa will have to be converted to floating-point form before the final multiplication to make this operation possible. This can usually be done by logical operations. The number can be shifted to an appropriate part of a word and an exponent can be inserted. For example, if the mantissa is 24 bits, the integer can be stored in these 24 bits and the exponent set to $+24$.

RECOGNIZING AND CONVERTING NAMES

The output from the name-recognizer subprogram should be a packed name suitable for entry or lookup in the name table. The packing used will depend on the amount of time available for the operation (if the assembler is very much input/output limited, then we are not particularly concerned with packing time), the space available in the name table, and possibly the method used for handling the lookup association in the name table. If space is not a problem, then the most straightforward technique is to pack the characters side by side in a binary representation, such as 6-bit BCD, into as many words as necessary. Thus if a 48-bit machine is used, if up to eight character names are allowed, and if a full word is to be used for a name, then all names can be made eight characters long by the addition of blanks on the right as necessary, and each character can be stored in a 6-bit representation from left to right across the 48-bit word.

In some cases, it might be desirable to use fewer bits to represent a name. Suppose, for example, that a 48-bit word was available and that names are restricted to six characters or less. If table entries are to include the name and 16 additional bits of information, then either two words will have to be used for each entry or the name will have to be represented in 32 bits or less. A six-character name with each character represented by 6 bits unfortunately requires 36 bits. The only possibilities for characters in the name are BLANK, 0,1, . . . 9, and A,B, . . . Z, or 37 different characters in all. These cannot be represented by less than 6 bits individually, but as a group of six character names, there are less than $37 * 37 * 37 * 37 * 37 * 37 = 2,565,726,409$ different names. Since the first character is restricted to be only a letter, and blanks cannot appear in the middle of a name, there are actually fewer.

Since $2^{32} = 4,294,967,296$ is greater than $37^6 = 2,565,726,409$, 32 bits can be used to represent all possible six-character names; the only problem is how. The representation has to be such that the conversion in either direction is straightforward. One simple method is to consider a six-character name (with blanks on the right if it is shorter than six characters) as a base-37 number representation. Each character 0,1, . . . 9,A,B, . . . Z, BLANK is assigned a unique value between 0 and 36, say, 0,1,2, . . . , 36 in the order given. The integer represented by the base-37 number is converted into binary. It will necessarily occupy less than 33 bits. For example, the name CAD31 is equivalent to $C * 37^5 + A *, 37^4 + D * 37^3 + 3 * 37^2 + 1 * 37 +$ BLANK which is equal to $12*37**5 + 10*37**4 + 13*37**3 + 3*37**2 + 1*37 + 36 = 851,531,763$. This number, stored as a binary integer, can be used to represent the name CAD31 in the table. It can be converted back to the alphanumeric form by converting back to base 37 and then recoding the characters into the standard form used in the machine (for example, BCD). If this method is used, then the recoding performed by the character table should be into the numeric value assigned to the alphabetic characters in order to minimize the time needed for the conversion. If this representation of names is used, six characters are packed into 32 bits for an average of 5.33 bits per character, which is not too much more than the minimum possible. In fact, there are 1,617,038,380 names of six or less alphanumeric characters that start with a letter. Therefore they can be represented by a minimum of 31 bits.

EVALUATING EXPRESSIONS IN THE ADDRESS FIELD

The final problem to be taken care of in the address field is to convert a string of names, numbers, and operators into a single number represented by the expression if it is a legal one, or to find out if it is illegal. When an expression is to be evaluated in pass I, it must normally be well defined; that is, all of the names must be previously defined in the name table. Therefore, we assume that each name has been looked up in the name table and replaced with a numeric value. The problem is to combine a string of numbers and operators. $123 + 456$ can be handled from left to right, as can $123 * 456 + 789$, but $12 + 34*56 + 78$ can neither be handled from left to right nor from right to left, that is, its value is neither $((12 + 34) *56) + 78$ nor $12 + (34 * (56 + 78))$. The reason is that the *hierarchy* of the multiply is *higher* than that of the plus operator, so that the multiply must be done before either plus.

Many standard techniques for translating arbitrary expressions are used in compilers. We can use one of the simplest of these for this case. Using the concept of hierarchy of operations, note that an operation should be performed if it is flanked by operators of no greater hierarchy. In this problem, there are only two hierarchies, the lower for plus and minus and the higher for multiply. Thus in $12 + 34*56 - 78$, the multiply can be done to get $12 + 1,904 - 78$, since it is flanked by the lower hierarchies of plus and minus. Now, both the plus and the minus operators are flanked by operators of no greater hierarchy (we can think of beginning and end of expressions as operators of lowest priority). In the case of equal hierarchies, the convention usually followed is *left to right*. Thus $1 - 2 + 3$ is $(1 - 2) + 3 = + 2$ rather than $1 - (2 + 3) = - 4$. The successive steps in reducing $12 + 34*56 - 78$ are:

$$12 + 34*56 - 78$$
$$= 12 + 1,904 - 78$$
$$= 1,916 - 78$$
$$= 1,838$$

It is not necessary to examine the complete string at every step. It can be scanned from the left until an operator can be performed. This can be sensed by comparing an operator with the operator on either side. Initially, we know that the first operator *(beginning of expression)* is not higher than the next one, so that we know that the next one $(+$ in $12 + 34*56 - 78)$ need only be compared with the following (*). If the following does not have a higher hierarchy, the plus can be performed. In this example, the multiply has a higher priority than the plus, so we continue the scan over the multiply. The fact that the scan continued indicated that the operator $(+)$ preceding the one currently being tested (*) has a lower hierarchy. Hence it is only necessary to compare the following one $(-)$ with the current one. (In the case of address expressions, we know that there is no higher hierarchy than multiply, so that this test is not strictly necessary.)

In the course of this scan, we passed over one operand (12) completely, and continued over the second (34) in order to look at the multiply operator. This can best be implemented using a stack technique. The basic recognizers extract numbers and operators one at a time from left to right. At any time, we wish to compare an operator with operators on either side. If the incoming items are placed in a stack if they are to be skipped over, the last items read are the ones immediately available. Initially, a mark meaning *beginning of expression* is placed in the stack. Items are recognized in turn and compared with the top two entries in the stack. Depending on the result of the comparison, either the items in the top of the stack are manipulated and a new comparison made, or the incoming item is placed on the stack and a new item is recognized. The comparison with the top items on the stack is to determine whether the last operator has a hierarchy at least as great as the incoming operand, this being the condition for execution of the last operator which is in one of the top two levels of the stack (because of the *last-in-first-out* operation of a stack). Let us follow an example through to see what sort of comparisons we must make. Suppose the string B 3 + 4 * 5 B is to be converted, where B stands for *beginning-of-expression* or *end-of-expression*. The pairs of lines below indicate the string state as items are removed from it, followed by the state of the stack where the top of the stack is on the right.

String 3 + 4 * 5 B	
Stack B	The first element is moved to the stack.
String + 4 * 5 B	
Stack B 3	Continue scanning.
String 4 * 5 B	
Stack B 3 +	Continue scanning.
String * 5 B	
Stack B 3 + 4	The * must be compared with the + in the second stack level. * has a higher hierarchy, so continue.
String 5 B	
Stack B 3 + 4 *	Continue scanning.
String B	

Stack B 3 + 4 * 5   The operator B has a lower hierarchy than the * in the
                      second stack level, so perform the multiply.
String B
Stack B 3 + 20   The operator B has a lower hierarchy than the + in the
                      second level, so perform the add.
String B
Stack B 23   The beginning-of-expression and the end-of-expression
                      characters are sensed together, so the evaluation is com-
                      plete. The answer is in the top of the stack.

We notice that the operations were generally in the second stack level when
they were compared with the incoming operation from the string. This would
not be true if there were errors in the expression or if other operations such as
unary minus or parentheses were allowed. Therefore the comparison should
check both the second and the top levels. When an operand (number) is
sensed as the input, it is put directly into the stack, since it is to be saved for
use in a later operation. Apparently, the rule to follow is to examine the next
item in the input and the top two levels of the stack and to perform the step
shown in Table 9.1 below.

This scheme is more complex than necessary for the simple address expressions that cannot involve parentheses, because there are only three hierarchies in total. If, however, we introduce parentheses, the scheme can be extended to cover the situation by adding to the second table. A pair of parentheses indicates that the expression inside the parentheses is to be evaluated
and then used as an operand in another operation. Therefore, when a left
parenthesis "(" is sensed in the input string, it should indicate that all of the
following input up to the matching right parenthesis has a higher hierarchy
than anything currently in the stack. Hence, a left parenthesis should be
placed into the stack immediately, as if it had a higher priority than any preceding operations. However, when another operation from the input is compared with a left parenthesis in the stack, the parenthesis must be given lowest

TABLE 9.1   Stack comparisons

INPUT	TOP STACK ENTRY	SECOND STACK ENTRY	ACTION
Number	—	—	Move input to stack.
Operator or	Number	Operator	Compare the hierarchies of the two operators.
Operator	Operator	—	If the input is higher, move the input to the stack, or else per-form the operator in the stack. The action of this operator is given in Table 9.2 below.
Operator	Number	Number	Error

priority so that the input operation is placed in the stack for future execution. When a right parenthesis is read from the input, it should be assigned the same hierarchical level as the left parenthesis in the stack, so that any operations in between will be performed.

The additional line needed in Table 9.2 must handle the left parenthesis which can get into the stack. Since it is given a low priority while in the stack, the only operations in the input string that can appear with it are right parenthesis and end-of-statement. The latter is an error caused by too many left parentheses. The beginning-of-statement may pop up to the top of the stack when too many right parentheses are present. Therefore, we must also change the first line of Table 9.2 as shown in Table 9.3.

The hierarchical level assigned to operators is shown in Table 9.4.

The greater the number, the higher the hierarchy. Consider the example 3*(4 + (5 + 6)*7) + 1. The successive states are

String 3*(4 + (5 + 6)*7) + 1B
Stack B
String *(4 + (5 + 6)*7) + 1B
Stack B 3   * is higher than B.
String (4 + (5 + 6)*7) + 1B
Stack B 3 *   '(' is higher than *
String 4 + (5 + 6)*7) + 1B
Stack B 3 *(
String + (5 + 6)*7) + 1B
Stack B 3*(4   + is higher than '('.
String (5 + 6)*7) + 1B
Stack B 3*(4 +   '(' is higher than +.
String 5 + 6)*7) + 1B
Stack B 3*(4 + (
String + 6)*7) + 1B

TABLE 9-2   *Stack operations*

OPERATION	ACTION
Beginning-of-statement	Terminate the computation, the answer is in the top of the stack.
+	If the first and third levels are numbers, add them, place the result in the third level, and discard the top two levels. If the second level is a number, discard the plus in the top level. (It is a unary plus sign.)
−	As for plus, except that a unary minus must change the sign of the number left in the top level.
*	If the first and third levels are numbers, multiply the first and third levels. Otherwise there is an error.

Note: Unary plus and minus are allowed in this table. They are sensed by also testing the third level.

TABLE 9-3   *Changes in Table 9-2 for handling parenthesized expressions*

OPERATOR	ACTION
Beginning-of-statement	If the input is end-of-statement, the answer is in the top of the stack. Otherwise there are too many right parentheses.
Left parentheses	If the input is a right parenthesis, delete it from the input string and delete the left parenthesis. Otherwise there are too many left parentheses.

Stack B 3*(4 +(5	+ is higher than '('.
String 6)*7) + 1B	
Stack B 3*(4 + (5 +	
String)*7) + 1B	
Stack B 3*(4 + (5 + 6	Now perform addition.
String)*7) + 1B	
Stack B 3*(4 + (11	Now eliminate '(' and ')'.
String *7) + 1B	
Stack B 3*(4 + 11	* is higher than +.
String 7) + 1B	
Stack B3*(4 +11*	
String) + 1B	
Stack B 3*(4 + 11*7	Now perform*.
String) + 1B	
Stack B 3*(4 + 77	Now perform +.
String) + 1B	
Stack B 3*(81	Now eliminate '(' and ')'.
String + 1B	
Stack B 3*81	Now perform*.
String + 1B	
Stack B243	+ is higher than B.
String 1B	
Stack B243 +	
String B	
Stack B243 + 1	Now perform +.
String B	
Stack B244	Here is answer.

TABLE 9-4   *Hierarchy levels*

OPERATOR	INPUT HIERARCHY	STACK HIERARCHY
BEGINNING	—	0
END	0	Never in stack
(	3	0
)	0	Never in stack
+	1	1
—	1	1
*	2	2

COROUTINES IN THE 370 AND PDP-11

It is suggested that the lexicographic scan should be a coroutine with the main process. The PDP-11 has a single instruction which will perform a coroutine transfer, swapping control between coroutines. This instruction is JSR PC, (SP) +, and it switches the contents of the control counter with the top of the stack. In actual execution, this instruction first forms the branch address by fetching the contents of the location in R6 (that is, SP). SP is then incremented by 2. Then the JSR is executed, causing the contents of SP to be decremented by 2 and the content of R7 (that is, PC) is stored in the address held in SP. The branch address is then put into the control counter PC, and execution continues.

The instruction BALR can be used in the 370 to switch between coroutines. Two registers must be reserved, one for each coroutine. Suppose register 10 is used for the lexicographic scan and register 11 for the main program. The main program would branch to the lexicographic scan by the instruction

```
BALR        R11,R10
```

which branches to the address in register 10, storing a return link in register 11. Similarly, the lexicographic scan would branch to the main program by

```
BALR        R10,R11
```

Before pass I is started, the contents of the top of the stack in the PDP-11 or registers 10 and 11 in the 370 must be initialized to the start of the respective pieces of code, then the appropriate one can be started.

9.2 Pass II

The purpose of pass II of the assembler is to convert the source language into binary, using the name table constructed in pass I to convert the addresses and a mnemonic table to convert the instructions. To do this, a copy of the source program must be read, a line at a time, and many of the steps of pass I repeated. The location field can be ignored because it was completely handled in pass I. The mnemonic field must be examined and a table lookup performed. In this pass, the mnemonic table must provide both a branch address or other indication of type of instruction or pseudo and, in the case of instructions, the binary code.

The address subfields must be converted into binary numbers for packing into the instructions or for use in pseudos. The code used in the pass I handling of pseudo addresses can be reused for this process. A location counter must be maintained in an identical manner to pass I. In this case, it is used to determine where to place the binary output (for load-and-go assemblers) or what location address to put on a card image (if the output is to be used as future input to a binary loader). Pass II is also terminated when the END pseudo is read. In many assemblers, the END pseudo can involve an address field which is used to provide a starting address at execution time. In the case of a load-and-go assembler, the last instruction executed will be a transfer to the address evaluated from the END pseudo. If the output of the assembler is input to a loader, then this address is placed in a suitable position on a card image.

The second pass can best be coded by breaking up the job into a number of subroutines to perform the basic tasks such as *read the next line, extract the mnemonic, search for the mnemonic in the mnemonic table, convert an address subfield to binary, accept a word of output for the location specified,* etc. A flowchart of pass II is shown in Figure 9.6. The result of one pass around the instruction loop is to construct one instruction and hand it to the output subroutine.

9.3 PSEUDOS

Pseudos are contained in the mnemonic table in passes I and II and cause a branch to an appropriate program to handle each separately. This section will discuss the methods used to handle each pseudo, and the restrictions that these methods place on the assembler user. In principle, the addition of a pseudo to an assembler is straightforward, since it only requires the addition of an entry to the mnemonic table and two sections of code, one to handle it during pass I and one to handle it during pass II. In fact, some assemblers allow the user to input code at the start of the first pass for the definition of new pseudos for his personal use. However, this frequently requires a fairly good knowledge of the implementation of the assembler itself. The user of a system program should not have to know details of implementation in order to use the program. If a reasonable number of pseudos is provided by the assembler, the use of a macro facility will frequently make it possible to construct mnemonics which have the effect of new pseudos.

9.3.1 Data loading pseudos

Typical data loading pseudos include DEC, OCT, and character input orders for many assemblers. The IBM 370 uses DC for all cases, while the PDP-11 uses .WORD, .BYTE, and .ASCII. During pass I, any name in the location field is treated exactly as a name in the location field of an instruction, since it is to be defined as the current value of the location counter. It is necessary to determine how many words of storage will be occupied by the data given in the pseudo, so that the location counter can be incremented accordingly during pass I. In DEC and OCT pseudos, this requires that the field be scanned to determine the number of data words provided by counting commas. A typical

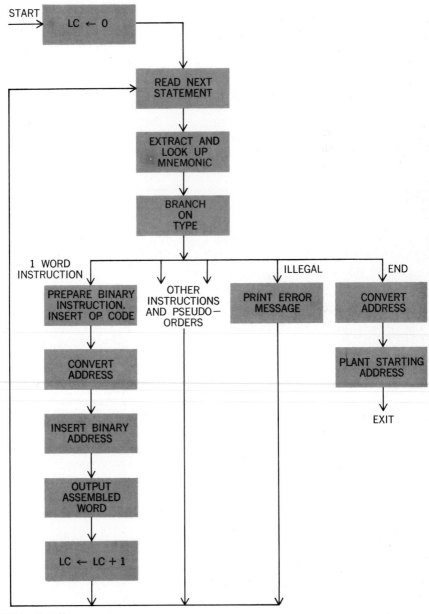

FIGURE 9.6   Pass II

character-conversion pseudo is BCD, whose address field contains the number of words of BCD information to be converted (or the number of characters in some assemblers), followed by a comma, followed by the Hollerith information. The assembler need only examine the length count at the start of the address field to determine the number of words required. Other character-loading pseudos use a character as a terminating mark for the string (thus ruling it out as a character in the string). In this case, pass I must count the characters in the string until this mark is found. The 370 DC instruction requires a more complicated scan. The first character determines the type of field following. It may be preceded with a repetition factor. For some characters, an L may follow with a length specification. Finally, the data will appear inside quotation marks. During pass I, the program must determine the boundary alignment and length of each field in the DC to calculate the location-counter change.

During pass II, the location field can be ignored, but the address field must be converted into binary according to the rules for the particular pseudo. At the same time, the location counter must be increased once for each word or byte produced. Conversion of character strings is straightforward, since the code used is either identical to the incoming code or can be converted by a character-table lookup. Octal or hexadecimal conversion can be done on the same basis, since each character supplies 3 or 4 bits, or it can be treated as an ordinary base-8 or -16 conversion problem similar to decimal.

9.3.2 Pseudos that affect the location counter

A number of pseudos affect the location counter and possibly cause names to be entered in the name table in pass I. The program used to modify the location counter in pass I and pass II can be identical; the program used to handle the entry of the names in pass I need not be used in pass II. Typical of these pseudos are BSS, BTS, or DS. BSS and BTS both cause the address-field value to be added to the location counter. Since BSS is an abbreviation of *Block Started by Symbol,* any name in the location field should be entered in the name table before it is incremented. BTS is an abbreviation of *Block Terminated by Symbol,* meaning that any name in the location field should be equated to the location of the last word of the block (that is, to one less than the contents of the control counter after it has been increased). The effect of the following sequence at the start of a program

A	BTS	356
B	BSS	24
C	BTS	51

is first to increase the location counter to 356 and enter A in the name table as 355; then to enter B in the name table as 356 and add 24 to the location counter, bringing it to 380; and finally to add 51 to the location counter, bringing it to 431, and entering C in the table as 430.

As long as the addresses in the address field are purely numeric, there are no problems. However, if a symbolic address is involved, then a value has to be assigned to it in order that the numeric value of the address can be calculated. In pass I, only those names that appeared before the line currently being examined are in the name table with numeric values. Therefore, if this method is to be used, names must be defined before they are used in any pseudos that affect the location counter in a manner dependent on their address field. For example, the following code could not be assembled

```
A           BSS        N
S           LOAD       A
N           EQU        10
```

because the value of the address N in the BSS pseudo is not known at the time it is read in pass I. The DS pseudo in the 370 is similar to the DC pseudo and can use the same piece of code in both passes, except that the DS does not actually produce object, whereas the DC must have the data specified in the address field.

9.3.3 Pseudos that affect the name table

It is desirable to be able to define names in the name table directly rather than by equating them to the current value of the location counter. Many names are not used as symbolic locations but as absolute integers or as symbolic names for index registers, etc. For example, a program may be written to process records of information coming in from a magnetic tape with a given logical number. It could be programmed so that the record size and the tape number are fixed in the program. Blocks would be defined by BSS pseudos with an absolute address. On the other hand, the program could, and should, be written to that the block size is a symbolic address, say BLKLGH, and the tape number a symbolic address, say, TAPENO. This program is assembled with these two addresses defined by use of the EQU pseudo. If the length of the block is 128 and the tape is number 3, then the pseudos

```
BLKLGH      EQU        128
TAPENO      EQU        3
```

would have to appear in the deck. Since BLKLGH appears as the address field of a BSS pseudo, the EQU which defines it must appear earlier in the deck. Therefore it would be conventional to put all the definitions at the front of the deck.

During pass I, the name in the location field of an EQU must be put into the name table together with the address calculated from the address field. It itself may contain symbolic names, so they must be defined prior to their use. That is,

```
A               EQU            B+1
B               EQU            10
```

is illegal, whereas

```
B               EQU            10
A               EQU            B+1
```

is allowed.

9.3.4 Other pseudos for special purposes

Particular machines often have a number of pseudos intended to assist the programmer in coping with some of the unfortunate features of the machine. (Don't look for "unfortunate features" in the index of your programming manual, they will probably be listed under "advanced features.") A common example of this type of pseudo arises in machines which have either a sub-word structure (such as two instructions or more per word) or a multiple-word structure for some instructions. There are frequently restrictions in the hard-ware which make it essential that some instructions appear in a special posi-tion within the word, such as at the start. In that case, a pseudo-instruction is needed which guarantees that the next instruction is located in this privileged position. Similarly, if multiple-word items are involved in operations—for example, doubleword arithmetic or transfers of blocks of a given size—there may be restrictions requiring that multiple-word items have to start in special positions such as on an even-word boundary or at a multiple of 2,048 charac-ters.

The purpose of an assembler is to save the programmer the details of specific addresses, so it must take care of such problems at the same time. Therefore, there may be pseudos that force the location counter to the next even value if it is odd currently, or that do the same for block structures. In the 370, the DS and DC pseudos can be used for this purpose. For example,

```
        DS           0F
```

would force the location counter to a fullword boundary, while

```
        DS           0D
```

would force it to a doubleword boundary. Since these cause no data to be loaded into any locations skipped over, they must not be used in the instruction stream. The pseudo CNOP is provided for this.

        CNOP   b,4

forces the location counter to the next fullword (b = 0) or the next middle of a fullword (b = 2). It assembles BR 0,0 instructions as necessary to fill up unused locations. This instruction branches on no conditions, hence it acts as a *no-operation* code. Similarly,

        CNOP   b,8

moves the location counter to the zero, second, fourth, or sixth byte of a doubleword as b is 0, 2, 4, or 6. This can be done at assembly by testing the bottom bits of the location counter. However, note that the loader must not relocate program in a way that would change the alignment. In the 370, this restricts relocation to multiples of doublewords.

The PDP-11 assembler provides the pseudos .EVEN and .ODD for similar purposes.

9.4 INTERMEDIATE LANGUAGE

In the brief discussion of pass II, it was noted that it is almost identical to pass I except for the job of outputting the binary object code and listing the translation. If the second pass is input/output limited, then this is an advantage, since pass II can be written by taking pass I, discarding the name table construction section, and adding the output section. However, if the computation time is significant, then we should consider the fact that the steps of reading, converting, and doing table lookups on the mnemonics are repeated in both sections, as is the work on the address fields of pseudos. Usually the most time-consuming part of the computation time is the name table searching, followed by the mnemonic table searching. The former cannot be reduced below one search per occurrence of a name; the latter can be reduced to one search per line of code, rather than the two presently used. In order to avoid a second search in pass II, enough information must be extracted from the table in pass I and saved for pass II use. The information required by pass II included the actual binary code for the instruction and an indication of how to treat the address field. This means that a string of information must be generated by pass I and saved (on auxiliary storage) for rereading by pass II. This string of information is a partial representation of the input code, so we call it an intermediate language—that is, intermediate between the assembly language source and the binary object language.

The use of an intermediate language is dependent on having a reasonably fast auxiliary storage device available for saving the language from pass I to pass II. If an intermediate language is to be used, then it is worth exploring the possibility of translating everything on the card into an intermediate form in order that the speed of subsequent passes can be improved. This can prove particularly valuable either if more than two passes are used (the additional passes will not have to reread the original input, which is neither densely packed nor particularly easy to read except in a character-oriented machine) or if it is not necessary to list the original input during pass II, in which case we can save rereading the original input completely.

If the input is to be translated into an intermediate language completely, then in addition to replacing the mnemonic by its binary equivalent and identifying information, it is necessary to convert the address field into a more convenient form for internal manipulation. To do this, numbers should be converted into binary and all names in the address field should be converted into a form that is more convenient to handle. If the name has already been defined, then it can be replaced by its address. In fact, there is no reason why the line should not be translated completely during pass I if the information is available. Some assemblers, typically for small paper-tape machines, allow the second pass to be skipped if all names are defined before they are used (that is, there are no forward references). In general, however, there will be forward references to names not yet defined, so the name cannot be converted to a number To avoid re-searching the table in pass II, the name can be replaced by the address of the entry in the table corresponding to the name. (This means that names must be entered when they are first encountered, although they may not be defined until they are encountered in the location field.)

It is impossible to give general rules to determine which organization of an assembler should be used. One example will be quoted to indicate the considerations used in planning the assembler. In this particular case, the instructions of the machine were variable length, and their length could not be determined until the address type was defined. Hence, unless predefinition of symbolic names which might affect the length of an instruction was required, it was not possible to determine the value of the location counter in pass I. Hence, during pass I, all that could be done was to build a table of all names used with enough information to determine the length of any instruction which used it. Pass II performed the task of a conventional pass I by rescanning the input, now being able to compute the value of the location counter and define the values of the symbolic names in the table. A third pass was needed to do the actual translation to binary and produce an optional listing. The source program was available on magnetic tape via the system input routine, but only about three cards were packed in a block, as opposed to about 25 that could be packed into the maximum-length block allowed by the hardware. However, there was a very fast drum available for auxiliary storage.

Some estimates of the computing time indicated that all passes would be completely input/output limited, so that computational time was unimportant. However, the second pass never needed to look at the original input if an intermediate language were available, and pass III did not, provided that the listing was not required (which happens in, perhaps, 5 percent of the uses of the assembler). Therefore, the first pass was used to construct a name table containing only the BCD form, and about 6 bits of information were used to tell the second pass how to determine the length of an instruction using the name. It also translated the input into an intermediate language in which all names had been replaced by their table address. This intermediate language was stored on the drum. In addition to enabling subsequent passes to read from the faster drum, the translation also achieved a reduction of about 10 to 1 in the number of words required to represent the information on one card. These steps allowed the second pass to run about 200 times faster than the first, a factor of 10 due to the reduction in number of words to be read, and a factor of 20 due to the speed of the drum over tape. This method also provided an additional benefit. The amount of main memory for the assembler was limited. The amount of information to store the length BCD names desired plus the amount of information needed to determine the address value and other important details about a name was more than the length of a word. Normally, two words would have been used for each name table entry. However, in pass I, the address information was not in the table, while in passes II and III the symbolic form of the name was not used. Hence, one section of the word was used to store both, reducing the need to one word per entry. (In order to provide a listing of all names used and their values after the translation was complete, a copy of the name table at the end of pass I was saved on the drum.)

The practical assembler will contain many features tailored to the particular environment. In many cases it is difficult to analyze the situation sufficiently to determine which of several ways are better, but typically the input/output considerations are the determining factors, so they should be examined first.

9.5 RELOCATION

The discussion above has not taken the problems of relocation into account. We recall from Chapter 3 that the assembler is expected to produce a relocation bit with each address, a bit which tells the loader whether the relocation used for that program at load time is to be applied to that particular address. In general, numerical addresses are taken to be absolute, whereas symbolic addresses may be absolute or relocatable. An address is determined to be relocatable if it is one which "moves" with the program, that is, if it is one which is defined by the contents of the location counter. In addition to the value of the name, the name table must contain a bit which indicates whether a name is relocatable or not. When a name is put into the table, this bit must be set to a 1. Any name appearing in the location field of an instruction is relocatable, as are names in the location fields of the pseudos BSS, BTS, DEC, OCT, BCD, and similar pseudos. This means that we always assume that the location counter is relocatable. (This is not essential, but it would mean that information would have to be given to the loader so that it could determine whether to relocate a section of code or not. This would allow the programmer to place code absolutely in memory, a facility that can cause more problems than it solves.) The pseudo that can define a nonrelocatable name is the EQU pseudo. N EQU 20 should set N to be nonrelocatable, since it may be used in a position where a nonrelocatable address is needed, for example, as an initial count for loading into an index register.

In order to determine whether the symbol in the location field of the EQU pseudo is relocatable, it is necessary to find out if the value of the address field is relocatable. This problem must also be solved for the address field of an instruction. Therefore a set of rules is needed which can be used to determine the relocatability of an expression used as an address. When this has been determined, it can be used to determine the relocatability of the object address of an instruction, of the location field of an EQU, and to determine if the other pseudos are valid. BSS and BTS should have nonrelocatable addresses, otherwise the loader cannot handle the object. ORG could be allowed either relocatable or nonrelocatable addresses (it is a problem, and its use should be avoided where possible since it is an anachronism in a system which is supposed to be taking care of all memory allocation).

An absolute (nonrelocatable) address can be constructed from any allowable expression involving numbers and absolute-value symbolic addresses. Thus $23*3 - 4*A$ is a valid absolute address if A is an absolute name. A relocatable address can certainly be formed by adding to or subtracting from a relocatable name any absolute amount. Thus, if B is a relocatable name, then $B - 34$ is also relocatable. Some assemblers restrict constructions to just those forms: absolute expressions and relocatable names plus or minus absolute expressions. However, it is convenient to allow combinations of relocatable addresses for some purposes. A particular example occurs when a table of words is to be input through the assembler and it is necessary to know how many items there are in the table, perhaps to set an index register for counting purposes. If the address of the first entry is A and of the last B, then the expression $B - A + 1$ is the number of entries. If more entries are added to the middle of the table by adding cards, it is not necessary to further modify the program, only to reassemble it. This is shown in the following example:

```
A          DEC        1
           DEC        5
           DEC        9
           . . .
```

```
B           DEC         63
N           EQU         B—A+1
```

Repunching the first or last cards if an additional first or last entry is to be made can be avoided by the coding:

```
A           BSS         0
            DEC         1
            . . . . .
            DEC         63
B           BSS         0
N           EQU         A—B
```

Thus, we would like to arrange that the difference of two relocatable-address expressions is an absolute expression. In this way, the expression A — B + C would be legal unless A and C were relocatable and B was absolute or vice versa. Although the address A + C may be meaningful to the programmer in some situations where both A and C are relocatable, it is not possible for the loader to handle it with only one relocation bit. If, in assembly, A and C are given the values 23 and 34 respectively, then A + C will assemble as 57. However, if the program is relocated so that A and C have the values 123 and 134 respectively, the address A + C must be doubly relocated to achieve the correct result of 257. With only one bit, the loader can only apply either single relocation or none. It would certainly be possible to design a loader which would allow double or even multiple positive or negative relocation, but its value to the user does not usually justify the cost.

Even with only single relocation, it is theoretically feasible to allow expression such as 2*A — B where both A and B are relocatable, since the total relocation is still single. In practice, however, it is doubtful that it would be worth the cost of writing the assembler program to handle it.

In addition to program relocation which adjusts addresses as the program is moved around in memory, other forms of relocation are desirable. Their need arises from various sources. One is the use of common variables between subroutines that are translated into binary separately. This can be handled by using common variables such as those provided in Fortran. The equivalent of labeled common requires that several different location counters be established, one for each labeled section. These problems also arise if CSECTs are allowed. A different relocation is associated with each location counter. If it is possible for a large number (more, say, than 8 or 16) of location counters to be established, it begins to become inefficient to associate relocation bits with each different location counter. Instead, a small field in the name table can be used to indicate which location counter should be used to relocate the name, if any. If up to 63 location counters were possible, 6 bits could be used in the field. The 64th possibility would indicate no relocation. Under those conditions, the 6-bit field could also be passed on to the loader so that it knew how to relocate an address.

If an unlimited number of location counters is possible, the length of the field becomes prohibitive. An alternative is to construct separate name tables, one for each location counter. Instead of passing relocation bits to the loader, additional information can be passed which lists the set of locations which should be relocated by a given location counter. Thus, if there were six CSECTs in a given job, the output from the assembler would consist of six sections of code that could be separately relocated and six lists of addresses for each section of code. Each list would give the position in its section of those locations whose contents should be relocated by the corresponding relocation amount.

A mechanism of this type can be used to handle external variables also.

9.5.1 Base register assignment in the system 370 assembler

This is a problem that arises in the 370 machines because of the use of base registers. During assembly, regular 24-bit addresses can be dealt with, but these must be converted to a 12-bit displacement and a base address. This can be done by storing, in 16 locations at assembly time, the value of each general-purpose register as declared by a USING pseudo. It is also necessary to note whether each register is available as a base register or not. When a relocatable address is used in an instruction, the difference between its value and the contents of each base register value is formed. The base register which results in the smallest displacement is assembled into the instruction. If no base register gives a displacement of less than 4,096, there is an error. Note that displacements will never be relocatable. Relocatable addresses in the 370 will arise from the A type constants in the DC pseudo.

Consider the following example of a section of 370 assembly language:

```
1              BALR      12,0
2              USING     *,12
3              L         11,A
4              USING     X,11
5              B         C
6   A          DC        A(X)
7   C          LA        4,X
               . . . .
8   X          DS        10F
               . . . .
```

If we assume that the first line is assembled into location 100 and that no base registers are currently known to the assembler, the assembler will convert the first instruction into 2 bytes of object code and advance its location counter to 102. Note that the execution-time effect of the BALR is to place 102 into register 12. The next pseudo in line two tells the assembler that it can assume that register 12 contains the current contents of the location counter, namely 102. At this time, the 16 locations in the assembler that tell the status of the base registers indicate that all but 12 are not allowed, and that 12 contains 102. (This would be a relocatable 102.) The next instruction uses an address A which, by pass II, will have been defined as 112 relocatable. It will check this against all base registers and find that it is a displacement of 10 from register 12, so that A will be assembled as register 12, displacement 10. At execution time, the third line of code puts the address X into register 11. The next pseudo in line four tells the assembler that it can assume that register 11 contains X from now on. Consequently it updates its list of register contents to so indicate. Note that X is not known until pass II, but that the base-register contents are not used until pass II when the instructions are converted to binary.

This simplified view does not allow for CSECTs and external variables, but small additions to the method will handle these problems.

9.6 ENTRIES AND EXTERNAL VARIABLES

When several sections of code are separately assembled or compiled but are to be loaded together, there must be some communication between them, both data and control. Common storage provides one mechanism for data communication, and it could conceivably be adapted to control communication. However, this would not be convenient for control usage, and it has unfortunate properties when used for data. These properties are due to the fact that it represents an absolute assignment of memory addresses by the programmer. In each separately translated section of code, variable storage must be assigned to the locations in common storage on an absolute basis so that they match between sections. Errors can easily arise in programs which contain many sections and a large amount of common storage. On the other hand, common storage is usually a more efficient mechanism for passing data to subroutines than using parameter techniques.

A symbolic linking technique that is efficient at execution time is needed for both data and control communication. Since the program sections are compiled separately, it is necessary that the loader be given the symbolic information and that the loader take care of linking it together. Chapter 3 discussed the transfer vector and the linking loader as two techniques that can be used for this purpose. This section will examine the implementation of these techniques in a typical two-pass assembler.

The information provided by the user to the assembler consists of source language statements such as ENTRY and EXTERNAL. Entry statements tell the assembler that the names in the address field are to be passed on to the loader, together with information telling the loader where the corresponding address is located relative to the code being translated. For example, the statements

```
          ENTRY      A,B
A         LOAD       =2
B         ADD        =3
```

at the start of a program indicate to the assembler that the symbolic addresses A and B are to be given to the loader with the relocatable addresses 0 and 1 respectively. Note that the names appearing in the address field of an ENTRY pseudo must be defined within the program in a relocatable manner. If several programs wish to access the same memory location by name, that is, to refer to it with the same name, rather than by placing it in the same location with the use of COMMON, then the pseudo EXTERNAL can be used. If symbolic addresses are defined as EXTERNAL by the statement EXTERNAL A,B, the assembler passes the names over to the loader with an indication of where they are used. In this case, some form of linking loader must be used.

The output from the assembler must consist of lists of entry points with their respective addresses, called names, and external names, with an indication of where they are used. These are usually placed in binary in front of the object program and must therefore be produced prior to pass II. Hence the major processing of these statements must occur in pass I. Pass II will only have to take care of providing an appropriate address for instructions using symbolic names called or declared as external. In the case of all three pseudos, the first pass has the option of either constructing separate tables of names used or using flags in the regular name table to mark those used in this manner. The latter may lead to slightly longer tables and hence to greater lookup time, but it usually leads to a simpler organization. Hence, we shall assume that all names are placed in one table.

9.6.1 Entries

During the first pass, the assembler must place any names in the address field into the name table if they are not already there. A bit must be allocated in each table entry to indicate entry names. This bit is set when the name is encountered in an ENTRY pseudo. Since it is preferable to allow the ENTRY pseudo to precede the definition of the name, the section of the assembler that enters names into the table when they are defined must allow for names to be in the table in an *undefined* state. This can be recognized by allocating a second bit which is set to a 1 when the name is defined.

Between pass I and pass II processing, each name in the name table must be examined. Any names that are marked as entry points are copied into the heading information of the object program together with their values.

9.6.2 External variables

If the use of external variables is restricted to situations in which the name is used by itself rather than in expressions, then the chain-linking loader described earlier can be used. However, if expressions involving external variables are allowed, then this method will not work. (The reason is that the address field of a translated instruction may contain the remainder of the expression. Thus, if the address is A + 7 where A is external, the address field will contain 7 and the value of A must be added to it.) In this case, the loader will have to accept a table of all uses of each external name. This provides for greater flexibility, but it slows down the loader by the increase in the size of the object deck.

External variables in 370 programs normally only appear in A or V fields of DC pseudos. In V fields, they may not be used in expressions, because the V field is also used to declare the external attribute. Typically, an external variable will only appear in one DC statement because of the base-register addressing.

9.7 MACROS

Macros were introduced in Chapter 4 as a method of inserting sections of code without the tedium of repunching the same cards over again. To recapitulate on the operation of a macro, there are two important phases: the definition phase when the set of statements defining the macro are read and stored in a suitable form, and the expansion phase when the name of a macro is used and is replaced with the set of statements representing that macro. This section will examine some of the methods that can be used to process macros. It will also mention some additional features that can be added to the macro facility.

Macros are usually handled as part of the assembler, since macros are most often used in assembly language. Macro expansion schemes have been defined for higher-level languages, but their use in such environments is usually of less value. This is because a higher-level language is supposedly adapted to the type of problems being solved, and hence macros are likely to achieve less compression of the source and little additional clarity. Assembly language is difficult to follow and lengthy to write, so macros can reduce the size of the source language and increase the clarity tremendously in long programs. The clarity can be improved even if a macro is only used once.

Macros can be expanded during pass I of the assembler so as to retain a two-pass assembler, or they can be expanded prior to pass I in what is called a *prepass*. In the latter case, it can be made optional, so that nonusers will not be penalized for the time of the extra pass. We shall discuss macros as though they are to be processed in pass I. This will introduce some restrictions of predefinition similar to the restrictions on the use of symbolic addresses in the EQU pseudos. Finally, we shall consider ways of removing these restrictions by using prepasses.

We recall that the definition of a macro is accomplished by preceding it with the pseudo MACRO and following it with the pseudo MEND. The macro definition may contain parameters which are names separated by commas. When the macro is used, its name appears in the mnemonic field, and the address field contains strings of information to be substituted for the parameters. The location field may contain a name which is to be assigned the current value of the location counter. The translator must be capable of saving the set of statements comprising the definition, recognizing the use of a macro name in place of a regular instruction or pseudo, expanding the macro so that the expanded form is available during both pass I and pass II, and making the substitutions for the parameters during the expansion. Whereas most parts of assembly are completely input/output limited, so that we can usually use simple techniques for the computational sections and ignore speed problems, macros provide a facility for generating large amounts of code from a few input statements. Thus one card can generate many object instructions. The translator will not be input limited during these sections, and it may not be input/output limited during pass II if the listing is not too verbose. Therefore, we need to be concerned about the speed of expansion methods used. In particular, we must decide whether to perform the expansion during pass I and to pass on an expanded form to pass II, or whether to reexpand during pass II. Decisions of this type inevitably depend on many factors and are very difficult to make. For example, if we decide to use a prepass technique to avoid some restrictions, then we shall see that the expansion must be done prior to pass I, so there is no decision to make. If we decide to run pass II from the original copy of the source language, perhaps because there are no suitable auxiliary devices to make additional copies, then we have to reexpand in pass II. On the other hand, if we are producing a second copy of the input, then it could either be in an unexpanded or an expanded form. The benefits of the former are that the source is typically shorter, of the latter that pass II processing time is saved.

This decision will also be influenced by the available storage space for the macro definitions during assembly. If large amounts of main memory are available, then most programs can be expected to be such that the macro definitions will never spill over into auxiliary storage. Although a limit on the number of lines of macro definition could be set, it is better to allow any program to be assembled that can be run within the system, so eventually provisions will have to be made for the program that contains more macro definitions than can be saved in the main memory. The additional macros will have to be saved on auxiliary storage devices. Accessing them may be slow, depending on the type of device available. Magnetic tape may have to be back or forward spaced to get to the definition, disk file arms may have to be moved, while drums require an average access time of half a revolution. These all serve to increase the processing time for a macro expansion. If the available devices are too slow, then it is probably better to expand in pass I so as to avoid taking up the time in pass II.

9.7.1 Expansion methods

During the first pass, the appearance of the pseudo MACRO must cause the assembler to stop the regular assembly process and enter a mode in which a copy of the input is kept for later use. The card images must be copied, one at a time, into a storage area until a MEND pseudo is encountered. The MACRO and MEND pseudo themselves need not be copied, but the information from the card following the MACRO must be saved in an index of the macro definitions. The name in the location field of the definition must be entered into this index, which is a subsidiary mnemonic table. The name of the parameters must also be saved, either in the index or at the front of the definition. After a MEND card has been read, the assembler returns to its normal state of examining each card for mnemonic type and handling it appropriately.

When the assembler checks the mnemonics it must also check for the presence of a macro. We must decide whether the user is allowed to redefine instructions and pseudos, or whether their names are permanent. In the latter case, the mnemonic table is scanned, and if the mnemonic is found there, that definition is accepted. Otherwise, the index of macro definitions must be scanned. If it is not there, an error exists; otherwise, expansion must take place. Note that this means that macros must be defined before they are used. In the former case, the macro index must be searched first. If it is not there, the mnemonic table is scanned in the regular way. In either case, when a macro has been located in the macro index, the expansion starts. The macro index must contain a pointer to the storage location of the macro definition. Simply stated, all that has to happen is that the read section of pass I must switch over and read the definition instead of the source input until the end of the definition is reached, at which time the read section must be switched back to the original source.

Perhaps the simplest way to program this is to provide a subroutine which reads the next source language statement, and to put a switch in this program which either reads from the actual source or from the definition. In this way, the remainder of pass I is not affected in any way. This subroutine must also take care of substituting the parameters provided by the user in the use of the macro. This can be a slow operation, since it is a character-string manipulation problem. Consider the macro definition

```
MACRO
COPY        B,C
LOAD        B+1,C
STORE       B,C
MEND
```

and the use

```
COPY        W+7,XSPEC
```

The definition contains the two statements LOAD and STORE with address fields. These address fields must be modified so that the result reads

```
LOAD        W+7+1,XSPEC
STORE       W+7,XSPEC
```

That is, the character string W + 7 and XSPEC must be substituted for B and C respectively.

This can be done by analyzing the definition when it is first read or by reanalyzing it each time. In the former case, the definition must be scanned when it is first read, and any occurrences of the parameters must be noted by replacing them with indicators showing which parameters they are. At expansion time, these indicators must be replaced with the character string provided by the user. In the latter case, the definition must be read at expansion time, and every name (including location and mnemonic fields) must be checked against the list of parameter names. If agreement is found, then the string provided by the user must be copied in place of the parameter. Since the program is not input limited during the expansion phase, it is preferable to do as much of the analysis as possible in the definition phase. A number of tricks can be used to speed up the processing during the latter phase. We shall examine one possible technique in more detail.

When the definition is read, the names of the parameters are placed in a table at the head of the definition. As each line of the macro is read, it is scanned to the end of the address field, starting from the location field. Names are extracted by doing a lexicographic scan looking only for *break* characters. These are characters which cannot be legitimate parts of names (for example, plus, minus, comma, multiply, blank, etc.). Each group of characters between break characters is compared with all of the parameter names. If agreement is found, that character string is replaced with an indicator constructed by using an internal code that is not a legal character. (Since there are fewer printing characters than bit combinations in most machines, this is possible.) The indicator consists of the special code followed by the number of the parameter (in the example above, B would be 0 and C would be 1). To save processing time during the expansion phase, those statements that contain parameters can be marked in an unused bit position. At expansion time, the character strings provided by the user (delimited by commas and blanks) are placed in a parameter value table in order. As each statement is read from the definition, the bit that indicates the existence of parameter is checked. If it is off, then the image is copied directly otherwise it is copied one character at a time. When the code indicating parameter use is sensed, the number following it is used to extract a character string from the parameter value table. This is copied in place of the parameter indicator. Then reading continues, one character at a time, from the definition statement until the end of the card is reached. This can cause problems because the length of the card image can change during expansion, so either the latter parts of the assembler must accept variable-length cards or the expansion section will have to insert or delete blanks to get the right length. As an example, the macro given above would appear in the macro definition table as

```
LOAD        &0+1,&1
STORE       &0,&1
```

where & (ampersand) has been used to represent the special code. When it is used by the statement

```
COPY        W+7,XSPEC
```

the two character strings W + 7 and XSPEC are listed in the parameter value table as entries 0 and 1 respectively. As the definition is read, the appearance of & causes the entry corresponding to the number following to be copied in its place to get

```
LOAD        W+7+1,XSPEC
STORE       W+7,XSPEC
```

During the expansion process, the output from the READ subroutine is processed by the assembler in order to control the location counter and build up the name table. It is possible that the assembler may encounter another macro name in the mnemonic field, since the definition has not been checked to see if it contains only legal mnemonics. This is normally allowed, and it is called *nested macro use*. One macro may be defined in terms of others. The mechanism is quite straightforward. The assembler recognizes the use of a macro in the usual way, so it conditions the read section to read from the macro instead of from the input. Unfortunately, it was already reading from a macro definition, although a different one. Since it should return to reading from the first macro when the expansion of the second has been completed, it is necessary to use a push-down list for saving the state of the read section when a macro is encountered by the assembler. Each time that a macro is encountered, the address field used for the macro is copied into the parameter value table of character strings (this may involve parameter replacement if a macro is currently being expanded). Then the current state of the read section is placed in a push-down stack, and reading of a new definition commences. When the expansion of a macro is complete, the previous state of the read section is restored. This includes restoring the state of the macro-parameter value table.

An example may help to clarify the picture. Suppose the input is

19	MACRO	
20	A	X,Y,Z
21	LOAD	X+4
22	Z	X,Y−1
23	STORE	X−4
24	ADD	=1
25	B	123,Y
26	STORE	R
27	MEND	
28	MACRO	
29	B	W,V
30	ADD	S+W,V
31	MEND	. . .
32	A	J,K,LOAD

(The lines are numbered for reference in the text below.)

When the assembler has finished processing line 31, the macro index table contains two entries, A and B. The definitions stored for A and B are

	DEFINITION		PARAMETER USE BIT
A1	LOAD	&0+4	1
A2	&2	&0,&1−1	1
A3	STORE	&0−4	1
A4	ADD	=1	0
A5	B	123,&1	1
A6	STORE	R	0
B1	ADD	S+&0,&1	1

The current entry in the push-down stack of the read section is

"Reading line 32, Source."

When the assembler reads the next card via the read section, it finds that the mnemonic field contains the macro A. Its parameters are J, K, and LOAD. It places these in a parameter value table and changes the state of the read section so that the macro A is being read. The state of the push-down stack for the read section is now

Top   "Reading line A1, macro A. "
Second "Reading line 33, source."

The parameter value table contains

ENTRY	CONTENTS
2	LOAD
1	K
0	J

As the read section passes on card images to the main assembler, the parameters are replaced by the entries in the parameter value table. Thus the images

LOAD	J+4
LOAD	J,K−1
STORE	J−4
ADD	=1
B	123,K

are generated. When the last statement is processed by the assembler, it recognizes the use of the macro B. The parameters are placed in the parameter value table (this can be done in a push-down fashion so that the previous entries are available later) and the read section is changed to a new state. The push-down stack for the read section is now

Top   "Reading line B1, macro B."
Second "Reading line A6, macro A."
Third   "Reading line 33, source."

while the table of parameter values is

ENTRY	CONTENTS
1	K
0	123
. . . .	(separation between levels)
2	LOAD
1	K
0	J

The next use of the read section causes the image ADD S+&0, &1 to be replaced by ADD S+123,K. Since that is the end of the macro B, the stack pops up, so that it now reads

Top   "Reading line A6, macro A."
Second "Reading line 33, source."

and the table contains

ENTRY	CONTENTS
2	LOAD
1	K
0	J

The last line of the macro A is passed on immediately from the read section to the assembler since it contains no parameters, and then the macro A is complete. Control pops up again so that the read section is back on the source stream.

Keyword parameters can be implemented by adding a small name table to the front of each macro definition. At the time that the macro is used, the key words can be constructed in the correct order. Undefined parameters can then be specified by the default definition, which should also be in the name table.

9.7.2 Macro expansion in a prepass

If macros were to be expanded during pass I, it was necessary to define a macro before its use. If this restriction is to be removed, it is necessary to add at least one extra pass in order to first accumulate all the macro definitions and then to expand them. If nested definitions were not used, it would be possible to locate all the definitions in a prepass and then to perform the expansion during pass I as above. However, nested definitions can cause additional definitions to appear as the result of expansion, requiring yet another pass. Therefore, it is simpler to complete the expansion prior to the first pass of the assembly, and to view the macro expander as a separate translator which accepts macro language as a source language and outputs assembler language as its object. Since the checking for valid assembler language is most easily accomplished by the assembler, the macro expander will not check for validity of the object program and should be viewed as a character-string manipulation program.

The macro expander can be implemented in much the same way as a macro assembler is implemented. Statements from card images are read one at a time, and the mnemonic field is checked. Any time that a macro definition is encountered, it is copied into a definition storage area and entered in a definition macro index. Any time that the use of a macro is sensed, the definition is copied, substituting for the parameters as above. If, during one pass, no new definitions are encountered, it is known that the expansion has been completed. If new definitions are encountered, then it is possible that they were used in an earlier section of the source, so additional passes may be necessary. These passes are made over the expanded version output from the last pass, using the macro definitions that have been accumulated thus far. It is highly desirable to minimize the number of passes in a translator, since the input read time accounts for most of the translation time. The solution proposed above requires at least two passes if any macros are used, one to find the definitions and the other to expand. This is similar to the two-pass assembler; one pass is used to find the definitions of the symbols and the other is used for replacement.

We commented early in the discussion of assemblers that it was possible to have a one-pass assembler if all names were predefined, and that some assemblers for simple paper-tape machines make provisions for a one-pass option. A similar technique can be used in a macro expander. If the user predefines all his macros, he should not be penalized for the flexibility available to other users. The translator can recognize that there are no earlier uses of the defined macros and avoid the extra pass. This is accomplished by constructing a table of all different mnemonics read in a pass over the source. Initially this is empty, and as each mnemonic is placed into the output from the translator, its mnemonic field is entered into a table (unless it is already there). When a definition is encountered, it is copied into the definition storage area in the usual way, and the table is checked to see if it has been used previously. If it has, a switch is set. At the end of the pass, this switch is tested. If it is still off, then no macros were defined which had been used previously, so no additional passes are necessary. This technique would only be worth while if the processing were I/O bound.

9.8 REMOVING RESTRICTIONS ON EQU AND BSS ADDRESS FIELDS

In the earlier discussion of these pseudos, the address fields were restricted to contain only names that had been predefined, so that they could be evaluated during pass I. If this restriction is to be removed, then a problem similar to that of macro expansion arises. An arbitrarily large number of passes may be necessary to evaluate all the name values. Consider, for example, the sequence

A	EQU	B
B	EQU	C
C	EQU	D
D	EQU	10

Four passes are needed to determine the value of A. On the first pass the value of D is found, on the second C, on the third B, and on the fourth A. It would be very expensive if the whole program were to be scanned in order to do this. Instead, during the first pass, those EQUs that cannot be evaluated can be copied into a separate storage area (there are usually few of these, so they can be kept in the main memory). At the completion of the first pass, the separate list of EQUs can be scanned as many times as necessary to complete the evaluation or to find out that no more can be evaluated, as could happen if there was a circular definition such as

```
A              EQU          B+10
B              EQU          2*A—30
```

(This does not define B as 10 and A as 20.) Since the list of EQUs is short, these scans are fast compared to a pass over the whole program.

If a BSS uses a name that has not yet been defined in its address field, then the location counter is no longer known, so that subsequent names defined by appearance in the location fields of instructions will not be determinate. This could be solved by noting that every future name can be expressed in terms of the address appearing in the pseudo plus a suitable displacement. For example, the code section

```
               BSS          M+T
               LOAD         A
               ADD          B
               TRA          C
A              BSS          N
B              BSS          2
C              STORE        B
               STORE        A
D              ADD          E
```
. . . .

is equivalent to

```
               BSS          M+T
               LOAD         A
               ADD          B
               TRA          C
               BSS          N
A              EQU          M+T+3
               BSS          2
B              EQU          A+N
               STORE        B
C              EQU          B+2
               STORE        A
               ADD          E
D              EQU          C+2
```
. . . .

and could be converted to this during the first pass, so that the mechanism for handling EQUs can be used to process it. Unfortunately, there are usually large numbers of names in location fields, so this will cause a large number of EQU statements to be generated, thus slowing down the assembly. To avoid this, we can introduce the idea of a location counter "relative" to a symbolic address. When a pseudo—such as BSS—that has an indeterminate address field is encountered during pass I, an *internal name* can be generated. This is a symbolic address that cannot be confused with one used by a programmer and is never seen by him. The location counter is marked as being relative to this name and is set to 0. An artificial EQU is generated, which equates this name to the expression in the address field of the pseudo (plus the previous contents of the location counter if the pseudo was a BSS). When any future names are defined by appearance in the location field, they are entered in the name table with both the numerical value of the control counter and the address of the name to which the location counter is relative. (This requires additional space in the name table.) Let us consider the example given above. If the internal names generated by the assembler have the form //0, //1, etc., then the effect of the code is as follows:

	BSS	M+T	M + T is not yet known, so the location counter is set to 0 relative to //0, and the statement //0 EQU M+T is generated.
	LOAD	A	
	ADD	B	
	TRA	C	By this time the location counter is 3 relative to //0.
A	BSS	N	A is entered as 3 relative to //0. A new symbol //1 is generated, and the statement //1 EQU //0+3+N is generated. The location counter is set to 0 relative to //1.
B	BSS	2	B is entered in the name table as 0 relative to //1. The location counter is increased to 2 relative to //1.
C	STORE	B	C is entered as 2 relative to //1.
	STORE	A	
D	ADD	E	D is entered as 4 relative to //1.
. . . .			Etc.

With this method, only one EQU will be generated for each use of a BSS with an indeterminate address field. At the end of pass I, the EQU list is repeatedly scanned in order to evaluate all entries.

PROBLEMS

1   Suppose that multiple positive or negative relocation was to be allowed by a single relocation address, perhaps the program start address. Discuss how the expression evaluator in 9.1.2 could be extended to calculate the relocation factor. It should be able to determine that the address

$$3*A - B$$

is doubly relocatable if A and B are relocatable singly, for example. What restrictions could be put on expressions in order to keep the problem reasonable? Would the address

N*A — (N — 1)*B

be allowed where A, B, and N are relocatable? What if A and B were relocatable but N was absolute?

2 How should the CSECT pseudo that is available in some assemblers be implemented?

3 Write a flowchart for the scan of the address field of the DC pseudo available in the 370 assembler, ignoring problems of conversion of single numbers into internal form.

4 How could the DS pseudo be included in the program described in question three?

5 Show that there are 1,617,038,306 names of six or less characters that start with a letter and contain only letters or digits. Suggest an algorithm for converting between such names and the integers between 0 and 1,617,038,-305 such that, if the names are in alphabetical order, their numeric equivalences are in numerical order.

6 Is code of the form

```
N          BSS          1
A          BSS          N
```

valid? Why?

7 What changes need to be made to the simple approach suggested for handling base registers in the 370 in Section 9.5.1 if CSECTs are allowed?

8 Suggest a mechanism for handling conditional assembly inside a macro definition. In particular, how should a branch (AGO in the 370 assembler) be handled? If conditional assembly is allowed outside of macro definitions, are there problems with assembly branches (equivalent to the AGO in the 370) if the branches are backward? How about forward?

10
SEARCHING AND SORTING

The need for associative memory devices is common to many applications. Some examples in the data processing field include the associating of account information for a given customer known by name (or account number), associating the address information with the symbolic address name in assemblers and compilers, and the association of employee statistics such as age, marital status, wage rate, etc., with the employee name. Outside of the computer, we meet two very common examples in the phone directory and the dictionary, both associating a set of information with a given word.

Because those associative memories that have been built are fairly expensive and relatively small, other techniques must be used in practice to simulate the associative memory. In a similar manner, the telephone numbers of all phones cannot be stored in an associative memory. The human can store a few in his head, perhaps a secretary can store a few more, but that is an expensive memory device. Instead one uses a telepone directory and performs a search for the name in order to get the number. This example is often a fruitful one to bear in mind as searching techniques are discussed, since a number of the techniques used to find a name in the telephone directory of a large city have their counterpart in computer techniques.

The basic operations needed in an associative memory are to:

Enter an item.
Remove an item.
Add to or modify an item already there.
Reference to obtain additional information when part of the item is known.

The frequency with which each of these actions is taken and the size of the total amount of information (called a file or data set) serve to determine the best way to simulate the associative memory. In some cases, such as the telephone directory, only one action is normally taken by the user — that is, to find additional information when the name is given. Hence, the alphabetic ordering technique is the best. Anybody who has tried to find the phone number of a Mr. Smith, say, in a very large city, not knowing the initials but knowing the address instead, knows that the telephone directory is not efficient for uses other than an alphabetical search.

Each item (called a record) in the file contains a set of information, such as name, address, telephone number. If one piece of information (called a field) in a record is always used to identify that record when the file is to be interrogated, that field is called a *key*. In some cases there can be more than one key for each item. If we wished to find the name of a person with a given phone number, then the phone number would be the key. Obviously the phone directory, although it could be used, is not a good way of doing this operation. The phone companies usually keep an *inverse* book where the entries are sorted in order of phone number, but this requires double the space for storing the information. The phone company also needs a list of phone numbers in terms of addresses. This means three directories, or three times the space. This is a case of *multiple keys.* The amount of information can be reduced by keeping only one complete directory, sorted, say, by name. The other two can contain the phone number and name and the address and name respectively, and they can be sorted by phone number and address respectively. The amount of storage space is reduced, but it now requires two lookups if the reference is by phone number or address. The second lookup in the name directory can be simplified if the reference to it is an entry number—that is, page, column, and row—so that no search is necessary.

Sometimes each record contains a fixed number of fields or can be conveniently arranged to have this form. We then talk of fixed-length records. The alternative is variable-length records. (Example: the file of people who have books checked out from a library may be variable length. Each record could consist of the user's name—the key—followed by a variable number of fields representing the books checked out to that person.) In general, variable-length records require more careful planning for efficient handling.

Requirements such as these must be examined in planning the simulation of associative memories. This chapter will discuss some of the simple techniques for programming associative memories with specific reference to their use by the assembler name table. Some of the methods discussed will not be valuable for most assembler implementations, and the reader is invited to consider their application to other problems.

10.1 SEQUENTIAL SEARCHING

Perhaps the simplest technique that can be applied to the name table problem is the sequential method. A table is constructed sequentially in memory, using as many words as necessary per entry. For example, three words may be needed for the assembler name table, the first containing the coded name, the second containing the address value (when it is defined), and the third containing flags for *defined, relocatable,* etc. This is shown in Figure 10.1. A table of N entries would then occupy $3N$ consecutive locations.

The four basic operations would be performed as follows:

1	Enter a new entry	A count of the number of entries N is maintained. The incoming entry is added to the bottom of the table (the next three words in memory) and N is increased by 1.
2	Remove an entry	This cannot be done without either leaving holes or moving other information, so in general it is not allowed in this scheme. (It is not necessary in the assembler name table.)
3	Modify an entry	The table of items is searched on the key, that is, each name (the first word of the group of three) is compared

with the desired name in turn until either a match is found or the end of the table is reached. This is the search part of the process. It yields the address of the three words of the entry or the fact that the record is not there. Using these addresses, other parts of the record can now be changed.

4 Locate information   This is done by searching on the key as above.

If deletion is to be allowed, then the hole left should be filled by moving the last entry in the table to the space and reducing N by 1.

This technique should only be used when tables are relatively small or the search time will be too long. Techniques exist to make this method faster by small factors, but not by enough that one should consider searching a table the size of a phone book a record at a time. One speed-up technique often used is the following. The search loop in a one-address machine can have the form

```
A          LOAD        NAME
           SUBTRACT    ENTRY(I)
           TEST FOR 0  AND BRANCH TO FOUND IF 0
           INCREASE I  AND BRANCH TO A IF I IS LESS THAN OR = TO N
```

This loop will take four instructions on many machines. If, instead of storing the name in the name table, the difference of the ith and the $(i - 1)$st name is stored (the name itself is stored as the first entry), then the code is

```
           LOAD        NAME
A          SUBTRACT    DIFFERENCE ENTRY (I)
           TEST        FOR 0 AND BRANCH TO FOUND IF 0
           INCREASE I  AND BRANCH TO A IF I LESS THAN OR = TO N
```

If the names are N(1), N(2), N(3), . . . , etc., the table entries are

```
N(1)
N(2)—N(1)
N(3)—N(2)
N(4)—N(3)
Etc.
```

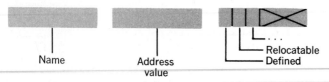

FIGURE 10.1   Name table entry

After the I-th pass through the loop, the accumulator will contain NAME — N(I). The (I + 1)st pass will subtract N(I + 1) — N(I) from this to get NAME — N(I + 1) as desired. The loop is now three instructions long on most machines. Some machines have a compare accumulator with memory instruction which does not change the accumulator. This can also be used to reduce the size of the loop. At least one early machine (the IBM 650) had a built-in table lookup instruction which took advantage of the rotating drum memory which was its main store.

10.1.1 Expected length of search

Consider an assembly input deck with N different names and suppose that each is used M greater than 1 times. If the definitions and uses are distributed evenly but no name is used before it is defined, then, at the stage where K names have been defined, we can expect a search to take about $K/2$ comparisons ("on the average" the search goes halfway down the table). This will be done M times before the next name is defined, or a total of $M*K/2$ comparisons will be made. Thus the total expected number of comparisons is about $M/2 + 2M/2 + 3M/2 = NM/2 = M(1 + 2 + 3 + \ldots + N)/2 = MN(N + 1)/4$. We say that the length of time is *asymptotic* to $MN^2/2$ (that is, the important or fastest-growing part of the time is $MN^2/2$). Thus if we double the number of names, the search time is quadrupled.

This estimate is not exact, but it is a good approximation. It is too small because names are used before they are defined and therefore the number of entries in the table increases very rapidly as the first part of the program is read. On the other hand, many programs refer most frequently to names that are defined near to the point at which they are used (transfers for example). It is therefore a better practice to search backward through the table, since the chances are good that the name is a recent entry and therefore near the bottom. This serves to lower the expected time of search, and the two effects may cancel each other out.

10.2 BINARY SEARCHING TECHNIQUES

The length of time used in the sequential search technique is due to a lack of information about the order of the items in the table. The phone book is ordered alphabetically, which gives us this very important facility—if a name is compared against an entry in the table and it does not match, then it is possible to tell immediately if the name should appear before or after the referenced entry in the table. This means, for example, that it is possible to eliminate half the entries in one step by simply comparing the name with the middle entry. If the name is larger (alphabetically), then the name will not be found in the first half of the table, so that the first half need not be searched further.

This technique is comparable to flipping open the phone book in the center and then deciding which half to concentrate on. Most people do not use this method directly because they have some idea from the name where it might be. For example, in looking up Brown, they know that they must start about one-twentieth of the way through. Such considerations can be taken into account in computer methods, and they will be discussed in the next section. In this section we wish to explore the advantages and disadvantages of *binary searching techniques,* which are the extension of the idea above.

Initially we start with a large table, T, of entries—say 1,024 entries as an example. We suppose that the keys in the table are sorted into order. When we wish to look up name S in this table, we compare it first with the middle entry (the 512th). See Figure 10.2. If the name S happens to match the middle entry, we are lucky and have completed the process. If not, then S is either larger or smaller than entry 512. If larger, we need look only at the top half of the table; if smaller, at the bottom half. In neither case are there more than 512 entries left to examine, and in either case the half that is left is itself a sorted table T1. Therefore the same technique can be applied again. That is, name S can be compared with the middle entry of the remaining table T1 (that is with the 256th or 768th entry of the original table). Again, we can tell whether it is in the top or bottom half of table T1, so, after two comparisons, we have narrowed the possibilities down to one-fourth of the original table. This process can be repeated until there is only one entry in the table to be searched, in which case a direct comparison will determine if it is name S or not. The example of a 1,024-entry table will take 10 or less steps, as can be seen from the calculation below.

NUMBER OF STEPS	NUMBER OF ENTRIES IN REMAINING TABLE
0	1,024
1	512
2	256
3	128
4	64
5	32
6	16
7	8
8	4
9	2
10	1

It is obvious that each additional step doubles the number of entries that can be taken care of. Thus if a total of n steps were to be taken, 2^n entries could be accommodated in the table. We need not restrict ourselves to tables which

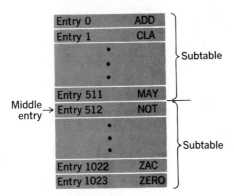

FIGURE 10.2 Binary searching

have a number of entries exactly equal to a power of 2. Other tables can be handled in two ways. The least efficient in storage space (but sometimes a faster program) is to fill up the table with "impossible" entries (for example, names that cannot be used by the programmer) until it is a power of 2 in size. When the size is a power of 2, addresses using fast shifting and logical orders can be constructed. The second method is simply to ignore the problem. The technique calls for the construction of the address of the middle of the remaining table. If the procedure saves two addresses L and M, L being the address one below the lowest entry in the remaining table and M the address one beyond the highest entry in the remaining table, the procedure is as follows:

1   If M = L + 1, then the entry is not in the table, stop.
2   Construct I = (L + M)/2 (as an integer by truncation).
3   Compare entry I with the name, and
a   if the entry is larger, set M equal to I;
b   if the entry is smaller, set L equal to I;
c   if the entry is equal, the name has been located, stop.
4   Repeat steps one through three.

Note that if the computer has a three-way compare for greater than, equal to, and less than (as the IBM 7094 has), then one may as well do all three comparisons indicated in step 3. If it has a two-way compare (greater than or equal to, for example) then it is probably worth changing the algorithm so that L is the address of the lowest entry. It then reads:

1   If M = L + 1, compare the name with entry L for equality and stop. (Entry L is either the name or the name is not in the table.)
2   Construct I = (L + M)/2 as an integer by truncation.
3   Compare entry I with the name, and
a   if the entry is larger, set M equal to I;
b   if the entry is less than or equal, set L equal to I.
4   Repeat steps one through three.

It may appear that many more steps will be taken in the second scheme above because searching always continues until only one entry is left, but it can be shown that this only increases the average number of searches by one for large tables.

Example

Suppose that we have a table with 13 entries which, for simplicity, we shall suppose are the letters A through M. Let us consider the problem of looking up entry H in the table. (Remember that we do not know that the entries are of this simple form, so H might be anywhere.) Suppose that the table starts in location T and takes one word per entry.

LOCATION	ENTRY
T+12	M
T+11	L
T+10	K
T+9	J
T+8	I
T+7	H
T+6	G
T+5	F
T+4	E
T+3	D
T+2	C
T+1	B
T	A

Initially, $L = T - 1$ and $M = T + 13$ if we use the method of three-way comparison. The steps are

$1 - 1$ M not equal to $L + 1$, therefore continue.
$1 - 2$ $I = (M + L)/2 = T + 6$.
$1 - 3$ Entry at $T + 6$ is G, less than H, hence set $L = I = T + 6$.
$2 - 1$ M not equal to $L + 1$.
$2 - 2$ $I = (L + M)/2 = T + 9$.
$2 - 3$ Entry at $T + 9$ is J, greater than H, hence set $M = I = T + 9$.
$3 - 1$ M not equal to $L + 1$.
$3 - 2$ $I = (L + M)/2 = T + 7$.
$3 - 3$ Entry at $T + 7$ is $H =$ desired name. Hence stop, we have found it.

If the letter I had been looked up, then four search steps—the maximum for this table—would have been taken.

10.2.1 Application of the binary search method to the assembler name table

The prerequisite for the use of the binary search technique is that the table be sorted into order. Keeping the table in order as it is generated is a slow process, since it is necessary to move existing information. On the average, half of the table will have to be moved for each new entry, hence the techniques discussed for the assembler are not directly applicable. What must be done is to first gather together a set of all entries to be made in the table. This can be done in pass I of the assembly. During pass I the table is unordered, so that no search of names used in address fields can be made and no check on double definition or nondefinition can be made. Between pass I and pass II, the defined names must be sorted into order. At this stage, double-definition errors will be caught when two entries with the same key are found. The names used in the address fields can be looked up by the binary search technique during pass II at the time of final translation. Because no table lookup is possible during pass I, pseudos such as BSS, EQU, etc., must either have absolute addresses or be delayed until after pass I. Use of this method obviously makes it less desirable to translate into an intermediate language during the first pass. Only the instruction mnemonic can be replaced by its binary form and any location names (which have already been processed) can be omitted.

10.2.2 Comparison of the binary search technique with the sequential search technique for an assembler name table

If the number of different names is N and each is used M times, then the sort at the end of pass I will take order of $N \log_2 N$ operations if a binary (two-way) internal merge is used. (This will be shown in the section on sorting below.) The searching during pass II for MN names will take order of $MN \log_2 N$ operations by a binary search technique. Thus the total is $(M + 1)N \log_2 N$ operations. This compares with $MN^2/4$ operations by a sequential search method. In addition, the comparison loop for the binary sort-and-search method is about twice as complex; thus we wish to compare $2(M + 1)N \log_2 N$ with $MN^2/4$. Suppose that $M = 4$. The result is shown graphically in Figure 10.3. It can be seen from this figure that as N increases, the binary search method becomes preferable.

10.3 SORTING

Much work has been done to find efficient methods of sorting, since it is an important part of many large business data processing problems. It is not our

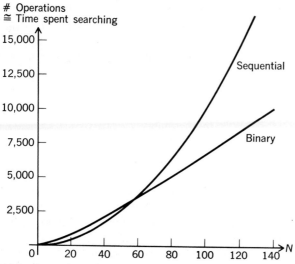

FIGURE 10.3   *Comparison of sequential and binary search times*

intent to go over this work in detail but rather to highlight the important features.†

Two related processes that are very important in data processing are sorting and merging. Sorting is the process which starts with a random file and finishes with a completely ordered file. Merging is the process which starts with several ordered files and produces a single ordered file. In practice, both processes have to be done to do a given job. For example, a bank which is updating its ordered file (on tape) of customer accounts with the day's transactions may first sort the day's transactions into order and then merge this file with the master file to produce a new master. This will make it unnecessary to read through the master file more than once. If the master file is much larger than the daily transaction file, this approach has obvious advantages. The use of large semirandom access devices such as disk files, which make the customer records available online, will modify such techniques. Sorting itself may involve merging, particularly if the number of entries is larger than can be accommodated in high-speed store. Typically, groups of entries that can be

†The most complete reference for sorting is D. Knuth, "The Art of Computer Programming, Volume 3," Addison-Wesley Publishing Company, Inc., Reading, Mass., 1973. Survey articles include W. A. Martin, Sorting, *Computer Surveys,* vol. 3, no. 4, December 1971, and C. Gotlieb, Sorting on Computers, in "Applications of Digital Computers," Freiberger and Prager (eds.), pp. 68–84, Ginn and Co., Boston, 1963.

held inside the main store are sorted by some technique and then written onto auxiliary store. When the whole file has been processed, the result is a collection of smaller sorted files. These are now merged. The first stage of this is called *internal sorting*. It is convenient to distinguish this phase because the class of methods that can be considered is larger than the class that can be used efficiently when an auxiliary store is used.

Internal sorting can be categorized in a number of ways. Three important classes of methods are those based on sequential searching, those based on merging, and those based on the radix representation of the key.

10.3.1 Sequential methods

A typical method in this category is the example invariably given in introductory Fortran texts. The first item in the file is moved to a location reserved for the smallest. It is then compared with each of the others in turn. If a smaller one is found, it is placed in the cell reserved for the smallest. When all of the keys in the file have been compared in this way, the smallest member is known. It is exchanged with the first member of the file and then attention is restricted to the remaining $N - 1$ members. The smallest of the reduced file is the second smallest of the whole file, so it is exchanged with the second member and so on. After M passes, the file would contain the first M members in order. After $N - 1$ passes, a file of N entries would be in order. The number of operations is proportional to $(N - 1) + (N - 2) + \ldots + 3 + 2 + 1 = N(N - 1)/2$ which is approximately $N^2/2$ for large N. All of the sequential search methods use KN^2 operations for some value of K. (We express this by saying that they are $O(N^2)$ methods, read *order of N^2* methods.) Thus as N increases, sequential methods increase very rapidly both for sorting and searching.

It is often convenient to sort a table *in place,* that is, without using additional storage space. This can be done sequentially by interchanging the nth entry with the nth largest, $n = 1, 2, \ldots, N - 1$. An alternative is to compare each entry with its neighbor in order, exchanging the two if they are in the wrong order. The largest will "float" to the top in this process. After at most $N - 1$ passes, the table will be in order. If the table is already partially sorted, this method will take fewer passes. The latter is called the *bubble sort.*

10.3.2 Merging methods

These are combination methods utilizing the sequential sort for smaller files and then merging techniques. One example of this is called the *quadratic selection process.* The original file of N records is broken into $\sqrt{N}$ subfiles, each with $\sqrt{N}$ records (or the nearest integer to $\sqrt{N}$). The subfiles are sorted into order by a sequential method (using approximately $(\sqrt{N})^2/2 = N/2$ comparisons each on $\sqrt{N}$ files for a total of approximately $N^{1.5}/2$ operations). The $\sqrt{N}$ subfiles are now merged by comparing the smallest of each to find the overall smallest (this takes $\sqrt{N}$ comparisons). This smallest is placed in its final position, and the process is repeated with it removed from its subfile. Since there are N records, this merging process takes $N^{1.5}$ operations for a total of 1.5 $N^{1.5}$ operations. We can therefore say that this is an $O(N^{1.5})$ method. The quadratic selection process is a special case of the *P-way merge*. In a *P*-way merge, the original file is split into P subfiles of N/P elements each. Each of these subfiles is sorted by some method, and then the *P*-ordered files are merged as in the quadratic selection process. This last operation takes order of $N*P$ operations. The subfiles of N/P elements could be sorted by any method. For example, another *P*-way merge could be used by breaking each subfile into sub-subfiles of $N/P/P$ elements. This process can be repeated until the sub-sub- . . . subfiles are small enough to be sorted sequentially.

An example of a *P*-way merge with P equal to 3 is given below. Initially, there are 18 items in the file. They are to be sorted into alphabetical order. Assume that the largest file that can be sorted rapidly by a sequential method is a two-item file. Hence the first step is to produce 3*3 files of two elements each.

If the initial file contains

SER DOG TYU EWB EDF ZUQ WFE QWE OUT DEG CAT WEB TOO WSS BSS TOM AAA QKX

the first pass produces 9 two-record sorted files equal to

```
DOG   SER
EWB   TYU
UWE   WFE
EDF   ZUG
DEG   OUT
CAT   WEB
TOO   WSS
BSS   TOM
AAA   QKX
```

The first group of these subfiles is merged as follows:

	INPUT FILES		OUTPUT FILE
	DOG	SER	
Start	EWB	TYU	
	UWE	WFE	
	. . .	SER	
Step 1	EWB	TYU	DOG
	UEW	WFE	

		SER						
Step 2	...	TYU	DOG	EWB				
	UWE	WFE						
	...	...						
Step 3	...	TYU	DOG	EWB	SER			
	UWE	WFE						
	...	...						
Step 4	...	...	DOG	EWB	SER	TYU		
	UWE	WFE						
	...	...						
Step 5	...	...	DOG	EWB	SER	TYU	UWE	
	...	WFE						
	...	...						
Step 6	...	...	DOG	EWB	SER	TYU	UWE	WFE
	...	...						

The next two groups of three subfiles are merged in a similar way, resulting in three subfiles, each sorted and containing six elements. These three subfiles are merged together to give a single sorted file of 18 elements. How many passes of merging are needed for a file of N elements? Assume that the number of records that are to be sorted initially is fixed at Q. Then if N is less than Q, only the initial sort pass is needed. If N is between Q and PQ, then one additional pass is needed. For each factor of P, one additional pass is needed. Hence the number of passes is the smallest integer at least as large as

$$1 + \log_P \frac{N}{Q}$$

The amount of work in each pass is proportional to NP, so the total work is proportional to

$$NP \left(1 + \log_P \frac{N}{Q}\right)$$

As N increases, this increases at a rate of $N \log N$. For a given N and Q, the optimum value of P can be calculated by differentiation. It can be seen that as N/Q becomes large (which is the case of interest when merging techniques are being discussed), then the value of P for which the total merge time is minimum is $\epsilon = 2.71828\ldots$. Since P must be an integer, 2 or 3 is optimum. In practice, merging from auxiliary storage devices is likely to be input/ output limited, so that the computation time is not as significant as I/O time. As P increases, the number of passes decreases but the computation time increases. Ideally, P should be increased until the computation time is equal to the I/O time. If magnetic tapes are being used, then it is probable that the physical number of tape drives available will be the limited factor, so the crudest rule of thumb is to use all tape drives available.

Merging techniques can be used for an internal sort by starting with files of length 1 which are necessarily sorted and performing P-way merges. Since the internal sort is not I/O limited, then a P of 2 or 3 should be chosen. In fact, a more careful analysis of the time for a given machine will usually suggest that P should be 2.

10.3.3 Radix methods

The key is usually expressed in some radix. For example, it may be expressed internally in binary, it may be a decimal number, or it may be an alphabetic name, which is radix 26. A radix method is one which takes account of the representation of the key in order to do the sorting. It can be likened to the method of alphabetizing a list of names by first sorting them into 26 piles based on the first letter, and then, treating each pile separately, alphabetizing them on the second letter, and so on. A familiar application of this technique is provided by the card sorter. A card sorter contains pockets for each row position on the card (12 pockets) plus a reject pocket which we shall ignore. It can be set to examine any particular column on the card. One pass through the sorter separates the deck according to the holes punched. Since it is easier to restack all cards together after a sort than to treat each subdeck separately, the least-significant digit of the representation of the key should be treated first. Suppose that a deck of cards contains record information to be sorted and the key is a 3-digit decimal number in columns 1 through 3. The deck should be first sorted on the basis of column 3 so that all cards are in order on column 3. Then the process should be repeated on column 2. At this time, the deck is in order on column 2 but not on 3. However, those cards with identical entries in column 2 are in order on column 3. After a third pass sorting on column 1, the deck is in order. An example of such a sort is given below. The deck input to the sorter is shown on the left, while the contents of each of the 10 pockets after the sort pass are shown to its right.

INPUT	0	1	2	3	4	5	6	7	8	9
436							436			
253				253						
856							856			
456							456			
457								457		
455						455				
364					364					
907								907		
004					004					
009										009
574					574					
276							276			
458									458	
473				473						
853				853						

The cards are stacked behind each other, those from pocket 0 in front, and on the second pass the reassembled file on the left below is sorted into the pockets shown:

INPUT	0	1	2	3	4	5	6	7	8	9
253						253				
473								473		
853						853				
364							364			
004	004									
574								574		
455						455				
436				436						
856						856				
456						456				
276								276		
457						457				
907	907									
458						458				
009	009									

On the third pass, it is sorted as shown below on the first digit:

INPUT	0	1	2	3	4	5	6	7	8	9
004	004									
907										907
009	009									
436					436					
253			253							
853									853	
455					455					
856									856	
456					456					
457					457					
458					458					
364				364						
473					473					
574						574				
276			276							

The result after reassembling into a single deck is:

004
009
253
276

364
436
455
456
457
458
473
574
853
856
907

This technique can be adapted to computer use. For internal sorting, there is no limit to the radix that could be used except that of the storage space required to provide at least one word for each pocket. It is not necessary to provide space for more than one entry in a contiguous location of memory, since subsequent entries in the same pocket could be chained together. If this technique is used for sorting files from auxiliary storage, then there must be at least as many output-file storage devices (for example, magnetic tape units) as there are pockets, so the radix used is limited. In addition, at least one input-file device is needed, and if unnecessary file-to-file copies are to be avoided, there should be as many input files as there are output files, so that on the next pass their roles can be switched.

The number of operations is proportional to the number of passes and the number of items N. The number of passes K is determined by the radix that can be used and the length of the key. To some extent, K is independent of the number of entries, except that it should be realized that the maximum number of entries is limited by the radix R and the number of passes K, because it is not possible to have more than R^K different keys keys consisting of K digits base R. Radix sorting is not very efficient unless the ratio of the number of keys used to the maximum possible number is large (close to 1). Roughly speaking, this is because the method is going through the motions of distinguishing between many more different keys than are actually present unless the ratio is large.

A sort using radix 2 called *radix exchange* has been developed for internal sorting. It has the property that very little temporary storage is required. Since the radix is 2, it is useful for binary machines in which the key is a fixed-point number. The unordered set of keys is scanned from the first entry, looking only at the most significant bit. When a 1 bit is found, the scan starts backward from the last entry until a key with a 0 first bit is encountered. The two entries are exchanged, and the scan continues. Two address pointers are used during this scan to remember where the forward and backward scans have reached. When the pointers meet, the file is in order on the first bit; that is, it has been divided into two subfiles based on the first bit. Each of these two subfiles can be sorted on the second bit to get four subfiles in order on the first 2 bits, and so on. If the key contains K bits, K address pointers will be needed for temporary storage.†

The radix exchange method described above is slow if the keys are long because the number of passes is proportional to the number of bits in the key. *Quicksort* and *quickersort* are the names of two similar methods that overcome this problem.‡

The first step in the radix exchange is to divide the table into two by putting all keys less than 1000000 . . . 0 at the top of the'table and all entries greater than or equal to this number below. This is done by scanning simultaneously from the top and bottom of the table so that keys can be exchanged when they are in the wrong relative order. Quicksort chooses one of the keys at random and uses this for the comparison instead of 100 . . . 0. Each key is examined, starting from the first, and compared with the random one chosen. When a larger one is found, the scan starts from the bottom of the table looking for a smaller one. When one is found, the larger and smaller are exchanged and the scan continues. This step is called *"partition" by Hoare*. It is described in Algol by

procedure partition (A,M,N,I,J): **value** M,N;
                    array A; **integer** M,N,I,J;
comment I and J are output variables, and A is the array (with subscript bounds M:N) which is operated upon by this procedure. Partition takes the value X of a random element of the array A, and rearranges the values of the elements of the array in such a way that there exist integers I and J with the following properties:

$$M \leq J < I \leq N \text{ provided } M < N$$
$$A[R] \leq X \text{ for } M \leq R \leq J$$
$$A[R] = X \text{ for } J < R < I$$
$$A[R] \geq X \text{ for } I \leq \quad \leq N$$

The procedure uses an integer procedure random (M,N) which chooses equi-probably a random integer F between M and N, and also a procedure exchange, which exchanges the values of its two parameters:

begin   **real** X; **integer** F;
                  F: = random (M,N); X: = A[F];
                  I: = M; J: = N;
up: **for** I: = I   **step** 1 **until** N **do**
                        if X $<$ A [I] **then go to** down;

†This method is described in P. Hildebrandt and H. Isbit, Radix Exchange, *Journal of the Association for Computing Machinery*, vol. 6, no. 2, pp. 156–163, April, 1959.
‡Described in C. A. R. Hoare and R. S. Scowen, Algorithms 64 and 271, *Communications of the Association for Computing Machinery*, vol. 4, p. 321, July, 1961.

```
            I: = N;
down:       for J: = J        step −1 until M do
                              if A[J]<X then go to change;
            J: = M;
change:     if I < J then      begin exchange (A[I], A[J]);
                                 I: = I + 1; J: = J − 1;
                                 go to up
                               end
else        if I < F then      begin exchange (A[I], A[F]);
                                 I: = I + 1
                               end
else        if F < J then      begin exchange (A[F], A[J]);
                                 J: = J − 1
                               end;
end         partition†
```

The result of applying "partition" to an array A is to break it into three sub-arrays of elements less than the one chosen at random, equal to it, and greater than it. This same algorithm can be applied to the subtables smaller and larger than the chosen element until they only consist of one element, at which time the table will be sorted. This is done by Hoare's Algol program

procedure   quicksort (A,M,N); **value** M,N;
         array A; **integer** M,N;
comment   Quicksort is a very fast and convenient method of sorting an array in the random access store of a computer. The entire contents of the store may be sorted, since no extra space is required. The average number of comparisons made is $2(M − N) \ln (N − M)$, and the average number of exchanges is one sixth this amount. Suitable refinements of this method will be desirable for its implementation on any actual computer;

```
begin          integer    I,J;
               if M < N then    begin partition (A,M,N,I,J);
                                quicksort  (A,M,J);
                                quicksort  (A, I, N);
                                end
end            quicksort
```

This provides a very nice example of recursion. Quicksort sorts a table. It first checks to see that there is more than one element; if not, the table is already sorted. It then breaks the table into three subtables and sorts the first and last by use of quicksort; the middle one contains equal elements, so it is already sorted.

The comments indicated that no extra storage space is required. From a data point of view this is true, but the user should be aware that recursive procedures require storage space for each of their variables and links. This method, therefore, does use kp extra storage locations, where p is the maximum depth of recursion, proportional to $\log (N − M)$, and k is a constant dependent on the implementation of the compiler.

---

†*Ibid.*

10.3.4 Internally sorting long records

In many business applications and in some system applications, the record is very long compared with the size of the key. Since the sorting methods discussed involve the movement of records from one part of memory to another several times, it is desirable to look for methods which avoid this movement or minimize it. We must first ask what is the desired form of the sorted file. There are three possibilities.

It might be sufficient that a chain of addresses pointing in order from one file to the next be available. This allows the file to be read in order, but it is not possible to access a particular entry such as the middle one without reading all previous ones in the chain. If this is the case, then the records need never be moved. An extra field must be allocated to each record stored. This will contain a chain address. Each file in memory is represented by a series of addresses linking one to another. As the files are changed, these address links are modified to reflect the new organization.

Suppose, for example, that the six files below were stored in the locations indicated (occupying 20 words each).

LOCATION	CONTENTS		LINK ADDRESS
100	JONES	DATA. .A	120
120	BROWN	DATA. .B	140
140	SMITH	DATA. .C	160
160	DAVID	DATA. .D	180
180	PETER	DATA. .E	200
200	BRYAN	DATA. .F	—

The link address is shown as it would be set up originally. It gives the file in the order in which it was read in. A sorting process, such as a three-way merge, might start by creating three ordered files of two elements each. These files start in locations 120, 160, and 200 (this information must be saved), and the records are modified to read

```
100  JONES   DATA. .A   —
120  BROWN   DATA. .B   100
140  SMITH   DATA. .C   —
160  DAVID   DATA. .D   140
180  PETER   DATA. .E   —
200  BRYAN   DATA. .F   180
```

The three-way merge is now performed by comparing the keys in locations 120, 160, and 200. BROWN in 120 is found to be the smallest, so it is put at the start of this final chain. The first file now has a starting address of 100, since the earlier entry was removed. The next comparison shows that BRYAN is the smallest of the three keys compared. Thus the entry in 200 is placed in the output file chain by putting 200 in the address link of the record in 120. The result at the completion of the merge is

100	JONES	DATA. .A	180
120	BROWN	DATA. .B	200
140	SMITH	DATA. .C	—
160	DAVID	DATA. .D	100
180	PETER	DATA. .E	140
200	BRYAN	DATA. .F	160

which tells us that the order of the file is 120,200,160,100,180,140. It is necessary to save the starting address, 120, of the chain in the memory. This file can now be accessed sequentially starting from the first member.

A second required form for a file occurs when it must be in alphabetical order. This can occur if the file has to be written onto an output device in order. This means that the records must be moved. To avoid moving them during the sort process, a technique such as the one used above can be employed. When the file has been alphabetized, it can be physically moved. This movement need not take more than one move of each record, which is an improvement over the number of moves that would have been used if the records had been moved in the sorting process.

A third form for a file occurs when it is only necessary to calculate the address of the *i*th entry for any *i*. This is sufficient for a binary search. In this form, the records can be separated into two pieces, the key and the remainder. The remainder can be left in fixed memory locations and only the keys sorted. In order that the key be connected to the remainder, an address pointer which points to the remainder of the record can be stored with the key. In the example above, the final form of the file would be

100	BROWN	DATA. .A	120	Brown's pointer points to his data, which is
120	BRYAN	DATA. .B	200	DATA. .B
140	DAVID	DATA. .C	160	
160	JONES	DATA. .D	100	
180	PETER	DATA. .E	180	
200	SMITH	DATA. .F	140	

The keys have been placed in order, but the remainder of the records have been left fixed. The address pointer contains the original address of the key before sorting occurred. This serves to link the key to the record.

Alternatively, a separate list of addresses pointing to the keys could be sorted on the key. The key could be accessed from this address by indirect addressing.

10.3.5 **Sorting from auxiliary storage**

The need for sorting from auxiliary storage is not likely to occur in the assembly process for any but the smallest machines, since the assembler name table can usually be kept in the main memory. Indeed, if it can't, then the assembly process must be designed very carefully so as to minimize the name table searching, for a search through a file contained on auxiliary storage can be very slow. In this section we shall discuss some of the criteria to be evaluated when planning a sorting job which will involve multiple passes over auxiliary storage files.

The characteristics of the machine that have the greatest effect on the sort times are the size of main memory available for the internal sort process and the type and number of auxiliary storage devices available for storing the information from one pass to another. Tape units are the most commonly available devices. Since the information is only available serially from a tape unit, methods used can only access information from the current position on each tape. Usually a variant of a P-way merge will be used. If $2P$ tape units are available, then a simple P-way merge can be done as follows. On the first pass over the unsorted file, groups of records are read into the main memory and sorted internally. They are written out onto P of the tapes, each tape receiving a sorted subfile in turn. At the completion of this process, the information has been spread over P of the tapes such that each tape contains a series of sorted subfiles. A P-way merge is now performed, reading the P input streams from these P tapes and generating an output stream of sorted subfiles P times as long. The output stream is split by placing successive subfiles onto each of the remaining P tapes. Thus the result of the second pass is another set of P tapes, each with longer sorted subfiles, and P tapes that are now free. The process can be repeated, merging from the tapes that have just been prepared onto the newly available tapes.

The longer the first subfiles are made, the fewer the passes that will be needed in the merging process. Consequently, it is important to use a method that uses a minimum amount of temporary storage during the internal sort so that a maximum amount is available for the subfile and necessary I/O buffers. If the key is binary and short, radix exchange may be the most suitable; but if the number of bits in the key is close to N, the number of entries, it will be as slow as sequential sorting or bubble sorting, neither of which require additional storage. A second parameter that is available to the user is the choice of the physical block size of the information written on tape. We call the number of records per block the blocking factor.

If the block size is made larger, then the percentage of tape occupied by record gaps is smaller, and hence the overall tape time is reduced. On the other hand, the longer the block, the more memory space required for each buffer, and hence the fewer buffers that can be used. Since there is some chance that the input can occur from one tape for some time, it is important that there be some backup of information in the memory before it is needed. The average amount of memory space not in use is half a buffer size for each of the P input buffers. This also argues for smaller buffers.

10.4 HASH ADDRESSING

The previous section dealt with techniques that depended on the table being ordered in memory but that did not require a knowledge of where a given name appeared in the table. This contrasts with the technique that a person uses in a phone book search. He knows, for example, that the entry for Mr. Brown will appear about $\frac{1}{20}$th of the way through the book. The strategy used could be to open the book at this point and then to scan forward or backward depending on the result of a comparison of the name Brown with the entry found at the $\frac{1}{20}$th point. The corresponding computer technique would be to construct an address based on an estimate of where the name being searched is likely to appear and then to start a sequential search forward or backward from that point. Let us illustrate this by an example. Suppose that the keys are 3-digit decimal numbers between 000 and 999 and that there are 100 entries in the table. If they are evenly distributed (that is, one key lies between each of 0 to 9, 10 to 19, . . . , and 990 to 999), then the address of the entry in the table would be given by the address

$A = T + K/10$ Truncated to an integer.

where the table is assumed to start in location T, require one location per entry, and where K is the key.

Unfortunately, the keys of a table will not be so evenly distributed in general, but the more that they approximate this distribution, the faster the method will be. In the worst possible case, it will not be worse than the sequential search method except that there is an additional calculation of a starting address and at some point the table has to be ordered. If it is a fixed table, such as the mnemonic table, then the sorting does not have to be done for each assembly. Therefore this is a better method than the sequential method, yet it retains most of the sequential method's simplicity.

If this method were to be used for the name table, then either the entries would have to be sorted between pass I and II (which means that no references to the table could be made in pass I unless a sequential technique were used), or else the table would have to be constructed in order. Constructing a table in order can be a time-consuming job if it has to be reordered after each new name is entered, because up to half of the entries in the table will have to be moved in order to make space for each new entry. This can be partially avoided if the table has blank spaces in it originally, so that there is a strong possibility that there will be a space for the next entry. The more spaces that are available in a given size table, the faster the entry process is likely to be. Let us return to the previous example where the keys are between 000 and 999. Suppose that there will be as many as 100 entries in the table, although initially there are none. Suppose that we allocate 200 locations for the table, so that it never becomes more than 50 percent dense. In this case, the probable address for an entry will be given by

$$A = T + K/5$$

When an entry is to be placed in the table, this address is calculated from the value of the key. If the addressed location is empty, the entry is placed in the table at that point. If the location is full, then the key is compared with the entry already in the table. If the table entry is larger, the next lower address $A - 1$ is examined. If this is empty, it is used to make the new entry. If its contents are larger, another step to the next lower address is taken. If it is smaller, then it is necessary to open up a space by moving everything, from this point down to the first blank space, down one position. If the original comparison showed that the table entry was smaller, then a similar process is followed in the upward (increasing address) direction. Let us examine the process when the entries 256 and 217 are added to the table after it already contains some entries. In the section of Table 10.1, the left-hand column gives the memory location, the next column contains the keys already entered, and the subsequent columns show the states of the table after the next two entries are made.

In step 1, entry 256 is added to the table. The probable address of the key

TABLE 10.1

LOCATION	KEY	AFTER STEP 1	AFTER STEP 2
T+40	201	201	201
T+41	203	203	203
T+42			
T+43	215	215	215
T+44	216	216	216
T+45			217
T+46	231	231	231
T+47			
T+48		246	246
T+49	246	255	255
T+50	255	256	256
T+51	257	257	257
T+52			
T+53	266	266	266

256 is T + $^{265}\!/_5$ = T + 51. Unfortunately, location T + 51 is already occupied by the key 257, which is larger than 256. Therefore, the entry in the next smaller location T + 50 is checked. It contains the key 255, which is smaller than 256. Therefore, 256 is entered into T + 50 and all entries from T + 50 down are moved down one location until the next blank in T + 48 is found. In step 2, the key 217, corresponding to the probable address T + 43, is entered. The present entries in T + 43 and T + 44 are both smaller than the key 217. However, the next table entry, T + 45, is empty. Therefore, 217 is entered into T + 45.

A table search process can be viewed as a means of calculating a function. The argument of the function is the key which is to be looked up, and its value is the address of the entry. If this function is known, that is, if for each key K we could calculate the address A by means of a function F such that A = F(K), then there is no need to perform a search through the table. In the technique discussed above, an approximation to F was formed by using a linear function F. It was linear because the table was to be ordered. However, if we ask what use was made of the ordering property, we shall see that it was only to determine whether to search backward or forward from the probable address if the entry and the searched name did not agree. We could just as well always search in the same direction, say in the direction of increasing address, in which case the ordering would not have been necessary. This has an additional advantage. Since the table does not have to be in order, it is not necessary to move previous entries. The method for finding a name by searching is now as follows:

1 Calculate an approximate address from the key by an approximate address function F', where A = F'(K).
2 Compare the name being searched for with the entry in location A.
3 If they agree, the entry has been found. Stop.
4 If the contents of the table are blank at location A, the entry is not in the table. Stop.
5 Otherwise, increase A by 1 and return to step 2.

A new entry is placed in the table as follows:

1 Construct the approximate address A = F'(K)
2 Check the contents of location A.
3 If they are not blank, increase A by 1 and return to step 2.
4 If they are blank, enter the new key in location A.

This will be illustrated by repeating the earlier example, this time using the new entry method.

In step one, the entry 256 is added to the table. Since the approximate address function gives location T + 51, which is not empty, the first blank location with a higher address is used, namely, T + 52. Note that the table is now out of order. When the entry 217 is made in step two, the process also has to

TABLE 10.2

LOCATION	KEY	AFTER STEP 1	AFTER STEP 2
T+40	201	201	201
T+41	203	203	203
T+42			
T+43	215	215	215
T+44	216	216	216
T+45			217
T+46	231	231	231
T+47			
T+48			
T+49	246	246	246
T+50	255	255	255
T+51	257	257	257
T+52		256	256
T+53	266	266	266

search forward two cells until a blank location is found. Note that, in this unordered technique, it is never necessary to move items already in the table; hence, the entry time is faster. However, the search time will be slower when the table becomes fairly dense, since it is necessary to search until a blank location has been found; in an ordered table, on the other hand, it was only necessary to search until either a blank location or a larger (or smaller if the search is backward) entry has been found. The unordered technique will never be slower than a sequential search.

In the above example we calculated an approximate address by means of a linear function of the key. In applications of this technique to assemblers and compilers, there is a high probability that the keys will not be distributed anywhere near uniformly over the range of possible keys. This will cause bunching in the table and slow down the search-and-entry process. Many assembly-language programs, for example, will contain names that start with the same three letters because these three letters serve to identify that section of code to the programmer. Since the ordering is not important, there is no reason why the approximate address function should be a monotonic function of the key. (A monotonic function is one which only increases—or decreases—as the value of the argument is increased.) Therefore, we should try to use an approximate address function that spreads the keys used fairly evenly over the locations used in the table. If the table is fixed, as the mne-monic table is, then various address functions can be tried until a reason-ably good choice between speed of calculation and speed of search is achieved. If the table changes, as happens in the case of the name table, then an address function must be chosen without prior knowledge of the entries. The idea generally used is to mix up or *hash* the key in some way so that keys assigned in any routine fashion are unlikely to fall in the same part of the table. Such an address is called a *hash address.*

Some examples of hash addresses that could be used in an assembler name table include multiplying the name by a constant after it has been packed into an internal representation such as BCD and just using a certain number of bits from the result, or using the bottom bits of the internal representation if it has been converted as a base-37 number. A common method for forming a hash address is to divide the packed form of the key by a prime number and use the remainder as the address displacement in the table. If the prime is p, the remainder will be between 0 and $p - 1$, allowing for p entries in the table.

Frequently the problem of *conflicts,* which occur when the space in the table is already occupied, is solved by calculating a second hash address and trying that location. One common technique is to use the quotient from the earlier division by the prime p and divide it by p or another prime. The result can then be used as an additional displacement from the present position in the table. Another solution to the problem of conflicts is to create a chain of additional entries with the same hash address and to search this chain sequentially.

10.5 CHAINING TECHNIQUES

In the previous sections, it has generally been assumed that the record positions in memory were in contiguous locations. This was necessary in methods that used address calculations such as the binary search method and the hash addressing technique. However, in sequential searching, it was only necessary that the successor of an entry be accessible directly. This was exploited in the discussion on sorting long records, where they were chained together in order to avoid moving them in memory. Chaining techniques can be exploited to advantage in a number of methods. This section will discuss various chaining techniques that can be used.

10.5.1 Sequential search with deletions

The method of sequential searching had a number of drawbacks. One was its inherent slowness, which was only offset by its simplicity. In some situations, it is desirable to replace names with the table address containing the related information. This means that deletion is not possible unless blank entries are permitted, since other entries may not be moved. Permitting blank entries slows down the entry process. If the entries are chained together in memory, the speed is not improved, but it is possible to remove entries from the chain without leaving blank entries in the table. This is shown in the following example. If the original table has the form

TABLE 10.3

LOCATION	KEY	LINK TO NEXT ENTRY
110	SAM	114
112	JOHN	120
114	BETTY	118
116		
118	PAT	112
120	BOB	

and the address 110 is indicated as being the start of the table, then the order of the table can be seen to be SAM, BETTY, PAT, JOHN, BOB, ... Suppose that the entry PAT is to be removed. We note that this entry is preceded by BETTY and followed by JOHN in locations 114 and 112 respectively. In order that the successor of BETTY be JOHN, the chain link from BETTY must be changed to the address of JOHN. That is, the chain address in location 114 must be changed from 118 to 112. The table now has the form

TABLE 10.4

110	SAM	114
112	JOHN	120
114	BETTY	112
116		
118	PAT	112
120	BOB	

It was not necessary to remove the key PAT in any way; it is omitted from any search process because the chain of link addresses does not pass through it. In this particular example, the first entry in the chain is also the first location of the table. If this entry were to be removed from the table, the first member of the chain would be in location 114. Therefore there must be a cell in memory which is used to hold the address of the first entry in the table.

If a new entry is to be added to the table, then it can be placed on the beginning or end of the chain. In the latter case, it is necessary to save the address of the last entry in the chain, so it is simpler to add a new entry to the beginning of the chain unless there are reasons for preferring the end.

When an entry is added to the chain, it is necessary to find an empty place in memory for recording the new record. Since the present records are not in contiguous locations, there may be holes in the table. Since we did not blank out a record when it was removed from the chain, it is not possible (or desirable) to scan through all locations looking for an empty position. Therefore, a method which will allow us to find empty positions must be introduced. This method must allow the positions made free when an entry is removed to be reallocated. A chaining principle can also be used for this by constructing a chained list of all free positions. The starting address of this chain must be kept in a known memory cell. When an item is to be added to the table, the first entry in the *free chain* (sometimes called the *free list*) is removed from that chain and used as a location for the new entry. When an item is removed from the table, its address can be added to the beginning of the free chain. Suppose our table is in the state

TABLE 10.5

| Table start . . . . 110 | | |
| Free chain start. . . . . . 118 | | |

LOCATION	KEY	LINK
110	SAM	114
112	JOHN	120
114	BETTY	112
116		0
118	PAT	116
120	BOB	0

The free chain contains locations 118 and 116. The 0 link in location 116 is used to indicate that it is the end of the chain. This only rules out location 0 as a possible table address. The table contains locations 110, 114, 112, and 120. Location 118 contains a nonblank key because it was previously used, but this key is not in the table because it is not in the table chain. If the key TOM were to be added to the table, then the procedure would be as follows. The new entry TOM is placed into the location given in the start of the free chain (118). Thus location 118 now contains TOM. The start address for the free chain is set to the link in location 118, the link in location 118 is set to the contents of the start of the table chain, and the new value of the start of the table chain is made equal to the old value of the start of the free chain. Thus the table has the form

TABLE 10.6

| Table chain start. . . . . 118 | | |
| Free chain start. . . . . . 116 | | |

LOCATION	KEY	LINK
110	SAM	114
112	JOHN	120
114	BETTY	112
116		0
118	TOM	110
120	BOB	0

If the entry BOB is now removed, the procedure is as follows. BOB is located in the table by a search. It is found in location 120. It is also noted that the preceding entry was in location 112. The link from location 120 (0) is copied into the link of the preceding location 112. The start of the free chain (116) is copied into the link of 120, and the address of the item being removed (120) is copied into the free-chain start storage cell. Thus the table becomes

TABLE 10. 7

Table start 118
Free chain start. 120

LOCATION	KEY	LINK
110	SAM	114
112	JOHN	0
114	BETTY	112
116		0
118	TOM	110
120	BOB	116

10.5.2 Radix techniques with chaining: trees

Methods of searching analogous to the radix sorting techniques can be constructed. In a telephone directory lookup, the user will typically locate the first letter of the name by some combination of scanning technique and address calculation method. The second letter is frequently located in a similar manner. One could imagine this process being made easier by providing a small 26-entry index at the front of the directory indicating where each set of entries with the same first letter starts. If this were mechanized on a computer, then a memory reference would be used to find the address of, say, the words starting with an R. The second letter could be handled in a similar way by providing 26 more tables, each with 26 entries. Thus a second memory reference would tell us where all words starting with, say, RE were stored. This could be continued, but the third level would take about 17,000 memory locations, which is no longer practical. The problem that not all two-letter combinations are used arises. As more letters are handled, then the probability that all combinations will be used decreases further. Therefore, instead of storing a table of all 26 possibilities for each new combination, a table of only those letters that actually occur should be stored. This table will have to be searched sequentially, since it is impossible to predict which letter will appear where; however, it is fairly short, in no case longer than 26 entries. Since the individual table may change in size by additions and deletions, it is also wise to use a chaining method for the tables of letters. Suppose, for example, that the words LOAD, ADD, MPY, AND, NOT, NOP, and NEG were to be stored in such a manner. The table could take the form

TABLE 10.8

Table start address 1000				
LOCATION	KEY	LINK TO NEXT ENTRY	LINK TO NEXT TABLE	ENTRY
1000	N	1001	1004	
1001	A	1002	1009	
1002	L	1003	1013	
1003	M	0	1016	
1004	O	1005	1006	
1005	E	0	1008	
1006	P	1007		NOP
1007	T	0		NOT
1008	G	0		NEG
1009	D	1010	1011	
1010	N	0	1012	
1011	D	0		ADD
1012	D	0		AND
1013	O	0	1014	
1014	A	0	1015	
1015	D	0		LOAD
1016	P	0	1017	
1017	Y	0		MPY

Note that any length names can be accommodated by this method, and that the search time will never be more than 26 times the number of characters in the word—usually very much less. It is evident that a large amount of additional storage can be used (18 locations to store seven items in this example). The percentage increase is less for larger tables. If, for example, all three letter keys are stored, 18,278 entries are used instead of the minimum of 17,576, which is only an additional 4 percent.

If this method is used for a name table, means of adding and searching must be provided. The spare locations in memory can be kept on a free chain, so that each time a new entry is made, another location can be obtained. The table is searched for the new entry, one character at a time, until a subtable is found in which the next letter is not present. This letter and subsequent letters must be added to the table. Suppose, for example, that the entry ABS is to be added to the table above. The search starts by comparing the first letter with the first table entry. The A does not match the N, so the next entry, from location 1001, is tried. This time the As match, so the search proceeds to the second character table starting in location 1009. The B is compared with the D in location 1009 and does not match. Hence it is compared with the next entry in 1010. The B does not match with the N either, and there is no next entry since the link to the next address is 0. Therefore, B must be added to this table. Suppose that the next locations available in the free chain are 1018, 1019, etc. The entry

1018	B	0	1019

is made in location 1018, while location 1010 (the last examined) is changed to

1010	N	1018	1012

by inserting the address of the new member of the subtable in the link to the next entry position. The S of ABS is entered in location 1019, and, since it is the last letter of ABS, this is the end of the chain.

1019	S	0	0	ABS

The table can accept keys in which one is an extension of another. If the entry ABST is made, the effect is to change location 1019 and add location 1020 to the table as follows:

1019	S	0	1020	ABS
1020	T	0	0	ABST

The data that have been stored in the table have a complex structure due to the chain addresses present. We refer to the structured storage arrangement as a *data structure*. The way it is stored in memory with chain addresses is just a way of representing this structure. We can visualize the structure presented above in the form of a *tree* as shown in Figure 10.4. It is drawn upside down in that the *root* of the tree is at the top of the figure. A tree consists of a set of *nodes* connected to each other by *branches*. It is such that there are no *closed circuits* in the branch connections, so that there is one and only one connection between any pair of nodes. The nodes may be labeled, as they are in the example. One node is special, and is called the root of the tree. The branches extend from this root to each of the nodes. A node that is only connected to one other node is called a terminal node. In the example, all of the nodes connected to the root correspond to the possible first letters of names entered in the table. Thus there are four *subnodes* of the root node corresponding to the letters N, A, L, and M. The nodes are so labeled. Each of these nodes has further subnodes corresponding to the possible second letters of the keys. Thus the first letter N can be followed by the letters O or E, so there are two subnodes under the node labeled N. The nodes which also correspond to actual entries in the table are further labeled with the name of the key. This

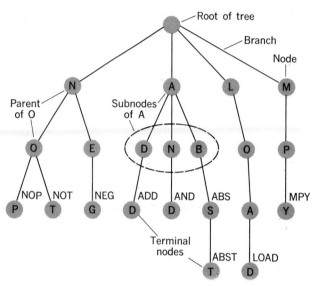

FIGURE 10.4   Tree structure

tree is represented in memory by using four elements for each node. They are the character at the node, the address of the next node to the right that is connected to the same *parent* node (the one immediately above as drawn) or 0 if there is no such node, the address of the leftmost subnode or 0 if there is none, and the actual entry if this is the last letter of an entry. (In practice, the latter would be the address of the record in storage corresponding to the key.) The data structure represented by the table above or by the tree in Figure 10.4 is an abstract entity which contains the data in a manner expressing certain relationships. A structure can be represented in many ways in a computer or on paper. We have shown just two ways for this particular structure.

10.5.3 Binary tree method

The binary search method is inflexible because it is necessary to store the information in order so that the address of any particular entry can be calculated. However, the information is only used in a particular sequence, namely: the middle entry, then the entry ¼ or ¾ of the way up, and so on. If the table were stored so that the middle entry were in a fixed position, and if from that position it was possible to get to either of the next two entries required, and from each of those to their two successors, etc., then it need not be stored in order. This suggests storing two pointers, or chain addresses, with each entry. The search mechanism consists of comparing the desired name with the entry in the fixed position reserved for the middle entry. If the desired name matches, there is nothing further to do. Otherwise, the search continues to

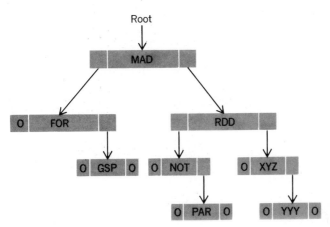

FIGURE 10.5   Binary tree

the entry pointed to by the appropriate one of the two pointers. Let us refer to these as the left pointer for entries that are less than the middle entry and the right pointer for those that are larger. Part of such a table is shown in Figure 10.5. Notice that it is a tree with two branches at every node and nodes labeled by a table entry. Storing the information this way for a binary search has the advantage that it is no longer necessary that the entry at the start (or root) of the table must be the middle entry. Whichever entry is used, it is only necessary that all other entries be to the left or right of it, depending on whether they are smaller or larger than it. Thus, in the figure, MAD is not the middle entry, but the search method would still work. If, for example, we were to look up PAR, we could check it against MAD. Since PAR is larger, we would check with the right-hand neighbor of MAD. PAR is less than RDD, so we would check it against NOT. It is larger, so the right-hand branch is taken, which leads to a match.

The search process can be handled easily with a recursive procedure. Suppose that each element is stored in an array with $N \times 3$ words, each containing a fixed-point number. Let $A[n,1]$ contain the integer representation of the key, $A[n,2]$ the index of the left or lower branch of the tree, and $A[n,3]$ the right or larger branch of the tree. An Algol form of the procedure is

```
procedure    search(A,key,pointer,result); value key,pointer;
             array A; integer key, pointer, result;
             begin if key = A [pointer,1] then result: = pointer;
             else          begin if key < A [pointer,1] then pointer : = A [pointer,2];
                                 else pointer : = A [pointer,3];
                                 if pointer=0 then result : = 0;
                                 else search (A,key,pointer,result);
                           end
end    search
```

The array indices are assumed not to include 0, so that it can be returned as the result if the key is not found. The procedure is called with pointer set to the root of the tree. Although the procedure uses recursion, it could easily be rewritten to avoid it, since it calls itself once at the very end of the procedure.

This method has the advantage that names can be added to the table at any time. If a new name is to be entered, a search process is followed which will finally come to the end of a chain, indicated in the figure by a 0-link address. If the name is found in the search, then it obviously should not be reentered. When the end of a chain is reached, the new entry can be added at that point. This makes the method very suitable for assembler use, if the space for the links is available. It has the additional advantage that it is trivial to print the table in alphabetical order when the time comes. It is not simple to remove a name from the table, since — unless it is the last name in a chain — it is necessary to replace it with another for comparison purposes in searching. If the names entered are in order, then the method is very bad because the tree would be one-sided. It is then as slow as a sequential search, but takes up more space.

10.6 TABLE METHODS SUITED FOR USE IN AN ASSEMBLER

There is no easy answer to the question of what method to use in an assembler. Choice of method will depend on the type of I/O equipment available and its speed relative to the speed of arithmetic, how much main memory is available for the storage, whether it is desirable to restrict symbolic names to a maximum length that is fairly short (six to eight characters), and other factors. If the assembler will be completely input/output limited, then the simplest technique may as well be used. Since the user usually likes to get an alphabetized listing of all names that he defines, the table will have to be sorted at some point, but it can be formed sequentially during pass I and searched sequentially in passes I and II. Unless programs with many names are expected, the simplest form of sequential search for the smallest name, the next-smallest name, and so on could be made during the listing of the name table, so that the list is in alphabetic order. If fast output is available, then the sequential search is not suitable. If the names are of fixed length, a hash addressing technique may prove to be best, but if names are allowed to be arbitrarily long, or effectively so, then a radix-based search using a tree structure is probably the best. It is not difficult to alphabetize such a tree by using a sequential sort on each of the subtables (that is, the sets of subnodes of a given node). If the arithmetic time is very slow compared to the input time, then a binary search should be considered.

An interesting assembly technique that can be used if the main memory available is so small that the name table must be placed on auxiliary storage is as follows. During the first pass, a list of all definitions and uses of names is generated. This list can be written as a file onto an auxiliary storage device. The entries in this list take one of the two forms:

1 Definition — name — value.
2 Usage — name — line number.

The first form is used when a name is defined by appearing in a location field. The second form is used when the name is used in an address field. The line number is the sequential number of the line of code on which the name is defined. At the completion of pass I, the list of names is sorted alphabetically. This brings the definitions and the usages of the same names together. The value of each name is placed in each usage at this time (and an alphabetical usage table giving all names, their values, and where they are used can be listed). Then the name list is re-sorted by line number (the definitions can be discarded). The result is a list of all name usages in the order in which they are used. Pass II consists of rereading the input and reading the name list at the same time. Each time that a name is used in the source, its value is available as the next entry in the name list.

The methods discussed are summarized briefly in Table 10.9.

TABLE 10.9

METHOD	HANDLES ARBITRARILY LARGE NAMES	SPEED	MEMORY REQUIRE-MENTS	CAN NAMES BE REMOVED	CAN NAMES BE LOOKED UP IN PASS 1
Sequential	No	Slow for large N	N spaces	Only if no pointers to the table are in use	Yes
Binary search	No	Fast for large N	N spaces, additional at sort time	No	No (except sequentially)
Hash address	No	Fast if a lot of memory allocated	$K*N$ where K greater than 1	No	Yes
Chained sequential	No	Slowest	Extra space for links	Yes	Yes
Radix tree	Yes	Medium	Usually about $1.25*N$	Yes	Yes
Binary tree	No	Close to binary	N spaces which hold names and two links	Difficult	Yes

PROBLEMS

1   Program a binary search for a table of length N.

2   Program a sequential search for a table of length N.

3   Write a program to build up a table of length N containing the integers 1 through N. Use the programs from questions one and two as subroutines to search, in turn, for each entry in the table. Use the system clock to find the total time for all references in the two cases. Run the program for various values of N (5, 10, 15, etc., stopping when too much computer time has been used) and plot the time of each method as a function of N.

4   Prove that the bubble sort (see Section 10.3.1) cannot take more than $N - 1$ passes for a table of length N.

5   Sketch a graph of the way in which the merge time for a P-way merge of a large file depends on P. Show the compute time and the I/O time separately. If I/O and compute are overlapped, indicate what P would be optimum. If I/O and compute are sequential rather than overlapped, what P is optimum based on the sketch?

6   Design a representation of a data structure similar to that in Figure 10.4 for internal computer storage. Assume that single words are to be used in the computer as elements in a table, and that each word contains a number of addresses. These addresses may be pointers to other table entries, to information to be stored, to individual letters, or they may be null. It is possible for the program to tell by the size of the address which is which. Perform the design in the three different cases where a computer word can contain (a) four addresses, (b) three addresses, or (c) two addresses.

7   Write a recursive subroutine which will make a new entry in the binary tree described in Section 10.5.3.

8   Rewrite the search program in Section 10.5.3 so that it is iterative rather than recursive.

11

AN INTRODUCTION TO COMPILING TECHNIQUES

The purpose of this chapter is to introduce the two basic methods of compiling, the bottom-up and the top-down methods, to indicate some of the problems that have to be tackled, and to whet the student's appetite for further reading. Two languages, Fortran and Algol, will be used as examples in the discussion below because, between them, they illustrate many of the problems that are present in compilers. It is not necessary that the reader be familiar with either language in detail. The presentation will not be complete because these notes are intended as steppingstones to more advanced work rather than as recipes for a cookbook compiler. To pursue the subject further, the student should consult the references below.†

11.1 FORMAT OF THE INPUT STRING

In most artificial languages (that is, languages designed for communication with a machine), the input to the compiler is a string of characters, perhaps from paper tape or punched cards. We can think of punched cards as being read, a character at a time, from left to right, so that there is no essential difference between punched cards and paper tape. If we are interested in lines of information, then we can assign a particular character on paper tape to correspond to the card boundary that occurs every 80 characters. This could be the carriage return, for example. Thus, whether we wish to consider the input as a string of characters or as a sequence of lines, there is no essential difference between paper tape and punched cards. However, compilers that were historically developed for card-oriented machines, such as Fortran for the IBM machines, tend to use card boundaries and fixed fields within cards as a part of the language, whereas languages developed by groups with a bias toward paper tape tend to ignore line boundaries and to use no fixed fields. An example of the latter is Algol. In Fortran, the first five columns are given over to a statement number and cannot be used for any other purposes except comments, which, in a sense, are not part of the language. In Algol, a statement without a label can start in the first character of the line. If a statement label is used, it is typed first, followed by a colon. The following Fortran and Algol codes are similar:

Fortran
```
        GO TO 17
    17  A = B
```

---

† D. Gries, "Compiler Construction for Digital Computers," John Wiley & Sons, Inc., New York, 1971, is a good textbook, while the following article is a survey and bibliography:
J. A. Feldman and D. Gries, Translator Writing Systems, *Communications of the Association for Computing Machinery*, vol. 11, pp. 77–113, February 1968.

Algol
          goto   L17; L17: A:= B;

Separate lines are not necessary for the Algol code, since the semicolon acts as a statement separator. Since L17 is also a valid variable name in Algol, it is not possible to determine whether the first three characters of the statement L17: A . . ., belong to a label or to a variable name until the colon has been read. In the Fortran code, the existence of a label can be determined by checking the first five columns of a card. This does not present a problem in compilation, but it does point up a possible difference in approach. In Fortran compilers, a number of problems can be solved by using the format of the input. Statement numbers can be detected and the range of a statement can be found by looking at card boundaries and continuation marks only. In Algol, it is necessary to examine the surrounding structure of the input to determine the meaning of all of the input. Statement labels can only be located at the beginning of a statement by looking for a following colon, and the end of a statement can only be detected by looking for an **end** or a semicolon in an appropriate position.

The fact that a Fortran program can easily be split into a sequence of statements whereas Algol can contain compound statements that are groups of statements has other effects on the type of compiler most suited to the job. A Fortran compiler usually contains an input section which reads one complete statement into a suitable buffer area, a section that determines the type of statement involved, a section that handles the statement number if there is one, and sections that compile object code for each possible type of statement. Consider, on the other hand, the Algol program section

```
begin real a real array, b[1:10]
for i := 1 step 1 until 10 do
               begin real array a [1:10];
               b[i] := i;
               . . . . . . . . . . . . . . . . . .;
               . . . . . . . . . . . . . . . . . .;
               end
    a := 3.5;
    . . . . . . . . . . . . . . .;
    end
```

The second "statement" in this program extends down to the first **end** because the block of program between the **begin** following the **do** and its matching **end** constitutes a single compound statement as far as the **for** statement is concerned. This means that if an error which causes the first **end** to be missed occurs, then the **for** statement will be extended down to the last **end** shown. In addition to extending the range of the **for** statement beyond the intended **end**, it can cause many apparent errors to be caught by a compiler. For example, the last assignment statement "a : = 3.5;" will be marked as an error because the variable "a" is used as an array name in the inner block, which was not terminated, but as a simple variable name in the outer block. This type of error will be propagated through the rest of the program because there will continue to be one **end** missing.

It is true that this type of error can occur in Fortran. A missing dimension statement, for example, could cause the statement "A(I) = I*I" to be interpreted as a function-definition statement, but the language is not as prone to such misconstructions. Because of this difference of degree rather than of kind, it is not as practical for Algol to have an input scanner to break up the string into separate statements identified as to type and then to pass control to a statement translator. A translator for Algol will be more continuous in nature. We shall see that this does not complicate the compiler particularly, but it is simpler to restrict ourselves initially to single statements under the assumption that the statement recognition has already been taken care of.

11.1.1 Key words and reserved words

The Algol example above contains two types of statements: those that start with a special word, such as **begin, end,** etc., and the arithmetic assignment statements such as "a[i]: = i;". The definition of Algol requires that words such as **begin** be special single characters. The lack of such characters on most card and paper-tape punches forces an implemented form of the language to use the usual alphabetic characters and either surround them by suitable characters to delimit the word or to *reserve* the word so that it cannot be used as an identifier by the programmer. These words are called *reserved words.* Words which determine statement type are called *key words* because they provide an immediate key to the statement type. Some Algol compilers use quotes around the key words, which are punched using the available upper case character set so that they appear as 'BEGIN,' 'END,' 'GOTO,' 'FOR,' etc., while others use reserved words and do not require the quotes. If reserved words are used, then the programmer must be careful in his naming of identifiers. The Algol statement

FOR I:=L STEP 1 UNTIL K DO GOTO M;

is a valid if stupid **for** loop. It is also an assignment statement placing the value of the variable "LSTEP1UNTILKDOGOTOM" into the variable "FORI" after blanks have been ignored. Fortran and Algol ignore blanks, PL/I does not. A user should not have to know about those features of a computer or language that he does not need, so it is undesirable for a language to have reserved words that the user must know before he can write any programs.

Although Fortran uses key words to determine statement type, and these words are not distinguishable from identifier names as they stand (unless they are longer than six characters), Fortran does not use reserved words. The structure of the overall statement makes the use clear. Thus

DO 1 I = 1,2

is a DO statement, whereas

DO 1 I = 1.2

is an arithmetic assignment statement.

FORMAT(6H) = S(IH)

is a FORMAT statement, whereas

FORMAT(IH) = S(IH)

is either an arithmetic assignment statement or a function definition, depending on its position in the program and whether a variable called FORMAT has been dimensioned.

Unfortunately, the differentiation between the different statements represented above is tedious, so a number of Fortran translators do use reserved words, preventing the programmer from dimensioning a variable named FORMAT, etc. If this is done, the recognition of different statement types is easy—as it is in Algol, where the key word can be recognized immediately.

Many statements that start with key words have a very restricted format and can be handled in a simple scan, one element at a time. An example of such a statement is the Fortran dimension statement. As each variable name is read, it can be entered in a table, and the corresponding size of the array can be stored with it. It presents no greater problems than the handling of the address field of an assembly-language instruction. Other statements, such as assignment statements, have a very free format and appear to present the most complex problems to the neophyte programmer. In fact, problems concerning memory allocation and subroutine parameter handling at execution time are among the more difficult parts of a compiler. These will be discussed briefly in Section 11.4 after we have studied the two main methods for recognizing the structure of the input string of characters.

11.2 BOTTOM-UP METHODS

These form the class of methods which consist of taking the input string, saying "I have no idea what this string of characters is," and attempting to put the characters together, one at a time, to find out what each part of the string represents. This is contrasted with the top-down methods, to be discussed in the next section, which start by saying "This string is going to be a *****" and then examining each character to attempt to form a "*****". The two methods could be applied to the assignment statement "AB = CD + E" in the following way:

Bottom up:

"A is a letter, B is a letter. A letter followed by a letter is a variable name.
C is a letter, D is a letter. A letter followed by a letter is a variable name.
E is a letter. A letter is a variable name.
A variable plus a variable is an expression.
A variable followed by an equal sign followed by an expression is an assignment statement. So we have an assignment statement."

Top down:

"This string is going to be an assignment statement (we think).

An assignment statement is a variable followed by an equal sign followed by an expression, therefore we need a variable.

A variable starts with a letter, so let's look for a letter.

A is a letter, so we are in good shape. A variable can continue with letters or digits. B is a letter, so AB is a variable. It can still continue with a letter or a digit. The next character " = " is neither, so the variable is AB. We now have the variable at the start of the assignment statement. We need an equal sign. This we have, so we now need an expression. An expression should start with a variable . . . a similar process finds that CD is a variable . . . It can contain a plus sign and another variable . . . a similar process locates the plus sign and the variable E . . . Thus we have an assignment statement."

There are many forms of bottom-up methods. Each involves the process of scanning the input string, a character at a time, trying to combine the new character with previously scanned characters to form more complex combinations. A form of bottom-up analysis was used in Section 9.1.2 in order to compute the value of address field expressions in an assembler language. That method, known as the *operator precedence* method, will be expanded to handle assignment statements. Precedence methods rely on the fact that certain of the characters can be recognized as operators and that consequently the other elements of the input can be recognized as operands. A precedence relationship, or hierarchy, between the operators enables the program to decide which operator should be compiled first. Fortunately, most algebraic languages have the property that operator precedence methods can be used, at least for the majority of their statement types. They are often the fastest methods of compiling arithmetic assignment statements.†

---

†Some of the basic ideas in this method were first presented by Samelson and Bauer, Sequential Formula Translation, *Communications of the Associa-*

The precedence methods use the ability to distinguish operands and operators. Conditions that a language must satisfy to make this possible are discussed in the Floyd paper cited above. In these notes, we are not concerned with general languages but with specific examples such as Fortran and Algol. It is evident that we can recognize operators and operands by a simple character scan of the input string, as was done in the assembler. From now on, we shall assume that a front-end subroutine will process the input and break it up into *tokens*, each token being either an operator or operand. If the operand is a constant, then it can be converted into binary; if it is a name, then it can be placed in an appropriate table. Name tables will require bits of information to indicate whether the name represents a simple variable, an array, or a subroutine, and whether it is real, complex, integer, etc. These entries can be made when the variable is first defined or used, and all occurrences of the name can be replaced by pointers to the table entry. Thus, by the time the detailed analysis of the statement starts, it has been converted from a character string to a more easily manageable string of tokens which can be represented in a convenient internal form.

11.2.1 Compilation of stack machine code

One of the principal reasons for our interest in stack machine code is that it can be easily compiled. Consider the problem of processing the input string of tokens, one at a time, in order to obtain a stack code. An expression such as A + B can compile as

```
LOAD        A
LOAD        B
ADD
```

In other words, the occurrence of operands causes a LOAD instruction to be compiled, and then the operation is compiled as the equivalent instruction. A + B*C can compile as

```
LOAD        A
LOAD        B
LOAD        C
MPY
ADD
```

---

tion for Computing Machines, vol. 3, no. 2, February 1960, while the idea of operator precedence methods for general languages was first explored by Floyd, Syntactic Analysis and Operator Precedence, *Journal of the Association for Computing Machines*, vol. 10, no. 3, pp. 316–333, July 1963.

The operands cause LOAD instructions to be compiled, while the operators cause arithmetic instructions to be compiled "as soon as they can be performed." This can be determined by a precedence technique similar to the one used in Chapter 9. As each operator is read from the input string, it can be compared with the last one not yet compiled. Thus, when the * (asterisk) is read, it is compared with the preceding + (plus) operator. Since * (asterisk) is "more important," that is, has a greater *precedence,* the plus is not yet compiled. The scan continues until the end of the statement, which is treated as an operator of low precedence, is recognized. This causes the multiply

TABLE 11.1

OPERATOR	PRECEDENCE IN INPUT	PRECEDENCE IN STACK
Beginning of string	0	0
End of string	0	Not possible
+ or −	2	2
* or /	3	3
**(single token)	4	4
(	5	1
)	1	Not possible

and then the add to be compiled. A precedence table can be constructed as was done in Chapter 9. We shall construct one for the common arithmetic operators and parentheses only, but any other allowed operators, such as the logical operators in Algol, can be added. In order to facilitate the testing of the operators, it is easiest to place them in a stack at compile time and to compare the top of the stack with the input operator. The rule used is similar to that used in Chapter 9. The next input token is examined. If it is an operand, it is compiled into a LOAD instruction. If it is an operator, its value is compared with the value of the top of the stack. (Initially the stack has no value, so that the beginning of the string can be entered immediately.) If the value in the stack is at least as high, it is compiled. If the input value is higher, it is placed into the stack. (Note that the value of the "(" token changes in this step.) When a "(" token is compiled, no code is generated, but the corresponding ")" in the input stream is removed. If there is none, then there is an error. A flowchart for this process is shown in Figure 11.1. This chart assumes that the input is syntactically correct. It does not, for example, detect an error which is due to two arithmetic operators next to each other.

Other elements in the language can be handled in a similar way, but we shall leave this as an exercise for the reader and examine problems that arise if the object code is for other than a stack machine. Note that there are two stacks: the execution stack, which is the accumulator stack of the machine used for operands at execution time; and the compile stack, which holds the operators not yet compiled at compile time.

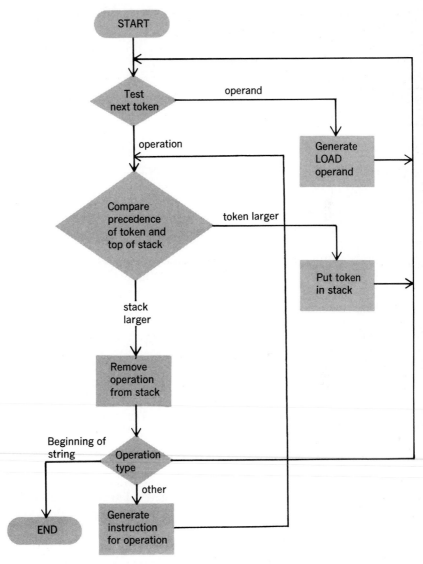

FIGURE 11.1 *Generating stack-machine code from tokens*

11.2.2 **Compilation of one-, two-, and three-address code**

The simplest way to handle other machine structures is to simulate the arithmetic stack in the machine. This can be done by setting aside an area of main memory to represent the stack. The bottom of the stack can be placed in location S, the next entry in location S + 1, and so on. Unfortunately, this leads to inefficient code, as can be seen from the one-address code to calculate A*B + C*D:

```
LOAD       A
STORE      S
LOAD       B
STORE      S+1
LOAD       S+1
MPY        S
STORE      S
LOAD       C
STORE      S+1
LOAD       D
STORE      S+2
LOAD       S+2
MPY        S+1
ADD        S
STORE      S
```

In two- or three-address code, each LOAD, STORE sequence can be replaced by a move, and each LOAD, Operation, STORE sequence by an arithmetic operation. Unfortunately, this is inefficient code for a number of reasons. Some of the inefficiencies of the one-address code can be removed by avoiding redundant sequences such as STORE S + 1, LOAD S + 1, but there is still a lot of inefficiency compared to the shortest code

```
LOAD       A
MPY        B
STORE      S
LOAD       C
MPY        D
ADD        S
```

This object code can be achieved by returning to the method used in Chapter 9. There, the compile stack stored both the operations and the operands. In the method above, only the operations were put in the compile stack, while the operands were assumed to be available in the accumulator stack. If the operands are kept in the compile stack, then their locations in memory rather than their values must be recorded, since the latter are not available at compile time. This can be illustrated by the following example: Compile A * B + C into code which will calculate its value in the accumulator of a one-address machine. Successive contents of the input and stack are shown below. The top of the stack is on the left. The generated code is also shown.

Input A * B + C | ("|" means beginning or end of string.)
Stack |
Code
Input * B + C |
Stack | A

Code
Input B + C |
Stack | A *
Code
Input + C |
Stack | A * B   + has lower precedence than *, so compile the * as LOAD
Code   A, MPY B.
Input + C |
Stack | Δ   Δ stands for the contents of the accumulator.
Code LOAD A
     MPY B
Input C |
Stack | Δ +
Code LOAD A
     MPY B
Input |
Stack |Δ + C | has lower precedence than +, so compile + as ADD C.
Code LOAD A
     MPY B
Input |
Stack | Δ
Code LOAD A
     MPY B
     ADD C

The beginning and the end of string atoms now cancel each other out, and we
see that code to calculate the desired value in the accumulator has been
generated. This method will break down if more than one use is made of the
accumulator. Consider the expression A * B + (C + D) * (E + F). The translator described above would generate

LOAD	A
MPY	B
LOAD	C
ADD	D
LOAD	E
ADD	F

and then it would not know how to handle the multiplication of the contents
of the accumulator by the accumulator. The first error was committed when
the LOAD C was performed without first saving the contents of the accumulator. Each time that a new LOAD instruction is generated, the current contents of the accumulator must be saved. This can be done by simulating an
execution stack in a temporary storage region. Suppose it is in locations S,
S + 1, etc. A count of the number of uses of the accumulator can be kept.
Each time that a LOAD is to be compiled, this counter can be increased by 1
and a STORE into the appropriate location in the stack can be compiled
before the LOAD. (This can be omitted for the first use of the accumulator.)

When two operands are indicated as being in the accumulator, the compiler knows that the first must be in the top level of the stack. It can use it from there and reduce the count by 1. The steps in the process are shown in the example below. (Intermediate results from steps that only copy from the input to the stack have been omitted.)

Input A * B + (C + D) * (E + F) |
Stack |
Count 0

Input + (C + D) * (E + F) |
Stack | A * B
Count 0   Compile LOAD A, MPY B. Add 1 to count.

Input + (C + D) * (E + F) |
Stack | Δ
Count 1

Input) * (E + F) |
Stack | Δ + (C + D
Count 1   Compile STORE S (= S + count − 1)
                                         since count > 0, LOAD C, ADD D.
                                         Add 1 to count.

Input) *(E + F) |
Stack | Δ + (Δ
Count 2   "Compile" (, resulting in an input)
                                         being removed.

Input * (E + F) |
Stack | Δ + Δ
Count 2

Input) |
Stack |Δ + Δ * (E + F
Count 2   Compile STORE S + 1 (= S + count −
                                         1) LOAD E, ADD F. Add 1 to count.

Input) |
Stack | Δ + Δ * (Δ
Count 3   "Compile" (.

Input |
Stack | Δ + Δ * Δ
Count 3   Since both operands are in the accu-
                       mulator, reduce count by 1 and compile
                       MPY S + 1 (= S + count − 1).

Input |
Stack | Δ + Δ
Count 2   Since both operands are in the accu-
                       mulator, reduce count by 1 and compile
                       ADD S (= S + count − 1).

Input |
Stack | Δ
Count 1   Now the result is in the accumulator.

Similar techniques can be developed for two- and three-address code. These are left as exercises for the reader.

We have not discussed how more difficult aspects of the object code are handled. How, for example, indexing or subroutine calls should be compiled. The methods discussed above can be extended to recognize the use of subscripts, subroutines, etc., in a simple way. The manner in which the object code should be produced depends on the efficiency of object code desired. Should, for example, index registers in the machine be used by the object program? Some compilers, usually those that are very fast at translation, will not make much use of special registers in the machine in order to have a simple compiler. Expressions used as indices can be evaluated, using the regular arithmetic instructions, and then placed into an index register or a memory location and used to fetch the desired value from memory by indexing or indirect addressing. Other translators, typically much slower at the translation task, spend a lot of time compiling object code which will make the best use of the hardware facilities of the machine.

The resulting code is usually considerably more efficient with the latter translators than the former. The methods used depend very much on the particular hardware configuration and will not be discussed here.

11.3 TOP-DOWN METHODS

Top-down methods use an approach in which the program attempts to find strings of characters in the input that satisfy the form that it thinks the input should take. If it is unsuccessful, then it will try for some other form. Thus, in looking at the total input that is supposed to be a program, it might first try to find an assignment statement at the start of the string. If it is unsuccessful there, it could next try for a DO statement (if the language is Fortran). Eventually it will either find a recognizable statement or the input is not a Fortran program, which must begin with a valid Fortran statement. It is necessary that we be able to state clearly the types of inputs that are permitted, so we shall first examine a way of defining formally the various correct input strings and then look at a simple way of building a program that will recognize correct strings and cause code to be compiled.

11.3.1 The Backus Normal Form definition of a language

It is desirable to be able to say precisely what are correct statements in an artificial language such as Fortran or Algol. Fortran is usually specified by listing each of the allowable statements in a table. Such a technique is adequate for statements such as GO TO. When arithmetic assignment statements are defined, most Fortran manuals will content themselves with the comment that they must be of the form $A = E$ where A is a variable name and E is an expression composed of variables and constants and $+$, $-$, $*$, $/$, $**$, $($, and $)$.

This definition of an expression appeals to our understanding of the meaning and form of expressions that we use every day, which is fine for teaching purposes; but it is of no value for describing to, say, a computer what is a correct expression, or for telling a person about a new artificial language. The Backus notation was first introduced for describing Algol in a formal manner. It is a notation that is suited to describing what might be called free-format languages, that is, ones in which such fixed-format ideas as card columns play no role. It is not, therefore, the best notation in which to describe Fortran, but it will be illustrated by describing familiar Fortran arithmetic assignment statements in *Backus Normal Form,* or *BNF.*

The Backus notation is a language which itself consists of statements which describe the way in which the source language (Fortran) may be written. To avoid confusion, the Backus language is called a *meta language;* it uses characters other than those used in the language being described. For example, in Fortran an arithmetic assignment statement is of the form *variable* followed by an = sign followed by an *expression.* This is written as < arithmetic assignment statement > :: = < variable > = < expression > . The characters < > and :: = are characters in the *meta language.* < and > are to be interpreted as a pair of parentheses surrounding a word in the meta language. The word represents a *phrase class name;* that is, it stands for a set of entities in the source language. Thus < variable > represent the class of all variables, in this case, in Fortran, while < expression > represents the class of all expressions. These have yet to be defined formally. Once they have, then the meta language statement above defines formally the class of all arithmetic assignment statements. It should be read as "any member of the class of 'arithmetic assignment statements' is of the form member of the class 'variable' followed by = followed by a member of the class 'expression.'" Any string of characters in the described language that satisfies this form may be an arithmetic assignment statement.

It may be necessary to express the fact that a particular phrase class can be formed in more than one way. For example, the variable above could be an identifier by itself (for example, ALPHA) or it could be an indexed variable. This is expressed either by use of the meta-language character | meaning "or" or by writing down both possibilities in separate meta statements. Thus, if the phrase classes < identifier > and < indexed variable > have been defined, variable can be defined either by

< variable > :: = < identifier > | < indexed variable >

or by

< variable > :: = < identifier >
< variable > :: = < indexed variable >

It might seem that in this way each class could be defined in terms of "smaller" classes until at some final point the classes are defined in terms of characters in the language being defined (Fortran). Consider Fortran identifiers. On many computers these can consist of six characters; the first must be a letter and the remaining may be letters or digits. Thus we could write

$<$ letter $>$ :: $=$ AlBlClDlElFlGlHlIlJlKlLlMlNlOlPlQlRlSlTlUlVlWlXlYlZ

$<$ digit $>$ :: $=$ 0l1l2l3l4l5l6l7l8l9l

$<$alphanum$>$:: $=$ $<$letter$>$ l $<$digit$>$

$<$ identifier $>$ :: $=$ $<$ letter $>$ l $<$ letter $>$ $<$ alphanum $>$ l $<$ letter $>$
                                  $<$ alphanum $>$ $<$ alphanum $>$ l
        $<$ letter $>$ $<$ alphanum $>$ $<$ alphanum $>$ $<$ alphanum $>$ l
        $<$ letter $>$ $<$ alphanum $>$ $<$ alphanum $>$ $<$ alphanum $>$
                                    $<$ alphanum $>$ l
        $<$ letter $>$ $<$ alphanum $>$ $<$ alphanum $>$ $<$ alphanum $>$
                                    $<$ alphanum $>$ $<$ alphanum $>$

Not a very convenient definition, and one which can certainly be expressed more concisely in English! If 8 or 10 character identifers were allowed, it would be even less pleasant. It happens that the Backus notation is not well adapted to describing languages in which restrictions such as "a maximum of six characters can be used for an identifier" appear, just as it is not useful for handling fixed-format characters. In Algol, however, identifiers may be of any length (although some translators restrict the user to six or eight to gain efficiency). A formal description of identifiers of any length cannot be achieved by writing down all cases! To get around this problem, *recursive definition* is used. This means that the definition may define something partly in terms of itself. As long as this does not involve an infinite loop, it is satisfactory. For example, Algol identifiers must also start with a letter and can contain letters and digits subsequently. Thus, if we have formed any legitimate identifier, we can form another by adding on any letter or digit, that is, any member of the class $<$ alphanum $>$. Therefore, together with the definitions of $<$ letter $>$, $<$ digit $>$, and $<$ alphanum $>$ above, an Algol identifier can be defined by

$<$ identifier $>$ :: $=$ $<$ letter $>$ l $<$ identifier $>$ $<$ alphanum $>$

That is to say, a letter is an identifier, and so is any identifier formed by following a shorter identifier with an alphanumeric character.

If we wish to know if A6Y is an identifier, then the steps are:

A is a letter and a letter is an identifier;

6 is a digit and a digit is an alphanum, A is an identifier and an identifier followed by an alphanum is an identifier, so that A6 is an identifier;

Y is a letter and a letter is an alphanum, A6 is an identifier and an identifier followed by an alphanum is an identifier, so A6Y is an identifier.

This can be illustrated graphically by the tree structure

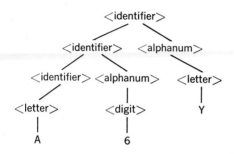

Terminal nodes of this tree are characters in the language; read from left to right they are as they appear in the source string. Nonterminal nodes are phrase class names such as letter, identifier, etc. The neighbors below them on the tree (those nodes connected by branches) correspond to one set of elements used on the right-hand side of the definition of the phrase class name. Thus, identifier appears with two subsidiary neighbors when it is defined as <identifier> <alphanum>;; it also appears with one subsidiary neighbor when it is defined as < letter >.

This breakdown into the structural form is called *parsing.* It is similar to the parsing that is done in natural languages such as English. Thus in English, we say that a sentence can be constructed as subject followed by a verb followed by its object, for example:

<sentence>	:: =	<subject> <verb> <> object>
<subject>	:: =	<definite article> <noun>
<object>	:: =	<definite article> <noun>
<verb>	:: =	throws
<noun>	:: =	boy I ball
<definite article>	:: =	the

Thus the sentence "the boy throws the ball" could be parsed in the tree form

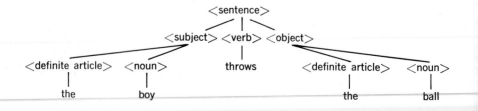

From this example, it is obvious that meaningless sentences can be constructed. For example, "the ball throws the boy" also parses. The formal description only deals with the structure of the language, not its meaning. In the same way it is possible to write quite reasonable Fortran statements that are illegal because of their meaning but are structurally sound. For example, A (15) = 34.1 is incorrect if A has not been appropriately dimensioned. We are only able to describe the structure, or *syntax,* of the language with BNF. The meaning, or *semantics,* must be described separately.

We would like to be able to define all correct statements in this formal manner. To simplify the discussion, we shall ignore indexing, subroutine calls, etc., and just concentrate on the expression on the right-hand side of an assignment statement.

An expression such as A * B — C/D should break down into a form that shows the multiplys and divides being performed before the minus. That is, it should have the general form

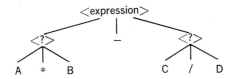

Therefore, the multiplication and division operators should combine in a parse first. Let us call the items that can take part in a multiplication or division *factors* as a phrase class name. We note that a factor can certainly be an identifier or a constant, so we can write

< factor > :: = < variable > | < constant >

We shall not further define constant. A number of factors can be multiplied together to form a more complex grouping. Let us call this a *term.* We could define

<term> :: = <factor> * <factor> | <factor> / <factor>

Unfortunately, this only allows for one multiplication or division. We could have a series of several. For example, A / B * C. Again, note that the A / B should be grouped first, since the value is formed by performing operators with equal precedence from left to right. Thus we should write

< term > :: = < term > * < factor > | < term > / < factor >

This defines term in terms of itself, just as identifier was defined recursively. As long as term is also defined as a factor by itself, this is acceptable. Thus we have as a final definition of term

< term > :: = < factor > | < term > * < factor > | < term > / < factor >

This means that the parse of A * B / C * D is

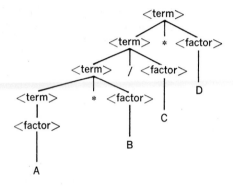

Now that we have defined the more complex group term, we can use it with the addition and subtraction operators to form expressions. By reasoning similar to that above, we write expression as

<expression> :: = <term> | <expression>
                    + <term> | <expression> − <term>

This omits a possible form of expression. Whereas * (asterisk) and / (slash) are always binary operations with two operands, + (plus) and − (minus) can be used as unary operations. For example, −A is an expression. We therefore must modify expression to read

< expression > :: = < term > |+ < term > |− < term > | < expression >
                    + < term > | < expression > − < term >

With these definitions, the expression A * B + DE can be parsed as

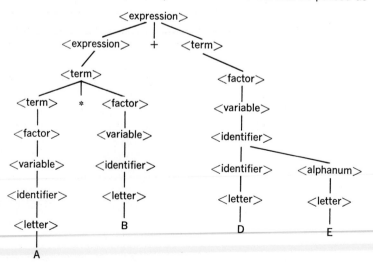

Now parentheses must be introduced. The purpose of parentheses is to override the implicit precedence of operators by an explicit statement of the order of evaluation and hence the order of parsing. Parentheses can be placed around any legitimate expression and its value can then be used as one operand at any of the binary operations. Thus we should include a parenthesized expression as one of the class factor by the definition

< factor > :: = < variable > | < constant > |(< expression >)

The expression A * (B + C) can then be parsed as

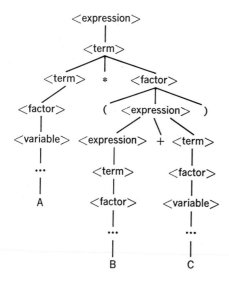

The definitions given above allow any expression containing arbitrary-length identifiers and the operators +, —, *, /, (, and) to be formed. It can readily be extended to allow the additional operators found in Fortran or Algol so as to provide a complete formal description of all strings of characters that are valid structurally, although possibly not meaningful.

The structure of Algol has been specified in just this manner in the standard description.†

11.3.2 Syntax-directed compilation

Earlier sections of this chapter discussed techniques for scanning the source language input in order to recognize the type of statement and structure

† See P. Naur et al., Revised Algol Report, *Communications of the Association for Computing Machinery*, vol. 6, no. 1, January 1963.

of that statement and to translate it into a lower-level language. Although the ideas used are conceptually simple, there is ample room for error in coding such techniques. Further, it is often desirable to make changes in the source language that can have considerable effect on the compiler. For this reason, a number of people have written compilers that work directly from formal descriptions of the source language. Such compilers can be loosely categorized into two classes:

1 Syntax-directed compilers. Syntax-directed compilers are those that are written by the programmer but have an obvious relationship with a formal syntax description such as the Backus Normal Form. This means that changes in the description are easily integrated into the compiler.
2 Compiler-compilers. The compiler that translates the source language into the object language is "written" by a compiler-compiler; that is, it is produced automatically from a formal description of the structure or syntax and a description of the meaning or semantics. Unfortunately, there does not yet exist any good formal way of describing the latter, so a number of different compiler-compilers exist, each with their own forms of description.

This section will examine the first type of compiler, the syntax-directed compiler. The next section will give a quick review of the extension to the semantic problem.

Let us first ignore the problem of translation into object code and deal with the question of the syntactical structure. Given an input string of characters, we wish to find out if it is a legitimate string and what structure it has; that is, we wish to construct a *syntax recognizer*.

Suppose that there already exist subroutines which will recognize some of the phrase classes in the language; for example, suppose the subroutines VARIABLE, EQUAL, and EXPRESSION recognize the class <variable>, the character =, and the class <expression> respectively. It should then be possible to use these to construct another subroutine to recognize the class <assignment statement> as:

```
ASSIGNMENT STATEMENT   CALL     VARIABLE
                       CALL     EQUAL
                       CALL     EXPRESSION
                       RETURN
```

(In practice, symbolic names must be reduced to an appropriate length!) If the three subroutines are *successful,* that is, if they recognize the appropriate quantities, then the assignment statement subroutine is successful; that is, it has recognized an assignment statement.

Let us be a little more precise about what is going on. Suppose that the source input string is in some available place such as core memory and that there is a pointer, p, which is pointing at the next character to be processed. Then the subroutines should move this pointer as they recognize sections of the language. Thus, when EQUAL is called and the pointer is in fact pointing at an equal sign, it should be moved on to the next character because EQUAL has been successful. What should happen if it is not pointing at an equal sign? Let us examine another case. In the last section, < variable > was defined as:

< variable > :: = < indexed variable > | < identifier >

In this case, <variable> should be recognized if either <indexed variable> or <identifier> is recognized. Suppose that <indexed variable> is called first and not recognized. In that case, the pointer p should be pointing to the same position as it was on entry to INDEXED VARIABLE, so that IDENTIFIER can be used. Also, it is necessary to distinguish between the *successful* and *unsuccessful* cases on exit from the subroutine. Let us provide a parameter for the unsuccessful exit, and, to save writing, drop the CALL mnemonic and use the subroutine name as the mnemonic below. Thus the recognizer for the class <variable> could take the form:

```
VARIABLE    ENTER
            INDEXED-VARIABLE   EXIT1
            RETURN
EXIT1       IDENTIFIER         EXIT2
            RETURN
EXIT2       ERROR
```

The mnemonic ENTER stands for a piece of program that performs those functions necessary to save registers at the start of a subroutine, *including* the pointer p. RETURN restores the registers *except* for the pointer p, since it is to be moved ahead. EXIT1 is a parameter for the subroutine INDEXED-VARIABLE, such that if the subroutine is unsuccessful, a branch to EXIT1 occurs. Similarly, if IDENTIFIER is unsuccessful, a branch to EXIT2 occurs. In this case, the subroutine VARIABLE has been unsuccessful (the characters do not represent either of the possibilities allowed for <variable>), so the return should be to the parameter supplied by the call on VARIABLE with the pointer p moved back to its position on entry to VARIABLE. The mnemonic ERROR stands for a piece of program that will do just that.

<Indexed variable> was not defined in the last section, but it can be defined as

<indexed variable> :: = <identifier> (<expression sequence>)
<expression sequence> :: = <expression> | <expression sequence> ,
                                                            <expression>

This raises two problems. The first arises because one possibility for <variable> is the beginning of another. Suppose that the program had been written as:

```
VARIABLE    ENTER
            IDENTIFIER           EXIT1
            RETURN
EXIT1       INDEXED-VARIABLE  EXIT2
            RETURN
EXIT2       ERROR
```

If the string AB(I) = C is scanned by this program, AB is successfully recognized by IDENTIFIER, so VARIABLE is successful. This returns to ASSIGN-
MENT STATEMENT, which tests for =. The next character is (, so EQUAL fails,
causing ASSIGNMENT STATEMENT to fail incorrectly and indicating that
AB(I) = C is not an assignment statement. There are two ways around this
problem:

1 The one used above (looking for the longer form first)
2 Combining the recognition of <identifier> by effectively writing

<variable> :: = <identifier> <index> | <identifier>
<index>   :: = (<expression   sequence>)

as

```
VARIABLE    ENTER
            IDENTIFIER    EXIT1
            INDEX         EXIT2
EXIT2       RETURN
EXIT1       ERROR
```

Whether or not <index> is recognized, the string has a valid identifier if
IDENTIFIER is successful. (Note that this method is faster for nonindexed
variables, since <identifier> only has to be recognized once.) It corresponds
to a BNF form

<variable> :: = <identifier> <trailer>
<trailer> :: = <index> |

The second problem is more serious. In its simplest form it can be seen in the
Backus form:

<expression sequence> = ◄ expression> | <expression sequence> ,
                                          < expression>.

Suppose this is "recognized" by the subroutine:

```
EXPSEQ      ENTER
            EXPRESSION  EXIT1
            RETURN
EXIT1       EXPSEQ        EXIT2
            COMMA         EXIT2
            EXPRESSION   EXIT2
            RETURN
EXIT2       ERROR
```

then the problem mentioned above arises; namely, that an <expression sequence> always starts with an <expression>, hence the comma is never read in the expression sequence program. If the order is reversed to be:

```
EXPSEQ      ENTER
            EXPSEQ      EXIT1
            COMMA       EXIT2
            EXPRESSION  EXIT2
            RETURN
EXIT1       EXPRESSION  EXIT2
            RETURN
EXIT2       ERROR
```

then chaos will result. First, note that all these subroutines will have to be recursive, so that recursive calling is not wrong per se, but it is wrong in this case since *no other element* is recognized first. Thus <expression sequence> is recognized if an <expression sequence> is recognized . . . ad infinitum. This problem arises whenever a phrase class is defined in such a way that it can start with a member of that same phrase class. The phenomenon that is causing this problem is known as *left recursion* and will cause trouble whenever a recursive approach is used.

The recursive approach in the syntax recognition problem is called the "top-down" approach because the top of the syntax tree is checked first. The alternative is the "bottom-up" approach or iterative method. This is essentially the method that was used intuitively in the "control-stack" method in a previous section. Left recursion does not cause a problem in an iterative method when the recognition technique corresponds to the sequence of questions:

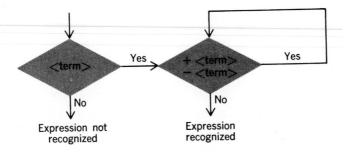

The iterative method can be combined with the top-down or recursive approach in the definition and subroutine for expression:

<expression> :: = <expression> < ± term> | <term>
< ± term> :: = + <term> | <term>

```
EXPRESSION  ENTER
            TERM        ERROR
```

LOOP	± TERM	RETURN	
	BRANCH	LOOP	(Regular branch order)
± TERM	ENTER		
	PLUS	M	
C	TERM	ERROR	
	RETURN		
M	MINUS	ERROR	
	BRANCH	C	

ERROR and RETURN have been used in the address field, meaning that a branch to a program which will cause the action to occur.

The sequence of subroutine calls for A — B + C are as shown below. Entering a subroutine is indicated by moving right, returning by moving left.

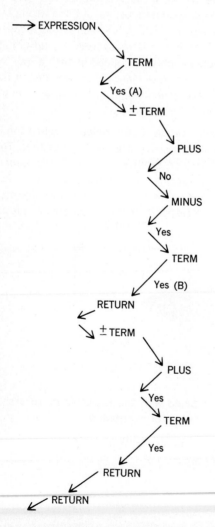

giving

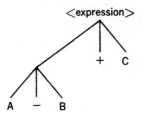

Thus to recognize the various forms of assignment statements formally described in the last section we can use the collection of programs:

```
ASSIGNMENT-STATEMENT    ENTER
                        VARIABLE            ERROR
                        EQUAL               ERROR
                        EXPRESSION          ERROR
                        RETURN
VARIABLE                ENTER
                        IDENTIFIER          ERROR
                        INDEX               RETURN
                        RETURN
INDEX                   ENTER
                        LEFT-PARENTHESIS    ERROR
                        EXPSEQ              ERROR
                        RIGHT-PARENTHESIS   ERROR
                        RETURN
EXPSEQ                  ENTER
                        EXPRESSION          ERROR
                        COMMA               RETURN
                        EXPSEQ              ERROR
                        RETURN
EXPRESSION              ENTER
                        TERM                ERROR
L1                      +TERM               E3
                        BRANCH              L1
E3                      —TERM               RETURN
                        BRANCH              L1
+TERM                   ENTER
                        PLUS                ERROR
                        TERM                ERROR
                        RETURN
—TERM                   ENTER
                        MINUS               ERROR
                        TERM                ERROR
                        RETURN
TERM                    ENTER
                        FACTOR              ERROR
L2                      *FACTOR             E4
                        BRANCH              L2
E4                      /FACTOR             RETURN
                        BRANCH              L2
*FACTOR                 ENTER
                        MULTIPLY            ERROR
```

	FACTOR	ERROR
	RETURN	
/FACTOR	ENTER	
	DIVIDE	ERROR
	FACTOR	ERROR
	RETURN	
FACTOR	ENTER	
	VARIABLE	E5
	RETURN	
E5	LEFT-PARENTHESIS	ERROR
	EXPRESSION	ERROR
	RIGHT-PARENTHESIS	ERROR
	RETURN	
IDENTIFIER	ENTER	
	LETTER	ERROR
L3	LETTER	E6
	BRANCH	L3
E6	DIGIT	RETURN
	BRANCH	L3
LETTER	ENTER	
	A	E7
	RETURN	
E7	B	E8
	RETURN	
E8	C	
	. . . . .	
E32	Z	ERROR
	RETURN	
DIGIT	ENTER	
	0	E33
	RETURN	
E33	1	E34
	RETURN	
E34	2	
	. . . . .	
E42	9	ERROR
	RETURN	

(In practice, recognizers for letters, digits, and other simple characters are worth hand coding for efficiency reasons.)

Implementation of the program is straightforward. A stack for storage on entry to a subroutine is maintained. Two items are entered into this stack by the ENTRY command; namely, the return link and the input string pointer. The RETURN command discards the string pointer and branches to the return link, whereas the ERROR command restores the string pointer before branching to the return link.

Notice that syntactical definitions may be ambiguous; that is, a given character string may have two different parses. For example, if two phrase classes are defined by

<sentence> :: = A <clause> | <clause> C

and

<clause> :: = AB | BC

then the sentence ABC can be either:

or

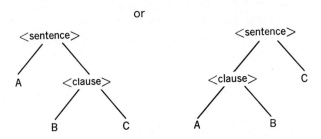

However, because the program must examine one first, the above technique
will find only one of these. For example:

SENTENCE	ENTRY		
	A	E3	
	CLAUSE	ERROR	
	RETURN		
E3	CLAUSE	ERROR	
	C		
	RETURN		
CLAUSE	ENTRY		
	A	E4	
	B	ERROR	
	RETURN		
E4	B	ERROR	
	C	ERROR	
	RETURN		

will declare ABC to be A <clause> rather than <clause> C. Some syntax-
directed compilers effectively examine all cases in parallel and thus detect
such ambiguities.

If the input string is illegal, then nothing is recognized. In practice, it is not
helpful to be told that the program is syntactically incorrect; it is desirable
to be told where the error most likely exists. It is not obvious in general how
to determine this, but in a statement oriented language such as Fortran it is
possible to narrow it down to at least a single statement. This can be handled
formally by defining an additional statement that is any character string followed by an end-of-statement. If this is given the bottom position in the analysis sequence, it will only be recognized when all other statements have failed.
The translation (yet to be discussed) can be an error message. To perform better error analysis, it is necessary to decide at what point in a recognizer a
syntactic structure has effectively been recognized. Any failures after that
would be considered errors. Thus, in Algol we could determine that a string
is an assignment statement after "variable : =" has been recognized. Any
subsequent failures would be called errors in expressions.

11.3.3 Semantics

The last section described the way in which a program could be written to take advantage of a syntactical definition of the language in order to recognize the structure of an input string. No mention was made of the way in which the input string was translated into an output string or object language. If the prescribed structure of the language bears any relation to its meaning or semantics, then we can expect to associate a meaning to each expansion or *production,* such as

<expression> :: = <expression> + <term>

which is presumably associated with the addition operation. (The Backus Normal Form syntax assigns no meaning to the character " + "; any meaning that you associate with it is due to its normal use in mathematics. We are free to define it to have any meaning, although we would be a little foolish to make it a nonstandard one!)

The meaning associated with a production can be specified by program instructions which translate or interpret the source language. Let us consider the translation of assignment statements into assembly language for a stack machine. (This object language has been picked because it is the easiest to derive directly from the production sequence recognized. More optimal 0 or 1 address objects require additional manipulations that tend to obscure the fundamentals.)

We are going to try to translate a statement such as

A3 = B + C1

into

```
LOAD        B
LOAD        C1
ADD
STORE       A3
```

The production tree for the statement is:

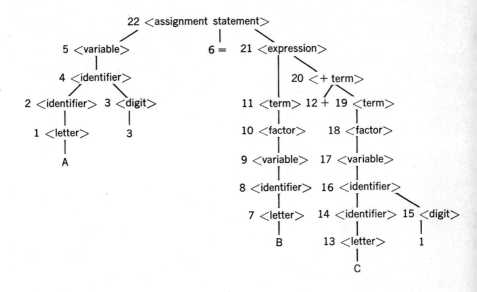

The numbers to the left of nodes are the order in which they are recognized. The obvious steps that must be taken in translation include the following:

1 Identifiers must be *packed* so that B, C1, and A3 are available for the object code.
2 By the time the variables B and C1 are absorbed into the expression, the orders LOAD B and LOAD C1 must have been compiled.
3 The ADD order must be compiled when <term> < + term> is formed.
4 A STORE order must be generated when the <assignment statement> is recognized.

An appropriate point at which to take care of step two is when a <variable> becomes a <factor>.

Suppose that, by some mechanism, the variable name recognized by <identifier> is available for use by other subroutines. In particular, define a subroutine CODE-LOAD which causes an object order LOAD variable name to be compiled. If the recognizer for <factor> is changed to

```
FACTOR      ENTER
            VARIABLE          E5
            CODE-LOAD
            RETURN
E5          LEFT-PARENTHESIS  ERROR
            EXPRESSION        ERROR
            RIGHT-PARENTHESIS ERROR
            RETURN
```

then, when <factor> is recognized in tree positions 10 and 18, LOAD B and LOAD C1 will be compiled in that order. The variable names B and C1 are packed at the time they are recognized by <identifier>. Again, suppose that there exists a pair of subroutines SET-NAME and PACK-NAME. SET-NAME forms a new packed name consisting of the last input character processed, PACK-NAME packs the last input character processed into the existing name. We now modify the <identifier> recognizer to read

```
IDENTIFIER    ENTER
              LETTER          ERROR
              SET-NAME
L3            LETTER          E6
L3A           PACK-NAME
              TRANSFER        L3
E6            DIGIT           RETURN
              TRANSFER        L3A
```

The result is that identifier recognition causes a name to be formed for use by the CODE-LOAD subroutine.

At the start of the statement, the identifier A3 is recognized and hence is packed as a name. It is not needed until after the right-hand side has been dealt with, so it must be saved. Many ways of doing this are available. For example, in the subroutine for <assignment-statement>, code can be placed after the recognition of <variable> which saves the variable. It can then be restored after <expression> has been recognized, immediately prior to compiling the STORE order. Another way, to be used below, is to make the cell which holds the name formed by SET- and PACK- a push-down stack. SET-NAME adds a new level to it. CODE-LOAD removes a level. In the same way, CODE-STORE removes a level and outputs the "STORE name" object code. With the addition of routines CODE-ADD, CODE-SUBTRACT, etc., to the recognizers for < + terms>, < − term>, etc., the program of the previous section will translate simple assignment statements that do not use indexed variables. <assignment statement> is modified to

```
ASSIGNMENT STATEMENT   ENTER
                       VARIABLE     ERROR
                       EQUAL        ERROR
                       EXPRESSION   ERROR
                       CODE STORE
                       RETURN
```

< + term> becomes

```
+TERM                  ENTRY
                       PLUS         ERROR
                       TERM         ERROR
                       CODE-ADD
```

etc.

The reader is urged to follow the compilation of a simple statement for himself. If the example A3 = B + C1 is used, the following sequence of subroutine calls results:

	OUTPUT CODE	NAME STACK CONTENTS
Variable		
Identifier		
Letter		
Return		
SET-NAME		A
Letter		
Error		
Digit		
Return		
PACK-NAME		A3
Letter		
Error		
Digit		
Error		
Return		
Return		
Equal		
Return		
Expression		
Term		
Factor		
Identifier		
Letter		
Return		
SET-NAME		B, A3
Letter		
Error		
Digit		
Error		
Return		
CODE-LOAD	LOAD B	A3
Return		
*Factor		
Multiply		
Error		
Return		
/Factor		
Divide		
Error		
Return		
Return		
+Term		
Plus		
Return		
Term		
Factor		

	OUTPUT CODE	NAME STACK CONTENTS
Identifier		
Letter		
Return		
SET-NAME		C, A3
Letter		
Error		
Digit		
Return		
PACK-NAME		C1, A3
Letter		
Error		
Digit		
Error		
Return		
CODE-LOAD	LOAD C1	A3
Return		
*Factor		
Multiply		
Error		
Return		
/Factor		
Divide		
Error		
Return		
Return		
CODE-ADD	ADD	A3
Return		
+Term		
Plus		
Error		
Return		
—Term		
Minus		
Error		
Return		
Return		
CODE-STORE	STORE A3	

(It is apparent by this time that a straightforward approach can lead to a very slow compiler! This is another case of the usual trade-off available between conceptual simplicity and speed.)

It can be seen from the above discussion that the artificial language translation program can be stated in a form that consists partly of a direct rewrite of the syntactical description and partly of subroutines executed when certain agreements are found between the input string and the syntax rules or productions. Because the first part is directly related to the syntax formalism, a number of compiler-compiler systems have been written which accept a formal description of the language and produce a working compiler or interpreter. Typically, these accept as input a set of BNF productions, that is, statements of the form

<assignment statement> :: = <variable> = <expression>

and allow any one of them to be *flagged* with the name of a program which is to be executed whenever the production or syntax rule is recognized. These programs can be written in a language suitable for compiler writing provided by the author of the compiler-compiler.†

11.4 MEMORY ALLOCATION

We have discussed how object code can be produced in a single pass over the source string. The code we produced above was symbolic in that we used the names of variables in the source language as the names of storage locations in the object language. We could next input the object code to an assembler and get binary machine code. To do this, we must also generate the pseudos necessary for the assembler to assign storage locations to variables. As an alternative, the compiler itself could assign storage during compilation and produce machine language directly. In this section we shall discuss the process of allocating memory space to variables as though the object code were assembly language. Generally, it is fairly simple to see how the compiler could be modified to produce machine language directly.

The problems of memory allocation are very different between Fortran and Algol. In Fortran, there is no block structure, and arrays have a fixed size. Consequently, DIMENSION statements can be translated into block reservation pseudos (the BSS or DS pseudos in various assemblers). Simple variables are not declared specifically in Fortran, but the first time that they are used, a pseudo can be generated to reserve a space. Since these locations should not be placed between lines of code, the actual generation of the pseudos should be delayed until all of the source has been translated. This can be done by putting the variable names into a table and scanning the tables at the end of the compilation pass to generate the required pseudos. If a one-pass compiler is required, then it is necessary to assign space to the variables immediately when they are defined. This can either be done in a separate area of memory (this is facilitated by the use of base registers as available in the IBM

---

†Examples of this are discussed in W. H. Burkhardt, Universal Programming Languages and Processors: A Brief Summary and New Concepts, *Proceedings of the Fall Joint Computer Conference,* vol. 27, part 1, pp. 1–20, 1965, and S. Rosen, A Compiler-Compiler System Developed by Brooker and Morris, *Communications of the Association for Computing Machinery,* vol. 7, no. 7, pp. 403–414, July, 1964.

370), or it can be done by compiling a transfer instruction to branch around the storage area.

Algol allows for a block structure such that one part of the program can reuse storage used by an earlier part. Consider the following section of Algol code:

```
. . .
begin          real array a[1 : 100];
. . . . . . .
end
. . . . .
begin          real array b[2 : n];
. . . .
end
. . . .
```

In the first block, 100 places must be reserved for the array "a." These locations are no longer needed after the matching **end** closes the block. In the next block shown, the array "b" requires $n - 1$ locations. These can reuse the locations no longer occupied by the array "a" plus additional locations if necessary. The second block also points out another problem. Since n is not known until execution time, it is not possible to assign storage until that time. We say that the allocation must be dynamic. For the moment, we shall ignore the problems introduced by subroutines (*procedures* in the Algol terminology). Since blocks can be nested within blocks, storage can be arranged in a stack fashion in memory. Suppose we have the following block structure with the storage requirements indicated:

block 1	20 locations
block 2	25 locations
block 3	n locations
block 4	3 locations
block 5	45 locations

Block 1 contains the other blocks and requires 20 locations. These could be locations S through $S + 19$. Block 2 requires 25 locations. These could be locations $S + 20$ through $S + 44$. Block 2 ends before block 3 starts, so block 3 could use locations $S + 20$ through $S + 19 + n$. Block 4 is inside block 3, so it must use locations $S + 20 + n$ through $S + 22 + n$. Block 5 can use locations $S + 20$ through $S + 64$ because it is only contained in block 1. These calculations must be performed at execution time, so the compiler must produce code at the beginning and ending of each block that assigns storage space. A location in memory can be assigned to each block to hold the address of the first word of storage assigned to that block. These addresses can be computed by code at the initiation of each block and can be loaded into index or base registers for use by the program.

The use of procedures complicates the problem because procedures can be called from within a block of code that does not contain the procedure. For example:

```
. . . .
procedure a
. . . . . . . . . . . . .
end
begin
. . .
call a
end
```

The call activates the block of code that is contained in the procedure, although it is not nested inside the innermost current block of code. This means that it is not possible to assign storage locations for base addresses by a simple stacking principle. If the fact that procedures can be used recursively is also taken into account, it is no longer possible to assign a unique location for a base address.

One solution is to assign a unique location to each block, to save its contents each time that the block is entered, and to restore it each time that it is left. It can be saved in a word in the dynamically assigned storage area for that block. Consider a procedure that has called itself. It has two storage areas currently in use, one for its first invocation and one for its second. The base address for the second is in a location associated with the procedure.

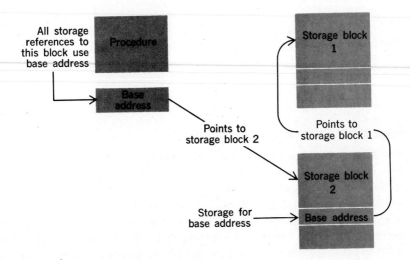

When the procedure exits from its second invocation, the base address can be restored from the copy in storage block 2 and the space in storage block 2 can be given back as free storage for future use.

11.5 ERROR DETECTION

An important part of a compiler is the code that detects errors and gives the user meaningful diagnostics. Whatever error detection is used, it is always possible for the user to give an input string that is only slightly different from a correct program but for which the compiler will give ridiculous error messages. A missing DIMENSION statement, for example, could cause a Fortran compiler to think that an indexed array is a subroutine name with parameters. Eventually there might be an error diagnostic based on that assumption. The compiler writer should try to detect many common errors, and, indeed, to correct those that are reasonably obvious, although a message should always be generated. The Fortran DO statement, for example, does not allow a comma between the statement number and the indexed variable. DO 1,I = 1,5 is incorrect: the first comma should not be present. However, the compiler should accept it as an alternative form, because it is very unlikely that the programmer meant other than DO 1 I = 1,5.

In general, bottom-up methods can be more easily changed to get sensible error messages. Top-down methods, as they stand, only give a "yes" or "no" answer. If the input is not a valid program (*well-formed string* is the technical jargon), then the method will simply say so. For a long program, that is not a very suitable diagnostic, so some other technique must be used. One method is to save the analysis that has proceeded the furthest prior to the failure to find a valid program. This could be assumed to be a correct analysis, so that the next character must either be incorrect or missing. If sensible rules to supply an alternative character can be generated, then the analysis can continue after indicating the phrase class that is being analyzed at the time of the failure.

11.6 CHOICE OF A COMPILATION TECHNIQUE

Preceding sections have only scratched the surface of the subject of compilation, so it is a little presumptuous to discuss the choice of "best" techniques. However, some general comments can be made at this stage. Top-down methods are generally more formal and consequently shorter and easier to program, debug, and document. However, error analysis tends to be more difficult. Bottom-up methods are usually faster in those cases where many levels of subroutines have to be called in order to produce a successful recognition. This is particularly the case in the recognition of an expression. Even with the simple form of expression discussed above, we saw that it was necessary for a top-down analysis to go through term, factor, variable, and identifier many times. In a practical language, there will be many more levels in an expression, and the overhead in computation time to enter each subroutine can be large.

In order to enjoy the best of both methods, it is sometimes worth employing both top-down and bottom-up methods. A bottom-up analysis subroutine with which to recognize expressions in the input string can be written. This can be used as part of a top-down syntax oriented analysis program for the recognition of all larger constructs.

PROBLEMS

1 What precedence should be given to the assignment sign if it were to be added to the operator precedence table of Section 11.2.1? How should the equal operation be handled during the compilation?

2 Suggest ways of including the Fortran logical IF statement in the precedence method of Section 11.2.1.

3 Change Figure 11.1 (page 419) so that it will detect errors in the input string of tokens which result from adjacent operands or operators using the same operator stack.

4 Change Figure 11.1 so that it will detect the use of unary plus and minus operators. To do this, you must state the rules under which you will allow a unary operator to be used, decide how to recognize it, and decide what to put in the stack for the unary operator. Assume that there is a stack machine operation NEGATE which forms minus the top of the stack in the stack.

5 Section 11.2.2 showed how a combined stack was used to produce one-address code. In that method, it was never necessary to look at more than the top three levels of the stack. In fact, the step to be performed could be stated in a chart showing the top three levels of the stack, the input token and the step. Thus one entry might say

STACK LEVEL				
THIRD	SECOND	TOP	INPUT	STEP
A	+,−, or (	A	* or /	Input to stack

Note: A stands for any operand.

Complete this table.

6 Modify the table produced in question five so that unary plus and minus are handled.

7 Add the exponentiation operator to the BNF description of expressions in Section 11.3.1. Do this by defining a new phrase class <primary> between <factor> and <variable>.

8 Write syntax descriptions of the Algol **if** and **for** statements.

9 Give a BNF description of all strings consisting of any number of "a" characters followed by the same number of "b" characters.

10 Write down all members of the phrase class list with not more than 13 characters, where list is defined by

<list> :: = A | (<list>, <list>)

11 Define recursive subroutines for the recognizers discussed in Section 11.3.2. Write macros so that the code given in that section can be used directly or with minor transliteration.

INDEX